Communications
in Computer and Information S

110659534

Joaquim Filipe   Mohammad S. Obaidat (Eds.)

E-Business and Telecommunication Networks

Third International Conference, ICETE 2006
Setúbal, Portugal, August 7-10, 2006
Selected Papers

 Springer

Volume Editors

Joaquim Filipe
INSTICC
Av. D. Manuel I, 27A - 2. Esq.
2910-595 Setúbal, Portugal
E-mail: j.filipe@est.ips.pt

Mohammad S. Obaidat
Monmouth University
Department of Computer Science
West Long Branch, NJ 07764, USA
E-mail: obaidat@monmouth.edu

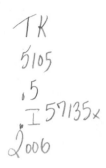

CR Subject Classification (1998): K.4.4, D.4.6, C.2

ISSN   1865-0929
ISBN-10   3-540-70759-X Springer Berlin Heidelberg New York
ISBN-13   978-3-540-70759-2 Springer Berlin Heidelberg New York

Springer is a part of Springer Science+Business Media

springer.com

© Springer-Verlag Berlin Heidelberg 2008
Printed in Germany

Typesetting: Camera-ready by author, data conversion by Scientific Publishing Services, Chennai, India
Printed on acid-free paper   SPIN: 12441211   06/3180   5 4 3 2 1 0

Preface

This book contains the best papers of the Third International Conference on E-business and Telecommunications (ICETE), which was held in 2006 in Portugal. This conference reflects a continuing effort to increase the dissemination of recent research results among professionals who work in the e-business field. ICETE is a joint international conference integrating four major areas of knowledge that are divided into four corresponding conferences: ICE-B (Int'l Conf. on e-Business), SECRYPT (Int'l Conf. on Security and Cryptography), WINSYS (Int'l Conf. on Wireless Information Systems) and SIGMAP (Int'l Conf. on Signal Processing and Multimedia).

The program of this joint conference included seven outstanding keynote lectures presented by internationally renowned distinguished researchers who are experts in the various ICETE areas. Their keynote speeches contributed to heightening the overall quality of the program and significance of the theme of the conference.

The conference topic areas define a broad spectrum in the key areas of e-Business and telecommunications. This wide view has made it appealing to a global audience of engineers, scientists, business practitioners and policy experts. The papers accepted and presented at the conference demonstrated a number of new and innovative solutions for e-business and telecommunication networks, showing that the technical problems in both fields are challenging, related and significant.

The conference received 326 submissions, with contributions from 53 different countries, in all continents, which really shows the success and global dimension of ICETE 2006. To evaluate each submission, a double-blind paper evaluation method was used: each paper was reviewed by at least two internationally known experts from our Program Committee. In the end, 98 papers were selected to be published and presented orally as full papers, corresponding to a 30% full paper acceptance ratio; 105 additional papers were published and presented, including short papers and posters. Then, a short list including only the very best and significant papers was selected to appear in this book.

We hope that you will find this collection of papers interesting and a helpful source of inspiration. In future years, ICETE will grow to become the main forum for all those interested in an integrative perspective of the areas of e-business and telecommunications, inter-relating knowledge on different theoretical and practical aspects of communication networks such as wireless information systems, security, signal processing and multimedia and e-business.

February 2008

Joaquim Filipe
Mohammad S. Obaidat

Conference Committee

Conference Chair

Joaquim Filipe, Polytechnic Institute of Setúbal / INSTICC, Portugal

Honorary Chair

Mohammad S. Obaidat, Monmouth University, USA

Program Co-chairs

Thomas Greene, MIT, USA (ICE-B)
Manu Malek, Stevens Institute of Technology, USA (SECRYPT)
Eduardo Fernández-Medina, UCLM, Spain (SECRYPT)
Javier Hernando, Polytechnic University of Catalonia, Spain (SECRYPT)
Pedro Assunção, Polytechnic Institute of Leiria, Portugal (SIGMAP)
Sérgio Faria, Polytechnic Institute of Leiria, Portugal (SIGMAP)
Luminita Vasiu, UK (WINSYS)
Rafael Caldeirinha, Polytechnic Institute of Leiria, Portugal (WINSYS)

Organizing Committee

Paulo Brito, INSTICC, Portugal
Marina Carvalho, INSTICC, Portugal
Hélder Coelhas, INSTICC, Portugal
Bruno Encarnação, INSTICC, Portugal
Vítor Pedrosa, INSTICC, Portugal
Mónica Saramago, INSTICC, Portugal

ICE-B Program Committee

Ajith Abraham, Korea
Antonia Albani, The Netherlands
Panagiotes Anastasiades, Greece
Gilbert Babin, Canada
Claudio Bartolini, USA

Morad Benyoucef, Canada
Hans Bjornsson, Sweden
Christos Bouras, Greece
Stephane Bressan, Singapore
Rongzeng Cao, China

Christer Carlsson, Finland
Barbara Carminati, Italy
Malu Castellanos, USA
Kwok Wai Cheung, China
Dickson Chiu, China
Soon Chun, USA
Jen-Yao Chung, USA
Michele Colajanni, Italy
Oscar Corcho, UK
Rafael Corchuelo, Spain
Teodor Gabriel Crainic, Canada
Alfredo Cuzzocrea, Italy
Wei Ding, China
Schahram Dustdar, Austria
Pascal van Eck, The Netherlands
Jinan Fiaidhi, Canada
Piero Formica, United Arab Emirates
Chiara Francalanci, Italy
Xiang Fu, USA
George Giaglis, Greece
Paul Grefen, The Netherlands
Volker Gruhn, Germany
Haresh Gurnani, USA
Mohand-Said Hacid, USA
Hardy Hanappi, Austria
G. Harindranath, UK
Manfred Hauswirth, Switzerland
Nina Helander, Finland
Martin Hepp, Austria
Birgit Hofreiter, Austria
Andreas Holzinger, Austria
Weihong Huang, UK
Patrick C.K. Hung, Canada
Ali Hurson, USA
Takayuki Ito, Japan
Arun Iyengar, USA
James Joshi, USA
Matjaz B. Juric, Slovenia
Sherif Kamel, Egypt
Robert Kauffman, USA
Werner Kiessling, Germany
Andy Koronios, Australia
Ibrahim Kushchu, UK
Anton Lavrin, Czech Republic
Elaine Lawrence, Australia

Lundy Lewis, USA
Dahui Li, USA
Yinsheng Li, China
Chin E. Lin, China
Kwei-Jay Lin, USA
Jie Lu, Australia
Tokuro Matsuo, Japan
Brian Mennecke, USA
Dunja Mladenic, Slovenia
Adrian Mocan, Austria
Ali Reza Montazemi, Canada
Aad van Moorsel, UK
Dan O'Leary, USA
Andrea Omicini, Italy
Cesare Pautasso, Switzerland
Krassie Petrova, New Zealand
Axel Polleres, Spain
Pak-Lok Poon, China
Dimitris Rigas, UK
Michael Rosemann, Australia
Demetrios Sampson, Greece
Detlef Schoder, Germany
Janice Sipior, USA
Il-Yeol Song, USA
Miguel Soriano, Spain
Katarina Stanoevska-Slabeva,
    Switzerland
Thomas Strang, Germany
York Sure, Germany
Thompson Teo, Singapore
Ramayah Thurasamy, Malaysia
Thanassis Tiropanis, Greece
Henry Tirri, Finland
Roland Traunmüller, Austria
Jan Vanthienen, Belgium
Vesna Bosilj Vuksic, Croatia
Bartel Van de Walle, The Netherlands
Krzysztof Wecel, Poland
Erik Wilde, Switzerland
Andreas Wombacher, The Netherlands
Jongwook Woo, USA
Lai Xu, The Netherlands
Soe-Tsyr Yuan, Taiwan
Han Zhang, USA

SECRYPT Program Committee

Robert Tolksdorf, Germany
Ambrosio Toval, Spain
Wade Trappe, USA
Wen-Guey Tzeng, Taiwan
Ulrich Ultes-Nitsche, Switzerland
Guillaume Urvoy-Keller, France
Huaxiong Wang, Australia
Yongge Wang, USA
Susanne Wetzel, USA
Duminda Wijesekera, USA

Chaoping Xing, Singapore
Shouhuai Xu, USA
Mariemma Yagüe, Spain
Jeff Yan, UK
Alec Yasinsac, USA
Sung-Ming Yen, Taiwan
Meng Yu, USA
Moti Yung, USA
Yuliang Zheng, USA
André Zúquete, Portugal

SIGMAP Program Committee

Karim Abed-Meraim, France
Driss Aboutajdine, Morocco
Patrice Abry, France
Ralf Ackermann, Germany
Abbes Amira, UK
Alessandro Amoroso, Italy
João Ascenso, Portugal
Jaakko Astola, Finland
Samir Attallah, Singapore
Noboru Babaguchi, Japan
Azeddine Beghdadi, France
Adel Belouchrani, Algeria
Amel Benazza-Benyahia, Tunisia
Mohammed Bennamoun, Australia
Younès Bennani, France
Shuvra Bhattacharyya, USA
Marina Bosi, USA.
Abdesselam Bouzerdoum, Australia
Jianfei Cai, Singapore
Lap-Pui Chau, Singapore
Liang-Gee Chen, Taiwan
Naveen Chilamkurti, Australia
Ryszard S. Choras, Poland
Paulo Correia, Portugal
Li Deng, USA
Petar M. Djuric, USA
Chitra Dorai, USA
Rob Evans, Australia
Anibal Ferreira, Portugal
Pascal Frossard, Switzerland
Marco Furini, Italy
Mathew George, Singapore
Fary Z Ghassemlooy, UK

Lorenzo Granai, UK
William Grosky, USA
Peter Händel, Sweden
Xian-Sheng Hua, China
Jenq-Neng Hwang, USA
Jiri Jan, Czech Republic
Philippe Joly, France
Chehdi Kacem, France
Mohan Kankanhalli, Singapore
Walter Kellermann, Germany
Hyoung-Joong Kim, Korea
Paris Kitsos, Greece
Stefanos Kollias, Greece
Hamid Krim, USA.
Murat Kunt, Switzerland
Pascal Larzabal, France
Fernando Lopes, Portugal
Wing-Kin Ma, Taiwan
Kai-Kuang Ma, Singapore
Antonio De Maio, Italy
Manuel Perez Malumbres, Spain
Hong Man, USA
Andreas Maras, Greece
Gloria Menegaz, Italy
Ajmal Mian, Australia
Majid Mirmehdi, UK
Robin Morris, USA
Antonio Navarro, Portugal
Haldun M. Ozaktas, Turkey
Raffaele Parisi, Italy
Luigi Paura, Italy
Andrew Perkis, Norway
Béatrice Pesquet-Popescu, France

Athina P. Petropulu, USA
Ioannis Pitas, Greece
Thomas Plagemann, Norway
Viktor Prasanna, USA
Maria Paula Queluz, Portugal
Anthony Quinn, Ireland
Rudolf Rabenstein, Germany
Matthias Rauterberg, The Netherlands
Giuseppe Ricci, Italy
Dimitris Rigas, UK
Abdulmotaleb El Saddik, Canada
Lauri Savioja, Finland
Raimondo Schettini, Italy

Timothy K. Shih, Taiwan
Eduardo da Silva, Brazil
Wladyslaw Skarbek, Poland
John Sorensen, Denmark
Ljubisa Stankovic, Montenegro
Yutaka Takahashi, Japan
Chintha Tellambura, Canada
Qi Tian, USA
Abdellatif Benjelloun Touimi, France
Vesa Valimaki, Finland
Kainam Thomas Wong, Canada
Habib Zaidi, Switzerland

WINSYS Program Committee

Alhussein Abouzeid, USA
Arup Acharya, USA
Rui L. Aguiar, Portugal
Ozgur Akan, Turkey
Salah Al-sharhan, Kuwait
Hakim Badis, France
Luis Orozco Barbosa, Spain
Luis Bernardo, Portugal
Mohammed Boulmalf, United Arab
   Emirates
Raouf Boutaba, Canada
Mihaela Cardei, USA
Claudio Casetti, Italy
Erdal Cayirci, Norway
Chung-Kuo Chang, USA
Xiaodong Chen, UK
Tibor Cinkler, Hungary
Alexander Clemm, USA
Reuven Cohen, Israel
Todor Cooklev, USA
Carlos Cordeiro, USA
Luis M. Correia, Portugal
Jun-Hong Cui, USA
Iñigo Cuiñas, Spain
Alfredo Cuzzocrea, Italy
Falko Dressler, Germany
Val Dyadyuk, Australia
Alfredo Goldman , Brazil
David Greaves, UK
Ibrahim Habib, USA

Richard Harris, New Zealand
Oliver Heckmann, Germany
Xiaoyan Hong, USA
Mario Huemer, Germany
Youssef Iraqi, Oman
Chung G. Kang, Korea
Andreas Kassler, Sweden
Michael Koch, Germany
Mladen Kos, Croatia
Srisankar Kunniyur, India
Wing Kwong, USA
Victor Peral Lecha, UK
Chin E. Lin, China
Antonio Liotta, UK
Justin Lipman, China
Pascal Lorenz, France
Antonio Loureiro, Brazil
Qusay Mahmoud, Canada
Kami Makki, USA
Stefan Mangold, Switzerland
Guoqiang Mao, Australia
Shiwen Mao, USA
Alan Marshall, UK
Enzo Mingozzi, Italy
Nader Mir, USA
Klaus Moessner, UK
Tomoaki Ohtsuki, Japan
Lisa Osadciw, USA
Andrzej R. Pach, Poland
Algirdas Pakstas, UK

Wen-Chih Peng, Taiwan
Dirk Pesch, Ireland
Edward Pinnes, USA
Andreas Pitsillides, Cyprus
Simon Podvalny, Russia
Nicholas Race, UK
Peter Reichl, Austria
Shangping Ren, USA
António Rodrigues, Portugal
Cesar Vargas Rosales, Mexico
Jörg Roth, Germany
Sana Salous, UK
Manuel García Sánchez, Spain
Hamid Sharif, USA

Khaled Shuaib, United Arab Emirates
Henrique Silva, Portugal
Jorge Sá Silva, Portugal
Andrej Stefanov, USA
George Tombras, Greece
Rafael P. Torres, Spain
Emmanouel Varvarigos, Greece
Enrique Vazquez, Spain
Yu Wang, USA
Hans Weghorn, Germany
Hongyi Wu, USA
Chunsheng Xin, USA
Gergely Zaruba, USA

ICE-B Auxiliary Reviewers

Alfons Huhn, Germany
Qinfang Li, Germany
Steffen Muhle, Germany
Alexander Sigel, Germany
Christian Schmitt, Germany

SECRYPT Auxiliary Reviewers

Jun Furukawa, Japan
Goichiro Hanaoka, Japan
Chien-Ning Chen, Taiwan
Kuo-Zhe Chiou, Taiwan
Chao-Chih Hsu, Taiwan
Fu-Hau Hsu, Taiwan
Hsi-Chung Lin, Taiwan
Rachel Akimana, Belgium
Daniel J. Bernstein, USA
Marc Joye, France
Claude Barral, France
Christophe Clavier, France
Damien Giry, Belgium
Guerric Meurice de Dormale, Belgium
Steve Kremer, France
Ozgur Gurleyen, UK
Wolfgang Dobmeier, Germany
Rolf Schillinger, Germany

Christian Schläger, Germany
Francisco Javier Lucas Martínez, Spain
Fernando Molina Molina, Spain
Miguel Ángel Martínez Aguilar, Spain
Celalettin Emre Sayin, Turkey
Abdulhakim Unlu, Turkey
Fabien Laguillaumie, France
Didier Alquie, France
Johann Barbier, France
Lutz Suhrbier, Germany
Franck Landelle, France
Xiaofeng Gong, UK
Toshihiro Tabata, Japan
Masakazu Soshi, Japan
Takeshi Okamoto, Japan
Sotiris Ioannidis, USA
C. Lambrinoudakis, Greece

SIGMAP Auxiliary Reviewers

Rong Duan, USA
Mohamed Rziza, Morocco
Odd Inge Hillestad, Norway
Stian Johansen, Norway
Anna Na Kim, Norway
Ana Luisa de Araújo Santos,Brazil
Danillo Bracco Graziosi, Brazil

José Fernando Leite de Oliveira,Brazil
Waldir Sabino da Silva Junior, Brazil
Alain Rakotomamonjy, France
Wei-Yin Chen, Taiwan
Chao-Chung Cheng, Taiwan
Li-Fu Ding, Taiwan

WINSYS Auxiliary Reviewers

Jun Liu, USA
Lei Tang, USA
Qunwei Zheng, USA
Adetola Oredope, UK
Johan Garcia, Sweden
Ana María Vázquez Alejos, Spain
Panagiotis Kokkinos, Greece
Michalis Oikonomakos, Greece

Christos Papageorgiou, Greece
Pablo Torío Gómez, Spain
Ioannis Baltopoulos, Greece
Atif Alvi, UK
Behzad Bastani, UK
Henry Robinson, UK
Susana Loredo, Spain
Lorenzo Rubio, Spain

Invited Speakers

David Marca, University of Phoenix, USA
Manu Malek, Stevens Institute of Technology, USA
Les Barclay, Barclay Associates Ltd., UK
Fernando Pereira, Instituto Superior Técnico – Instituto de Telecomunicações,
    Portugal
Jan Jürjens, Technische Universität München, Germany
Anisse Taleb, Ericsson AB, Sweden
Tom Greene, M.I.T., USA

Table of Contents

Part III: SIGMAP

Part IV: WINSYS

PART I
ICE-B

Towards Automated Service Trading

Manuel Resinas, Pablo Fernandez, and Rafael Corchuelo

ETS Ingenieria Informatica, University of Seville, Spain

Abstract. The service-oriented architecture is a promising means to support out-sourcing amongst real-time enterprises. In this context, SLAs (Service Level Agreements) are essential because they grant guarantees about how a service must be provided or consumed. We define service trading as the process of locating, selecting, negotiating, and creating SLAs. Although automating the service trading process is a key characteristic of a real-time enterprise, to the best of our knowledge it has not been completely addressed yet.

In this article, we propose a conceptual framework for automated service trading. Therefore, our goal is not to implement a concrete architecture but to develop a framework that can be used to define, compare and analyse the interoperability of different service trading architectures. The novel contributions of this paper are threefold: we identify the roles and interactions that are necessary to carry out this automated service trading, we motivate and introduce the idea of trading protocols, and we define the elements that are necessary to support an automated decision-making in service trading.

Keywords: Service Oriented Computing, SLAs, Trading.

1 Introduction

In recent years, we have witnessed how new technologies are enabling the emergence of a new age of enterprises that quickly adapt to their ever-changing business environments but keep their costs under control. This is the main characteristic of what has been called *real-time enterprises*. Two elements are the key to achieve this vision: the management and analysis of the information collected by the enterprises related to their business environment, and the ability to use products or services offered by other enterprises as components for further innovation.

The service-oriented computing paradigm [1] and the service-oriented architectures based on web services are the mechanims used to support this idea of using services offered by other companies as pieces of our systems. In this context, SLAs (Service Level Agreements) are a key point because they grant guarantees about how a service will be provided or consumed by establishing both functional and non-functional requirements that must be fulfilled by both parties during the service execution. Additionally, SLAs allow providers to deploy an automated provision of services based on the SLAs agreed with their customers [2].

We define service trading as the process of locating, selecting, negotiating, and creating SLAs. The service trading is a subprocess of a more general *contracting process* that was already defined in [3]. Although there are infrastructures to provision SLAs

J. Filipe and M.S. Obaidat (Eds.): ICETE 2006, CCIS 9, pp. 3–14, 2008.

and services [2] that agree with them automatically, there is little support, to the best of our knowledge, to tackle the service trading process, which is still mostly a human-centric process. However, automating the service trading process is a key characteristic of a real-time enterprise.

In this paper, we take the ideas exposed in [3] as a starting point and propose a conceptual framework for automated service trading. The framework is divided into six organisations[1] (discovery, information, selection, agreement making, binding, and trading), and each one cares for a specific subgoal in the whole service trading process. Our goal is not to implement a concrete architecture but to develop a conceptual framework that can be used to define, compare and analyse the interoperability of different service trading architectures.

Our work advances the state of the art in service trading in the following. First, we clearly identify the roles that are necessary to carry out this service trading as well as the relationships between them. Second, we motivate and introduce the trading protocols, which are a specification of the global behaviour of the trading system from a temporal point of view. And third, we define the elements that are necessary for an automated decision-making in the service trading process. This bridges the two key elements of a real-time enterprise mentioned before: the management and analysis of the information collected by the enterprises as the basis of the decision-making, and the ability to use services offered by other enterprises through the automated creation of SLAs.

The structure of this article is the following. Next, in Section 2, we briefly introduce the organisational metaphor and we describe the conceptual framework. Section 3 compares our framework with other proposals developed by both the industry and the academy, and we conclude and enumerate future work in Section 4.

2   Conceptual Framework

Several phases have been identified on the contracting process [3] (as it is shown in the left part of Figure 1): The first step that appears in the figure is outside the contracting process and it has been called preparation phase. This step involves the creation of the offer by the provider of the service and the analysis of its functional and non-functional requirements by the consumer. In the contracting process itself, first step is defined as information phase whose goal is to match service providers with potential consumers and vice versa. In the next phase, they may start a negotiation with those consumers or providers to find a mutually acceptable agreement. At the end of this phase the result is the creation of an agreement on the execution of a service between a provider and a consumer. In the fourth phase, both service provider and service consumer set up a deployment plan to make it possible to follow all terms established in the agreement settled in the previous phase. The last phase in the contracting process is the fulfilment phase. This phase involves the fulfilment of the obligations established in the agreement and in the monitoring of the whole process in order to ensure that both parties observe the agreement correctly.

---

[1] We borrow this term from the GAIA methodology[4]. An organisation does not amount to a company or a department but to a number of agents that work together.

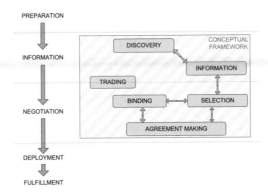

Fig. 1. Conceptual framework

The conceptual framework proposed in this article is focused on the information and negotiation phases. Therefore, on the one hand, input to the framework consists in the requirements gathered during preparation phase. We call *user preferences* to this set of information developed in the preparation phase; additionally, it is worth pointing out that our idea of *user* is independent of the nature of the stakeholder, i.e. whether user stands for a service consumer or a service provider. On the other hand, the output of the framework is a established SLA. This SLA can be used to drive the further deployment and fullfilment phases.

In order to deal with the complexity of the service trading problem, we use the organisational metaphor [4] where organisations are outlined developing a general architectural characterization of the problem. In so doing, our model is composed of six organisations (depicted in the central-right part of Figure 1) that interact amongst each other.

As an introduction to the conceptual framework, we can sketch the global behaviour of organisations as following: The discovery organisation performs the process of locating a set of potential providers or consumers according to a number of functional and non functional requirements; candidates discovered, are then passed to the information organisation in order to gather detailed information about the characteristics and preferences of each potential party. This information is subsequently used by the selection organisation to create and select a set of promising agreement proposals with other parties. Proposal selected are also analysed to decide whether we would start a negotiation process with other parties or produce a take-it-or-leave-it offer. This instructions are delegated to the agreement making organisation responsible to actually negotiate or propose the agreement to other party. During this procedure, agreement making organisation interact with the binding organisation by asking for approval to make or accept binding offers. In so doing, the responsiblity of the binding organisation can be seen as to determine when an offer may be accepted.

Finally, the main goal of the trading organisation is to specify a choreography that will regulate how the whole process is carried out, that is, it cares of starting the search for parties, submitting offers, waiting for responses, starting negotiations or sending binding offers. Additionally, trading organisation monitorise the market (making use of the discovery organisation) in order to decide when the agreement search should be started.

The remainder of this section describes each organisation detailing their goals and the roles that can be identify on them.

2.1 Trading

In general, service trading is a process whose details change from scenario to scenario depending on the type of parties involved and the temporal requirements to be met. In order to deal with these issues, it is necessary an orchestration of the different stages in the trading process.

The trading organisation focuses on the global behaviour from a temporal point of view. Its goal is the coordination of the remain layers so as to implement a trading protocol.

To understand what a Trading Protocol is, we use a simple real-life example: A public bidding where an institution looks for a service provider and devises a trading protocol that consists of the following stages: the announce of the bidding, a deadline for the submission of proposals, a period of resolution and, finally, the communication of results. The trading protocol also states temporal constraints for each stages.

Building on these ideas, the trading organisation should address the following issues: (i) A taxonomy of Trading Protocols, (ii) a repository with implementations for each Trading Protocols, (iii) the management of the life-cycle of the elements in the system, including a mechanism for the instantiation of the actors that implement the trading protocol, and (iv) a definition of the temporal parameters that will control the behaviour of other organisational. These parameters would be passed to the actors of those organisations.

This organisation is composed of the following roles:

- The *Trading Protocol Selector* role analyses user preferences to decide which of the known trading protocols best suits to the temporal contraints especified on the preferences.
- The *Customer Manager* role is in charge of interacting with the environment in order to handle user preferences. Consequently, this role transmit the appropriate part of these preferences to the rest of the roles. Additionally, this role is the responsible for trigger the search based on market status and knowledge harvested from pervious searches. Once a given search is about to start, this role is asisted by the *Trading Protocol Selector* to invoke the approporiate actors that would develop the trading protocol used on the search.

2.2 Discovery

In the discovery organisation the main aim consist in locating potential parties demanding (or supplying) a service that other party provides (or needs). In order to deal with the issues related with discovery, we can identify the following requirements:

- An infrastructure for a taxonomy of services. Each demand or provision of service should be catalogued based on the taxonomy; the classifying criteria may include both functional and non-functional features.
- A method for registering new trading events. An example of such an event would be the fact that an entity is searching for service providers of a given type (as specified in the taxonomy).
- A way to store access points to the different actors that generate events.
- A method for subscribing to events. This is necessary to feed the knowledge base used to decide when an agreement search must be started or the results of a previous search must be refined. This information might also be useful for some negotiation strategies.
- A protocol to exchange and propagate events amongst organisations.
- An addressing specification to provide a mechanism to access and identify actors.

Roles in this organisation include:

- The *Discovery Service* role represents an abstraction of the discovery infrastructure that should be refined in further concrete models. Different infrastructures can be selected from a wide range of models: from a centralized paradigm to a distributed one.
- The *Market Mediator* role is in charge of adapting local knowledge model in a given party to the appropriate discovery infrastructure. This adaptation make independent the characteristics of market modelized by the discovery service to the rest of organisations.
- The *Tracker* role is the active part that make use of the discovery service to search for some particular trading event.
- The *Advertiser* role is the complementary role for *Tracker* generating trading events to be searched. This trading events, should be parametrized with the most significative user preferences that can be made public.

2.3   Information

The goal of this organisation is to manage the public information about the user preferences and the potential candidates found by the discovery organisation. The amount and type of information collected from each candidate may be different; however, at a conceptual level the information should include, at least, the public features about the service demanded/supplied. In addition, some information can be harvested from external sources, e. g., information about the reputation of the candidate.

Roles in this organisation include:

- The *Inquirer* role polls the different *Informant*s located by the Discovery organisations. In this process, this role can select different strategies of quering, depending on the intraction standard and the type of information needed to match user preferences.
- The *Informant* role is the responsible for publish all the public user preferences that can be usefull to other parties in order to evaluate the possibilities to become a business partner.

Both *Inquirer* and *Informant* must implement a compatible specification of a format to express functional and non-functional features of services and a procedure to query and to inspect services. In addition, the *Inquirer* must provide an integration of the service features format with the taxonomy of the discovery layer.

2.4   Selection

The aim of the selection organisation is to choose a set of candidate parties with whom a negotiation process can be started or to whom an agreement proposal can be submitted. The selection starts with a set of information about potential parties coming from several sources: information provided by the information organisation after an active search, agreement proposals received from other parties, and non-successful offers [2] coming from the binding organisation, so that they can be processed again.

The selection process is carried out by the following roles:

- The *Proposal builder* role creates agreement proposals based on the information gathered by the information organisation. Then it sends these agreements proposals to the *Proposal collector*.
- The *Proposal collector* receives the agreement proposals generated by the *Proposal builder* as well as the agreement proposals coming from other parties through the *Proponent* role and submits them to the *Proposal filter*. Optionally, it can kept them until an event occurs. For instance, they can be kept until the negotiation phase finishes.
- The *Proponent* role represents the party that is submitting us a proposal.
- The *Proposal filter* role is in charge of filtering the agreement proposals collected by the *Proposal collector* and the non-successful offers coming from the binding organisation. The filter criteria are not unique but, in most cases, they depend on the preferences given by the user and the status of the whole service trading process. After this process, several proposals are rejected and the others are sent to the *Proposal dispatcher* role.
- The *Proposal dispatcher* sends the proposal to the most appropriate *Agreement Maker*. One system may have several *Agreement Makers* with different characteristics and one of them may be better than the others for certain conditions. For instance one *Agreement Maker* can implement auction protocols, another one can implement bilateral negotiation protocols, and another one can implement just a take-it-or-leave-it protocol.

2.5   Agreement Making

The goal of the agreement making organisation is to provide a mechanism to create agreements, possibly through an automated negotiation process, that are acceptable to all the parties involved in them. Therefore, the result of this organisation is an agreement that specifies the terms under which the service shall be executed. This may include both functional and non-functional terms.

---

[2] These offers are non-successful because either they were not good enough for us or the other party rejected them.

Consequently, the requirements of the agreement making organisation are: it must support an agreement format that must be understood by both parties and that allows them to identify the terms of the agreement; it must implement at least one protocol to create agreements and, optionally, to negotiate them; it must provide decision making mechanisms to evaluate the offers received and generate their own bids or counteroffers if necessary, and it must offer a way to create reliable and non-repudiable agreements.

The protocols to create agreements can range from a very simple form of communication such as the submission of an offer by one party and its acceptance o rejection by the other one, to a more complex form based on negotiation protocols. A negotiation protocol establishes the rules that govern the negotiation and the way the communication amongst the parties involved in the negotiation is carried out. The most common negotiation protocols are based on the submission of offers and can be categorised into auctions [5] (e.g. English, Dutch or Vickrey) and bilateral negotiations. Bilateral negotiations involve the exchanging offers and counteroffers between the two parties carying out the negotiation [6].

The decision-making mechanisms determine the way the parties involved in the negotiation process behave. There are four parts that sould be implemented in these decision-making mechanisms: (i) an offer evaluation, usually carried out through the definition of utility functions to each term of the agreement; (ii) a decision on which response shall be sent to the counterparty; (iii) a construction of a counteroffer if necessary [7,8,9], and (iv) a model of the world and of our opponents in order to improve our negotiation capabilities [10].

We have identified three roles in this organisation:

- The *Agreement Maker* is the role that implements our agreement creation mechanism. Therefore, it must understand an agreement format and support at least one protocol to create agreements. This role can act almost as a proxy if it just implements a take-it-or-leave-it agreement creation protocol. However, it can be very complex if it understand several negotiation protocols and has to create bids or counteroffers. There is no restriction on the number of *Counter-parties* that the *Agreement Maker* can be negotiating simultaneously.
- The *Counter-party* role represents the party that we are trying to reach an agreement with. This role must implement the same communication protocol and agreement format as the *Agreement Maker*.
- The *Notary* role must guarantee that the agreement created between the two parties is reliable and non-repudiable.

2.6 Binding

The goal of the binding organisation is to determine when a binding offer must be submitted and whether a binding offer that has been received should be accepted. In addition, this organisation must establish when these decisions are going to be made. For example, one option is to make the decision as the offers are received; another possibility is to make the decisions at some points in time that has been previously set. These points may be dynamically selected, depending on changing conditions of the environment such as the frequency of arrival of offers, or statically determined based on temporal constraints imposed by the *trading protocol*, or a combination of them both. Therefore, the responsibilities of this organisation are not only to determine whether a binding offer must be accepted or submitted but to establish when these decisions shall be made as well.

The decisions made in this organisations are based on several factors and they may vary depending on whether it is a service consumer who is making the decision or it is a service provider. Nevertheless, we can divide these factors in three groups: First, User preferences about the contents of the agreement. For instance, constraints about the values of the terms of the agreement or an utility function indicating the importance of these terms to the user. Second, user preferences about the agreement process. Some examples are the deadline and the eagerness to reach an agreement. Third, external factors that may prevent a party to commit to an agreement. For instance, the provider's capability to accept new agreements or the existence of dependencies amongst the agreements a service consumer wants to reach.

This organisation is composed of three roles:

- The *Commit Handler* role has the final decision on whether to bind to an offer or not and it is also in charge of determining when these decision are made. To make these decisions it takes into account the user preferences about the contents of the agreement and the agreement process and it consults other roles about the feasibility of committing to an agreement.
- The *Capacity Planner* role analyses the provider's capability to provision a certain agreement and recommends the *Commit Handler* to commit or not to that agreement. This role is specific to the concrete deployment of the service provider.
- The *Demand Planner* is the role that plans the search of multiple agreements. For instance, a service consumer may want to reach agreements on different services, and there may exist dependencies between those services. These dependencies can be like *"I want either an agreement on all different services or no agreement at all"*. The *Demand Planner* is in charge of enforcing these restrictions.

The most important decisions of the whole system take place in this organisation because it is where it is decided when to commit to an agreement. Therefore, in a real-time enterprise, the roles in this organisation are likely to be very complex and supported by additional components that manage and analyse the information collected by companies using methods such us data mining, forecasting or stochastic modelling.

3 Related Work

In this section, we analyse related proposals from two points of view: First, we focus on different conceptual architectures or frameworks that address the interoperability of web services. Second, we give an overview of current technologies that can be used to develop different parts of the organisations identified in our framework.

Since web services and service-oriented computing paradigm were introduced, some architectural research has been developed. The comparative analysis carried out amongst them, focuses on automating the service trading; particularly, in Table 1 we

Table 1. Comparative analysis of conceptual frameworks

Phases Architectures	Discovery	Information	Selection	Agreement Making	Binding	Trading
WSA [11]	+	~				
OGSA [12]	+	+		+	~	
WSMO-Full [13]	+	~	+	+		
SWSA [14]	+	~		+		
Ours	+	+	+	+	+	+

study, for each of the proposals, if the organisational goals indentified in our conceptual framework are addressed.

Web Service Architecture (WSA)[11] is the reference architecture built by W3C. Due to the abstraction level of this conceptual architecture, SLAs automation creation is marginaly dealt and the only issues directly handled are discovery ones. However, in the last couple of years, an extended web service architecture [15] have addressed Information problem in terms of standards for metadata interchange.

In the area of integration and virtual organisations, an evolved grid paradigm has emerged in the last years: the service grid. There is a wide range of on-going standarising work in this context. As part of this work, a conceptual architecture has been developed: the Open Grid Service Architecture (OGSA)[12]. This approach tries to address a highly distributed scenario of collaborative stakeholders. Concerning our organisational goals, OGSA deals with all organisations that involves some kind of interaction (Discovery, Information and Agreement Making) in an explicit way. Nevertheless, organisations centered in decision-making mechanisms (Selection and Binding) are not well defined and the needed elements have not been identified. However, in OGSA there are some references to the capacity planning issues.

The Semantic Web has influenced several research fields; particularly, semantic approaches have boosted several open research efforts in the web services field. One of the most active is the Web Service Modelling Ontology (WSMO) that comprises a group of especifications and systems for dealing with semantic web services. In particular, there is a conceptual architecture called WSMO-Full that describes the abstract background of WSMO. In this approach, interactions related to the information organisation are not clearly isolated and no further architectural element is outlined. However, there are some subtle references to additional information needs after a discovery phase. WSMO-Full[13] is more centered on decision making than other architectures and they explicitly propose a selection after the discovery of potential candidates. Nevertheless, it does not identify the issues related to the decision-making in the binding organisation. WSMO-Full supports the creation of agreements and defines contract agreement choreographies that are protocols for message interactions between at least one service requestor and at least one service provider. However, unlike our trading protocols they do not cover all phases of service trading but only the creation of agreements, and they are more focused on the messages exchanged rather than the temporal behaviour of the system.

Following the idea of semantic web services, a joint effort of several research groups in the area have developed a more general and abstract conceptual framework called

Semantic Web Service Architecture (SWSA)[14]. SWSA completely covers discovery and agreement making. However, information issues are not addressed in a explicit architectural concept, although some higly related requirements are defined. Additionally, some matchmaking mechanisms are stated as part of their discovery phase. Nonetheless, this matchmaking is only about the advertised information of the service, while in our proposal, there is an additional selection carried out by the selection organisation that chooses amongst concrete agreement proposals instead of just advertised information.

We have analysed how different approaches differ based on the organisational outlining of our framework. Additionally, another significant difference amongst frameworks is the way they integrate the behaviour of service consumer and service provider into the overall architecture: on the one hand, WSMO-Full is aligned with our approach and the elements of its architecture are independent of the nature of the stakeholders, i.e. whether the are service consumers or service providers. On the other hand, SWSA strongly links the behaviour of active roles to the service consumer side while the more passive roles correspond to the service provider.

Several standards have emerged to enrich the basic web service stack. Table 2 shows a distribution of stadards over the conceptual organisations identified.

Concerning the discovery organisation, there are three specifications that can be used to implement its requirements: (i) UDDI can be used as a flexible repository that can be used to store the access points of elements and the taxonomies used by the discovery organisation. (ii) WS-Notification [16] can be used to subscribe and broker notification events. (iii) Lastly, WS-Adressing [15] provides an specification of the references/locations of web services by means of a standardization of the concept of *endpoint references*.

There are a number of standards that deal with the exchange of service descriptions, from both a functional and a non-functional point of view and they can be used in the implementation of the information organisation. For instance, WS-MetadataExchange [15] and WS-InspectionLanguage. Alternatively, WS-Agreement [17] uses a template-driven procedure, and those templates can be seen as a mean of expressing the preferences of a given party.

The most significant specification that covers most aspects included in the agreement making organisation is WS-Agreement [17]. It allows to specify the structure of an agreement document, so that it must be used together with one or several domain-specific vocabularies to give the proper semantic to the terms of the agreement. Furthermore, it defines a protocol and a web service-based interface to create, represent and allow the monitoring of agreements.

Table 2. Related standards

Discovery	Information	Agreement Making	Trading
UDDI	WS-MetadataExchange	WS-Agreement	WS-CDL
WS-Notification	WS-InspectionLanguage	FIPA Protocols	BPEL
WS-Addressing	WS-Agreement		

However, WS-Agreement just defines a take-it-or-leave-it protocol. To use more complex negotiation protocols, other specifications must be implemented. For instance, WS-AgreementNegotiation[3] [18], which builds on WS-Agreement and specifies a bilateral negotiation protocol, or the negotiation protocols defined by FIPA [19].

Concerning the trading organisation, depending on the complexity of the trading protocol used, different approaches are possible. For complex coordinations, there are workflow standard such as BPEL [15] or choreography languages such as WS-CDL[20]. In the case of simple cases, an alternative to implement Trading Protocols would be the specification of ad-hoc elements in the concrete architecture build upon the conceptual framework.

4   Conclusions and Future Work

This paper focuses on the problem of service trading. In this context, our main aim is to achieve an effective background for the development of automated discovering, selection and negotiation of SLAs. To this end, a conceptual framework is developed and compared with related conceptual approaches.

The main contributions of this article are:

- A decomposition of the automated service trading problem outlining a set of abstract roles and organisations. Unlike other proposals, which are centered in the interactions between parties, we also identify the neccesary elements for the automated decision making.
- The conceptual framework presented aims to define and compare different trading architectures. Furthermore, the conceptual background developed can be used to analyse potential interoperability amongst architectures.
- We introduce the concept of Trading Protocol as a method for defining the temporal features and behavioral stages of trading scenarios. These protocols drive the choreography of the different elements and allow a temporal match procedure among SLA demands/offers of stakeholders.

Additionally, it is worth pointing out that an automation of the service trading process, shall benefit not only a cross-organisational scenario but also an intra-organisational (integration) one: SLAs have been associated traditionally with cross-organisational transactions where a company must enforce a certain level of service to their partners; however, real-time enterprises paradigm, in most cases, is built upon the integration of a complex organisation; in this context SLAs are starting to be an important issue to be addressed amongst the subsystems involved. In this integration scenario, the rationalisation of the usage of resources inside the organisation argues for SLAs to be managed as automatically as possible. In so doing, new promising fields such as the Service Grid [12] are aligned with an hybrid scenario cross/intra-organisational where SLAs are comparatively important.

Further work to be done in this field is to develop a reference architecture making use of the conceptual framework presented. This architecture has been outlined in [21] although some refinement and implementation must still be developed.

---

[3] Still in a very early stage of development.

References

1. Curbera, F., Khalaf, R., Mukhi, N., Tai, S., Weerawarana, S.: The next step in web services. Commun. ACM 46, 29–34 (2003)
2. Ludwig, H., Gimple, H., Dan, A., Kearney, R.D.: Template-based automated service provisioning-supporting the agreement-driven service life-cycle. Technical Report rc23660, IBM Research Division (2005)
3. Ludwig, H.: A conceptual framework for building e-contracting infraestructure. In: Corchuelo, R., Wrembel, R., Ruiz-Cortes, A. (eds.) Technologies Supporting Business Solutions. Nova Publishing (2003)
4. Zambonelli, F., Jennings, N.R., Wooldridge, M.: Developing multiagent systems: The gaia methodology. ACM Trans. Softw. Eng. Methodol. 12, 317–370 (2003)
5. Ströbel, M., Weinhardt, C.: Montreal taxonomy for electronic negotiation. Group Decision and Negotiation 12, 143–164 (2003)
6. Sierra, C., Faratin, P., Jennings, N.R.: A service-oriented negotiation model between autonomous agents. In: Padget, J.A. (ed.) Collaboration between Human and Artificial Societies 1997. LNCS, vol. 1624, pp. 17–35. Springer, Heidelberg (1999)
7. Faratin, P., Sierra, C., Jennings, N.R.: Negotiation decision functions for autonomous agents. Int. Journal of Robotics and Autonomous Systems 24, 159–182 (1998)
8. Faratin, P., Sierra, C., Jennings, N.R.: Using similarity criteria to make trade-offs in automated negotiations. Artificial Intelligence 142, 205–237 (2002)
9. Karp, A.H., Wu, R., Chen, K.Y., Zhang, A.: A game tree strategy for automated negotiation. In: ACM Conference On Electronic Commerce, pp. 228–229 (2004)
10. Zeng, D., Sycara, K.: Bayesian learning in negotiation. Int. J. Hum.-Comput. Stud. 48, 125–141 (1998)
11. W3C WSAG: Web services architecture (2004), http://www.w3.org/TR/ws-arch/
12. Globus Alliance: Open grid service architecture (2005),
    http://www.globus.org/ogsa/
13. Preist, C.: A Conceptual Architecture for Semantic Web Services. In: McIlraith, S.A., Plexousakis, D., van Harmelen, F. (eds.) ISWC 2004. LNCS, vol. 3298, pp. 395–409. Springer, Heidelberg (2004)
14. Burstein, M., Bussler, C., Zaremba, M., Finin, T., Huhns, M.N., Paolucci, M., Sheth, A.P., Williams, S.: A semantic web services architecture. IEEE Internet Computing 9, 72–81 (2005)
15. Weerawarana, S., Curbera, F., Leymann, F., Storey, T., Ferguson, D.F.: Web Services Platform Architecture. Prentice-Hall, Englewood Cliffs (2005)
16. Graham, S.G., Hull, D., Murray, B.: WS-BaseNotification Specification (2005),
    http://docs.oasis-open.org/wsn/wsn-ws_base_notification-1.3-spec-pr-01.pdf
17. Andrieux, A., Czajkowski, K., Dan, A., Keahey, K., Ludwig, H., Pruyne, J., Rofrano, J., Tuecke, S., Xu, M.: WS-Agreement specification (2004)
18. Andrieux, A., Czajkowski, K., Dan, A., Keahey, K., Ludwig, H., Pruyne, J., Rofrano, J., Tuecke, S., Xu, M.: WS-AgreementNegotiation specification, draft (2004)
19. FIPA: FIPA Contract Net Interaction Protocol Specification,
    http://www.fipa.org/specs/pesspecs.tar.gz
20. Group, X.P.W.: Soap specification (2003),
    http://www.w3.org/TR/soap12-part0/
21. Resinas, M., Fernandez, P., Corchuelo, R.: Automatic creation of agreements in a service-oriented scenario. In: Columbus, F. (ed.) Progress in Computer Network Research, pp. 41–62. Nova Science Publishers (2006)

SAGA: An Adaptive Infrastructure for Secure Available GRID on Ad-Hoc Networks

Manel Abdelkader[1], Noureddine Boudriga[1],
and Mohammad S. Obaidat[2]

[1]University of November 7th at Carthage, Tunisia
[2]Department of Computer Science, Monmouth University,
W. Long Branch, NJ 0764, U.S.A.
obaidat@monmouth.edu
http://wwwmonmoth.du/mobaidat

Abstract. Security management is a major issue in grid computing systems. One approach to provide security is to implement techniques such as encryption and access control on all grid elements. The overhead generated by such an approach may however limit the advantages of grid computing systems; particularly, when the network experiences different types of variations. This paper examines the integration of the notion of adaptive grid service along with security management and accounting. It also provides a fault tolerance technique to build grid systems that are intrusion tolerant.

Keywords: System security, grid computing, ad hoc networks, adaptive infrastructures.

1 Introduction

Recently, Grid computing has emerged as an attractive area characterized by large scale resource sharing, innovative applications and high-performance capabilities. The Grid problem has been defined as a flexible, secure, coordinated resource sharing among dynamic sets of individuals, institutions, and resources. In such settings, one can come across authentication, authorization, resource access, resource discovery, and quality of service (QoS) provision challenges.

Until recently, the main priority for grid developers has been to design working prototypes and demonstrate that applications can be developed over a grid environment with a restricted support to application-level fault tolerance in computational grids. Limited work also has addressed the integration of quality of service (QoS) and security while allocating resources. However, failure detection services were among the main supportive tools in developing grid environments; but, neither solution has considered the intrusion detection and intrusion tolerance [1, 2], nor did they provide schemes for the management of GRID resources when variability in the network dynamics is experienced.

Several recent studies have investigated security and trust management while allocating Grid resources [3-5]. Quite a few models have been proposed to quantify trust in Grid applications, including fuzzy model that was provided for e-commerce applications by

J. Filipe and M.S. Obaidat (Eds.): ICETE 2006, CCIS 9, pp. 15–27, 2008.
© Springer-Verlag Berlin Heidelberg 2008

[6]. Even though these studies have made interesting contributions, they did not address situations where multi-level trust is required, which is a natural assumption in environment where businesses are provided.

Wireless ad-hoc networks do not rely on a pre-existing network infrastructure and are characterized by a wireless multi-hop communication. Wireless ad-hoc networks are increasingly used in situations where a network must be deployed rapidly without an existing infrastructure. Unlike fixed wired network, wireless ad-hoc networks may have many operational limitations such as the transmission range, bandwidth, and energy. Additionally, wireless ad-hoc networks are vulnerable to more threats than those observed for the wired network, due to the dynamic nature of the routing infrastructure and the mobility of nodes. Applications of ad-hoc networks are emerging tremendously. New applications are nowadays getting more interest including target sensing, tactical battlefield and GRID computing.

Different features and challenges are introduced by the deployment of a GRID system over wireless ad-hoc networks. Among these features, one can consider the provision of protection to the whole GRID structure, the completion of the GRID execution, and the need for authentication and access control to resources, processes and messages involved in the GRID execution. In fact, to ensure distributed resources provision, different nodes in the wireless ad-hoc network should contribute, in the presence of the fact that each node of this structure does not have to know (or communicate directly with) all the other participants in the service provision.

Typically, wireless ad-hoc networks raise additional challenges to the provision of intrusion tolerant GRID systems, for which the effectiveness of wired solutions can be limited. To access a GRID service, a node needs to be under the coverage of an access point. In addition, a node agreeing to participate in a GRID service needs to stay connected until the service has terminated; otherwise a procedure for its replacement should be implemented. This is induced by the fact that a GRID architecture may vary in terms of time, location, and even availability. Security mechanisms must be deployed in order to counter threats against GRID over wireless ad-hoc networks. While cryptography-based mechanisms provide protection against some types of attacks from external nodes (with respect to the GRID service), they cannot be able to protect against malicious internal nodes, which may already have legitimate cryptographic keys. Therefore, mechanisms are necessary to provide intrusion tolerance for GRID applications.

The work presented in this paper aims at developing a general framework for the implementation of Grid applications in ad-hoc networking. The framework provides a generic extension mechanism for integrating multi-level trust management, QoS, and intrusion tolerance functionalities into Grid applications and handle variations in topology and availability. It consists of three models: a) a resource management scheme, which is responsible for resource description, request handling, and service continuity; b) an intrusion tolerance scheme; which integrates a scheme for event passing, a model for event correlation, and an alert notification procedure; and c) an accounting scheme, which includes the definition of a third party role, payment authentication, and payment processing.

We have addressed, in [8], the design of a GRID architecture on ad hoc networks, which includes service discovery, service request and service allocation. In addition, we have introduced the notion of real-time control and management of trust in ad hoc nodes. This work can be considered as a first step in the development of SAGA. In the present paper, we extend this architecture by addressing other issues for the GRID service provision, the availability of GRIID services and the tolerance to attacks and failure. Considering the high variability of ad hoc topology, we also discuss the role of rescue plans to ensure GRID service provision continuity.

The remaining of this paper is organized as follows. Section 2 provides a definition and architecture for the GRID system. Section 3 develops the main characteristics of SAGA service continuity and system flexibility to cope with ad-hoc variability and node autonomy. Section 4 defines an approach to integrate intrusion tolerance capabilities in Grid computing systems and the management of multi-level trust. Section 5 discusses an application of SAGA to micro-payment environment. Finally, section 6 concludes this paper.

2 Adaptive Infrastructure

Resource and connectivity protocols facilitate the sharing of individual resources in Grid systems. These protocols are designed so that they can be implemented on top of a large spectrum of resource types defined at a Grid layer, called Fabric layer (as depicted by Figure 1). They also can be used to construct a wide range of services and applications. Figure 1 depicts a layered Grid architecture for ad-hoc networks and its relationship to the Internet protocol architecture. Our architecture presents some similarities with the one discussed in [8], but it builds a number of useful services for GRID continuity and protection.

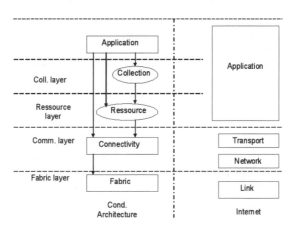

Fig. 1. Layered Grid architecture

The *Grid Fabric layer* provides the resources to which shared access is mediated by Grid protocols. A resource may be a logic entity, a storage resource, a network resource or a computational resource. The Fabric layer provides a resource-specific description of capabilities such as: (a) mechanisms for starting, monitoring and controlling of the resulting processes and controlling the resources allocated to these processes; (b) mechanisms for storing and retrieving files and (c) management mechanisms that allow control over resources allocated to processes and data transfers.

The *Communication layer* defines the communication and authentication protocols required for Grid-specific transactions. While communication protocols enable the exchange of data between fabric layer resources, the authentication protocols build on communication services to provide security services, such as authentication and integrity of users and resources and tolerance to intrusions. The communication layer should provide mechanisms for delegation, integration of local security and trust management.

The *Resource layer* builds on top of the connectivity layer for the secure negotiation, initiation, monitoring, accounting and billing of sharing operations on individual resources. Therefore, resource layer protocols are concerned entirely with individual resources and ignore issues of global state and atomic actions. Examples of resource layer protocols include information protocols, which collect information about the structure and state of a resource, and management protocols, which are used to negotiate access to shared resources while specifying resource requirements and the operation to be performed.

The *Collection layer* contains protocols and services that are able to capture interactions across the collection of resources. Example of services include (but are not restricted to): (a) the directory services that allow Grid users to discover resources; (b) the brokering services that allow users to request the allocation of one or more resources and the scheduling of tasks related to these resources; (c) software discovery services that help discovering and selecting execution platforms (or nodes) based on user/application parameters and (d) collaboration services that support accounting GRID services.

In Grid systems with distributed resources and task ownership, it is important to consider quality of service and security while discovering, allocating, and using resources. The integration of QoS has been examined with resource management systems by different studies. However, little work has been done for the integration of security considerations. Most cases have assumed that security is implemented as a separate subsystem from the Grid and the resource management system.

In a previous work, [8], we have developed a scheme to search and use resources and access a GRID application. In particular, we have demonstrated that after finding the resource responding to the node requirements on security and QoS, the requester delegates to this resource the rights to use other resources that may be needed during service provision. In this section, we recall the major features of this scheme and extend it to provide an adaptive behaviour that takes into consideration the variability of network topology, autonomy of nodes and security requirements.

Figure 2 depicts a Grid service setup. Three tasks are basically involved in this process:

1. A node requesting a Grid service discovers the ad-hoc nodes that are able to allocate tasks and resources to establish the desired service.
2. Upon receiving the request, a node willing to be involved in the Grid service answers the request by sending a response specifying the accepted tasks, the amount of resources it can allocate, the security level of the process (engaged in that node), the cost and whether the node will act as a service provider or service operator.
3. On receiving the responses, the requestor selects the set of nodes that will be engaged in the provision of the grid service. A negotiation may take place between

the requestor and a respondent before completing the service established. The negotiation involves QoS parameters, resources parameters and security services.

Features of the aforementioned process include the following three items:

- A service operator is a node that is in charge of offering the service using its own resources and the resources it can request on behalf of the requester. Therefore, the original requester does not need to know the identity of nodes involved in that share. In this case, the service operator is called delegated requestor.
- A service provider designates a node that acts as a server. It allocates the resources needed to the contracted tasks. It can leave the Grid on a simple message informing the requestor of its leave. It also can be dropped from the established Grid for various reasons, including security needs or renegotiation.
- Nodes contributing to a grid service are autonomous in the sense that they act as ad-hoc network node. They can move out of radio coverage, power off, or be attacked.

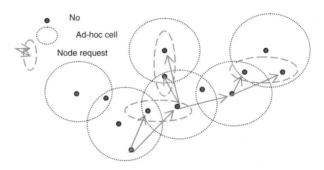

Fig. 2. Grid application on Ad-hoc network

Illustrative Example. An application of Grid can be demonstrated by a micro-payment system for packet service delivery similar to the one provided in [10] and which has the following properties:

- The application is only employed for paying packets forwarding: a node desiring to send a set of packets to a given set of destinations can request the delivery of these packets to other nodes that are known to be on the routes to destinations (neighbours or close cluster heads).
- Each node involved in the delivery has a prior knowledge of the routes that the packets it sends should follow.
- Each node should be able to know the costs of all paths leading to destination and details of costs for each intermediate nodes (or at least the costs to pay to the next nodes involved in the delivery).

3   Adaptive Grid Behaviour

To fulfill its objectives, a Grid service has to cope with the ad-hoc topology variability, node autonomy, and security intrusiont. The continuity of Grid service and the guarantee of the offered quality of service should be maintained as long as it is needed; otherwise correcting measures should be taken to correct any deviation. Measures fall into two classes: predictive and reactive.

3.1 Predictive Infrastructure Modification

When a server S (service provider or service operator) realizes that it cannot continue acting within a Grid to a requestor R, it starts searching for a replacement resource that can replace it and provide the remaining part of its agreement with R. This can be done as follows:

Resource Reservation. To perform the replacement task, S uses the delegation firstly given by R. It starts by negotiating with the servers it has involved in its offers to R. Let S_m, $1 \leq m \leq n$ be these servers; S checks with resources S_m, $1 \leq m \leq n$, whether one of them can fulfil the QoS agreement of the Grid service provided to R. If there is a server, say S_m, S presents to S_m the tasks required by the client R, the state of their execution, the remaining jobs and the related QoS information including the period of time t after which S will make the transfer to S_m, and S_m reserves the necessary resources to be used after t. Then, S gives S_m the list of the other resources participating to the execution of the job J_R requested by R.

Announcement. After that, S informs the resources involved with it about their new manager S_m to which they should send the results related to J_R after t. On the other hand, S informs its cluster head CH_S and the cluster head of R, CH_R, about this modification. CH_S liberates the connection between S and R. However, CH_R starts building a new route between R and the new server S_m. Further, the cluster head of S_m, $CH_{S(m)}$, starts to establish new routes between S_m and the other elementary resources. At the end of this phase, one can say that the 3-tuple $(R, S, \{S_m, 1 \leq m \leq n\})$ is replaced by the 3-tuple $(R, S_m, \{S_i, i \neq m \text{ and } 1 \leq i \leq n\})$ in the Grid service.

Job Transfer. Before making the transfer to S_m, R generates a new delegation credential to S_m to be used after time t. In this credential, R allows S_m to execute job J_R on its behalf and search for the required resources. When t expires, S transfers to S_m all the information and the results related to J_R. If S_m finds that it needs more resources, it uses the delegation credential given by R to search them. Thus, the job transfer is done from S to S_m without disturbing the execution of J_R and with respect to the QoS required by R.

3.2 Reactive Infrastructure Modification

The interruption of the GRID service provision may occur suddenly. Neither the resource, nor the requester has prior knowledge about this interruption. This case is critical and happens after a node crash or a damaging attack on a node involved in the Grid service provision. To handle this situation, appropriate mechanisms need to be made available (at the cluster heads) to discover and handle any disconnection at any step of Grid service provision period.

To react to sudden modifications, the cluster observing a disconnection of a server S should inform the sources requesting a Grid service to S that S became unavailable. This can be performed because a cluster head acts as a router in ad-hoc networks. It also can maintain the routes established by nodes belonging to its cluster. However, since it cannot distinguish between the users and the data transmitted on the different routes, we propose the introduction of a new field in the header of IP packets, called *Grid-index field*, to distinguish between routes used in GRID applications. In fact, each application would be characterized by a unique number A_i that should be maintained on all the routes related to the same application. This field is written by the first node initiating a GRID application and is maintained on all the routes to GRID servers.

Using this field, one can select an access to a GRID application by the IP address of the source, the IP address of the destination and the value A_i contained in the new field. Therefore, every cluster head can select and manage different groups of routes where each group is attached to a GRID application and contribute to the reaction to disconnections as follows:

Announcement. When server S stops suddenly to offer a GRID service to a requestor R, the first node that can notice the interruption would be the cluster head of S, CH_S. In addition, CH_S can distinguish the different GRID applications to which S is involved by using its routing table. After CH_S has realized the unavailability of S, it extracts from its routing table the different addresses of the nodes present in routes related to job J_R. Then, CH_S informs all the actors involved with S in the Grid service provision that S (let us call these servers again S_m, $1 \leq m \leq n$) is no longer available so that they can they can suspend the execution of tasks related to J_R during a period τ and free their resources to use them for other purposes during a period of time of length τ. This allows resources exploitation ever when S is unavailable. Finally, CH_S informs the requester R about the abrupt interruption.

Information Collection. In this phase, CH_S requests from all servers S_m, $1 \leq m \leq n$ reports on the usage related to the Grid service involving S. A report should contain the nature of the task, the state of the execution, the intermediate results and the remaining tasks scheduled, if needed. Each report should refer to the server responsible of the execution of job J_R. S then collects all the reports and sends them to the immediate requester R.

Resource Discovery. When receiving the intermediate reports, R should start a new request for new nodes (and resources) that are able to replace S and continue J_R execution. R begins by communicating with servers S_m, $1 \leq m \leq n$. It starts with the resource that may provide a better QoS in a secure manner [8]. If one among servers S_m accepts the replacement, R sends it the set of collected reports execution reports. In addition, R generates a new delegation credential allowing S_m to start service recovery. If no node in $\{S_m, 1 \leq m \leq n\}$ is able to accept the request, R can get back to the selection phase of S and asks whether one node among those competing with S can still handle the replacement, otherwise, it restarts the discovery process with the initial request published during the selection phase of S.

In the case where an agreement is concluded, R presents to the new server the different intermediate reports related to J_R, if a server S_m is selected, or the initial request, if no S_m is willing the replacement.

Service Recovery. Three cases should be considered:

1. If one server S_m is selected for the replacement of S, the recovery process described in the preventive case is applied. In this case, the 3-tuple $(R,S,\{S_m, 1\leq m\leq n\})$ is replaced by the 3-tuple $(R, S_m,\{ S_i, i\neq m \text{ and } 1\leq i\leq n\})$ in the Grid service, and new routes are built.

2. If a server, say S', that has competed with S is selected, the procedure used in the first case is involved, provided that S' plays the role of S_m. In this case, the 3-tuple $(R,S,\{S_m, 1\leq m\leq n\})$ is replaced by the 3-tuple $(R, S',\{S_i, 1\leq i\leq n\})$

3. If a new server T, servers $S_m, 1\leq m\leq n$, are dropped and the 3-tuple $(R,S,\{S_m, 1\leq m\leq n\})$ is replaced by the 3-tuple $(R, T,\{T_i, 1\leq i\leq t\})$ and new routes are built appropriately.

By receiving the identity of the new job manager, the servers involved in cases a) and b) give the priority to suspended tasks and continue their. In case 3, the server delete all computation made for the Grid service. We should note, however, that service recovery is only possible before the expiration of τ and the release of resources immediately after τ has expired, if no resume is engaged.

4 Secure Infrastructure

In this section, we show what makes the presented infrastructure secure. In fact, security mechanisms integrated in our solution protect GRID applications from different types of attacks such as those related to integrity violation, denial of service, and node defacement. However, the intrusion tolerance provided with SAGA guarantees robustness against a set of attacks that should be maintained.

A. Security Provision

Since the integration of digital credentials such as the X.509 public key certificates ensures mutual authentication between ad-hoc nodes, provides efficient digital signature, and protect the message exchange related to Grid service provision, SAGA assumes the nodes contributing to Grid services have digital credential allowing them to authenticate each other, provide confidentiality and protect ad-hoc nodes. Therefore, integrity of transmitted messages is ensured. Furthermore, a delegation service is guaranteed through specific credential definition. A delegation credential specifies identities of delegating and delegated nodes, delegated rights, and delegation validity. It may also address information related to accounting. Protection of delegation credentials is ensured by a digital signature. This allows the verification of authenticity, integrity and non repudiation of the delegated rights.

On the other hand, Intrusion tolerance in SAGA is guaranteed through the use of:

1. Preventive mechanisms that are based on the notion of trust level, which classify applications according to their requirements on security and behaviour. The management of trust guarantees that requesting nodes (to access a Grid service) are authorized only when they present a level of trust higher or equal to the level required to access the service
2. Detection mechanisms that allow the employment of cooperative local intrusion detection systems (IDS), which detect appropriate events and exchange security alerts
3. Recovery mechanisms allow dynamic trust management which is responsible for maintaining the trust level of node according to their behaviour and the attack they are subject to.

The basic idea behind the trust management assumes that the trust level of a node (or application) seen by a second node is initially defined by the digital credential of the node and can be decreased with the reporting alerts.

B. Protection Against Denial of Service

The deployment of an adaptive GRID on ad hoc networks introduces new types of attacks. Those attacks are related to the nature of information and messages exchanged between nodes participating in GRID service provision. Among these attacks, one can mention the denial of service attack (DoS) that can target the adaptive GRID. The following special attacks are important to protect SAGA against:

Erroneous-Alert Attacks: These attacks are launched to force reactive infrastructure modification. Such an attack operates as follows:

- A hacker interrupts all the messages transmitted between the server S and its cluster head CH_S during a period of time lasting sufficiently long.
- After a certain period of time, CH_S realizes that S is no longer reachable and begins the reactive procedure which induces the abortion of the GRID jobs handled by S and the waist of resources on the ad-hoc network.

This attack induces the augmentation of the execution delay of a GRID service. When repeated on different servers, these attacks might generate a distributed denial of service and endanger the system availability. Different protections can be used against these attacks. Protections may include; but are not limited to: (a) the duplication of the role of CH_S; (b) an effective control of the reachability of S (CH_S asks the remaining nodes of its cluster to try to reach S, for example) and (c) keeping the role and communication made by S confidential. In fact, when the reachibility of S is under investigation, CH_S should not generate the alerts related the needed reaction, it saves the reports and messages to deliver to S until investigation completion and delivers them appropriately.

Alert-Absence Attacks: The attacks target the reactive infrastructure. They operate as follows:

- When a server S involved in a Grid service is no longer available, its cluster head CH_S generates an alert to inform elementary resources to suspend the execution of jobs managed by S.
- A hacker interrupts the transmission of the alert. The resources involved with S (S is a service operator) continue to be reserved for S although S is no longer available.

These attacks may induce several damages including: (a) useless resource locking and other jobs are delayed; (b) loss of intermediate reports that continue to be sent to CH_S where they are deleted or ignored and (c) unacceptable overhead for the network and all the nodes contributing to the Grid service routing.

A protection against these attacks aims at imposing that every resource involved with server S should receive an acknowledgment from S after sending an intermediate report. Those acknowledgments should be protected and should refer to the report they are acknowledging.

Service Interruption Attacks: These attacks can target the predictive and reactive infrastructure modification. They aim at interrupting the initialization of a Grid service, blocking the communications between a service operator and the resources (or nodes) $\{S_i\}_{1 \le i \le n}$ involved with it, replaying sensitive messages, or modifying the value of the new Grid-index field that we have added to the packet header (see Section 2). Regarding the latter attack, one can perform it as follows:

- A hacker can distinguish the application that has a Grid-index A_i. Then it can interrupt all the communications related to this application by modifying the Grid-index field content.
- It also can copy all messages, reports and transported results related to the application associated with index A_i.
- The hacker also can change the index A_i and so neither S nor the nodes $\{S_i\}_{1 \le i \le n}$ can reach each other. This induces the starvation of the GRID application and the loss of network resources.

To protect against these attacks, various mechanisms can be added including the protection of the integrity of the Grid-index content, the insertion of protected nonce (a sequence number or time stamp) and IPSec.

5 SAGA Application

In this section we illustrate the use of the scheme presented in the previous sections. We consider an interesting domain of applications that can take place on an ad hoc network. This is a distributed application, referred to as micro-payment on ad-hoc environment.

In [10], authors propose a protocol employing micro-payment techniques. The protocol allows each ad hoc node involved in packets relaying to be paid by the sender as it provides the service. It allows paying all nodes in the path to a given destination without the requirement to contact a third trust party or a bank to issue a new payment contract. The main steps of this protocol are described as follows:

1. A user buys prepaid tokens through his/her terminal from a broker whose main purpose is to aggregate micro-payments between entities. The user starts by generating an unbalanced one-way binary tree and sends the set of N defined anchors to the broker.

2. The broker generates a set of N secret endorsement values; one for each anchor value that was sent by the user. A broker endorsement consists of an anchor value, a random number corresponding to the endorsement value, the length of the hash chain, the value of a hash in the chain, the identity of the user that purchased the chain and the expiration date of the chain.

   All of the above fields are signed with the private key of the broker. The Grid service associated with this application assumes the following:

- When it is desired to set up a call to a remote destination (or asset of call to remote destinations). The user should have knowledge of the total costs involved in forwarding the related packet through the ad hoc network. Each node in the path to destination(s) must indicate its charge for packet forwarding.
  - With every packet or message sent by the user, the user should attach the cost of transmission. Every node in the established route extracts the value of the cost required. The unit defined to pay the different nodes is a single hash token. Thus, every node presents the number of tokens it wants for the forwarding.

The integration of this application in a Grid infrastructure should introduce some modifications for the sake of flexibility. In fact, we propose the integration of this application to pay the use of different resources used in a Grid application (i.e., Grid accounting). Modifications assume that the requester R knows only the set of immediate servers $\{S_i\}_{1 \leq i \leq n}$ and it is not supposed to identify the set of the other nodes contributing to the execution of the Grid service. In addition, a Grid application can offer other services than packets forwarding, which means that every node should determine dynamically the cost that it requires to contribute to the Grid service.

To manage the new assumptions, we assume that a server S_i (e.g.;, service provider) is responsible for paying for the resources, $\{S_{i,j}\}_{1 \leq j \leq ni}$, that it can get involved in. In fact, after determining the set of resources with which S_i will collaborate, S_i asks for a total cost including the use of all resources needed to perform the tasks it is assigned. S_i collects all the costs and adds them to its local costs. The total cost is then sent to the applicant R. Based on the delegation credentials initially generated and the trust levels of R and S_i. R presents an appropriate set of tokens to S_i. These tokens are encrypted with the public key of S_i. Then, S_i manages these tokens to cover its own cost and the costs of $S_{i,j}$, for $1 \leq j \leq n_i$. When paying a contributing $S_{i,j}$, S_i should encrypt the required tokens by the public key of $S_{i,j}$. In addition tokens should no longer go together with each packet.

We assume that after collecting the tokens corresponding to a service provision, a server presents these tokens to the broker which is responsible for concluding the payment. Before making the transfer, the broker should wait for a period of time. This period is fixed by the administrator allowing the reception of any objection. In fact, if a node takes the tokens without achieving the tasks for which it was paid, the payer could protest against concluding the payment. If this period of time expires without receiving any objection, the transfer is concluded and the server is paid.

Finally, new security features should be considered according to the SAGA model. They include:

- In the case of predictive modification, before a server S withdraws, it should pay all the contributing resources for the jobs they are involved with S. Furthermore, S should return the unused tokens to requester R. The latter will give other tokens to the new server S'. The operation of giving new tokens can be kept as it was defined in [10].
- In the case of reactive modifications, the contributing resources $\{S_i\}_{1 \leq i \leq n}$ to a withdrawing server S should inform R about the last payment they obtained. R informs the broker to revoke the remaining tokens and use new tokens to continue GRID service provision. In this case, we believe that there is a need to tolerate very limited token losses since the applicant can not define precisely when S was gone away. Two reasons can justify our tolerance. This assumption can be made since micro-payment is a field where such assumptions are accepted, when they are limited. In fact, this kind of payment reduces the possible losses since it divides the payment amount into small values. In addition, the trust management provided in SAGA can require that a node, which does not conclude its agreements without signalling it, will see a decrease in its trust level. This will impact its further works.

6   Conclusions

In this paper, we addressed the issue of adaptive behaviours in a Grid service provision. Our approach builds systems called SAGA that are able to define a framework for the design of Grid application that are secure, tolerant to intrusion and can cope with the variable nature of ad-hoc networks.

The framework provides a generic extension mechanism for integrating multi-level trust management, QoS, and intrusion tolerance functionalities into Grid applications and handle variations in topology and availability.

References

1. Casanova, W., Cirne, H., Dail, M., Faerman, S., Figueira, J., Hayes, G., Obertelli, J., Schopf, G., Shao, S., Smallen, N., Spring, A., Su, A., Zagorodnov, D.: Adaptive computing on the Grid using AppleS. IEEE Transactions on parallel and distributed systems 14(4), 369–382 (2003)
2. Song, S., Hwang, K.: Dynamic Grid security with trust integration and optimized resource allocation. In: Int. Symp. On High-performance distributed computing, Honolulu, June 4-6 (2004)
3. Butt, A., Adabala, S., Kapadia, N., Figueiredo, R., Fortes, J.: Fine-grain access control for securing shared resources in computational Grids. In: 2002 Proc. Int. Parallel and distributed processing symposium (IPDPS 2002), April 2002, pp. 159–165 (2002)
4. Azzedin, F., Maheswaran, M.: Towards trusted-aware resource management in Grid computing systems. In: Proc. 2nd IEEE/ACM Int. Symp. on cluster computing and the Grid (2002)

5. Czajkowski, K., Foster, I., Kesselman, C.: Resource co-allocation in computational Grids. In: Proc. 8th IEEE Int. Symp. on high-performance distributed computing (HPDC-8), pp. 219–228 (1999)
6. Gefen, D., Rao, V.S., Tractinsky, N.: The conceptualization of trust, risk, and their relationships in e-commerce. In: Proc. 36th Hawaii Int. Conf. on System science (HICSS 2003) (2003)
7. Foster, I., Kesselman, C., Tuecke, S.: The anatomy of the Grid: Enabling scalable virtual organizations. Int J. Supercomputer applications (2001)
8. Abdelkader, M., Boudriga, N.: Intrusion Tolerant GRID in Ad-Hoc Networks. In: 12th IEEE International Conference on Electronics, Circuits and Systems, ICECS 2005, Tunis, December 11-14 (2005)
9. Liu, R., Lloyd, E.L.: A Distributed Protocol For Adaptive Link Scheduling in Ad-hoc Networks. In: Proc. of IASTED Int. Conf. on Wireless and Optical Comm (WOC 2001) (2001)
10. Tewari, H., O'Mahony, D.: Multiparty Micropayments for Ad Hoc Networks. In: IEEE Wireless Communications and Networking Conference, WCNC 2003 (2003)

Variable Quantity Market Clearing Algorithms

Jarrod Trevathan and Wayne Read

School of Mathematics, Physics and Information Technology, James Cook University, Australia
{jarrod.trevathan,wayne.read}@jcu.edu.au

Abstract. Market clearing is the process of matching buy and sell bids in securities markets. The allocative efficiency of such algorithms is important, as the Auctioneer is typically paid a commission on the number of bids matched and the volume of quantity traded. Previous algorithms have concentrated on price issues. This paper presents several market clearing algorithms that focus solely on allocating quantity among matching buy and sell bids. The goal is to maximise the number of bids matched, while at the same time minimise the amount of unmatched quantity. The algorithms attempt to avoid situations resulting in unmarketable quantities (i.e., quantities too small to sell). Algorithmic performance is tested using simulated data designed to emulate the Australian Stock Exchange (ASX) and other world stock markets. Our results show that it is difficult to avoid partial matchings as the complexity of doing so is NP-complete. The optimal offline algorithm for partial quantity matching is used as a benchmark to compare online matching strategies. We present three algorithms that outperform the ASX's strategy by increasing the number of bids matched, the amount of quantity matched, and the number of bids fully matched.

Keywords: Continuous double auctions, online auctions, share trading, competitive analysis.

1 Introduction

Securities markets such as the New York Stock Exchange[1] and the Australian Stock Exchange [2] (ASX), employ a form of auction referred to as a *Continuous Double Auction* (CDA). A CDA has many buyers and sellers continuously trading a commodity. Buy and sell bids accumulate over time and must be cleared. The method by which buy and sell bids are matched is referred to as a *market clearing algorithm*. In general, two bids can only be matched if: 1) both bids are currently active (i.e., they haven't expired or previously been cleared); and 2) the price of a buy bid equals or exceeds the price of a sell offer.

The efficiency and performance of a clearing algorithm is important. An algorithm must be able to cope with large numbers of bids, and make timely decisions which maximise the benefits for buyers and sellers. Furthermore, the Auctioneer/Broker typically gains commission on the *number of bids cleared*, and the *volume of quantity traded*. As a result, the algorithm must also strive to maximise both of these factors.

---

[1] http://www.nyse.com
[2] http://www.asx.com.au

J. Filipe and M.S. Obaidat (Eds.): ICETE 2006, CCIS 9, pp. 28–39, 2008.
© Springer-Verlag Berlin Heidelberg 2008

Stock exchanges have been fully automated since the early 1990s (see [2]). The ASX uses a computerised clearing system referred to as the Stock Exchange Automated Trading System (SEATS). SEATS imposes a strict time-based priority on matching bids. Bids are ordered according to price, and are then matched based on their arrival times. Larger bids are not given priority over small bids.

Alternate strategies for market clearing have been discussed by [9,6]. [7] show that in some situations, the Auctioneer can increase the profit from a sale (i.e., the price difference between a buy and sell bid). This is achieved by not matching bids immediately, but rather waiting for a better match to possibly eventuate. [7] also describe how profit producing matches can subsidise loss producing matches to increase the total number of bids matched.

The market clearing model used by [7] mainly attempts to maximise the amount of surplus generated by the matching process. In doing so, the model only considers price, and assumes that the quantity of each bid is *one* unit. If a bidder desires to bid for more than one unit, then they must enter a number of bids equal to the amount of the quantity. (e.g., five separate bids are required to bid for a quantity of five units.)

This approach is not very practical when the amount of quantity transacted is large. For example, in the case where a bidder desires $10,000$ units, it is unlikely they would be willing to expend time and effort to submit $10,000$ bids. While software bidding agents and other automated methods could be used to alleviate this situation, there are further issues regarding allocating quantity among bids. For example, a bidder may desire n units, but the market is only able to clear ρ units, where $\rho < n$. This may leave the bidder with an *unmarketable quantity*. An unmarketable quantity, is a quantity that is too small to sell, after taking into account Auctioneer commission, and other associated costs.

In this paper, we propose the idea of a *variable quantity market clearing algorithm*. Once bids have been ordered according to price, a variable quantity market clearing algorithm is used to efficiently allocate quantity among matching buy and sell bids. The algorithm attempts to match up as many bids as possible, with as little or no unmatched quantity outstanding. The primary goal is to avoid situations that result in unmarketable quantities.

This paper presents several variable quantity market clearing algorithms. The first algorithm shows why it is difficult in practice to avoid unmarketable quantities. The second algorithm gives the optimal offline solution in terms of avoiding unmarketable quantities. The third algorithm is online, and is the approach used by SEATS. The remaining algorithms are online, and try to outperform Algorithm 3, using differing strategies including; waiting until a bid is ready to expire before matching, subsidising short falls in allocation, and giving priority to bids with smaller quantities.

The algorithms have been tested on simulated data designed to emulate the workings of the ASX. Each algorithm is assessed according to the number of bids matched, the volume of quantity traded and how much unmarketable quantity is produced. We show that it is possible to out-perform SEATS in terms of these goals.

This paper is organised as follows: The CDA model and goals of the algorithms are discussed in Section 2. Section 3 presents several market clearing algorithms for matching variable quantities of an item. A comparison of the algorithms is given in Section 4, and Section 5 provides some concluding remarks.

2   Preliminaries

This section presents a CDA model for describing variable quantity market clearing algorithms. The goals for a clearing algorithm are discussed, and basic statistics are introduced for measuring how an algorithm performs in terms of these goals.

2.1   Model

The algorithms presented in this paper are based on a *temporal clearing model*. This consists of a set of buy bids, B, and a set of sell bids, S. Each bid $v \in B \cup S$ has the components $(type, t_i, t_j, p, q)$.

$type = \{buy, sell\}$ denotes the type of the bid. It is common in securities markets to refer to a buy bid as a *bid* and a sell bid as an *offer*.

A bid, v, is introduced at time $t_i(v)$, and removed at time $t_j(v)$, where $t_i(v) < t_j(v)$. A bid, v, is said to be alive in the interval $[t_i(v), t_j(v)]$. To be a candidate for a particular matching, two bids must have a period where their arrival and expiration times overlap. Two bids $v, v' \in B \cup S$ are said to be *concurrent*, if there is some time when both are alive simultaneously.

p denotes the price of a bid. In order to run the clearing algorithm, bids are first ordered according to price. The definition of concurrency now extends to two bids that met the criteria for matching based on price. This allows us to concentrate on matching quantities rather than prices. The problem now becomes the opposite extreme of the price-matching problem from [7].

$q \in [q_{min}, q_{max}]$ denotes the quantity, and $q(v)$ is the quantity desired by bid v. q must be greater than zero and an integer, i.e., it is not possible to buy or sell a fraction of a quantity.

The temporal bidding model is abstracted as an incomplete interval graph. An incomplete interval graph is a graph $G = (V, E)$, together with two functions t_i and t_f from V to $[0, \infty]$ such that:

1. For all $v \in V$, $t_i(v) < t_f(v)$. (i.e., the entry time is less than the exit time.)
2. If $(v, v') \in E$, then $t_i(v) \leq t_f(v')$ and $t_i(v') \leq t_f(v)$. (i.e., bids are concurrent.)

An incomplete interval graph can be thought of as an abstraction of the temporal bidding problem. The fact that bids come in two types (buy and sell) and have prices attached to them is ignored. Instead a black box "E" is used, that given two bids v, v', outputs whether or not they can be matched. This generalisation provides a simple framework for describing and developing clearing algorithms.

2.2   Goals

The quantity matching algorithms presented in this paper have the following goals:

Maximise Number of Matches. The first goal is to maximise the number of matches between buy and sell bids. This is important as the Auctioneer typically gains a commission based on the number of bids matched.

The *Bid Match Ratio* (BMR) is used to measure the number of bids matched, α, in relation to the total number of bids, n. This is calculated as:

$$BMR = \alpha/n \times 100$$

where $0 \leq \text{BMR} \leq 100$.

Maximise Volume of Quantity Matched. The second goal is to maximise the amount of quantity matched. The Auctioneer also typically gains a commission proportional to the volume of quantity cleared.

The *Quantity Match Ratio* (QMR) is used to measure the amount of matched quantity, δ, in relation to the total quantity, γ. This is calculated as:

$$QMR = \delta/\gamma \times 100$$

where $0 \leq \text{QMR} \leq 100$.

Maximise Full Quantity Matches. A *full* match occurs when a bid has had its entire quantity matched and cleared. A *partial* match occurs when a bid which is in the process of being matched, expires with an outstanding quantity that hasn't been filled. The Auctioneer must strive to satisfy the entire quantity of a bid, so that a bidder is not left with an unmarketable quantity.

The *Full Match Ratio* (FMR) examines the bids that were fully matched, ϵ, against the total number of matches, ζ. This is calculated as:

$$FMR = \epsilon/\zeta \times 100$$

where $0 \leq \text{FMR} \leq 100$.

2.3   Analysing Efficiency

Within both Computer Science and Finance, many problems reduce to trying to predict the future. For example, cache/virtual memory management, process scheduling, or predicting future returns for an asset. Such problems become trivial if the future is known (i.e., the stream of future memory requests or tomorrow's newspaper), but typically we only have access to the past.

An offline problem provides access to all the relevant information to compute a result. An online problem continually produces new input and requires answers in response. Offline problems have the benefit of perfect knowledge, anas such they generally outperform online problems (if designed properly).

An *offline* clearing algorithm learns of all bids up front. That is, all bids must be submitted before a closing time. The algorithm is then able to match bids at its discretion. An *online* clearing algorithm only learns about bids as they are introduced over time. The online algorithm has the added complexity of bids expiring before they can be matched.

Securities markets employ both types of algorithms. For example, the online algorithm is used during trading hours and the offline algorithm is used after hours while bids accumulate over night.

Competitive analysis allows an online algorithm to be compared based on its ability to successfully predict the future. The efficiency of an online solution is compared to the optimal offline solution. The closer an online algorithm performs to the optimal offline algorithm, the more 'competitive' the algorithm is.

An algorithm, A, is said to be *c-competitive* if there exists some constant b, such that for every sequence of inputs σ:

$$cost_A(\sigma) \leq c \ cost_{OPT}(\sigma) + b$$

where OPT is the optimal offline algorithm. In developing an online algorithm, the goal is to attain a *competitive ratio*, c, as close to one as possible. The worse the performance of an algorithm, the larger c is.

In this paper, an optimal offline solution is presented for clearing variable quantities. Several online strategies are discussed, and their performance is compared based on their competitive ratios. Related literature on how competitive analysis has been applied to online auctioning can be found in [4,5,1].

3   Quantity Clearing Algorithms

This section presents several market clearing algorithms for matching variable quantities of an item.

3.1   Algorithm 1

The initial goal for this algorithm is to either match quantities entirely, or not at all (i.e., bids are *indivisible*). This effectively eliminates the possibility of unmarketable quantities.

For example, a buy and sell bid each for 1 unit, can be matched. In addition, a buy bid for 2 units can be matched to two sell bids that are for 1 unit each. However, if a buyer is demanding 2 units, and there is a seller supplying only 1 unit, then neither of the bids can be matched.

Matching indivisible quantities is similar to the Knapsack problem. Consider the case where there is a buy bid v for a quantity $q(v) = n$. In order to match this bid, the algorithm is required to select either a single sell bid v' offering n units, or some combination of n or less sell bids, where the collective quantity on offer sums exactly to n. The complexity of the algorithm for matching indivisible quantities is dominated by this step.

The problem of trying to find a subset of integers from a given set, that sums to a particular value, is referred to as the *subset sum problem*. The subset sum problem is considered to be hard, and there are no known algorithms to efficiently solve it. The quandary of matching indivisible quantities can be reduced to the subset sum problem. The subset sum problem is NP-complete, and therefore the indivisible quantity matching problem is also NP-complete. As a result, it is not feasible to construct an efficient algorithm that does not deliver unmarketable quantities.

Even if this algorithm were practical, it does not necessarily perform well in terms of the number of bids matched, as it is too restrictive. The costs of unmarketable quantities must be weighed against the benefits of relaxing the indivisibility constraint. Doing so allows the clearing process to benefit the majority of bidders, while at times delivering an undesirable result to a minority. The problem now becomes how to limit the extent of unmarketable quantities.

3.2   Algorithm 2

This algorithm is offline and allows bids to be *divisible*. A particular bid is matched with as many other candidate bids as required to satisfy it. If there is not enough available quantity, the bid is considered as *partially matched*. A partial matching can result in bidders holding unmarketable quantities. The goal of this algorithm is to match as many bids as possible and minimise partial matchings.

A greedy strategy is employed which successively subtracts the smaller bid quantity from the larger opposite bid quantity. The algorithm keeps track of the current unmatched buy and sell quantities at each stage of the algorithm using two variables, α_b and α_s. Once a particular bid has been allocated its exact quantity, it is cleared (i.e., moved to the set M). The algorithm is as follows:

1. $\alpha_b = \alpha_s = 0$.
2. While there are more vertices in G
   (a) if α_b and $\alpha_s = 0$ then
       i. get next v and v' from G
       ii. if $q(v) > q(v')$ then
           $\alpha_b = q(v)$
       iii. else
           $\alpha_s = q(v')$
   (b) else if $\alpha_b > 0$ then
       i. get next v' from G
       ii. if $\alpha_b > q(v')$ then
           A. $\alpha_b = \alpha_b - q(v')$
           B. place edge between v and v', move v' to M
       iii. else
           A. $\alpha_s = q(v') - \alpha_b$
           B. place edge between v and v', move v to M
   (c) else if $\alpha_s > 0$ then
       i. get next v from G
       ii. if $\alpha_s > q(v)$ then
           A. $\alpha_s = \alpha_s - q(v)$
           B. place edge between v and v', move v to M
       iii. else
           A. $\alpha_b = q(v) - \alpha_s$
           B. place edge between v and v', move v' to M

As all bids are concurrent, the proposed solution is equivalent to summing the volumes of buy and sell bids, and subtracting the smaller from the larger. This algorithm is the optimal solution for matching variable quantities, and is the basis for the operation of the forthcoming online algorithms.

3.3 Algorithm 3

This algorithm is online and uses the same strategy as Algorithm 2. Bids have entry and expiration times. When a bid is introduced, it is matched with as many other bids as possible. However, when expiration time is reached, the bid is cleared regardless of whether it has been fully matched. That is, if a bid is in the process of being matched when it expires, its outstanding quantity remains unfilled.

This is the actual approach used by SEATS and most of the world's securities markets. It is simple, fair and performs relatively well. However, this algorithm performs significantly worse than the previous algorithm, and can result in many bids expiring partially matched.

3.4 Algorithm 4

Algorithm 4 aspires to out-perform the previous algorithm. When a bid expires in Algorithm 3, there may be a significant amount of residual unmatched quantity. In addition, bids that arrive later, but expire earlier have to wait on earlier bids, with later expiration times. Algorithm 4 modifies the previous algorithm by waiting till a bid is about to expire, before matching it with as many other bids as possible based on expiry time.

3.5 Algorithm 5

Algorithm 5 uses an inventory of quantity to offset the unfilled portions of partially matched bids. We refer to this as *subsidising*.

To acquire an inventory, the Auctioneer must first collect surplus quantity. A *surplus* occurs when the quantity on offer is greater than the quantity being bid for. If a buy bid demands a quantity less than the quantity offered by a sell bid, then the Auctioneer pays for the surplus. The surplus quantity is placed in an inventory that can be used at a later date to subsidise shortfalls in allocation. A *shortage* occurs when there is less quantity on offer than the amount bid for. Determining the extent to subsidise shortages requires choosing a threshold, which is the maximum amount that can be subsidised. This is denoted by θ.

The algorithm proceeds in a similar manner to the previous online algorithms. However, when a bid is about to expire, it becomes a candidate for subsidisation. Let I denote the current inventory of quantity held by the algorithm. The subsidisation process is as follows:

1. if v is type *sell* then
   (a) if $(I + q(v) < \theta)$ then
       $I = I + q(v)$
   (b) else
       $temp = \theta - I$
       $I = I + temp$
       $q(v) = q(v) - temp$
2. else if v is type *buy* then
   (a) if $(I < q(v))$ then
       $q(v) = q(v) - I$

(b) else
$$I = I - q(v)$$
$$q(v) = 0$$
3. Move v to M

The choice of θ depends on the risk the Auctioneer is willing to take. If θ is set too small, the Auctioneer will not be able to significantly influence the clearing process. However, if θ is set too large, the Auctioneer might be left holding a large quantity at the close of trade, which is undesirable.

The *Remaining Inventory Ratio* (RIR) is used to measure the extent of remaining quantity held by the Auctioneer at the close of trade. The RIR is calculated as follows:

$$RIR = I/\theta \times 100$$

where $0 \leq RIR \leq 100$.

3.6   Algorithm 6

A problem with the greedy approach of Algorithms 2 and 3 is that a large number of smaller bids may be waiting on a earlier, larger bid to clear.

In economic systems it is usually the case that a smaller number of individuals own the most. Likewise, in share trading there tend to be more bids for smaller quantities compared to larger bids. Large bids are often due to financial institutions such as superannuation schemes or managed funds that pool the capital of many smaller investors. An Auctioneer can take advantage of the above situation by clearing the smaller bids first. This will increase the number of bids matched while leaving the volume traded unchanged.

Algorithm 6 gives priority to smaller bids. That is, if a large bid is in the process of being matched, it is 'pre-empted' when a smaller bid arrives. This is analogous to the problem of process scheduling where many processes compete for CPU time. In shortest job first scheduling, the process with the shortest time is given priority to use the CPU.

In terms of market clearing, quantity represents CPU time and bidders are the processes. However, matching bids is two sided and therefore more complicated than process scheduling. That is, the set of buy bids represents a set of processes, and the set of sell bids represents another set of processes. When a large buy bid is matched to several smaller sell bids, the buy bid is equivalent to the CPU for that instance in time (and vice versa).

4   Comparison

This section provides a comparison of the market clearing algorithms. Each algorithm is assessed on its ability to achieve the goals outlined in Section 2.2. These goals are: maximise the number of matched bids (BMR), maximise the volume of quantity matched (QMR), and maximise the number of fully matched bids (i.e., avoid partial matchings)(FMR).

The *Research Auction Server* at James Cook University, is an online auction server used to conduct research into online auctioning [see [8]]. The auction server contains a

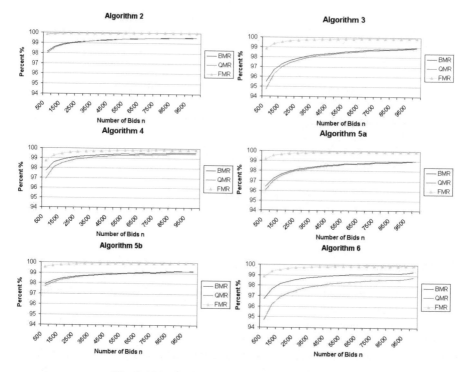

Fig. 1. Algorithmic Performance on Simulated Data

simulation environment for testing computational aspects related to auctioning online. This includes emulating the workings of the ASX by generating the kind of bidding data that exists in share markets. The clearing algorithms were tested in this setting using the simulated data.

The input parameters for a test are the number of bids, n, the maximum quantity allowable for a bid, q_{max}, and the total time, t. Time is split into discrete units representing seconds. Entry and Exit times are randomly generated between time period one and t. Bids are randomly allocated quantities between one and q_{max}. For now, it is assumed that entry/exit times and quantities are uniformly distributed among bidders, and there is an even number of buy and sell bids (i.e., # buy = # sell = $n/2$).

Figure 1 shows the individual results for each algorithm (except Algorithm 1). Each algorithm was tested using varying numbers of bids up to a maximum of $n = 10,000$, with $q_{max} = 1000$. The online algorithms are shown for a six-hour time period (i.e., $t = 21,600$ seconds). This is consistent with the trading hours of the ASX and most share markets.

In general, all algorithms run in a time proportional to n. Furthermore, the larger the value of n, the better the performance. Additionally, online algorithms tended to perform better with smaller values of t. The size of q_{max} does not significantly affect the running time or the performance of the algorithms.

For each algorithm, trendlines are calculated using the *method of least squares*. The resulting equations for each algorithm are listed in Table 1. The smaller the value of the

Table 1. Comparison of Variable Quantity Market Clearing Algorithms

Type	BMR	QMR	FMR	RIR	Competitive Ratio
Alg. 2 offline	$0.43 \ln(n)$	$0.47 \ln(n)$	$0.05 \ln(n)$	-	Optimal
Alg. 3 online	$1.05 \ln(n)$	$1.23 \ln(n)$	$0.29 \ln(n)$	-	2.44
Alg. 4 online	$0.51 \ln(n)$	$0.71 \ln(n)$	$0.30 \ln(n)$	-	1.18
Alg. 5a online	$0.81 \ln(n)$	$0.91 \ln(n)$	$0.21 \ln(n)$	50.61%	1.88
Alg. 5b online	$0.43 \ln(n)$	$0.48 \ln(n)$	$0.11 \ln(n)$	50.13%	1.00
Alg. 6 online	$0.77 \ln(n)$	$1.20 \ln(n)$	$0.29 \ln(n)$	-	1.79

coefficient of $\ln(n)$ for the BMR, QMR and FMR, the better the performance. Competitive analysis is used to compare the performance of the online algorithms to the optimal offline algorithm. The BMR is used to determine an algorithm's competitive ratio.

Algorithm 2 is the optimal offline strategy for matching divisible bids. Only a small percentage of bids were partially matched. This algorithm is the benchmark to which all online algorithms are compared. This algorithm is $1 - competitive$.

Algorithm 3 is online, and orders bids strictly according to entry time (the approach used by SEATS). This algorithm performs significantly worse than the offline algorithm. This algorithm is $2.44 - competitive$.

Algorithm 4 waits until a bid is about to expire before matching it. This strategy is a significant improvement on Algorithm 3. The reason for this is that by waiting, the algorithm is essentially acting similar to the offline algorithm. Although this algorithm doesn't have perfect knowledge about future bids, delaying matching allows the algorithm to gather more information, which it can use to optimise its matching decision. However, Algorithm 4's FMR does not fare much better than Algorithm 3. This algorithm is $1.18 - competitive$.

Algorithm 5 uses an inventory of quantity to subsidise deficit quantity trades. Two tests were conducted with differing values of θ. The first test (referred to as Algorithm 5a), examined the effect of minimal subsidisation. The second test (referred to as Algorithm 5b), used excessive subsidisation. Both tests were also assessed on the amount of inventory remaining at the end (i.e., the RIR, see Section 3.4).

Algorithm 5a uses minimal subsidisation where $\theta = 1000$. This algorithm improved upon Algorithm 3 (i.e., SEATS) with regard to its BMR and QMR. This algorithm achieved a better FMR than both previous online algorithms. This algorithm is $1.88 - competitive$.

Algorithm 5b uses excessive subsidisation where $\theta = 5000$ ($5 \times q_{max}$). This algorithm's performance approaches Algorithm 2 in terms of BMR and QMR. It also attains an excellent FMR. This algorithm is $1 - competitive$. If subsidisation were without bound, eventually all bids would be matched.

The amount of remaining inventory (i.e., RIR) for Algorithm 5a and 5b were 50.61% and 50.13% respectively. This shows that over time, the clearing algorithm will always be holding an inventory that is half full (i.e., $\theta/2$). While excessive subsidisation may achieve significant results, the practicality of subsidising must be weighed against the level of risk the Auctioneer is willing to take.

Algorithm 6 prioritises bids with smaller amounts of quantity. This algorithm out performs Algorithm 3 (SEATS) in terms of its BMR, and improves on using minimal subsidisation. The QMR and FMR are marginal improvements on Algorithm 3. This algorithm is $1.79 - competitive$. This result is consistent with the goals of the algorithm. That is, we strived for an increase in the BMR by matching a larger number of smaller bids. In doing so, the amount of matched quantity would be roughly the same.

5   Conclusions

A market clearing algorithm's performance greatly affects the revenue earned by the Auctioneer, and the welfare of the bidders. Previous literature on market clearing only addresses price issues, and neglects concerns regarding allocative efficiency.

This paper presents several market clearing algorithms that focus solely on allocating quantity among matching buy and sell bids. The algorithms attempt to avoid situations resulting in unmarketable quantities (i.e., quantities too small to sell).

We show that it is difficult to avoid partial matchings, as the complexity of doing so is NP-complete. The problem of matching bids with indivisible quantities reduces to the subset sum problem. The subset sum problem is a renowned NP-complete problem. As a result, an efficient algorithm cannot be constructed to avoid partial matchings.

An optimal offline algorithm is presented for matching bids with divisible quantities. The algorithm employs a greedy strategy. Each bid is matched with as many other bids as required to satisfy it. This approach achieves a high match rate. However, the algorithm can result in a limited number of bidders receiving partial matchings.

SEATS and most of the world's stock exchanges use an online version of the previous algorithm. Bids are strictly ordered by price and time. Larger bids are not given priority over smaller bids. This algorithm is simple and fair. However, it performs significantly worse than the optimal offline solution.

We propose several alternate methods for clearing variable quantities. The goal is to out-perform the approach used by SEATS. Algorithmic performance is tested using simulated data designed to emulate the ASX. Competitive analysis is used to compare the performance of an online algorithm to the optimal offline solution.

The first of our proposed algorithms showed that there is some benefit in waiting rather than matching with the first available quantity. Waiting until a bid is about to expire before matching, makes the algorithm function more like its offline counterpart. This algorithm performs significantly better than SEATS.

The next algorithm collects surplus quantity to subsidise shortfalls in allocation. With minimal subsidisation, this algorithm can deliver less partial matchings than SEATS. With excessive subsidisation, this algorithm can approach the efficiency of the optimal offline solution. However, the level of subsidisation must be weighed against the potential to be left holding a large inventory at the end of matching.

Alternately, the final algorithm gives priority to bids with smaller quantities. If a bid is in the process of being matched, it is pre-empted by a bid with a smaller quantity. This approach strongly outperforms SEATS in terms of the number of bids matched. However, it only offers a minor improvement in delivering less partial matchings.

In a rigid environment such as a share market, these mechanisms may not be deemed as initially fair. However, our results show that over time, the proposed algorithms can attain a better outcome than SEATS.

The tests assume there are an even number of buy and sell bids with a uniform distribution of quantity. In reality this would not occur. Increasing the number of either type essentially increases the volume on offer for one type in relation to the other. This degrades performance regardless of the algorithm employed. In the extreme case there will be all of one type and none of the other, which in this case the BMR and QMR would be zero. Having an even number of each type of bid is a neutral point. Skewing the number of bids one way or the other is detrimental to performance.

Bids are uniformly distributed across time. In reality, there may be periods of high bidding volume and also low volume periods. Future work involves using a Poisson probability distribution to model the frequency of the bids. This should help show how the algorithms perform on bursty data.

It would be intuitive to test the algorithms on real stock market data. However, we have found such data difficult to obtain. There exist many commercial securities market data providers such as Bourse Data [3] who sell real-time and historical market data. However, the market depth provided only lists the aggregate quantity at a price level and not the individual bids.

References

1. Bagchi, A., Chaudhary, A., Garg, R., Goodrich, M., Kumar, V.: Seller-Focused Algorithms for Online Auctioning. In: Dehne, F., Sack, J.-R., Tamassia, R. (eds.) WADS 2001. LNCS, vol. 2125, pp. 135–147. Springer, Heidelberg (2001)
2. Economides, N., Schwartz, R.: Electronic Call Market Trading. Journal of Portfolio Management 21(3), 10–18 (1995)
3. Kao, M., Tate, S.: Online Difference Maximisation. SIAM Journal of Discrete Mathematics 12(1), 78–90 (1999)
4. El-Yaniv, R., Fiat, A., Karp, R., Turpin, G.: Competitive Analysis of Financial Games. In: Proceedings of the 33rd Symposium on Foundations in Computer Science, pp. 327–333 (1992)
5. Lavi, R., Nisan, N.: Competitive Analysis of Incentive Compatible Online Auctions. In: Proceedings of the 2nd ACM Conference on Electronic Commerce, pp. 233–241 (2000)
6. Sandholm, T., Suri, S.: Market Clearability. In: Proceedings of the Seventeenth International Joint Conference on Artificial Intelligence (IJCAI), pp. 1145–1151 (2001)
7. Sandholm, T., Blum, A., Zinkevich, M.: Online Algorithms for Market Clearing. In: Proceedings of the 13th SIAM Symposium on Discrete Algorithms (SODA), pp. 971–980 (2002)
8. Trevathan, J., Read, W.: RAS: a system for supporting research in online auctions. ACM Crossroads 12(4), 23–30 (2006)
9. Wellman, M., Wurman, P.: A Parameterization of the Auction Design Space. In: Proceedings of the Second International Conference on Autonomous Agents (AGENTS), pp. 301–308 (1999)

---

[3] http://www.boursedata.com.au

Modeling the Dynamics of Social Networks

Victor V. Kryssanov[1], Frank J. Rinaldo[1], Evgeny L. Kuleshov[2],
and Hitoshi Ogawa[3]

[1]Faculty of Information Science and Engineering, Ritsumeikan University
Kusatsu, Shiga, Japan
kvvictor@is.ritsumei.ac.jp, rinaldo@is.ritsumei.ac.jp
[2]Department of Computer Systems, the Far-Eastern National University,
Vladivostok, Russia
kuleshov@lemoi.phys.dvgu.ru
[3]Department of Information and Communication Science, Ritsumeikan University
Kusatsu, Shiga, Japan
ogawa@airlab.ics.ritsumei.ac.jp

Abstract. Modeling human dynamics responsible for the formation and evolution of the so-called social networks – structures comprised of individuals or organizations and indicating connectivities existing in a community – is a topic recently attracting a significant research interest. It has been claimed that these dynamics are scale-free in many practically important cases, such as impersonal and personal communication, auctioning in a market, accessing sites on the WWW, etc., and that human response times thus conform to the power law. While a certain amount of progress has recently been achieved in predicting the general response rate of a human population, existing formal theories of human behavior can hardly be found satisfactory to accommodate and comprehensively explain the scaling observed in social networks. In the presented study, a novel system-theoretic modeling approach is proposed and successfully applied to determine important characteristics of a communication network and to analyze consumer behavior on the WWW.

Keywords: Social networks, Power law, Human response time, Consumer behavior.

1   Introduction

Understanding the mechanisms underlying the formation and evolution of social (communication, entertainment, financial, and the like) networks is crucial in many fields of human activity, ranging from software development, to market analysis, resource distribution and deployment, and to catastrophe prognosis and prevention (see [18], for a comprehensive survey). Recently, there is an increasing number of reports that the dynamics of social networks reveal statistical properties conforming to the power law [11], [5], [19], [2], [21]. Striving to find a universal model for the human behavior apparently responsible for the observed statistics, researchers have been quick to affiliate social networks with the familiar Zipfian phenomena [18], [4].

J. Filipe and M.S. Obaidat (Eds.): ICETE 2006, CCIS 9, pp. 40–51, 2008.
© Springer-Verlag Berlin Heidelberg 2008

There exist a rich variety of stochastic processes leading to a power, heavy-tailed (e.g. Zipf, Zipf-Mandelbrot, or Pareto) form of the probability distribution of an observed random variable [17]. Only a small fraction of these processes, however, would be considered relevant to discuss in a social, economic, or anthropological context peculiar to the development of social networks. Even fewer processes have actually been explored as possible generating mechanisms for the network dynamics and tested against real-world data.

Adamic and Huberman [2] gave an explanation for the power-law distribution of the consumer activities in a global e-market, such as the World-Wide Web (WWW). The proposed model exercises the well-studied multiplicative growth stochastic mechanism for the network expansion but carries no implication about the human behavior. Barabasi [5] suggested a version of the preferential selection mechanism to describe the dynamics observed in a university e-mail network. While he did propose a model for human communicative behavior, which is, effectively, choice based on priorities, this model requires making rather implausible assumptions (e.g. about uniformly distributed priorities) and yet demonstrates poor predictive results even for the data originally used in the study (see Figure 1; also[23]). Johansen [11] derived an empirical formula, which provides a good approximation for the general response rate of a human population, working with the same data as the previous author (Figure 1). Another example of the empirically grounded approaches to modeling the dynamics of social networks is a modification of the Zipf-Mandelbrot law – the formula suggested by Krashakov et al. [12] to characterize the popularity of Web-sites that apparently has a predictive power better than the classic (e.g. the "pure" power or Zipf law) models. The latter two studies, however natural, offer little insight on why the observed networks exhibit scale-free properties.

In the absence of a sufficiently universal alternative to the power law (see [22], for a relevant discussion), the above mini-survey is quite indicative of the current situation with the understanding and modeling of the dynamics of social networks. Whenever the true mechanism underlying the observations is not known, the most probable scenario is that any process generating heavy-tailed data is either "by default" (i.e. with a minimal, if any, attention to statistical hypothesis testing and model validation) attributed to (a version of) one of the well-studied power-law generating mechanisms, such as multiplicative growth, preferential attachment, optimal coding, etc. or simply approximated with an empirical "a la Zipf" formula having an arbitrary interpretation that can hardly be discussed in a context different from mere curve fitting.

In the presented study, the authors aim to improve upon this, in essence theoretical, deficiency and focus on the development of a reasonably universal approach that would provide a distinct modeling perspective and have a potential to deliver a plausible and verifiable explanation of scale-free phenomena discovered in diverse social networks.

The next section gives a general mathematical framework. It is applied to analyze possible reasons of the power law patterns in the observed behavior of complex systems. Two experiments are then conducted to determine the dynamic structure of social networks, based on the proposed theory, and their results are briefly discussed. The study's conclusions are drawn, and plans for future research are outlined.

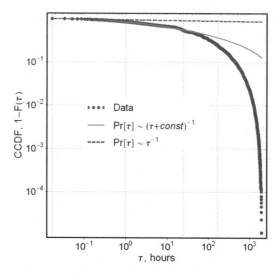

Fig. 1. Problems with explaining the heavy-tailed activity pattern in e-mail communications: while the empirical formula (solid line) derived by Johansen [11] provides a better approximation for the distribution of τ, the time taken by an individual to reply to a received e-mail, than Barabasi's model (dashed line) based on an activity-prioritizing mechanism [5], it gives no clue about the generating process (for details on the data, see [8])

2   System-Theoretic Framework

In this section, we will analyze the observed behavior of the so-called complex systems – the conglomerates (physical, social, cognitive, cybernetic, or the like) whose internal mechanisms and structure by some reason cannot be inspected in full. Power-law phenomena are very often associated with (produced by, observed in, etc.) such systems.

Let us consider a system Ω defined in a very general sense, i.e. as the object of investigation (not necessarily physically grounded). An observable O is a property of the system Ω that can be investigated in a given context. We will assume that Ω exists in different states and that different states of the system release themselves as different outcomes of observations (measurements, etc.) associated with observables O. The latter means that the system states (or behavior, seen as state change) are in principle conceivable through their representations resulting from observations of O.

We will seek to determine the distribution of the occurrence number of different representations associated with a given observable across increasing expenditures of time. In so doing, we will assume that a) the same state can have different representations, and b) different states can have the same representation. The analysis will be in three steps.

Step I: to characterize the occurrence number (or rate) of different representations of one (identical) state for the same observable O_0.

<u>Case 1</u>: Let the process of system state representation implement an efficient encoding procedure so that $\bar{k}_0 t_r = const$, where $\bar{k}_0$ is the expectation of a discrete random

variable K_0 revealing the occurrence number of different representations, and t_r is the average time of state representation.

To estimate $f_{K_0}(s)$ the probability mass function (PMF) of K_0, we will maximize its entropy $H = -\Sigma_s f_{K_0}(s) \ln f_{K_0}(s)$, $s = 1, 2, \dots$, subject to constraints $\Sigma_s f_{K_0}(s) = 1$ and $\Sigma_s s f_{K_0}(s) = \overline{k}_0$. This will give us "the least biased estimate possible on the given information" [10].

The optimization problem is solved using a Lagrangian approach. The Lagrangian function is defined as

$$\mathcal{L}(f_{K_0}) = -\sum_s f_{K_0}(s) \ln f_{K_0}(s) + \gamma(1 - \sum_s f_{K_0}(s))$$

$$+ \lambda(\overline{k}_0 - \sum_s s f_{K_0}(s)), \tag{1}$$

where γ and λ are coefficients, with optimality conditions $\partial\mathcal{L}/\partial f_{K_0}(s) = 0$, $\partial\mathcal{L}/\partial\gamma = 0$, and $\partial\mathcal{L}/\partial\lambda = 0$ [7]. From the first and second conditions, one can then derive

$$f_{K_0}(s) = \Pr[K_0 = s \mid \lambda] = (e^\lambda - 1)e^{-s\lambda} \tag{2}$$

where $s = 1, 2, \dots$. Since $\overline{k}_0 = \sum_{s=1}^{\infty} s f_{K_0}(s) = e^\lambda/(e^\lambda - 1) = 1/f_{K_0}(1)$ and $\overline{k}_0 \gg 1$, $f_{K_0}(1) \ll 1$ and $\lambda \ll 1$, and therefore $\lambda \approx 1/\overline{k}_0$.

Case 2: Let us now consider a different-type system and impose a conservation constraint for the representation (observation) time by requiring that at any time, only one but not necessarily the same property of the system is evaluated. In other words, we will assume that there are multiple competing observables for the same state. We will also assume that these observables are independent. (To simplify technicalities, the following discussion will mainly be built around the continuous case, i.e. for k_0 the continuous counterpart of K_0, yet with the customary abuse of the notation when the same symbol is used to refer to a random variable and to its value.)

For θ a period of time, w_0 the rate of the representation change is given as $w_0 = k_0/\theta$. Under the above assumptions, the dynamics of w_0 can be modeled using a system of differential equations defined as follows:

$$\frac{dw_i}{dt} = a_i \left(\rho\mu - \sum_{n=0}^{N} w_n \right) + \eta_i \tag{3}$$

where μ is the investigated state rate (characterizes the "true," as opposed to the observed, behavior of the system), N is the number of competing observables, $i = 0, 1, \dots, N$; $\eta_i(t)$ is a Gaussian noise (e.g. due to measurement errors) with average zero, some $a_i(t) > 0$, and ρ is a parameter to account for the efficiency of the representation process (i.e. the system state may principally be only to an extent available for observation).

Equations (3) describe a diffusion process in the vicinity of a hyperplane $\rho\mu = \Sigma_n w_n$ formed by $N+1$ observables with w_n representation rates, whose values are (approximately) uniformly distributed in the interval $[0, \rho\mu]$. Due to the hyperplane condition, there can be only N mutually independent observables, say $O_1,...,O_N$. $\Sigma_n k_n = \Sigma_n w_n \theta = \theta\rho\mu$ by definition. The probability that $k_n \geq k_0$, $n = 1,...,N$, can be calculated as a product of the marginal distributions $f(k_n) = 1/\theta\rho\mu$, that then yields $\Pr[k_1 \geq k_0,...,k_N \geq k_0] = (1 - k_0/\theta\rho\mu)^N$. Probability theory defines the cumulative distribution function (CDF) for some x_0 taken from the set of all random variables that obey a given probabilistic law as $F(x_0) = \Pr[x_1 < x_0,...,x_N < x_0]$. In this context and for $N \gg 1$, one can write:

$$F(k_0) \propto 1 - (1 - k_0/\theta\rho\mu)^N \approx 1 - e^{-k_0\lambda} \tag{4}$$

where parameter $\lambda = t'_r(\theta\rho)^{-1}$ is, up to the constant $1/\theta\rho$, determined by $t'_r = (\mu/(N+1))^{-1}$ the representation time averaged over the observables (note that generally, t_r of Case 1 is not equal to t'_r).

At this point, we would like to note that while there would be a number of modeling scenarios both, similar to and different from those of Case 1 and 2, which would produce an exponential form for the distribution sought, the approaches discussed above have two important implications. First, the models defined with Equations (2) and (4) both stipulate that under other similar conditions, more often met representations correspond, on average, to system states with a shorter representation time. Second, for an occurrence number significantly greater than 1, the parameter $\lambda \ll 1$.

Step 2: to characterize $k(t)$ the representation occurrence number of many different states for the same observable O_0.

For the system Ω, the measured stochastic variable k will be a sum of random variables $k_0 + k1_0 + k2_0 + ...$, where the summands are due to different states having identical representations. The statistical properties of k will then depend on the parameter λ that can naturally vary (e.g. as a result of a variation in the average representation time for different states). Let $g(\lambda)$ be the probability density function (PDF) of λ. For a large number of states investigated by means of O_0, $f(k)$ the PDF of k is defined as a $g(\lambda)$ parameter-mix of $f(k \mid \Lambda = \lambda)$:

$$f(k) = f(k \mid \Lambda = \lambda) \bigwedge_\Lambda g(\lambda) = \int_0^\infty g(\lambda)P(k_0)d\lambda \tag{5}$$

where $P(k_0)$ is the PDF of k_0 discussed in Step 1.

Step 3: to generalize the result of Step 2.

The random variable k may reflect more than one (presumably associated with the observable O_0) property of the system Ω, while the system mechanisms controlling the observable may be heterogeneous in time (e.g. owing to environmental perturbations).

This can provoke the existence of more than one probability distributions for λ. When M the number of statistically independent factors influencing the observation (or the system behavior) is finite, $P(k)$ the PDF of the occurrence number of system state representations can be estimated as

$$P(k) = \sum_{i=1}^{M} c_i f_i(k) \tag{6}$$

where weights c_i give the likelihood to observe the influence of the i-th factor on the random variable k, and each $f_i(k)$ is specified with Equation (5) and is determined by the (sub)system parameters as it was discussed in Step 1.

3 When the Power Law?

The analytic framework formulated in the previous section is fairly general and can be applied to analyze the behavior of virtually any complex system. It should be emphasized however, that the focus of the developed model is on the frequency (count) of observed activities rather than on their durations. Most of the modeling approaches discussed in the introduction are therefore not directly comparable to the one proposed in this study. Given the fact that in social systems, there often exists a detectable (though not always easily formalizable) connection between the frequency of a certain activity and its duration, it appears interesting to explore under what conditions Equation (6) may produce a power form of the probability distribution.

An acute reader would have already noticed that the substitution of the exponential PDF into Equation (5) yields a Laplace transform of the product $\lambda g(\lambda)$:

$$f(k) = \int_{0}^{\infty} \lambda e^{-k\lambda} dG(\lambda) \tag{7}$$

where $G(\lambda)$ is the CDF of λ.

This is a very nice result since it, owing to Bernstein's theorem [6] stipulates that if $f(k)$, the PDF of the observed variable, is completely monotone, i.e. all its derivatives exist and $(-1)^n f^{(n)}(k) \geq 0$ for any integer $k > 0$ and $n \geq 1$, there can always be found some proper $G(\lambda)$ in effect describing the internal (i.e. not directly observed, "true") dynamics of the system. There is a large class of probability distributions for λ (e.g. originated from or simply approximated with the Beta of the Second Kind probability distribution $g(\lambda) = (\Gamma(p+q)/\Gamma(p)\Gamma(q))\lambda^{p-1}(1+\lambda)^{-(p+q)}$, where $\Gamma(\cdot)$ denotes the Gamma function, $p > 0$ and $q > 0$ are parameters, which encompasses many commonly used distributions, such as the Log-Normal, Gamma, Weibull, etc. – see [16], 1995) that will cause "fat" tails of the observed data $f(k) \propto k^{-\beta}$ for some $\beta > 0$ as $k \to \infty$ [1]. This asymptotic property will, however, not necessarily be maintained for small k.

Generally, the developed model dictates that in the case of a homogeneous (i.e. assuming the existence of one PDF $g(\lambda)$) system, candidate distribution functions for the description of the statistical properties of k and λ should satisfy Equation (7). In view of this, an interesting exercise would be to find a family of probability functions satisfying the Laplace transform (7). Unfortunately, no closed analytic forms for $g(\lambda)$ exist in many cases of long-tailed $f(k)$.

Equation (6) further stipulates that in order for $P(k) \propto k^{-\beta}$, either all the summands should have an identical "heavy-tailed" form (that would indicate certain self-similarity existing in the system) or at least one of the summands should have a power form with an exponent β_i small enough to dominate the asymptotic behavior of the other distributions.

4 Modeling the Dynamics of Social Networks

To verify the proposed model against real-world data and explore its predictive and analytic capabilities, two experiments have been conducted.

4.1 Experiment 1

Data used in the experiment is a sample representing the timing of e-mails sent and received by a group of ~10000 people at a university in Europe during a period of ~80 days. The corresponding server log-file was obtained from the authors of Reference [8]. Specifically, we have focused on the time taken by an individual to reply to a received message – the human response rate; there have been extracted ~24000 of reply times from the file. It was reported elsewhere [8], [11], [5] that power-law generating mechanisms could be behind the formation of the distribution of this data, as it exposes the characteristic (yet noisy) heavy-tailed pattern (see Figure 1; also the inset in Figure 2).

The discretization time interval for the delays with reply was set to 1 minute. No other preprocessing has been done. The investigated system in this case is the social system that existed at the university, and the observed property is the perturbed (by incoming e-mails) communication timing. It is expected that delays with reply to received e-mails reveal the rate of the system internal state change (e.g. in its simplest form, from "e-mail is not replied" to "e-mail replied").

The two-parameter Gamma distribution $g(\lambda) = b^{v}\lambda^{v-1}e^{-b\lambda}/\Gamma(v)$, where $\lambda \geq 0$, $b > 0$, $v > 0$, and $\Gamma(\cdot)$ denotes the Gamma function, was chosen to characterize the system's hidden dynamics, because this is a simple form well describing cognitive processes and "mental" reaction time [15]. This form can, and possibly should, be considered for $g(\lambda)$ regardless what is the "true" mental architecture triggering one or another investigated human activity [24]. Taking into account the discrete nature of the observed variable value count and after substitution of the corresponding PMF and PDF into Equation (5), Equation (6) is specialized to

$$P(k) = \sum_{i=1}^{M} c_i \left(\frac{b_i^{v_i}}{(k-1+b_i)^{v_i}} - \frac{b_i^{v_i}}{(k+b_i)^{v_i}} \right), k = 1, 2, \ldots \quad (8)$$

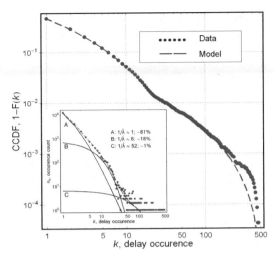

Fig. 2. Estimation of the dynamic social structure based on an analysis of the traffic in a university e-mail network

that is thus the probability mass function of the occurrence of a human response rate. Note that each of the summands has the form of the discrete Lomax distribution.

Figure 2 depicts the complementary cumulative sums calculated for the data and the model (8) with parameters c_i, b_i and v_i obtained by a numerical maximum likelihood method and $M = 3$ as yielding the smallest value of Akaike's Information Criterion, $AIC = -2\log(L(\hat{\phi} \mid x)) + 2n$, where $\log(L(\hat{\phi} \mid x))$ is the log-likelihood maximized with parameters $\hat{\phi}$ (for the PMF (8), $\hat{\phi} = \{\hat{c}_{i \neq 1}, \hat{b}_i, \hat{v}_i\}$, $i = 1,...,M$) for a given sample x, and n is the number of estimable parameters (for $M = 3$, $n = 8$). AIC is a fundamental measure assessing the relative Kullback-Leibler distance between the fitted model and the unknown true mechanism, which actually generated the observed data [3]. Taking into account the information known from the original report [8] about the structure of the social system in focus, models with M the number of components ranging from 1 to 4 have been tried in the experiment. The second-best model had $M = 2$, $n = 5$ and was therefore simpler, but with an AIC value by 90 greater than in the case of $M = 3$ it had to be omitted from further consideration [20].

4.2 Experiment 2

To explore the dynamic structure of an e-market on the World-Wide Web, a data sample representing the activity of America Online (AOL) users (acting as consumers of the services provided by Web sites) has been obtained from the authors of Reference [2]. The sample covers approximately 120000 sites accessed by 60000 users during one day.

Figure 3 shows the results of the modeling of the consumer activity dynamics with formula (8). It is assumed that a hit to a particular site corresponds to a specific mental or "goal" state, and that these states are common (i.e. shared) within the population (from a generic anthropological viewpoint, this seems a natural assumption). As no a priori information was available on the structure of the social system examined, four prediction models have been probed by varying the value of M from 1 to 4. The two models displayed in the figure are statistically justified by the data and perform practically equally well.

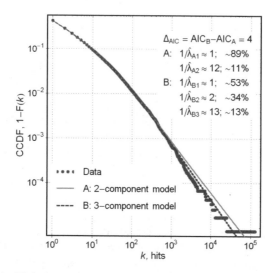

Fig. 3. Modeling the Web site (server) visiting rate (hits) observed on December 1, 1997, in a segment of the WWW. (For details on the data, see [2].)

5   Discussion

It is quite illustrative that while a "pure" form of the power law would fail to reasonably accurately predict probabilities for the entire ranges of the data used in the experiments, as the corresponding complementary cumulative sums visibly do not form single straight lines on the double-logarithmic plots, the model specified with Equation (8) produces sound fits.

For the university e-mail network, Pearson's χ^2 test does not reject the model with a significance level $\alpha = 0.001$ that might be considered good enough in the case of noisy data. An objection would, however, be made that the proposed model overfits the data: the large number of its parameters creates a situation when the fit may be driven by the random fluctuations rather than by the "true" statistical properties of the data.

The values of c_i the parameters obtained in the first experiment suggest that the examined social system has an internal structure: there are two subsystems with different dynamics responsible for the generation of approximately 81 and 18% of the observed variety in delays with reply to an e-mail; about 1% of the occurrences – for the most typical and shortest delays – are probably caused by factors other than social (e.g. owing to an auto-reply function of the e-mail clients or the processing of long mailing lists) and may be excluded from consideration.

The larger, "static" subsystem – A in the inset of Figure 2, where the distributions are built for the data, the model, and the model's 3 components – produces on average longer yet unique delays (for a gamma-distributed λ, the estimate of its mean $\hat{\lambda} = v/b$). The second subsystem – B – is approximately 4 times smaller (or 4 times observationally less influential) and 6 times more dynamic (and hence, as it could be speculated, is more constrained and/or has stronger social ties). These size estimates principally conform to the ones reported in the original work [8] and independently obtained through somewhat intricate analysis of the individual communications present in the sample. This, along with the fact that the obtained parameters behave just as it is implied by the model (back to Section 2), can be considered as strong evidence in support of the hypothesis that Equation (8) does describe the system behavior but not merely approximates the data.

In the second experiment, the models with two and three Lomax-distributed components are not rejected by Pearson's test with $\alpha = 0.1$. The difference in AIC calculated for these models implies that neither should be favored in the absence of information other than obtained from the data. Nevertheless, both of them suggest that approximately 10% of the observed variety in the site popularity is due to mental states (and corresponding activities) most often experienced (pursued) by the consumers at the e-market. The latter does not appear implausible in the light of the Internet demographic survey for 1997 by Nielson Media Research (http://www.nielsenmedia.com) stating that 73% of the consumers used the WWW to search for information about products and services by means of accessing a small number of Web portals and search engines, such as Yahoo®, etc.

It is understood that for any "complete" validation of the proposed model, many more experiments are required but are beyond the limits of this paper. Additional cross-checking and verification are, however, still indispensable because technically, derivation of the Lomax (Pareto Second Kind or General Pareto) distribution as a gamma mix of exponentials was first reported several decades ago [9] but did not receive due attention in complex system research.

One supportive argument for the proposed approach is that it does not contradict the findings about the dynamics of social networks reported in the literature, but instead generalizes them. The widely held form of the power law $P(k) = v b^v / k^{v+1}$ can be obtained from Equation (8) for $k \gg b$ by Taylor series expansion (the minuend – by small $(b-1)/k$, and the subtrahend – by small b/k) under the assumption that the investigated system is homogeneous (i.e. by setting $M = 1$).

Let us now consider an asymptotic approximation of the model, which is also the continuous counterpart of Equation (8):

$$P_c(k) = v b^v (k + b)^{-v-1} \tag{9}$$

From

$$R(x) = l \int_x^\infty P_c(k)dk = l b^v (b + x)^{-v} \tag{10}$$

where $R(x)$ gives r the rank of a unit of size x, $x_{(1)} \geq x_{(2)} \geq \cdots \geq x_{(r)} \geq \cdots \geq x_{(l)}$, in a set of l objects, one can easily obtain

$$f_r = bl^{-1+1/v} r^{-1/v} - bl^{-1} \tag{11}$$

where f_r is the relative occurrence frequency of the r-th popular unit. When $r \gg u$, this result coincides with the empirical formula $f_r = d + q(u+r)^{-\alpha}$, d, q, and u are some constants, obtained by the authors of Reference [12]. Moreover, the negative values of d empirically calculated in the latter study are generally in agreement with what would be estimated based on the sample size by applying formula (11), where $b, l > 0$ by definition.

As a final remark, let us mention that a lognormal distribution is often discussed as an alternative to the power law when describing the dynamics of complex systems [17]; [23]. Given $k \gg b$ and some m, $2m \gg \ln k$, Equation (8) can be approximated as

$$P(k) = \frac{vb^v e^{\frac{vm}{2}}}{k} e^{-\frac{(\ln k + m)^2}{2m/v}} \tag{12}$$

that gives its lognormal asymptotic form.

6 Conclusions

Having defined the overall goal as to deliver a universal but simple and accurate theoretical model for the observed behavior of a large class of complex systems, in this particular paper we focused on the formation of the dynamics of social networks and on methods for the network structure analysis. A mathematical model correctly describing these phenomena would help optimize resource and service allocation as well as economic and management policies for companies in both the traditional and electronic business sectors, and also for organizations involved in collaborative activities, such as distribution of funds, innovation and know-how exchange, and so on.

We have applied the apparatus of statistical physics to describe the emergence of social networks. The network dynamics was defined in terms of its structure (i.e. how many subsystems are there and what is, as observed, their influence on the overall dynamics) as well as parameters of its elementary constituents (these parameters are the mental reaction time and, possibly, response times of external systems coupled with or simply affecting the social network). In the presented experiments, the proposed model has demonstrated a prognostic potential far superior to any of the classical modeling approaches. At the same time, the model proved to be quite encompassing but natural and thus easy to interpret and validate.

In our prior research reported elsewhere, the system-theoretic framework was successfully applied to capture the structure of different languages and to compare the efficiencies of text- and hypermedia- based communication [14], [13]. In future studies, we plan to explore various authorship networks.

Acknowledgements

The authors would like to thank, without implicating, Lada A. Adamic and Jean-Pierre Eckmann for providing the data used in the research.

References

1. Abate, J., Whitt, W.: Modeling service-time distributions with non-exponential tails: Beta mixtures of exponentials. Stochastic Models 15, 517–546 (1999)
2. Adamic, L.A., Huberman, B.A.: The nature of markets in the World Wide Web. Quarterly Journal of Electronic Commerce 1, 5–12 (2000)
3. Akaike, H.: Information measures and model selection. International Statistical Institute 44, 277–291 (1983)
4. Barabasi, A.-L., Albert, R.: Emergence of scaling in random networks. Science 286, 509 (1999)
5. Barabasi, A.-L.: The origin of bursts and heavy tails in human dynamics. Nature 435, 207–211 (2005)
6. Bernstein, S.N.: Sur les functions absolument monotones. ACTA Mathematica 51, 1–66 (1928)
7. Cover, J., Thomas, J.A.: Elements of Information Theory. John Wiley&Sons, New York (1991)
8. Eckmann, J.-P., Moses, E., Sergi, D.: Entropy of dialogues creates coherent structures in e-mail traffic. PNAS 101, 14333–14337 (2004)
9. Harris, C.M.: The Pareto Distribution As A Queue Service Discipline. Operations Research 16, 307–313 (1968)
10. Jaynes, E.T.: Information theory and statistical mechanics. Physical Review 106, 620–630 (1957)
11. Johansen, A.: Probing human response times. Physica A 338, 286–291 (2004)
12. Krashakov, S.A., Teslyuk, A.B., Shchur, L.N.: On the universality of rank distributions of website popularity. Computer Networks (in press, 2006)
13. Kryssanov, V.V., Kakusho, K., Kuleshov, E.L., Minoh, M.: Modeling hypermedia-based communication. Information Sciences 174, 37–53 (2005)
14. Kuleshov, E.L., Krysanov, V.V., Kakusho, K.: The distribution of term frequency in texts. Optoelectronics, Instrumentation and Data Processing 41, 81–90 (2005)
15. Luce, R.D.: Response Times. Their Role in Inferring Elementary Mental Organization. Oxford University Press, New York (1986)
16. McDonald, J.B., Xu, J.Y.: A Generalization of the Beta of the First and Second Kind. Journal of Econometrics 66, 133–152 (1995)
17. Mitzenmacher, M.: A Brief History of Generative Models for Power Law and Lognormal Distributions. Internet Mathematics 1, 226–251 (2003)
18. Newman, M.E.J.: Power laws, Pareto distributions and Zipf's law. Contemporary Physics 46, 323–351 (2005)
19. Oliveira, J.G., Barabasi, A.-L.: Darwin and Einstein correspondence patterns. Nature 437, 1251 (2005)
20. Sakamoto, Y., Ishiguro, M., Kitagawa, G.: Akaike information criterion statistics, KTK Scientific. KTK Scientific, Tokyo (1986)
21. Scalas, E., Kaizoji, T., Kirchler, M., Huber, J., Tedeschi, A.: Waiting times between orders and trades in double-auction markets. Physica A (in press)
22. Solow, A.R., Costello, C.J., Ward, M.: Testing the Power Law Model for Discrete Size Data. The American Naturalist 162, 685–689 (2003)
23. Stouffer, D.B., Malmgren, R.D., Amaral, L.A.N.: Comments on The origin of bursts and heavy tails in human dynamics. arXiv:physics/0510216 (2005)
24. van Zandt, T., Ratcliff, R.: Statistical mimicking of reaction time data: Single-process models, parameter variability, and mixtures. Psychonomic Bulletin & Review 2, 20–54 (1995)

Reputation Management Service for Peer-to-Peer Enterprise Architectures

M. Amoretti, M. Bisi, M.C. Laghi, F. Zanichelli, and G. Conte

Distributed Systems Group - Dip. di Ingegneria dell'Informazione
Università degli Studi di Parma, Italy
{amoretti,laghi,zanichelli,conte}@ce.unipr.it,
matteo.bisi@sigrade.it

Abstract. The high potential of P2P infrastructures for enterprise services and applications both on the intranet (*e.g.* project workgroups) and on the Internet (*e.g.* B2B exchange) can be fully achieved provided that robust trust and security management systems are made available.

This paper presents the reputation system we have devised for SP2A [1], a P2P framework which supports secure role-based peergroups and service interactions. Our solution includes decentralized trust and security management able to cope with several threats. The underlying analytical model is introduced and discussed, together with a simulation-based evaluation of the robustness against malicious negative feedbacks.

Keywords: Service Oriented Architectures, Peer-to-Peer, Security, Reputation Management.

1 Introduction

Ubiquitous access to networks is deeply changing the ways enterprises organize and perform their business both internally and externally. Intranets and the global Internet allow for seamless and almost instantaneous information and knowledge sharing within organizations thus enabling more efficient processes and activities and giving rise to novel forms of interaction and supporting applications.

Peer-to-peer (P2P) technologies have gained world-wide popularity due to the success of file-sharing applications (and the predictable reactions of copyright holders) and their decentralized nature appears promising also to the purposes and applications of enterprises. P2P-based instant messaging and file-sharing can be effectively exploited on an intranet to support for example projects workgroups, distributed offices and distributions chains for documents and archives. Internet-enabled inter-firm collaboration can benefit from a P2P approach as well. Business-to-business exchanges are becoming increasingly important and many B2B communities organize themselves to be more competitive in specialized industry sectors by increasing the efficiency of their procurement and supply chains. By leveraging upon P2P technologies, the common tasks of searching for new business partners and exchanging transaction information (*e.g.* quotations) can be improved in terms of instant information, control over shared data (mantained at each P2P node) and reduced infrastructure costs.

J. Filipe and M.S. Obaidat (Eds.): ICETE 2006, CCIS 9, pp. 52–63, 2008.

The vision of unmediated, instantaneous trading as well as more realistic P2P-based B2B communities can be approached only if enterprise-level solutions are made available to cope with the fundamental trust and security issues. *Identity trust*, namely the belief that an entity is what it claims to be, can be assessed by means of an authentication scheme such as X.509 digital identity certificates. *Provision trust*, that is the relying party's trust in a service or resource provider, appears more critical as users require protection from malicious or unreliable service providers. Unlike B2B exchanges based on centralized, third party UDDI directories which offer trustworthy data of potential trading partners (*i.e.* service providers), P2P decentralized interaction lends itself to trust and reputation systems mainly based on first hand experience and second-hand referrals. This information can be combined by a peer into an overall rating or reputation value for a service provider and should influence further interaction with it.

In this paper we present the reputation system we have devised for SP2A [1], a P2P framework which supports secure role-based peergroups and service interactions. Our system includes decentralized trust and security management able to cope with several threats, starting from *impersonification*, which refers to the threat caused by a malicious peer posing as another in order to misuse that peer's privileges and reputation. Digital signatures and message authentication are typical solutions for this kind of attack. As malicious peers can engage in *fraudulent actions*, such as advertising false resources or services and not fulfilling commitments, a consistent reputation management system has been introduced in our P2P framework which also forbids *trust misrepresentation* attempts. In a peer-to-peer system, the most difficult threat to discover and neutralize is *collusion*, which refers to a group of malicious peers working in concert to actively subvert the system. To face this danger, the default policy provided by our security framework is *role-based group membership based on secure credentials (SC policy)*. Based on this strategy, a group of peer can filter what actions its members can perform. This paper focuses on reputation management, which was left as open issue in our previous work [2].

Next section 2 outlines the issues of reputation management systems and the choices available for centralized and decentralized implementation. The analytical model underlying our reputation management is described in section 3. An emulation scenario is then presented, first describing a four roles configuration example (section 4) and then discussing the obtained results (section 5). Section 6 reports on some relevant work in the area of reputations systems for P2P systems. Finally, a few conclusive remarks and an indication of further work conclude the paper.

2   Reputation Management in Role-Based Peergroups

A role-based peergroup can achieve stability only if each participant (which is supposed to be authenticated and authorized) bases its actions on previous experience and/or recommendations, *i.e.* which define the reputation of the other participants. Reputation and trust are orthogonal concepts, which require, in a peer-to-peer context, complex management mechanisms such as node identification and digitally signed certificates exchange [3].

Our model considers both *peer reputation* and *service reputation*. A peer can provide more than one service, each of them with its own reputation which contributes to the overall reputation of the peer. Peer reputations may have non-zero initial value, fixed by a trusted third party. Based on peer's behaviour, the reputation value changes with time, and represents the trustworthiness of peers on the basis of their transaction with other nodes. Each peer, at the end of an interaction with another member of the group, can provide its feedback about each consumed service; the feedback is used to update the reputation of the provider peer.

Two issues arise: where are to be stored the reputation information, and how to guarantee their integrity. Several solutions can be adopted:

1. a stable and recognized peer stores and manages the reputation information of all group members (*centralized* solution);
2. each peer stores its experience against other peers, and when others ask for reputation information of a particular peer, it provides an answer based on its stored information (*local* solution);
3. the reputation storage is partitioned into several small parts, which are stored in all peers; that is, every peer equally manages some part of the whole reputation information (*global* solution);
4. only stable, recognized and highly-reputed peers are reputation collectors (*mediated* solution).

It can be easily seen that not all these solutions are equally scalable, efficient and robust.

Solution 1 is easy to implement as a Centralized Reputation Management Service (CRMS), but it does not scale well, *i.e.* it could work only for small peergroups. Solutions 2, 3 and 4 require a Distributed Reputation Management Service (DRMS).

The local solution is slightly efficient and lacks robustness. If a peer wants more objective reputation about another peer, it should ask as many peers as necessary, thus generating a lot of messages in the peer-to-peer network. Moreover, if the reputation information is concentrated in few very active customer peers, the reputation system becomes broken when these are not online.

The global solution is very attractive, in particular if the reputation management system is implemented as a Distributed Hash Table (DHT). In this case, the peer which is responsible for a specific reputation information is determined with a hash function within $O(1)$ time, and its location is found within $O(\log N)$ time.

The mediated solution should be appropriated for unstructured networks, with few highly connected and stable nodes, *e.g.* scale-free topologies [4].

3   Analytical Model

In this section we illustrate an analytical model which defines the fundamental parameters which are involved in the evolution of the reputation, for each role which can be taken in a peergroup based on our SC policy.

The reputation Rep of a peer is the difference between the number of positive feedbacks and the number of negative feedbacks. Feedbacks take values $+1$ and -1 with probability p and $q = 1 - p$ respectively. Thus, the sequence of feedbacks that a peer receives can be considered as a generalized random walk, a stochastic process which becomes nearly normal after long time.

When a peer joins the secure peergroup, and each time it is promoted or demoted, it receives an initial reputation value which is stored by the reputatation management service. We consider the following parameters:

- *total votes* $n = n_+ + n_-$, which represents the sum of received feedbacks;
- *good ratio* $R = \frac{n_+}{n_+ + n_-}$, which is the number of positive feedbacks, versus n; R is a fundamental parameter for the analytical model, because its instantaneous value allows to define the *dependability degree* of the peer.

The domain of R and n can be easily obtained from their definitions:

$$0 \leq R \leq 1, n \geq 0$$

Depending on values of R and n, we can consider four different conditions for each role a peer can take, which are listed below.

- $n \geq n_{th}$, where $n_{th} \geq 0$ is the *confidence threshold*, evaluated on all received feedbacks. The reason of considering such a threshold is that the dependability of the reputation value of a peer depends on the total number of performed transactions (the more they are, the more the value is dependable).
- $n < n_{th}$ means that the peer has recently joined the group, thus the reputation value must be weighted to consider a potentially less dependability.
- $R \geq R_{th}$, where $0 \leq R_{th} \leq 1$ is the *trust threshold*. In this case, the peer can be trusted.
- $R < R_{th}$, on the other side, means that the peer cannot be trusted and should be demoted.

From the definitions of n and R, we obtain

$$Rep = n_+ - n_- = (2R - 1)n \tag{1}$$

from which we can derive the *role preservation condition*

$$Rep \geq (2R_{th} - 1)n \tag{2}$$

Suppose that R, in the steady state, is characterized by little variations around an average value. A sudden increase or decrease of R may be considered as a suspect event. If an abrupt increase or decrease of R lasts for a significant time interval, possibily leading R to its upper or lower threshold (R_{th}^u or R_{th}^l, respectively), an attack may be in progress.

In order to avoid misleading demotions or promotions, a simple but effective solution is to introduce two *braking windows*, one for the upper threshold and one for the lower threshold, within which R is increased by R_b, defined as a non-linear function of R with the following properties:

- R_b is positive and between R_{th}^l and R_w^l
- R_b is zero between R_w^l and R_w^u
- R_b is negative between R_w^u and R_{th}^u

Figure 1) illustrates an example of a particular $R_b(R)$ function.

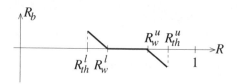

Fig. 1. An example of $R_b(R)$ with decreasing shape and braking windows of the same size

The mechanism of the braking windows is general, although the window size should be different for each role, namely decreasing with the importance of the peer.

It is possible to compute from previous parameters the rate r_{bad} with which one or more (possibly cooperating) malicious peers can provide negative feedbacks without affecting the peer's role. Above this rate value, the peer is soon demoted for insufficient good ratio, according to the rules which have been illustrated above.

We first consider the case with no braking windows. In the time unit Δt, the average number of received feedbacks is defined as

$$\Delta n = \Delta n_+ + \Delta n_- + \Delta n_{bad}$$

where Δn_+ and Δn_- are honest feedbacks, while Δn_{bad} represents deceptive negative feedbacks, sent by malicious peers. For sake of simplicity we suppose that no deceptive positive feedbacks are received, and $\Delta n_+ \geq \Delta n_-$. The reputation decreases if

$$\Delta n_{bad} > \Delta n_+ - \Delta n_- \tag{3}$$

i.e.

$$r_{bad} = \frac{\Delta n_{bad}}{\Delta n} > 2R - 1 \tag{4}$$

At the trust threshold, this means $r_{bad} > 2R_{th} - 1$.

If there are the braking windows, the adjusted good ratio is

$$R' = R + R_b(R)$$

thus the value of r_{bad} which leads to peer demotion becomes

$$r_{bad} > 2[R + R_b(R)] - 1 \tag{5}$$

4   Four-Role Configuration Example

We now apply the analytical model to an example of a four-role reputation policy of a service-sharing system. For each role we set the initial values for the parameters we illustrated in section 3, considering for simplicity only the lower threshold and the related braking window. In details, the list of roles is:

– admin - the peer is highly-reputed, and trusted by the group founder, or it is the group founder itself; the actions it is allowed to perform are: service sharing/discovery, group monitoring, voting for changing member ranks, store reputation information (if the mediated solution is adopted);

– newbie - the peer is a new member; it only can search for an admin peer, to ask for a promotion;

– searcher - the peer is allowed to search for services and to interact with them;

– publisher - the peer can search for services but also publish its own services in the peergroup.

Each **admin** peer has the following configuration:

$$
\begin{cases}
n_{+,init} = 50 \\
n_{-,init} = 10 \\
n_{init} = n_{+,init} + n_{-,init} = 60 \\
R_{init} = \dfrac{n_{+,init}}{n_{+,init} + n_{-,init}} = 0.8 \\
Rep_{init} = n_{+,init} - n_{-,init} = 40 \\
R_{th} = 0.6 \\
R_w = 0.8 \\
R_b(R_{th}) = 0.075
\end{cases}
$$

For example, we assume $\Delta n_+ = 9.6$ and $\Delta n_- = 2.4$ in the average, *i.e.* $\Delta n = 12$ feedbacks per time unit. Without braking window, the number of deceptive negative feedbacks per time unit must be $\Delta n_{bad} < 3$, since $r_{bad} < 2R_{th} - 1 = 0.2$. With the braking window, the number of deceptive negative feedbacks per time unit must be $\Delta n_{bad} < 6,46$, since $r_{bad} < 2(R_{th} + R_b(R_{th})) - 1 = 0.35$. Thus the braking window makes the system more robust.

Each **publisher** peer has the following configuration:

$$
\begin{cases}
n_{+,init} = 35 \\
n_{-,init} = 10 \\
n_{init} = n_{+,init} + n_{-,init} = 45 \\
R_{init} = \dfrac{n_{+,init}}{n_{+,init} + n_{-,init}} = 0.\overline{7} \\
Rep_{init} = n_{+,init} - n_{-,init} = 25 \\
R_{th} = 0.6 \\
R_w = 0.75 \\
R_b(R_{th}) = 0.04
\end{cases}
$$

Compared with previous case, the braking window for a publisher is smaller: 0.15 versus 0.2. With this window, the maximum tolerable rate of deceptive negative feedbacks is $r_{bad} = 28\%$.

Each **searcher** peer has the following configuration:

$$
\begin{cases}
n_{+,init} = 25 \\
n_{-,init} = 10 \\
n_{init} = n_{+,init} + n_{-,init} = 35 \\
R_{init} = \dfrac{n_{+,init}}{n_{+,init} + n_{-,init}} = 0.714 \\
Rep_{init} = n_{+,init} - n_{-,init} = 15 \\
R_{th} = 0.6 \\
R_w = 0.7 \\
R_b(R_{th}) = 0.025
\end{cases}
$$

For a searcher, whose braking window is 0.1 large, the maximum tolerable rate of deceptive negative feedbacks is $r_{bad} = 25\%$.

Finally, each **newbie** peer has the following configuration:

$$
\begin{cases}
n_{+,init} = 15 \\
n_{-,init} = 10 \\
n_{init} = n_{+,init} + n_{-,init} = 25 \\
R_{init} = \dfrac{n_{+,init}}{n_{+,init} + n_{-,init}} = 0.6 \\
Rep_{init} = n_{+,init} - n_{-,init} = 5 \\
R_{th} = 0.6 \\
R_w = 0.65 \\
R_b(R_{th}) = 0.005
\end{cases}
$$

Thus a newbie, which is characterized by the smallest braking window (0.05), can tolerate at most $r_{bad} = 21\%$.

5   Emulation Results

SP2A is an abstract framework but also a Java middleware for the development and deployment of service-oriented peer-to-peer architectures. Using its simple API, we realized a centralized reputation management service able to emulate the interaction of that service with an hypothetical network of peers which provide positive and negative feedbacks. We emphasize that our purpose was not to evaluate reputation retrieval and maintainance performance, obviously radically different in the cases of centralized and distributed services. The deployed testbed allowed us to verify the correctness of the proposed analytical model as well as the tuning of the parameter values for the four-role secure group configuration.

The reputation management service maintains a reputation table, and randomly assigns feedbacks to peers, with $\Delta n = 12$ as assumed in section 4. All emulations started with each peer having $R = R_{init}$, and lasted the time necessary to observe significant results (we set $\Delta t = 1$ minute). We tracked the evolution of the reputation value Rep for each peer, and we computed the average behaviour for each role. We initially emulated a peergroup of righteous peers, in which positive and negative feedbacks per unit time are distributed with $R_{avg} = R_{init}$. Then, we performed several emulations of a system in which some peers provided deceptive negative feedbacks with increasing rate. For each role, we found the maximum tolerable rate of malicious negative feedbacks, over which the target peer is demoted, or banned from the peergroup if its role is newbie.

In general, to know if the role preservation condition $Rep \geq (2R_{th} - 1)n$ will be fulfilled, in a stable condition with fixed r_{bad} and R_{avg}, we need to compare the average slope of the current reputation curve, with the average slope of the minimum reputation curve representing $Rep(R_{th})$ (using, for example, the least squares method). There are two possible situations:

- $\frac{d}{dt}Rep \geq \frac{d}{dt}Rep_{th}$: the curves diverge, $i.e.$ the reputation of the peer increases more quickly than the minimum reputation, under which the peer is demoted;

- $\frac{d}{dt}Rep < \frac{d}{dt}Rep_{th}$: the curves converge, $i.e.$ in a non-infinite time the peer will be demoted.

Also note that both curves depend on r_{bad}, because $\Delta n = \Delta n_+ + \Delta n_- + \Delta n_{bad}$.

Starting from $R = R_{init}$, the good ratio decreases if the number of negative feedbacks per time unit is higher than the number of positive feedbacks. In particular, this eventuality can arise if $r_{bad} > 0$. In our emulations, for each role we set a braking window (according to the parameters illustrated in section 4), which enters the game when $R < R_w$, and contributes to maintain $\frac{d}{dt}Rep \geq \frac{d}{dt}Rep_{th}$.

Figure 2 illustrates the average evolution of an admin peer's reputation over the emulation time interval. If no malicious peers provide deceptive negative feedbacks, the measured reputation of the target peer is represented by the fat continuous curve. Comparing this curve with the graph of the reputation which we obtain if $R = R_{th}$ (the thin continuous curve in the figure), we can observe that they diverge, thus we expect that the peer will not be demoted unless $r_{bad} = 0$. In the same figure, dotted curves refer to the case of $r_{bad} = 20\%$; they still diverge. Finally, dashed curves show the limit over which the role preservation condition is not fulfilled, $i.e.$ $r_{bad} = 35\%$, the same we computed with the analytical model.

The most interesting emulation results for the publisher role are illustrated in figure 3, which compares the case of no malicious peers (continuous lines) with the case of deceptive negative feedbacks with $r_{bad} = 29.4\%$ rate (dashed line). We can observe that, in the latter case, the average slopes show that the curves eventually converge. We measured $max\{r_{bad}\} = 28\%$, over which the publisher is demoted in a non-infinite time. Also this result is compatible with the analytical model.

Figures 4 and 5 illustrate, respectively, emulation results for the searcher and the newbie roles. We measured a maximum malicious feedbacks rate $r_{bad} = 25\%$, for a searcher peer. The figure illustrates what happens when this rate is overthrown, $i.e.$ the reputation curves (average and minimum) converge. For a newbie peer, the measured maximum rate of deceptive negative feedbacks is $r_{bad} = 21\%$. The figure illustrates a less dangerous situation. Both these emulations gave satisfactory results, which respect the numerical constraints obtained with the analytical model.

All results are summarized in table 1. The first and second columns report the analytical results, respectively for a reputation management service without and with braking windows. The third column reports the emulation results, which refer to a reputation management service with braking window and target peer with righteous behaviour,

60   M. Amoretti et al.

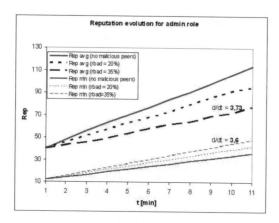

Fig. 2. Average and minimum reputation dynamics, for an admin peer, for different rates of malicious negative feedbacks

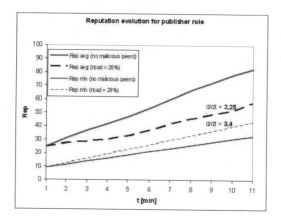

Fig. 3. Average and minimum reputation dynamics, for a publisher peer, for different rates of malicious negative feedbacks

i.e. a peer which would maintain the initially assigned good ratio R_{init} in absence of malicious negative feedbacks.

6 Related Work

There have been several studies about managing reputation in P2P networks, most of them related to content sharing, which is currently the killer application for these architectures. A reputation management system in DHT-based structured P2P networks is proposed in [5]; this model uses file reputation information as well as peer reputation information, and the system uses a global storage for reputation information, that is available when evaluator is not on-line. The reputation information consists, as in our model, of two values representing the number of positive and negative feedbacks.

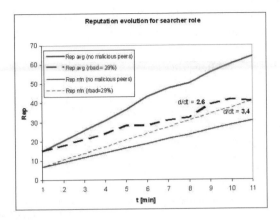

Fig. 4. Average and minimum reputation dynamics, for a searcher peer, for different rates of malicious negative feedbacks

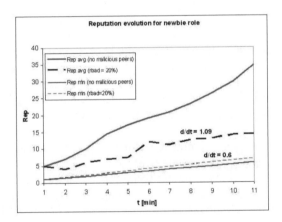

Fig. 5. Average and minimum reputation dynamics, for a newbie peer, for different rates of malicious negative feedbacks

In [6] a reputation management system for partially-decentralized P2P systems is described, in which the reputation information is managed by supernodes. The authors assume that the supernodes are selected from a set of trusted peers, and they share a secret key used to digitally sign the reputation data. Good reputation is obtained by having consistent good behaviour through several transactions. The proposed scheme is based on four values associated to each peer and stored at the supernode level; two of them are used to provide an idea about the satisfaction of users, and the others express the amount of uploads provided by the peer. The reputation information is updated according with the peer transactions of upload and download. In a posterior work [7] the same authors propose an algorithm to detect malicious peers which are sending inauthentic files or are lying in their feedbacks. They distinguish righteous peers from those which share

Table 1. Maximum tolerable malicious feedbacks rate r_{bad}: analytical results without and with braking window, and simulated results

Role	th_{norec}	th_{rec}	sim_{rec}
A	20%	35%	35%
P	20%	28%	28%
S	20%	25%	25%
N	20%	21%	21%

inauthentic files and provide false feedbacks about other peers. The model introduces the concept of suspicious transaction, that is a transaction whose appreciation depends on the reputation of the sender and the concept of credibility behaviour, as an indicator of the liar behaviour of peers. These schemes are able to detect malicious peers and isolate them from the system, but do not consider the tolerable rate of malicious negative feedbacks, and suppose that supernodes are always trustworthy.

A distributed method to compute global trust values, based on power iteration, is illustrated in [8]. The reputation system aggregates local trust values of all users, by means of an approach based on transitive trust: a peer will have a high opinion of those peers which have provided authentic files and it is likely to trust the opinions of those peers, since peers which are honest about the files they provide are also likely to be honest in reporting their local trust values. The scheme is reactive, *i.e.* it requires reputations to be computed on-demand, through the cooperation of a large number of peers. This introduces additional latency and requires a lot of time to collect statistics and compute the global rating.

The protocol proposed in [9] aims to distinguish malicious responses from benign ones, by using the reputation of the peers which provide them. The protocol relies on the P2P infrastructure to obtain the necessary reputation information when it is not locally available at the querying peer. The outcomes of past transactions are stored in trust vectors; every peer maintains a trust vector for every other peer it has dealt with in the past. The trust query process is similar to the file query process except that the subject of the query is a peer about whom trust information is inquired. The responses are sorted and weighted by the credibility rating of the responder, derived from the credibility vectors maintained by the local peer, which are similar to the trust vectors.

In [10], the use of a scheme named ROCQ (Reputation, Opinion, Credibility and Quality) in a collaborative content-distribution system is analyzed. ROCQ computes global reputation values for peers on the basis of first-hand opinions of transactions provided by participants. Global reputation values are stored in a decentralized fashion using multiple score managers for each individual peer. The final average reputation value is formed by two aggregations, first at the score managers and second at the requesting peer.

All these works consider the situation in which a peer with a bad reputation is simply isolated from the system, while the analytical model we are proposing describes different roles for peers, associated with different actions. So a peer with a suspect malicious behaviour can be first demoted, and eventually isolated from the system.

7 Conclusions

In this work we have illustrated the analytical model of a reputation management service for role-based peergroups. The model defines some parameters and indicators, such as the maximum tolerable rate of malicious negative feedbacks. We applied the reputation model to an example of four-role security policy, giving a parameter set for each role, and computing the theoretical values for the main indicators. These results have been confirmed by those we obtained from several emulations exploiting a centralized reputation management service.

Further work will follow two main directions. In order to improve the analytical model, we need to compare the effectiveness of different functions for realizing the braking windows. Once the analytical model is verified and all of its parameters are tuned, we will investigate an efficient and robust distributed solution for reputation storage and retrieval by means of simulations and prototypes.

Acknowledgements

This work has been partially supported by the "STIL" project of Regione Emilia-Romagna, and by the "WEB-MINDS" FIRB project of the National Research Ministry.

References

1. Amoretti, M., Zanichelli, F., Conte, G.: SP2A: a Service-oriented Framework for P2P-based Grids. In: 3rd International Workshop on Middleware for Grid Computing, Co-located with Middleware (2005)
2. Amoretti, M., Bisi, M., Zanichelli, F., Conte, G.: Introducing Secure Peergroups in SP2A. In: HOTP2P 2005, San Diego, California, USA (2005)
3. Ye, S., Makedon, F., Ford, J.: Collaborative Automated Trust Negotiation in Peer-to-Peer Systems. In: Fourth International Conference on Peer-to-Peer Computing (P2P 2004) (2004)
4. Barabási, A.-L., Albert, R.: Emergence of Scaling in Random Networks. Science 286, 509–512 (1999)
5. Lee, S.Y., Kwon, O.H., Kim, J., Hong, S.J.: A Reputation Management System in Structured peer-to-peer Networks. In: The 14th International Workshops on Enabling Technologies:Infrastruture for Collaborative Enterprise (2005)
6. Mekouar, L., Iraqui, Y., Boutaba, R.: A Reputation Management and Selection Advisor Schemes for peer-to-peer Systems. In: The 15th IFIP/IEEE International Workshop on Distributed Systems: Operations and Management (2004)
7. Mekouar, L., Iraqui, Y., Boutaba, R.: Detecting Malicious Peers in a Reputation-based peer-to-peer System (2004)
8. Kamvar, S.D., Schlosser, M.T., Garcia-Molina, H.: The Eigentrust Algorithm for Reputation Management in peer-to-peer Networks. In: The 12th International World Wide Web Conference (2003)
9. Selcuk, A.A., Uzun, E., Pariente, M.R.: A Reputation-Based Trust Management System for peer-to-peer peer-to-peer Networks. In: IEEE International Symposium on Cluster Computing and the Grid (2004)
10. Garg, A., Battiti, R., Cascella, R.: Reputation Management: Experiments on the Robustness of rocq (2005)

A New Approach for the Trust Calculation in Social Networks

Mehrdad Nojoumian and Timothy C. Lethbridge

School of Information Technology and Engineering, University of Ottawa
Ottawa, ON, K1N 6N5, Canada
mnojoumi@site.uottawa.ca, tcl@site.uottawa.ca

Abstract. This paper aims at the trust calculation in social networks by addressing some major issues: Firstly, the paper evaluates a specific trust function and its behaviors, and then it focuses on the modification of that trust function by considering diverse scenarios. After that, the paper proposes a new approach with a specific functionality. The main goals are to support good agents strongly, block bad ones and create opportunities for newcomers or agents who want to show their merit in our society although we can not judge them. Finally, a mathematical discussion by a new trust function is provided with ultimate results.

Keywords: Trust, Reputation, Social Networks.

1 Introduction

One of the major challenges for electronic commerce is how to establish a relationship of trust between different parties and how to form a reputation scheme as a global vision. In many cases, the parties involved may not ever have interacted before. It is important for participants such as buyers, sellers and partners to estimate each other's trustworthiness before initiating any commercial transactions.

According to [4], *"Trust"* is a personal expectation an agent has about another's future behavior, it is an *individual quantity* calculated based on the two agents concerned in a present or future dyadic encounter while *"Reputation" is* perception that an agent has of another's intentions, it is a *social quantity* calculated based on actions by a given agent and observations made by others in a social network. From the cognitive point of view [19], trust is made up of underlying beliefs and it is a function of the value of these beliefs. Therefore, reputation is more a social notion of trust. In our lives, we each maintain a set of reputations for people we know. When we have to work with a new person, we can ask people with whom we already have relationships for information about that person. Based on the information we gather, we form an opinion about the reputation of the new person.

To form a pattern for agents, we should consider a *"social network"* which is a social structure made of nodes and ties. Nodes are individual actors within the networks, and ties are relationships between the actors. In E-commerce, social network refers to an electronic community which consists of interacting parties such as people or businesses.

J. Filipe and M.S. Obaidat (Eds.): ICETE 2006, CCIS 9, pp. 64–77, 2008.

Another concept is *"reputation systems"* which collect, distribute and aggregate feedback about participants' past behavior. They seek to address the development of trust by recording the reputations of different parties. The model of reputation will be constructed from a buying agent's positive and negative past experiences with the aim of predicting how satisfied the buying agent will be with the results of future interactions with a selling agent. OnSale exchange and eBay are practical examples of reputation management. OnSale allows users to rate and submit textual comments about sellers. The overall reputation of a seller is the average of the ratings obtained from his customers. In eBay, sellers receive feedback (-1, 0, +1) for their reliability in each auction and their reputation calculated as the sum of those ratings over the last six months. The major goal of reputation systems is to help people decide whom to trust and deter the contribution of dishonest parties. Most existing online reputation systems are *centralized* and have been designed to foster trust among strangers in e-commerce [16].

To extend reputation systems, a *"social reputation system"* can be applied in which a buying agent can choose to query other buying agents for information about sellers for which the original buying agent has no information. This system allows for a *decentralized* approach whose strengths and weaknesses lie between the personal and public reputation system.

For creating a *"reputation model"*, researchers apply various approaches. For example in [3], an agent maintains a model of each acquaintance. This model includes the agent's abilities to act in a trustworthy manner and to refer to other trustworthy agents. The first ability is *"expertise: ability to produce correct answers"* and the second one is *"sociability: ability to produce accurate referrals"*. The quality of the network is maximized when both abilities are considered.

The other essential factor is *"social behavior"*. This refers to the way that agents communicate and cooperate with each others. Usually, in reputation systems good players are rewarded whereas bad players are penalized by the society. For instance, if A_1 encounters a bad partner (A_2) during some exchange, A_1 will penalize A_2 by decreasing its rating and informing its neighbors. In a sample proposed approach [1], A_1 assigns a rating to A_2 based on:

1. Its direct observations of A_2
2. The rating of A_2 as given by his neighbors
3. A_1's rating of those neighbors (witnesses)

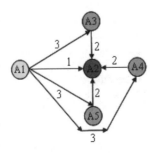

Fig. 1. A sample rating assignment

As you can see, this approach seeks to create trust based on local or social evidence; *"local trust"* is built through direct observations while *"social trust"* is built through information from others.

The purpose of this paper and our major motivations are to evaluate the behavior of a specific trust function and propose a new approach for the modification of the trust calculation. The rest of this paper is organized as follows. Section 2 reviews the existing literature on the trust and reputation systems. Section 3, illustrates the behavior of a specific trust function and its modification by proposing a new approach. Section 4, presents a new trust function and shows the final results. Finally in section 5, some concluding remarks are provided.

2 Literature Review

In this section, we review many interesting approaches in various research projects in order to form a clear vision of trust and reputation systems.

Trust is one of the most important parameters in electronic commerce technology. According to [17], if you want to maximize the amount of trade and of agents' utility functions, the seller's trust should be equal to the buyer's trustworthiness; this shows the impact of trust in E-commerce. [11] summarize existing works on rating and reputation across diverse disciplines, i.e., distributed artificial intelligence, economics, and evolutionary biology. They discuss the relative strength of the different notions of reputation using a simple simulation based on *"Evolutionary Game Theory"*. They focus on the strategies of each agent and do not consider gathering reputation information from other parties.

A *"Social Mechanism"* of reputation management was implemented in [20]. This mechanism requires that users give a rating for themselves and either have a central agency (direct ratings) or other trusted users (collaborative ratings). [7] present an approach which understands referrals as arising in and influencing *"Dynamic Social Networks"* where the agents act autonomously based on local knowledge. They model both expertise and sociability in their system and consider a weighted referral graph. [9] show how social network analysis can be used as part of the *"Regret Reputation System"* which considers the social dimension of reputation. [10] propose an approach to establish reputation based on the *position of each member* within the corresponding social networks. They seek to reconstruct the social networks using available information in the community.

[6] develop a *"Graph Based Representation"* which takes a strong stance for both local and social aspects. In their approach, the agents track each other's trustworthiness locally and can give and receive referrals to others. This approach naturally accommodates the above conceptualizations of trust: social because the agents give and receive referrals to other agents, and local because the agents maintain rich representations of each other and can reason about them to determine their trustworthiness. Further, the agents evaluate each other's ability to give referrals. Lastly, although this approach does not require centralized authorities, it can help agents evaluate the trustworthiness of such authorities too.

To facilitate trust in commercial transactions *"Trusted Third Parties"* [18] are often employed. Typical TTP services for electronic commerce include certification, time stamping, and notarization. TTPs act as a bridge between buyers and sellers in electronic marketplaces. However, they are most appropriate for closed marketplaces. Another method is from *"Social Interaction Framework (SIF)"* [15]. In SIF, an agent evaluates the reputation of another agent based on direct observations as well through other witnesses.

[13] present a *"Coalition Formation Mechanism"* based on trust relationships. Their approach extends existing transaction-oriented coalitions, and might be an interesting direction for distributed reputation management for electronic commerce. [14] discuss *the trust that is needed to engage in a transaction.* In their model, a party engages in a transaction only if its level of trust exceeds its personal threshold. The threshold depends on the type of the transaction and the other parties involved in the transaction.

In [5] an agent maintains a model of each acquaintance. This model includes the acquaintance's *reliability* to provide high-quality services and *credibility* to provide trustworthy ratings to other agents. [2] discuss the effect of reputation information sharing on the *efficiency and load distribution of a P2P system*, in which peers only have limited or no information sharing. In their approach, each node records ratings of any other nodes in a reputation vector. Their approach does not distinguish the ratings for service (reliability) and ratings for voting (credibility) and does not consider how to adjust the weight for voting.

[12] use a model to manage trust in a P2P network where no central database is available. Their model is based on *"Binary Trust"*. For instance, an agent is either trustworthy or not. In case a dishonest transaction is detected, the agents can forward their complaints to other agents. Recently, a new P2P reputation system is presented in [8] based on *"Fuzzy Logic Inferences"* which can better handle uncertainty, fuzziness, and incomplete information in peer trust reports. They demonstrate the efficacy and robustness of two P2P reputation systems (*FuzzyTrust* and *EigenTrust*) at establishing trust among the peers.

In the next section, we evaluate the behavior of the proposed trust function in [1] and offer a new approach for the trust calculation.

3 Trust Function

In this section, we evaluate a specific trust function by [1] and assess its behavior. In the proposed scheme, after an interaction the updated trust rating T_{t+1} is given by the following formulas (Table 1) and depends on the previous trust rating where:

$\alpha >= 0, \beta <= 0$

Table 1. Trust function from [1]

T_t	Cooperation
> 0	$T_t + \alpha (1 - T_t)$
< 0	$(T_t + \alpha)/(1 - \min\{|T_t|, |\alpha|\})$
$= 0$	α
T_t	Defection
> 0	$(T_t + \beta)/(1 - \min\{|T_t|, |\beta|\})$
< 0	$T_t + \beta (1 + T_t)$
$= 0$	β

The following diagram (Figure 2) shows the behavior of the Yu trust function, it is convergent at points (+1, +1) and (-1, -1). The above curve is for the cooperation and the other one is for the defection. This function also crosses axis Y at the following points: α =0.1 and β =-0.2 where T_t is equal to zero.

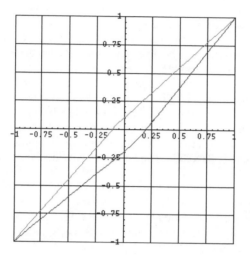

Fig. 2. Yu trust function diagram (α =0.1 & β =-0.2)

3.1 Evaluation of the Yu Trust Function

To see the exact properties of the Yu trust function, refer to the Table 2, which shows T_t and its corresponding value (T_{t+1}) in the interval [-1, +1].

Figure 3 illustrates the behavior of the proposed trust function in cooperation situations. It shows the reward values in the interval [-1, +1]. The main critique here is for cooperation in the interval (0, +1] but the behavior of the function in the interval [-1, 0) is fine. Consider the two following scenarios for cooperation:

a) If the participant is a trustworthy agent (e.g. T=0.8) and shows more cooperation, the function increases the trust value a little bit (0.02), but if it is not very trustworthy (e.g. T=0.2) and shows cooperation, the function enhances the trust value a lot (0.08). These are not good properties.

b) If the participant is a corrupt agent (e.g. T=-0.8) and shows cooperation, the function increases the trust value a little bit (0.02) and if agent's trust value is e.g. T=-0.2 and shows cooperation, the function enhances the trust value more (0.09) in comparison to the previous situation. These are good properties.

Table 2. Trust function's behavior, α =0.1 & β=-0.2

T_t	Plus	T_{t+1}	T_t	Minus	T_{t+1}
1	0	1	1	0	1
0.9	0.01	0.91	0.9	-0.03	0.87
0.8	0.02	0.82	0.8	-0.05	0.75
0.7	0.03	0.73	0.7	-0.08	0.62
0.6	0.04	0.64	0.6	-0.1	0.5
0.5	0.05	0.55	0.5	-0.13	0.37
0.4	0.06	0.46	0.4	-0.15	0.25
0.3	0.07	0.37	0.3	-0.18	0.12
0.2	0.08	0.28	0.2	-0.2	0
0.1	0.09	0.19			
			0.16	-0.21	-0.06
0	0.1	0.1	0.12	-0.21	-0.09
			0.08	-0.21	-0.13
-0.02	0.1	0.08	0.04	-0.21	-0.17
-0.05	0.1	0.05			
-0.08	0.1	0.02	0	-0.2	-0.2
-0.1	0.1	0	-0.1	-0.18	-0.28
-0.2	0.09	-0.11	-0.2	-0.16	-0.36
-0.3	0.08	-0.22	-0.3	-0.14	-0.44
-0.4	0.07	-0.33	-0.4	-0.12	-0.52
-0.5	0.06	-0.44	-0.5	-0.1	-0.6
-0.6	0.04	-0.56	-0.6	-0.08	-0.68
-0.7	0.03	-0.67	-0.7	-0.06	-0.76
-0.8	0.02	-0.78	-0.8	-0.04	-0.84
-0.9	0.01	-0.89	-0.9	-0.02	-0.92
-1	0	-1	-1	0	-1

Figure 4 demonstrates the behavior of the proposed trust function in defection situations. It shows the penalty values in the interval [-1, +1]. The main critique here is for defection in the interval [-1, 0) but the behavior of the function in the interval (0, +1] is fine. Consider the two following scenarios for defection:

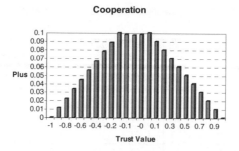

Fig. 3. Yu trust function's behavior in cooperation

c) If the participant is a trustworthy agent (e.g. T=0.8) and shows defection, the function decreases the trust value a little bit (-0.05), but if it is not very trustworthy (e.g. T= 0.2) and shows defection, the function decreases the trust value a lot (-0.2) which are good properties to some extend.

d) If the participant is a corrupt agent (e.g. T=-0.8) and shows more defection, the function decreases the trust value a little bit (-0.04) and if agent's trust value is e.g. T=-0.2 and shows defection, the function decreases the trust value more (-0.16) in compare to the previous state. These are not good properties.

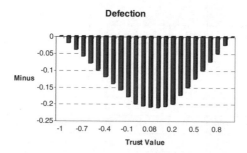

Fig. 4. Yu trust function's behavior in defection

Therefore, this paper's major critique is for cooperation in scenario "a" and defection in scenario "d". They show bad behaviors of the trust function. In the next section, a sample improved function is provided to modify the trust calculation for the social networks.

3.2 Modification of the Trust Function

To modify the trust function in [1], we consider six possible situations (Table 3). If trust value is less than β then the agent is a *bad* participant, if it is greater than α then the agent is a *good* member of the society, otherwise ([β , α]) we can not judge the agent. We just suppose it is a member who is looking for some opportunities. By considering both cooperation and defection factors, we have the following rules:

(1) If a bad agent cooperates, then we *encourage* it a little bit, e.g. by the factor $X_E \in (0.01, 0.05)$

(2) If we encounter with an agent who is looking for a chance by cooperating, then we *give it some opportunities* by the factor $X_{Give} = 0.05$

(3) If a good agent cooperates, then we *reward* it more than the encouragement factor:

$X_R \in (0.05, 0.09) > X_E \in (0.01, 0.05)$

(4) If a good agent defects, then we *discourage* it a little bit, e.g. by the factor $X_D \in (-0.05, -0.01)$

(5) If we encounter with an agent that we can not judge it while it is defecting, then we *deduct its credit value* by the factor $X_{Take} = -0.05$

(6) If a bad agent defects, then we *penalize* it more than the discouragement factor: $|X_P| \in | (-0.09, -0.05)| > |X_D| \in | (-0.05, -0.01)|$

If the agent has an excellent trust value (e.g. 0.99) and shows more cooperation, we increase the trust value in a way that it would be convergent to 1. On the other side, if the agent has a poor trust value (e.g. -0.99) and shows more defection, we decrease the trust value in a way that it would be convergent to -1. Therefore, the new trust function is also in interval [-1, +1]. This function covers all the above proposed rules, more detailed behaviors are provided in Table 4.

Table 3. Six possible situations for interaction

Trust Value	Cooperation	Defection
$T_{Bad\ Agent} \in [-1, \beta)$	*Encourage*	*Penalize*
No Judgment: $[\beta, \alpha]$	*Give/Take*	*Opportunities*
$T_{Good\ Agent} \in (\alpha, +1]$	*Reward*	*Discourage*

In the next section, the result of the new trust function in different intervals with various scenarios is illustrated; moreover, a quadratic regression is provided in order to find a simpler approximating formula for the new trust function.

Table 4. Modified trust function, α =0.1 & β=-0.1

T_t	Plus	T_{t+1}	T_t	Minus	T_{t+1}
-1	0.005	-0.995	**-1**	**0**	**-1**
-0.9	0.01	-0.89	**-0.975**	**-0.024**	**-0.999**
-0.8	0.015	-0.785	**-0.95**	**-0.047**	**-0.997**
-0.7	0.02	-0.68	**-0.925**	**-0.07**	**-0.995**
-0.6	0.025	-0.575	-0.9	-0.09	-0.99
-0.5	0.03	-0.47	-0.8	-0.085	-0.885
-0.4	0.035	-0.365	-0.7	-0.08	-0.78
-0.3	0.04	-0.26	-0.6	-0.075	-0.675
-0.2	0.045	-0.155	-0.5	-0.07	-0.57
-0.1	0.05	-0.05	-0.4	-0.065	-0.465
-0.05	0.05	0	-0.3	-0.06	-0.36
0	0.05	0.05	-0.2	-0.055	-0.255
0.05	0.05	0.1	-0.1	-0.05	-0.15
0.1	0.05	0.15	-0.05	-0.05	-0.1
0.2	0.055	0.255	0	-0.05	-0.05
0.3	0.06	0.36	0.05	-0.05	0
0.4	0.065	0.465	0.1	-0.05	0.05
0.5	0.07	0.57	0.2	-0.045	0.155
0.6	0.075	0.675	0.3	-0.04	0.26
0.7	0.08	0.78	0.4	-0.035	0.365
0.8	0.085	0.885	0.5	-0.03	0.47
0.9	0.09	0.99	0.6	-0.025	0.575
0.925	**0.07**	**0.995**	0.7	-0.02	0.68
0.95	**0.047**	**0.997**	0.8	-0.015	0.785
0.975	**0.024**	**0.999**	0.9	-0.01	0.89
1	**0**	**1**	1	-0.005	0.995

4   Results

In this part, a detailed evaluation of the new trust function with its regression is presented. First of all look at the Figure 5. It illustrates the behavior of the new function in cooperation situations. This diagram shows the value that trust function adds to the trust value each time according to the following scheme:

[-1, β)   →   *Encourage*

[β, α]   →   *Give Opportunities*

(α, +1]   →   *Reward*

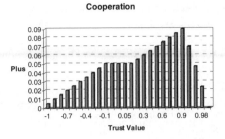

Fig. 5. New function's behavior in cooperation

Figure 6 also illustrates the behavior of the new function in defection situations. This diagram shows the value that trust function deducts from the trust value each time according to the following scheme:

$[-1, \beta)$ →   *Penalize*

$[\beta, \alpha]$ →   *Take Opportunities*

$(\alpha, +1]$ →   *Discourage*

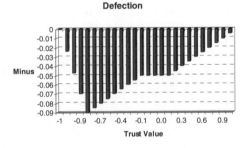

Fig. 6. New function's behavior in defection

The last two diagrams show important properties. They complete behaviors of each other.

In interval $[\beta, \alpha]$ they neutralize each other (if $\beta = \alpha$) to provide opportunity for new agents that their past behaviors are not available (newcomers) and also agents who want to pass the border between bad players and good ones. They must prove their merit in this area; otherwise they will be stuck in this region, because we add or deduct the trust value with the same rate, for instance |0.05| (we can play with α and β to change the interval, e.g. [-0.2, +0.1]).

In interval $[-1, \beta)$, we penalize bad agents more than the rate that we encourage them. This means that we try to avoid and block bad participants in our business, at the same time we provide a chance by interval $[\beta, \alpha]$ for the agents who want to show their merit, if they reach this area then we behave more benevolently.

In interval (α, +1], we reward good agents more than the rate that we discourage them. This means that we try to support good players in our business and keep them in our trustee list as much as we can and as long as they cooperate, although they will be guided to the interval [β, α] if they show bad behaviors continuously.

The other important scenario is related to the value of the transactions, suppose a good agent cooperates for a long time in cheap transactions (e.g. $100) to gain a good trust value and after that he tries to defect for some expensive transactions (e.g. $1000). The solution is that we can consider a coefficient (λ) for the value of a transaction and then increase or decrease the trust value according to the λ. For example, if the transaction value is $100 then: λ=1 and if it is $1000 then: λ=10; therefore, if an agent cooperates for 5 times on the cheap transactions (λ=1) then we add his trust value 5 times. If he defects after that on an expensive transaction (λ=10) then we deduct his trust value 10 times continuously. So, by this approach we have a more reliable trust function which depends on the transaction value.

In Figure 7, you can see a quadratic regression that approximates the new trust function (Table 4) with 99.9% accuracy.

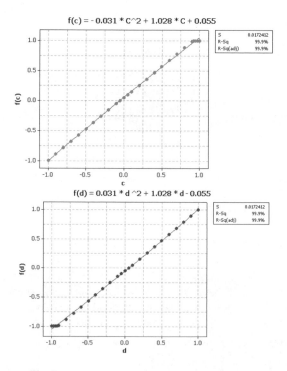

Fig. 7. Quadratic regression for the new function

The quadratic approximation to the trust function is as follows and you can see its diagram in Figure 8:

$$\begin{cases} T_{t+1} = \omega * T_t^2 + \theta * T_t + \sigma \\ Cooperatio\, n : \omega = -0.031, \theta = 1.028, \sigma = 0.055 \\ Defection : \omega = 0.031, \theta = 1.028, \sigma = -0.055 \end{cases}$$

Where:

$T_t \in [-1,+1]$

$\alpha = 0.1$ & $\beta = -0.1$

$X_E \in (0.01, 0.05)$

$X_{Give} = 0.05$

   $X_R \in (0.05, 0.09) > X_E \in (0.01, 0.05)$

   $X_D \in (-0.05, -0.01)$

   $X_{Take} = -0.05$

   $|X_P| \in |(-0.09, -0.05)| > |X_D| \in |(-0.05, -0.01)|$

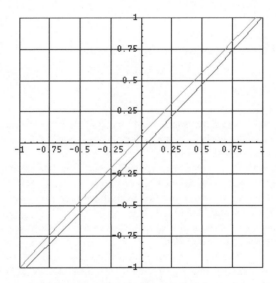

Fig. 8. New proposed trust function

Above function is simpler and has better behavior in comparison to the trust function in [1], which is more complex with some irrational behaviors. On the other hand, this function satisfies the proposed approach in this paper, although we can use the cubic regression with more sample points to achieve better accuracy. In the next section, some discussion and concluding remarks are provided.

5   Conclusions

In this paper, we evaluated a specific trust function for social networks. The paper showed the behavior of that function and proposed a new mathematical approach to modify a previously published trust formula [1]. A mathematical discussion with various scenarios was provided to demonstrate the behavior of the new trust function. The paper used a bottom-up approach to create a new trust function; and it provided sample points according to the function's behavior for certain values of 8 constants used to parameterize our approach. We also provided a quadratic approximation to simplify calculation of the function, with only minor cost in accuracy. Alternative approximations would be needed if any of the eight constants were changed.

Another important factor is to consider both *expertise* (ability to produce correct answers) and *sociability* (ability to produce accurate referrals) in social networks. Usually, the goal of a trust function is to calculate expertise, but we should also consider another function for the calculation of sociability. If we do so, then we can evaluate our social networks by those two functions. As a future work, we would like to work on the computation of sociability. Our purpose is to evaluate social behaviors of agents by considering both functions at the same time and apply a two dimensional function for this assessment.

Acknowledgements

We appreciate the anonymous reviewers for their comments.

References

1. Yu, B., Singh, M.P.: A social mechanism of reputation management in electronic communities. In: Proceedings of Fourth International Workshop on Cooperative Information Agents, pp. 154–165 (2000)
2. Marti, S., Carcia-Molina, H.: Limited reputation sharing in P2P systems. In: Proceedings of the ACM Conference on Electronic Commerce, pp. 91–101 (2004)
3. Yu, B., Singh, M.P.: Distributed reputation management for electronic commerce. Computational Intelligence 18(4), 535–549 (2002)
4. Mui, L.: Computational models of trust and reputation. PhD thesis in Electrical Engineering and Computer Science, MIT (2002)
5. Yu, B., Singh, M.P., Sycara, K.: Developing trust in large-scale peer-to-peer systems. In: First IEEE Symposium on Multi-Agent Security and Survivability (2004)
6. Yolum, P., Singh, M.P.: Service graphs for building trust. In: Proceedings of the International Conference on Cooperative Information Systems, vol. (1), pp. 509–525 (2004)
7. Yu, B., Singh, M.P.: Searching social networks. In: Proceedings of the 2nd International Joint Conference on Autonomous Agents and Multi-Agent Systems (AAMAS). ACM Press, New York (2003)
8. Song, S., Hwang, K., Zhou, R., kwok, Y.: Trusted P2P transactions with fuzzy reputation aggregation. IEEE Internet Computing 9(6), 24–34 (2005)
9. Sabater, J., Sierra, C.: Reputation and social network analysis in multi-agent systems. In: Proceedings of First International Joint Conference on Autonomous Agents and Multi-agent Systems, pp. 475–482 (2002)
10. Pujol, J.M., Sanguesa, R., Delgado, J.: Extracting reputation in multi-agent systems by means of social network topology. In: Proceedings of First International Joint Conference on Autonomous Agents and Multi-agent Systems, pp. 467–474 (2002)

11. Mui, L., Mohtashemi, M., Halberstadt, A.: Notions of reputation in multi-agents systems: a review. In: Proceedings of First International Joint Conference on Autonomous Agents and Multi-agent Systems, pp. 280–287 (2002)
12. Aberer, K., Despotovic, Z.: Managing trust in a peer-2-peer information system. In: Proceedings of the Tenth International Conference on Information and Knowledge Management (CIKM 2001), pp. 310–317 (2001)
13. Breban, S., Vassileva, J.: Long-term coalitions for the electronic marketplace. In: Proceedings of Canadian AI Workshop on Novel E-Commerce Applications of Agents, pp. 6–12 (2001)
14. Tan, Y., Thoen, W.: An outline of a trust model for electronic commerce. Applied Artificial Intelligence 14, 849–862 (2000)
15. Schillo, M., Funk, P., Rovatsos, M.: Using trust for detecting deceitful agents in artificial societies. Applied Artificial Intelligence 14, 825–848 (2000)
16. Resnick, P., Zeckhauser, R., Friedman, E., Kuwabara, K.: Reputation systems: facilitating trust in internet interactions. Communications of the ACM 43(12), 45–48 (2000)
17. Brainov, S., Sandholm, T.: Contracting with uncertain level of trust. In: Proceedings of the First International Conference on Electronic Commerce (EC 1999), pp. 15–21 (1999)
18. Rea, T., Skevington, P.: Engendering trust in electronic commerce. British Telecommunications Engineering 17(3), 150–157 (1998)
19. Castelfranchi, C., Falcone, R.: Principle of trust for MAS: cognitive anatomy, social importance, and quantification. In: Proceedings of Third International Conference on Multi Agent Systems, pp. 72–79 (1998)
20. Chavez, A., Maes, P.: Kasbah: An agent marketplace for buying and selling goods. In: Proceedings of the 1st International Conference on the Practical Application of Intelligent Agents and Multi-agent Technology (PAAM), pp. 75–90 (1996)

PART II
SECRYPT

Spoofed ARP Packets Detection in Switched LAN Networks

Zouheir Trabelsi and Khaled Shuaib

College of Information Technology, UAE University, Al-Ain, UAE
trabelsi@uaeu.ac.ae

Abstract. Spoofed ARP packets are used by malicious users to redirect network's traffic to their hosts. The potential damage to a network from an attack of this nature can be very important. This paper discusses first how malicious users redirect network traffic using spoofed ARP packets. Then, the paper proposes a practical and efficient mechanism for detecting malicious hosts that are performing traffic redirection attack against other hosts in switched LAN networks. The proposed mechanism consists of sending first spoofed packets to the network's hosts. Then, by collecting and analyzing the responses packets, it is shown how hosts performing traffic redirection attack can be identified efficiently and accurately. The affect of the proposed mechanism on the performance of the network is discussed and shown to be minimal. The limits of current IDSs regarding their ability to detect malicious traffic redirection attack, based on spoofed ARP packets, in switched LAN networks are discussed. Our work is concerned with the detection of malicious network traffic redirection attack, at the Data Link layer. Other works proposed protection mechanisms against this attack, but at the Application layer, using cryptographic techniques and protocols.

Keywords: Intrusions Detection Systems, Spoofed ARP, ARP Cache Poisoning, Packet Sniffers.

1 Introduction

Traditionally, research in the area of information and communication security focused on helping developers of systems prevent security vulnerabilities in the systems they produce, before the systems are released to customers. In addition, in most studies on network security, only external attacks were being considered. All of these areas are of the outmost importance when it comes to information and communication security, but need to be complemented with research supporting those developing detection and recovery mechanisms, and studying internal threats. *MiM* attack is used by malicious internal users to sniff the network traffic between target hosts, in switched networks. Malicious users can tap in on the network traffic for information without the knowledge of the networks legitimate owner. This information can include passwords, e-mail messages, encryption keys, sequence numbers or other proprietary data, etc. Often, some of this information can be used to penetrate further into the network, or cause other severe damage. This underlines the importance of reliable *MiM* attack detection techniques that can aid network administrators, in detecting malicious sniffing activities in switched networks.

J. Filipe and M.S. Obaidat (Eds.): ICETE 2006, CCIS 9, pp. 81–91, 2008.

Today, IDSs, such as Snort [2], have become a standard part of the security solutions, used to protect computing assets from hostile attacks. IDSs are able to detect many types of attacks, such as denial of services (DoS) attacks and IP spoofing attacks. But, their ability and reliability to detect some particular attacks are still questionable, notably the *MiM* attack. IDSs must be able to detect the *MiM* attack since malicious sniffing activities in switched networks rely on this attack [7], [8]. This paper discusses the limits of the main IDSs regarding the detection of the *MiM* attack, provides an understanding of how *MiM* attack works, and proposes a novel efficient mechanism for detecting *MiM* attack-based sniffing activities in switched networks. The proposed detection mechanism is based mainly on the generation of spoofed packets which are sent to the network's hosts. By collecting and analyzing the response packets, it will be possible to identify hosts performing *MiM* attack against the other hosts in the network. Even though, the proposed mechanism injects additional spoofed packets in the network, the network will not be flooded and its performance will not be affected, since the number of the injected packets is relatively very limited. In addition, it will be shown that the proposed mechanism does not disturb the network activities of the hosts.

The rest of the paper is organized as following: Section 2 provides an overview of the related work done in this area. Section 3 gives a brief understanding of some networking concepts to lay the groundwork for what follows. Section 4 discusses the ARP cache poisoning attack. Section 5 discusses the *MiM* attack and how it is used for malicious sniffing activities in switched network. Section 6 presents an efficient mechanism for detecting hosts sniffing switched networks. Section 7 presents a tool, called *AntiMiM*, for detecting malicious sniffing hosts in switched networks, based on the proposed detection mechanism. Section 8 discusses the affect of the proposed detection mechnaism on the network performance. Finally, conclusions are made and some directions for future research are provided in section 9.

2   Related Work

Although few tools and some newer IDSs can detect ARP anomalies, most of them do not specially target the ARP cache poisoning attack and the *MiM* attack. Those attacks are interesting to detect because they are highly intentional. No virus or worms use it, so when such attacks are in effect, there is certainly some human controlling them. Besides, most IDSs rely on Sniffer-based sensors to detect those attacks, greatly restricting their effectiveness in switched networks.

Arpwatch [1] is a tool that aims to keep sysadmins informed (usually via email) about changes in the IP/MAC mappings. This catches many interesting events, such as IP addresses being changed (by authorized personnel or not), MAC addresses being changed (either by software reconfiguration or by physically replacing Ethernet card), new machines being added to the network (because of gratuitous ARPs), common misconfigurations (like IP address conflicts), etc. To do that, *Arpwatch* monitors Ethernet activity and keeps a database of Ethernet MAC address/IP address pairs. By sniffing the network, *Arpwatch* tries to detect any packet that has an Ethernet MAC address/IP address pair which does not appear in *Arpwatch's* database. However, *Arpwatch* can't tell these non-malicious events apart from intentional ARP spoofing attacks. On large busy networks with overworked or lax sysadmins, where typically hundreds of ARP anomalies are reported daily, many real serious attacks may pass unchecked. In addition, *Arpwatch's* detection technique presumes that the host running *Arpwatch* has access to a monitoring port on the Switch (usually, known under the name of *SPAN* port, or *mirroring* port). Therefore, it would be more interesting and efficient to detect any ARP anomalies without the use of any access privilege or special ports on the Switches. In addition, there is usually a substantial performance impact when port mirroring is in effect; this strategy makes ARP spoofing detection based on sniffing not quite viable on switched networks. *Snort* is an open source network intrusion prevention and detection system utilizing a rule-driven language, which combines the benefits of signature, protocol and anomaly based inspection methods. *Snort* is able to detect ARP cache poisoning attack by checking each packet contents. If the analyzed packet has an Ethernet MAC address/IP address pair which does not appear in *Snort's* database, then the system administrator is alerted. Like *Arpwatch*, *Snort* is an intrusion detection sensor, that is, it should have access to a monitoring port or be placed in a location where it can see all the incoming and outgoing network traffic.

3 Background

This section is aimed at providing a brief understanding of Address Resolution Protocol (ARP) and ARP cache.

3.1 ARP Protocol

To map a particular IP address to a given hardware address (MAC address) so that packets can be transmitted across a local network, systems use the Address Resolution Protocol (ARP) [3]. ARP messages are exchanged when one host knows the IP address of a remote host and wants to discover the remote host's MAC address. For example, if host 1 wants host 2's MAC address, it sends an ARP request message (Who has?) to the broadcast MAC address (FF:FF:FF:FF:FF:FF) and host 2 answers with his addresses (MAC and IP). Basically, an ARP message on an Ethernet/IP network has 8 important parameters: Ethernet header source and destination MAC address, Ethernet type (=0x0806 for ARP message), ARP message header source and destination IP address, source and destination MAC address, operation code (1 for request), (2 for reply). It is important to mention that there is nothing specifying that there must be some consistency between the ARP header and the Ethernet header. That means you can provide uncorrelated addresses between these two headers. For example, the source MAC address in the Ethernet header can be different from the source MAC address in the ARP message header.

3.2 ARP Cache

Each host in a network segment has a table, called ARP cache, which maps IP addresses with their correspondent MAC addresses. There are two types of entries in an ARP cache, namely: Static entries which remain in the ARP cache until the system reboots and Dynamic entries which remain in the ARP cache for few minutes (this depends on the operating system (OS)) then they are removed if they are not referenced. New ARP requests allow to add them again in the ARP cache. Static entries mechanism is used unfortunately in small local area network (LAN). However, in large networks, the deployment and updates of static entries in the ARP caches of the hosts are non practical networking tasks. New entries in the ARP cache can be created or already existing entries can be updated by ARP request or reply messages.

4 ARP Cache Poisoning Attack

ARP cache poisoning attack is the malicious act, by a host in a LAN, of introducing a spurious IP address to MAC address mapping in another host's ARP cache. This can be done by manipulating directly the ARP cache of a target host, independently of the ARP messages sent by the target host. To do that, we can either add a new fake entry in the target host's ARP cache, or update an already existing entry by fake IP and MAC addresses.

4.1 Static ARP Cache Update

An efficient technique to protect an ARP cache against the ARP cache poisoning attack is to use static entries in the ARP cache. That is, the entries in the ARP cache cannot be updated by ARP request and reply packets, and do not expire. But, this can provide a wrong believe of security under some OSs, such as Windows 2000 and SunOS Solaris 5.9. In fact, those OSs marks static entries in their ARP caches, but authorize their updates by ARP request and reply packets. Consequently, such entries cannot be considered as static entries, but solely permanent entries in the ARP caches.

4.2 Dynamic ARP Cache Update

In principle, to corrupt the entries in the ARP cache of a target host, a malicious host generates ARP request or reply messages including fake IP and MAC addresses. However, in practice, the success of this malicious activity depends on the operation system of the target host. A malicious host may attempt to send fake ARP reply messages to a target host even though the malicious host did not receive any ARP request message from the target host. If the OS of the target host accepts the fake ARP reply message from the malicious host without checking whether or not an ARP request message has been generated before, then the received ARP reply message will corrupt the ARP cache of the target host with a fake MAC/IP entry. Alternatively, the malicious host may attempt to send ARP request messages, instead of ARP reply messages.

Table 1 shows the result of an experiment we performed on several common OSs. The objective of this experiment is to identify which OSs with dynamic entries in the ARP caches are vulnerable to the ARP cache poisoning attack. Table 1 indicates clearly that: All tested OSs, except Windows 2000 and Free BSD 4.11, do not allow the creation of a new entry by an ARP reply message and all tested OSs allow the creation of a new entry by an ARP request message. However, if the entry exists already in the ARP cache, all tested OSs allow its update by an ARP reply (even in the absence of an ARP request) or request message. Therefore, when using ARP reply messages, the ARP cache poisoning attack becomes difficult to realize against most OSs. However, it remains indeed possible when using ARP request messages. Most common OSs are still vulnerable to the ARP cache poisoning attack [6]. Malicious

Table 1. Update of dynamic entries in the ARP caches using ARP request and reply messages

	Windows XP		Windows 2000		Windows 2003 Server		Linux 2.4		Linux 2.6		Free BSD 4.11		SunOS Solaris 5.9	
Does the entry exist in the ARP cache?	Yes	No	Yes	No	Yes	No	Yes	No	Yes	No	Yes	No	Yes	No
ARP request	✓	✓	✓	✓	✓	✓	✓	✓	✓	✓	✓	✓	✓	✓
ARP reply	✓	X	✓	✓	✓	X	✓	X	✓	X	✓	✓	✓	✓

✓   : Means that the ARP request or reply message is accepted by the system and therefore allows the update or the creation of an entry.

X   : Means that the ARP request or reply message is rejected by the system and therefore does not allow the update and the creation of an entry.

users can first use ARP request messages to create fake MAC/IP entries in the ARP caches of their target hosts. Then, fake ARP reply massages are used to maintain the existence of the fake entries in the ARP caches of the target hosts.

5   The MiM Attack

In shared networks, when the Network Interface Card (NIC) is set to the promiscuous mode all the traffic can be sniffed, since each packet is broadcasted to all hosts. However, in a switched network, even by setting their hosts' NIC cards into the promiscuous mode, hackers cannot capture all the traffic in the network, because all packets sent by a host will be received only by the destination host, unless it is a broadcast packet. The *MiM* attack allows a malicious user to sniff a switched network. The attack consists into re-routing (redirecting) the network traffic between two target hosts to a malicious host. Then, the malicious host will forward the received packets to the original destination, so that the communication between the two target hosts will not be interrupted and the two hosts' users will not notice that their traffic is sniffed by a malicious host.

To do that, the malicious user should first enable his host's IP packet routing (IP packet forwarding), in order to become a router and be able to forward the redirected packets. Then, using ARP cache poisoning attack, the malicious user should corrupt the ARP caches of the two target hosts, in order to force the two hosts to forward all their packets to his host. It is important to notice that if the malicious host corrupts the ARP caches of two target hosts without enabling its IP packet routing, then the two hosts will not be able to exchange packets and it will be a DoS attack. In this case, the malicious host does not forward the received packets to their legitimate destination. This is extremely potent when we consider that not only can hosts be poisoned, but routers/gateways as well. All Internet traffic for a host could be intercepted by performing a *MiM* attack on the host and the network's router. The *MiM* attack is performed as follows (where C is the malicious host, and A and B are the two target hosts): Host C enables its IP packet routing and corrupts the ARP caches of hosts A and B, using ARP cache poisoning attack. Figure 1 (a) shows the initial entries in the ARP caches of hosts A and B, before the ARP cache poisoning attack. After the attack, host A associates host

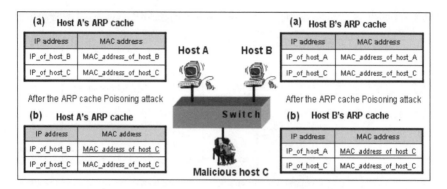

Fig. 1. The entries of the ARP caches of hosts A and B before and after the ARP poisoning attack

B's IP with host C's MAC, and host B associates host A's IP with host C's MAC (Figure 1 (b)). Consequently, all the packets exchanged between hosts A and B will first go to host C. Then, host C forwards them to the legitimate destination (host B or host A).

6   Detection of MiM Attack

To perform a *MiM* attack, the malicious host should enable the IP packet routing and corrupt the ARP caches of its target hosts. Therefore, if IP packet routing is enabled in a host, then it is a suspicious host. Only routers and some servers need to enable the IP packet routing since they have to perform packets routing. But still, we need to prove that the suspicious host has performed also ARP cache poisoning attacks against target hosts. In section 6.1, we discuss an efficient technique for detecting any host in the network with enabled IP packet routing. Hosts with enabled IP packet routing are called *suspicious hosts*. Then, in section 6.2, we discuss a technique for detecting, among the *suspicious hosts,* those that have performed ARP cache poisoning attacks against other hosts in the network.

6.1   Detection of Hosts with Enabled IP Packet Routing

The following is a technique based on an algorithm for detecting any host with enabled IP packet routing, in a switched network. The technique consists of two phases and assumes that there is a host in the network, *Test host*, used to do all the tests needed during the two phases.

Phase 1: *Generation of trap ICMP echo request packets.* In this phase, the *Test host* sends a trap ICMP Ping packet to a given target host in the network. Usually, if a host A (whose IP address is IP_A and MAC address is MAC_A) wants to Ping a host B (whose IP address is IP_B and MAC address is MAC_B) in a network, then host A should send to host B an ICMP echo request packet. A Ping packet is used to detect whether or not a host is connected to the network [4], [5]. For host A, there is no reason and it is meaningless to send a Ping packet to itself, since this means that host A wants to know whether or not it is connected to the network. Usually, hosts use other mechanisms to perform any networking tests on their NIC cards, such as the use of Loop IP addresses (e.g.:127.0.0.1). When host A wants to send to itself a Ping packet, it should set the *"Destination MAC address"* field in the Ethernet header and the *"Destination IP address"* field in the IP header to the values *"MAC_ A"* and *"IP_A "*, respectively. However, the *Test host* attempts to Ping itself, using a *trap* ICMP echo request packet. In fact, the *Test host* wants to send this packet to each host in the network. Therefore, the value of the *"Destination MAC address"* field in the Ethernet header of the trap ICMP Ping packet is set to the MAC address of the target host in the network (*MAC_Target_host*). The value of the *"Destination IP address"* field in the IP header of the packet is kept as usual, that is the IP address of the *Test host* (*IP_Test_host*). The values of the main fields of the trap ICMP Ping packet are as shown in Table 2.

Table 2. Trap ICMP Ping packet

Ethernet header	
Source MAC address =	*MAC_ Test_host*
Destination MAC address =	*MAC_ Target_host*
Ethernet Type =	*0x0800 (IP message)*
IP header	
Source IP address =	*IP_Test_host*
Destination IP address =	*IP_Test_host*
ICMP header	
Type =	8 (echo request)
Code =	0

The NIC card of each target host in the network will receive a trap ICMP Ping packet sent by the *Test host*. Since, the MAC address in the *"Destination MAC address"* field of the trap packet matches the MAC address of the target host, then the packet will be accepted by the target host and sent to the IP layer for processing. Since, the IP address in the *"Destination IP address"* field does not match the IP address of the target host, then the target host will either discard or forward the packet to the host whose IP address is specified in the *"Destination IP address"* field. If the target host is set to do IP packet routing, then the packet will be forwarded to the *Test host,* otherwise, the packet is discarded. Table 3 shows the results of an exercise we performed on several common OSs. This experiment confirms that when the IP packet routing is enabled all tested OSs forward the received trap ICMP Ping packet.

When the target host is set to do IP packet routing, it will forward the original packet with the same IP and ICMP headers, but with a different Ethernet header, as a router did. The destination MAC address will be set to the MAC address of the *Test host*, and the source MAC address will be set to the MAC address of the target host.

Phase 2: *Detection of the hosts with enabled IP packet routing.* All hosts that send back the received trap ICMP packets to the *Test host*, have enabled IP packet routing, and consequently are considered as *suspicious hosts*. In order to capture the forwarded trap ICMP packets sent by the target hosts, the *Test host* may use a Sniffer or any program that allow to capture ICMP Ping packets (echo request) whose *"Destination IP address"* field is set to the IP address of the *Test host*.

Table 3. Responses of the tested OSs after receiving the trap ICMP Ping packet

	Win-dows XP		Win-dows 2000		Win-dows 2003 Server		Linu x 2.4		Linu x 2.6		Free BSD 4.11		SunO S So-laris 5.9	
Enabled IP packet rout-ing?	Yes	No	Yes	No	Yes	No	Yes	No	Yes	No	Yes	No	Yes	No
The target host forwards the trap ICMP Ping packet to the original host?	Yes	No	Yes	No	Yes	No	Yes	No	Yes	No	Yes	No	Yes	No

6.2 Detection of ARP Cache Poisoning Attack

In section 6.1, we discussed a technique for detecting the hosts with enabled IP packet routing. Those hosts are classified as *suspicious hosts*. In the following section, we discuss a technique for detecting the hosts, among the *suspicious hosts*, that have performed ARP cache poisoning attack against other hosts in the network. If a host has enabled IP packet routing (*suspicious host*) and has performed ARP cache poisoning attack against other hosts in the network, then we can conclude that the host is most likely sniffing the network traffic. This technique consists into corrupting the ARP cache of a *suspicious host* in order to force it to forward to the *Test host* the packets received from its victim hosts. It will be demonstrated that by analyzing the traffic generated by a *suspicious* host, it is possible to identify whether or not the *suspicious host* has performed ARP cache poisoning attacks against target hosts in the network.

We assume that A, B, C, D and E are the hosts of a network. Hosts A and B are exchanging network traffic. The IP packet routing in host D is enabled. In addition, host D has corrupted the ARP caches of the two hosts A and B, in order to sniff their traffic. However, the ARP cache of host C is not corrupted since it is not the target of the malicious host D. Host E is the *Test host*. The detection technique described in section 6.1 allows us to identify host D as a suspicious host, since its IP packet routing is enabled. The initial values of the entries (IP/MAC) in the ARP caches of hosts A, B, C and D, before the process of the corruption of the ARP cache of any *suspicious host*, are:

The ARP cache of host A (corrupted ARP cache) i.e. IP_B – MAC_D, the ARP cache of host B (corrupted ARP cache) i.e. IP_A – MAC_D, the ARP cache of host C i.e. IP_A – MAC_A and IP_B – MAC_B and the ARP cache of host D i.e. IP_A – MAC_A and IP_B – MAC_B.

For each suspicious host, we corrupt first its ARP cache, using ARP cache poisoning attack. To do that, the *Test host E* sends fake ARP requests to the *suspicious host* D. So that, all the entries IP/MAC in the ARP cache of host D will have the MAC address of the *Test host* E as MAC address (MAC_E). After this attack, the entries in the ARP cache of the *suspicious host* D become corrupted: The ARP cache of host D (corrupted ARP cache) i.e. IP_A – MAC_E, IP_B – MAC_E and IP_C – MAC_E.

Consequently, any packet sent by host A to host B will go first to the *suspicious host* D, since the ARP caches of hosts A and B have been corrupted before by the *suspicious host* D (Figure 2: arrow (1)). Then, the *suspicious host* D forwards the

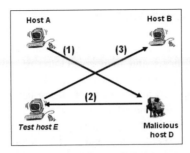

Fig. 2. The network path of the packets sent by host A to host B

received packet to the *Test host* E, since the ARP cache of the suspicious host D has been corrupted by the *Test host E* (Figure 2: arrow (2)). Finally, the *Test host E* takes a copy of the received packet and forwards it to the legitimate destination host, which is host B (Figure 2: arrow (3)).

By analyzing the packet sent by the *suspicious host* D to the *Test host* E, we can easily reveal that the source IP address in the IP header of the packet (2) is of host A, but the source MAC address in the Ethernet header of the packet is of the *suspicious host* D; however it should be equal to the MAC address of host A. Consequently, we have the prove that the *suspicious host* D has corrupted before the cache ARP of host A in order to sniff its traffic. If the *Test host* receives only legitimate packets from the *suspicious host* D, that is the packets' source IP is host D's IP and the packets' destination IP is the *Test host* E's IP, then we can conclude that the *suspicious* host D has enabled IP packet routing but it is not sniffing any network traffic. Host D may have enabled IP packet routing by accident without any intention to perform malicious sniffing activities against other network hosts. The whole process of detection is then repeated for the remaining identified suspicious hosts.

7 The AntiMiM Application

Based on the proposed detection techniques, an application, called *AntiMiM*, has been developed using Visual C++6.0 and WinpCap Library. The application detects any host sniffing the switched network using the *MiM* attack. *AntiMiM* application has been evaluated against the two IDSs *Arpwatch* and *Snort*. The application does not require a monitoring port (SPAN) to run, unlike *Snort* and *Arpwatch*. In addition, *Snort* and *Arpwatch* are not able to detect the network's hosts with enabled IP packet routing. Finally, *AntiMiM* does not require a predefined database of valid IP/MAC entries, like *Snort* and *Arpwatch*. The database is used to verify whether or not a given IP/MAC pair found in a captured packet belongs to the database. Usually, such a packet is used when performing ARP cache poisoning attack. When *Snort* or *Arpwatch* are used to detect ARP cache poisoning attack, the network administrator should provide them with a database of valid IP/MAC pairs. The generation of such a database is times consuming. In addition, in large networks, the database may include erroneous entries. When a new host is connected to the network, or a host gets a new MAC address (after changing its NIC card) or IP address, the database should be updated.

8 Network Performance Analysis

The proposed detection mechanism uses two techniques that attempt to send spoofed packets to the network's hosts and then collect the response packets for analysis. Therefore, for the efficiency of the proposed mechanism, it is important to compute the number of packets injected in the network. If the network is flooded with heavy traffic, then its performance may be affected.

We assume that there are n hosts in the network including the *Test host* used to perform all the tests (refer to sections 6.1 and 6.2). The proposed mechanism detects first, among the n hosts, the hosts with enabled IP packet routing, using the technique discussed in section 6.1. We assume that m hosts with enabled IP packet routing have been identified (called *suspicious hosts*). Hence, the *Test host* will send $(n-1)$ trap ICMP echo request packets to the $(n-1)$ hosts in the network. Only, m hosts will forward back the received packets, since they have enabled IP packet routing. Therefore, $((n-1) + m)$ packets are injected in the network, while detecting the hosts with enabled IP packet routing.

Then, the proposed mechanism attempts to detect among the m identified suspicious hosts, the hosts that have performed ARP cache poisoning attack against the other hosts. When the technique of the section 6.2 is used, the *Test host* sends fake ARP requests to the suspicious hosts in order to corrupt all the entries in their cache. Since there are n hosts including m suspicious hosts in the network, and the maximum number of IP/MAC entries in an ARP cache is $(n-1)$, the *Test host* needs to generate $((n-1)*m)$ fake ARP request packets. In addition, since the ARP cache entries are supposed to expire if they are not referenced within few minutes (typically between tens of seconds to a few minutes, according to the OS), then the *Test host* should keep sending fake ARP requests periodically. As long as the *Test host* keeps doing this, the suspicious hosts will not issue ARP requests for that IP addresses, since their ARP cache entries will always be within the timeout threshold. Therefore, if the *Test host* waits a period of 10 seconds, for example, and then sends again the $((n-1)*m)$ fake ARP packets, and the detection process will take 1 minutes, then the *Test host* will inject $(((n-1)*m)*6)$ packets in the network.

Consequently, the use of the proposed techniques does not degrade the network performance since they do not flood the network with heavy traffic. On the other hand, the techniques are independent from the Switch brand and model, since they are based on the attack of the ARP caches of the suspicious hosts.

9 Conclusions

Throughout this paper, we demonstrated that sniffing is still a big thread even in a switched network. This is against the belief that switched network are safe from sniffing activities.

Most of the works done in the area of malicious sniffing activities detection, deal with Sniffers in shared networks. Few IDSs, mainly *Snort* and *Arpwatch*, tried to detect malicious sniffing activities in switched networks. The limits of those IDSs regarding their ability to detect properly *MiM* attacks have been discussed.

The paper proposes a mechanism for detecting sniffing hosts in switched networks. The hosts use the *MiM* attack, to sniff switched network. The proposed mechanism consists into sending spoofed packets to the network's hosts. By collecting and analyzing the responses packets, it has been demonstrated how malicious sniffing hosts can be identified efficiently and accurately. The mechanism does not degrade the network performance when injecting packets into to the network, since the number of injected packets is relatively very limited.

Future works will be to make an IDS plug-in version of the proposed mechanism, such as *Snort* plug-in, and to lower the false positive/negative ratios when the hosts use personal firewalls to filter the incoming and outgoing traffic.

References

1. `ftp://ftp.ee.lbl.gov/arpwatch.tar.gz`
2. `http://www.snort.org`
3. Plummer, D.C.: An Ethernet Address Resolution Protocol-Converting Network Protocol to 48 bit Ethernet Address for Transmission on Ethernet Hardware, RFC-826 (1982)
4. Postel, J.: Internet Control Message Protocol, RFC-792 (1981)
5. Stevens, R.: TCP/IP Illustrated: vol. 1 (2001)
6. Sanai, D.: Detection of Promiscuous Nodes Using ARP Packets (2004), `http://www.securityfriday.com`
7. Trabelsi, Z., et al.: Detection of Sniffers in an Ethernet Network. In: Zhang, K., Zheng, Y. (eds.) ISC 2004. LNCS, vol. 3225, pp. 170–182. Springer, Heidelberg (2004)
8. Trabelsi, Z., et al.: An Anti-Sniffer Based on ARP Cache Poisoning Attack. Information System Security Journal 13(6) (2005)

Efficient All-or-Nothing Encryption
Using CTR Mode

Robert P. McEvoy and Colin C. Murphy

Department of Electrical & Electronic Engineering
University College Cork, Ireland
{robertmce,cmurphy}@eleceng.ucc.ie

Abstract. All-or-Nothing Encryption is a useful technique which can heighten the security of block ciphers. It can also be used to design faster symmetric-key cryptosystems, by decreasing the number of required encryption operations at run-time. An open problem in the literature regards the speed of all-or-nothing encryption, which we address in this paper by combining two techniques from the literature, forming a new all-or-nothing mode of operation. Trade-offs in the implementation of this design are considered, and theoretical proofs of security are provided.

Keywords: All-or-Nothing Transforms, CTRT, CTR Mode, Efficient Symmetric-Key Encryption, MANETs.

1 Introduction

All-or-Nothing Transforms were originally proposed by Rivest, as a method to hinder brute-force key search attacks on block ciphers such as DES [16]. Essentially, All-or-Nothing Encryption consists of two stages. By applying an All-or-Nothing Transform (AONT) to a plaintext message, a 'pseudo-message' is formed. This pre-processing stage is not considered encryption, however, as the AONT does not utilise a secret key. An All-or-Nothing Encryption (AONE) mode is formed when an AONT output is encrypted using a symmetric block cipher. The resulting cryptosystem has the property that a brute-force attacker must decrypt *all* of the ciphertext blocks when testing each key. Hence, an exhaustive key-search attack on an AONE mode is slowed, in proportion to the number of blocks in the ciphertext.

However, modern symmetric-key cryptosystems are based on block ciphers with longer key lengths than DES, such as AES (minimum 128 bits). An attack on AES-128 is beyond the capability of modern computers, and it is believed that 128-bit symmetric keys will be secure until after the year 2030 [9].

A second, more currently relevant application of AONTs relates to increasing the efficiency of block-cipher based encryption schemes [10]. In this scheme, an AONT is applied to a plaintext message as above, but only some (as opposed to all) of the pseudo-message blocks are subsequently encrypted. The AONT mixes the plaintext in such a way that all of the pseudo-message blocks are required in order to invert the transform and regain the plaintext. Therefore, fewer secret-key encryptions and decryptions are required.

J. Filipe and M.S. Obaidat (Eds.): ICETE 2006, CCIS 9, pp. 92–106, 2008.

In order for this 'efficient encryption' application of AONTs to be worthwhile, the AONT used must itself be quickly and efficiently computable. In [16], an AONE mode was presented where the time penalty for encryption was a factor of three greater than standard CBC mode encryption, along with an open question as to whether this latency could be improved. Desai [6] proposed an AONT construction which reduced the relative penalty to a factor of two. In this paper, a new AONE mode is considered for the first time, combining Desai's AONT and the well-known CTR mode of encryption. We show that when our design is used, the penalty for AONE can, under certain circumstances, be reduced to the negligible cost of just one xor operation.

The rest of this paper is organised as follows. The following section defines AONTs, and surveys related work. In Section 3 we present the new all-or-nothing encryption mode, analyse its efficiency, and consider some applications where it would be beneficial. Section 4 focuses on the provable security of the scheme, and conclusions are given in Section 5.

2   All-or-Nothing Transforms

2.1   Definitions

Informally, an All-or-Nothing Transform f maps a sequence of plaintext blocks $x_1, x_2, \ldots, x_n$ to a sequence of pseudo-message blocks, denoted $y_1, y_2, \ldots, y_m$. As put forward in [16], AONTs should possess four properties:

- Given the sequence of pseudo-message blocks, one can invert the transform to retrieve the plaintext blocks.
- Both the AONT and its inverse should be efficiently computable.
- All AONTs should be randomised, in order to avoid chosen-message and known-message attacks.
- Most importantly, if any one of the pseudo-message blocks is unknown, it should be computationally infeasible to invert the AONT, or determine any function of any plaintext block.

Since the original proposal, several other authors have published formal AONT definitions in the literature. The definitions differ in the strength of the security notions which each author uses.

Desai [6] defined a new notion of security for AONTs, called 'non-separability of keys', which captures the requirement for an adversary to decrypt every block of ciphertext before gaining any information about the underlying key. In addition, Desai required his AONTs to be secure in the 'indistinguishability of encryptions' sense, which is a notion defined in [2]. Furthermore, the AONT pseudo-message should be indistinguishable from a random string. We adopt these notions of security in our constructions.

2.2   Applications

In this paper, we focus on the use of AONTs for efficient encryption in symmetric-key block cipher cryptosystems. This is discussed further in Section 3. Another application of AONTs has already been mentioned in Section 1, namely the original application of impeding brute-force key search attacks. In their respective theses, Boyko [4] and Dodis [7] both give excellent surveys of potential AONT applications. These include remotely keyed encryption, gap secret sharing and protecting against partial key exposure. Subsequent publications have proposed the use of AONTs in electronic voting protocols [11], 'multiple encryption' schemes [19], and secure file deletion schemes [15].

2.3 Constructions

This paper deals specifically with the CTR-Transform (CTRT) of [6], which is described in Section 3, where it is used in our proposed efficient symmetric-key AON encryption scheme. Several other candidate constructions for AONTs have been proposed in the literature. These are listed below, with references for the interested reader.

– Package Transform [16]
– OAEP [4]
– Exposure-Resilient Function-based Transforms [8]
– Quasigroup-based AONTs [13]
– 'Extended-Indistinguishable' AONTs [18]
– Error-Correcting Code-based AONTs [5]

3 CTRT-CTR Encryption

This section introduces our new mode of all-or-nothing encryption, which we call 'CTRT-CTR'. In essence, it combines Desai's CTRT AONT [6] with the popular CTR mode of block cipher encryption [12]. Indeed, it is surprising that this mode has not been suggested already in the literature. We show that CTRT-CTR affords fast AON encryption, that is not attainable with other AONTs discussed in the literature to date.

3.1 Package Transform

Before examining the CTR Transform, it is instructive to first consider Rivest's original AONT proposal, the 'Package Transform' [16]. Since the package transform is based on a block cipher F, the plaintext message x being processed is broken up into fixed-sized blocks of data, labelled $x_1, x_2, \ldots, x_n$. A random key K' is chosen for the AONT, from a large enough keyspace to deter a brute force attack. Note that this key is not a 'secret key', and it does not have to be shared explicitly with the recipient of the message via public-key cryptography. The pseudo-message y is calculated as follows:

$$y_i = x_i \oplus F_{K'}(i) \tag{1}$$

for $i = 1, \ldots, n$, where $F_{K'}(\cdot)$ denotes encryption with the block cipher F using the key K', and $\oplus$ denotes bit-wise xor. To complete the package transform, a further pseudo-message block y_{n+1} is added:

$$y_{n+1} = K' \oplus h_1 \oplus h_2 \oplus \cdots \oplus h_n \tag{2}$$

where

$$h_i = F_{K_0}(y_i \oplus i) \tag{3}$$

for $i = 1, \ldots, n$, and K_0 is a fixed, publically known key. In effect, the final pseudo-message block comprises a hash of all the previous pseudo-message blocks, xored with the random key K'. To invert the transform, the receiver simply calculates the random key, and uses it to decrypt the first n pseudo-message blocks:

$$K' = y_{n+1} \oplus h_1 \oplus \cdots \oplus h_n \tag{4}$$

$$x_i = y_i \oplus F_{K'}(i) \tag{5}$$

for $i = 1, \ldots, n$. Rivest observed that if the package transform was combined with an ordinary encryption mode such as CBC, the time to encrypt would increase threefold, as three passes through the block cipher encryption would be required. Rivest set the task of reducing this latency as an open problem, which Desai solved using the CTR transform.

3.2 CTR Transform

In the CTR ("counter") Transform, as in the case of the package transform, a random key K' is chosen, and the plaintext is transformed via:

$$y_i = x_i \oplus F_{K'}(i) \tag{6}$$

The final pseudo-message block is given by:

$$y_{n+1} = K' \oplus y_1 \oplus y_2 \oplus \cdots \oplus y_n \tag{7}$$

Clearly, CTRT operates in the same fashion as the package transform, with one block cipher encryption stage omitted. In fact, Equations (6) and (7) are equivalent to Equations (1) and (2) with $h_i = y_i$. The final pseudo-message block is composed of the random key K' xored with all of the previous pseudo-message blocks. Intuitively, this may seem less secure than the package transform, yet it is proven secure within the model and definitions used by [6]. Using CTRT, Desai reduced the cost of All-or-Nothing Encryption to just a factor of two greater than CBC mode, hence answering the open problem of [16].

3.3 CTRT-CTR Mode

In the CTR mode of encryption [12], the sender maintains an l-bit counter ctr, where l is the block length of the underlying cipher F. The value of ctr can be transmitted in the clear to the receiver when sending the ciphertext. A plaintext $x_1, x_2, \ldots, x_n$ is encrypted with a shared secret key K to a ciphertext $z_1, z_2, \ldots, z_n$ according to:

$$z_i = x_i \oplus F_K(ctr + i) \tag{8}$$

for $i = 1, \ldots, n$. Decryption is performed on the receiver side according to:

$$x_i = z_i \oplus F_K(ctr + i) \tag{9}$$

for $i = 1, \ldots, n$.

Here we propose combining the CTR mode of encryption with the CTRT transform, via:

$$z_i = y_i \oplus F_K(ctr + i) \tag{10}$$
$$= x_i \oplus F_{K'}(i) \oplus F_K(ctr + i) \tag{11}$$

for $i = 1, \ldots, n$. For the final ciphertext block:

$$z_{n+1} = K' \oplus y_1 \oplus \cdots \oplus y_n \oplus F_K(ctr + n + 1) \tag{12}$$

To decrypt a message encrypted with CTRT-CTR, the receiver first calculates pseudo-message blocks:

$$y_i = z_i \oplus F_K(ctr + i) \tag{13}$$

for $i = 1, \ldots, n$, and uses their xor to uncover the random key K':

$$K' = z_{n+1} \oplus F_K(ctr + n + 1) \oplus \bigoplus_{i=1}^{n} y_i \tag{14}$$

A second pass is then required, where K' is used to retrieve the plaintext message blocks x_i:

$$x_i = y_i \oplus F_{K'}(i) \tag{15}$$

CTRT-CTR encryption is illustrated for block i ($i \neq n + 1$) in Figure 3.3.

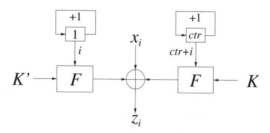

Fig. 3.3. CTRT-CTR Mode Encryption, Equation (11)

3.4   Latency Considerations

The attraction of CTR-CTRT lies in its suitability for pre-calculation and parallelisation. With reference to Equation (11), it can be seen that all of the variables to be encrypted by F are potentially known by the sender *before* the plaintext block x_i becomes available. Therefore, the sender can use idle clock cycles to pre-compute $F_{K'}(i) \oplus F_K(ctr + i)$. When x_i becomes available, it can be quickly encrypted on-the-fly using a single l-bit xor. Therefore, given the necessary processing/memory resources, CTRT-CTR can acutely reduce the run-time cost of AON encryption.

This saving is possible because the CTRT and CTR mode do not operate directly on the plaintext blocks (other than with the xor operation), and each ciphertext block is independent of the others. To the best of our knowledge, no other AONT in the literature possesses this property. Output Feedback Mode (OFB) is another block cipher encryption mode in which the plaintext blocks are not operated on directly. Hence, an efficient All-or-Nothing encryption scheme could also be built using CTRT and OFB mode. Indeed, CTR mode is a simplification of OFB mode, where the input block to the encryption algorithm is updated using a counter, rather than using feedback [14].

Of course, not all implementations of AONE systems will have the capacity for full pre-calculation and storage of the $F_{K'}(i) \oplus F_K(ctr + i)$ 'one-time pad'. Below we present four implementation scenarios, beginning with the fastest. These are summarised in Figure 3.4.

(1) **Full Pre-processing:** In this scenario, we assume that the sender A has knowledge of the secret key K before the plaintext x becomes available. A computes $F_{K'}(i)$ and $F_K(ctr + i)$ during idle clock cycles, requiring $l(2n + 1)$ bits of memory storage. The run-time latency for encryption is negligible (i.e. one l-bit xor).

(2) **Partial Pre-processing:** Here we assume that A does not know K before x becomes available. Because A chooses K', the $F_{K'}(i)$ values (i.e. the AONT part) can be calculated in advance, but the $F_K(ctr + i)$ must be computed during run-time. The latency in this scenario is the same as for ordinary CBC mode encryption, and nl bits of storage are required.

(3) **Online Parallel processing:** In this case, A has no capability (or perhaps desire) for storage, but has two block cipher encryption engines at its disposal. These may be dedicated hardware cores, or microprocessors configured to perform F efficiently. This scheme runs at the same speed as ordinary CBC encryption, but requires no storage.

(4) **Online Processing:** In this worst case, A performs no pre-processing, and has one F-processor available to it. Then the cost is the same as Desai's proposed CTRT-ECB scheme, i.e. twice that of CBC encryption. Memory of nl bits is also required to store intermediate results.

We note that the savings from using CTRT-CTR mode are forthcoming only on the transmission side. Receiver B must perform decryption in two stages, as described in Equations (13)-(15) (Equation (14) can be calculated cumulatively to save memory). This penalty is no worse than that for a receiver decrypting Desai's CTRT-ECB mode, however.

3.5   Efficient All-or-Nothing Encryption

CTRT-CTR mode can be further enhanced using the 'efficient encryption' method (United States Patent 5,870,470) introduced in Section 1, and pioneered in [10]. This technique takes advantage of the fact that an AONT cannot be inverted unless all of the pseudo-message blocks are known. Knowledge of some of the pseudo-message blocks should not reveal any information about the plaintext. Therefore, it should be possible to encrypt only a subset (as opposed to all) of the pseudo-message blocks, and still maintain the same level of security. The provable security of this remarkable scheme is investigated in Section 4.

The efficient CTRT-CTR encryption scheme would proceed as follows. Sender A applies the CTRT to the plaintext, as described by Equations (6) and (7). A then chooses

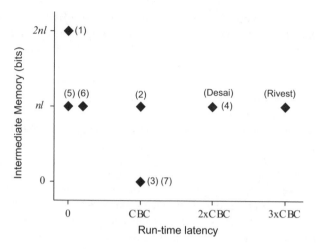

Fig. 3.4. Performance Trade-offs with AONE

a subset of the pseudo-message blocks to encrypt, whose indices are given by $\mathcal{S}$, where $\#\mathcal{S} = r, 1 \leq r \leq n$. Of course, $\mathcal{S}$ must be made public so that receiver B can decrypt the ciphertext. To form the ciphertext z, A computes:

$$z_i = \begin{cases} y_i \oplus F_K(ctr + i) & \text{for } i \in \mathcal{S} \\ y_i & \text{for } i \notin \mathcal{S} \end{cases} \qquad (16)$$

The efficient encryption method allows even faster implementations of CTRT-CTR. Assuming $r = 1$ (i.e. just one pseudo-message block is encrypted), the scenarios described in Section 3.4 become:

(5) Full Pre-processing: Run-time latency of one xor (negligible), $l(n + 1)$ bits of memory.
(6) Partial Pre-processing: Run-time latency of one xor and one encryption, nl bits of memory.
(7) Online Processing: Run-time latency approximately that of ordinary CBC encryption (as $r << n$), regardless of multiple processors. No extra memory is required.

Figure 3.4 summarises the latency/memory trade-off associated with implementing CTRT-CTR in software or hardware. Fast, efficient All-or-Nothing Encryption is clearly attainable if the application justifies the added processing and storage costs. The best results are obtained by combining CTRT-CTR (or CTRT in any encryption mode) with the efficient encryption system of [10]. Fewer encryption operations are necessary, therefore the system's power consumption is lower. However, the performance bonus must be traded off against the costs associated with using this patented method.

3.6 Applications

CTRT-CTR encryption would clearly be beneficial in applications where fast on-the-fly AON encryption is required, such as secure mobile telecommunications networks,

MANETs (Mobile Ad-Hoc NETworks), or wireless ad hoc sensor networks. MANETs are mainly used in highly mobile and hostile environments, where data confidentiality is important. Typical examples of nodes in a MANET include units where processing power and battery life are limited, such as backpack radios, handheld devices, and vehicle computers [3]. Constrained environments such as these are well suited to secure, efficient all-or-nothing encryption schemes such as CTRT-CTR.

CTRT-CTR is also especially useful in protocols where the existing encryption mechanism is a block cipher (e.g. AES), as the encryption software/hardware can be re-used to perform the AONT, deeming implementation of additional algorithms unnecessary.

4 Proofs of Security

The provable security of the proposed CTRT-CTR scheme is now considered. We also analyse how the security changes when we incorporate CTRT-CTR and Johnson et al.'s efficient encryption technique. For convenience, the definitions and notation used in our theorems rely heavily on those used by [6]. In particular, we employ the framework used in Theorem 3 and Lemma 14 of that work, and extend those results.

4.1 Existing Security Results

Desai proved his results in the Shannon model ('ideal model') of a block cipher [17]. In essence, the Shannon model states that each new key to the block cipher defines an independent random permutation $F_k(\cdot)$. Desai defined a notion of security for AONTs, based on indistinguishability from a random string. The experiment (or 'game') used to capture this notion is as follows:

AONT. Let $\Pi' = (\mathcal{E}', \mathcal{D}')$ be an AONT of block length l. For adversary A and bit $b = 0$ or 1 define $\mathrm{Exp}_{\Pi'}^{\mathrm{aon}}(A, b)$ as:

```
01  (x, s) ← A(find);
02  y₀ ← ℰ'(x);       \\ All-or-nothing Transform
03  y₁ ← {0,1}^|y₀|;  \\ Random |y₀|-bit string
04  d ← A^y(guess, s);
05  return d.
```

The advantage function of Π' is defined as:

$$\mathrm{Adv}_{\Pi'}^{\mathrm{aon}}(t, m) = \max_A \{\Pr[\mathrm{Exp}_{\Pi'}^{\mathrm{aon}}(A, 0) = 0] - \Pr[\mathrm{Exp}_{\Pi'}^{\mathrm{aon}}(A, 1) = 0] \} \tag{17}$$

where A runs with time complexity t, and $|y_0| = |y_1| = ml$ (i.e. m l-bit blocks). The notation $A^{\mathcal{Y}}$ means that A has access to an oracle $\mathcal{Y}$, taking an index $j \in \{1, \ldots, m\}$ and returning $y_b[j]$, where $y_b = y_b[1], \ldots, y_b[m]$. At most m queries are allowed to $\mathcal{Y}$ during the guess stage. In addition, s denotes state information generated by the results of A's queries.

Based on any $m - 1$ blocks of the challenge, adversary A has to decide whether the challenge is a real AONT output, or a randomly chosen string. Equation (17) measures A's maximum probability of success in this game, which should be negligible.

Indistinguishability of encryptions [2] is an important security notion for block cipher encryption schemes, described below:

IND. Let $\Pi = (\mathcal{K}, \mathcal{E}, \mathcal{D})$ be an encryption mode. For adversary A and bit $b = 0$ or 1 define $\text{Exp}_{\Pi}^{\text{ind}}(A, b)$ as:

```
01 F ← BC(k, l);        \\ Choose block cipher at random
02 a ← K(1^k);          \\ Choose key of length k
03 (x_0, x_1, s) ← A^{F,F^{-1},E^{F_a,F_a^{-1}}} (find);
04 y ← E^{F_a,F_a^{-1}}(x_b); \\ Apply encryption mode
05 d ← A^{F,F^{-1},E^{F_a,F_a^{-1}}} (guess, y, s);
06 return d.
```

The advantage function of Π is defined as:

$$\text{Adv}_{\Pi}^{\text{ind}}(t, m, p, q, \mu) = \max_A \{ \Pr[\text{Exp}_{\Pi}^{\text{ind}}(A, 1) = 1] - \Pr[\text{Exp}_{\Pi}^{\text{ind}}(A, 0) = 1] \} \tag{18}$$

where A runs with time complexity t, p is the maximum number of queries allowed to F/F^{-1}, $|y| = ml$, and q is the maximum number of queries allowed to $\mathcal{E}^{F_a, F_a^{-1}}$, these totalling at most μ bits.

In this game, A is given a ciphertext, and must determine which of two plaintexts it corresponds to. If the encryption mode is secure in the **IND** sense, A's success probability should be negligible. Theorem 3 of [6] quantifies this success probability when the encryption mode is an all-or-nothing ECB mode. He proved that if $n \geq 2$:

$$\text{Adv}_{\Pi}^{\text{ind}}(t, m, p, q, \mu) \leq 2m\, \text{Adv}_{\Pi'}^{\text{aon}}(t', m) + \frac{2mp}{2^k} + \frac{2m}{2^l} \tag{19}$$

where n is the number of l-bit plaintext blocks, $t' = t + (\frac{\mu}{l} + m - 1).T + \mathcal{O}(ml + pl + \mu)$, and T is the time taken to decode a ml-bit string using $\mathcal{D}'$. In the specific case where the AONT is CTRT, Desai also proved that for $k \leq l$ and $m + p \leq 2^{k-1}$, then:

$$\text{Adv}_{\text{CTRT}}^{\text{aon}}(t, m, p) \leq \frac{m^2 + 8p}{2^k} \tag{20}$$

where k is the key length of the underlying block cipher, and t, m and p are as defined above.

4.2   Security of AONT-CTR Encryption

We extend the result of Equation (19) to evaluate the **IND**-security of the CTR mode of all-or-nothing encryption. Note that all m pseudo-message blocks are encrypted using CTR mode in this case. The security of the 'efficient AON encryption' scheme of Section 3.5 is considered in Section 4.3.

Theorem 1: Let $\Pi = (\mathcal{K}, \mathcal{E}, \mathcal{D})$ be an all-or-nothing CTR mode in the Shannon model, using AONT $\Pi' = (\mathcal{E}', \mathcal{D}')$. Then for $n \geq 2$:

$$\text{Adv}_{\Pi}^{\text{ind}}(t, m, p, q, \mu) \leq 2m\, \text{Adv}_{\Pi'}^{\text{aon}}(t', m) + \frac{2p}{2^k} + \frac{2m}{2^l} \tag{21}$$

where $t' = t + (\frac{\mu}{l} + m - 1).T + \mathcal{O}(ml + pl + \mu)$ and all other variables are as defined in Section 4.1.

Proof: A new game **COLL** is defined as follows:

COLL. Let $\Pi = (\mathcal{K}, \mathcal{E}, \mathcal{D})$ be an AONT-CTR mode. For adversary A define $\mathrm{Exp}_{\Pi}^{\mathrm{coll}}(A)$ as:

01 $a \leftarrow \mathcal{K}(1^k)$;   \\ *Choose key of length k*

02 $(x, s, \mathrm{Elist}_F) \leftarrow A^{F, F^{-1}, \mathcal{E}^{F_a, F_a^{-1}}}$ (find);

03 $y \leftarrow \mathcal{E}^{F_a, F_a^{-1}}(x)$; \\ *Apply AONT-CTR*

04 $\mathrm{Elist}_G \leftarrow A^{F, F^{-1}, \mathcal{E}^{F_a, F_a^{-1}}}$ (guess, y, s);

05 for $i, j \in [m]$ {

06 if$(i \neq j \wedge y[i] = y[j]) \vee (y[i] \in \mathrm{Elist}_F \cup \mathrm{Elist}_G)$

07 then $d \leftarrow 1$, else $d \leftarrow 0$; }

08 return d.

The success function of Π is defined as:

$$\mathrm{Succ}_{\Pi}^{\mathrm{coll}}(t, m, p, q, \mu) = \max_A \{\Pr[\mathrm{Exp}_{\Pi}^{\mathrm{coll}}(A) = 1]\} \qquad (22)$$

where A runs with time complexity t, $[m]$ denotes the set $\{1, \ldots, m\}$, and all other variables are as defined in Section 4.1. $\wedge$ and $\vee$ denote logical AND and OR, respectively. Elist_F and Elist_G ('Encryption lists') contain the answers to A's $\mathcal{E}^{F_a, F_a^{-1}}$ queries during the find and guess stages.

This **COLL** experiment measures the probability of collision between ciphertext blocks, across queries. We proceed to relate $\mathrm{Succ}_{\Pi}^{\mathrm{coll}}$ to $\mathrm{Adv}_{\Pi'}^{\mathrm{aon}}$ by a contradiction argument. Later, we will relate $\mathrm{Succ}_{\Pi}^{\mathrm{coll}}$ to $\mathrm{Adv}_{\Pi}^{\mathrm{ind}}$, and arrive at the theorem statement by substitution.

Consider an **AONT** adversary A, built using a **COLL** adversary B. Because A has no oracles other than $\mathcal{Y}$, it must simulate B's oracles. The A(find) algorithm (i.e. **AONT** line 01) becomes:

A(find) :

01 $a \leftarrow \mathcal{K}(1^k)$; \\ *Choose key of length k*

02 $Tlist \leftarrow \{\}$; \\ *Initialise* Tlist

03 $(x, s) \leftarrow B(\text{find})$;

04 $s' \leftarrow (s, x, a, \mathrm{Tlist})$;

05 return (x, s').

where Tlist is similar to B's Elist, except that it holds the pseudo-message blocks returned from queries to $\mathcal{E}^{F_a, F_a^{-1}}$, and the corresponding block indices. $A^{\mathcal{Y}}$(guess, s) (i.e. **AONT** line 04) becomes:

$\mathbf{A}^{\mathcal{Y}}(\text{guess}, (\mathbf{s}, \mathbf{x}, \mathbf{a}, \mathbf{Tlist}))$:

01 $j \leftarrow [m]$;   \\ *Choose index j at random*

02 for $i \in [m] \wedge i \neq j$ {

03    $y[i] \leftarrow \mathcal{Y}(i)$; \\ *Retrieve challenge block i*

04    $\mathrm{Tlist} \leftarrow \mathrm{Tlist} \cup \{(y[i], i)\}$;

05    $z[i] \leftarrow y[i] \oplus F_a(ctr + i)$; }

06 for $i \in [| \mathrm{Tlist} |]$ {

07    $(block, index) \leftarrow \mathrm{Tlist}[i]$;

08    $\mathrm{Elist}[i] \leftarrow block \oplus F_a(ctr + index)$; }

09 $z[j] \leftarrow \{0, 1\}^l \backslash \mathrm{Elist}$;

10 $\mathrm{Tlist} \leftarrow \mathrm{Tlist} \cup B(\text{guess}, z, s)$;

11 for $i \in [| \mathrm{Tlist} |]$ {

12    $y[j] \leftarrow \mathrm{Tlist}[i]$;

13    $x_i \leftarrow \mathcal{D}'(y)$; \\ *Inverse AONT*

14   if $(x_i == x)\{d \leftarrow 0$; return $d\}\}$

15 $d \leftarrow 1$; return d.

In lines 01 to 05, $A^{\mathcal{Y}}(\text{guess})$ forms all but one block of B's challenge ciphertext z, based on the $m-1$ blocks of its own challenge y that it receives from $\mathcal{Y}$. For the missing block $z[j]$, A must choose a random string, but has to ensure that B has not seen this block already in its find stage, otherwise a collision would be guaranteed. This requirement is met by lines 06 to 09. Finally in lines 11 to 15, A searches incrementally through Tlist, inserting a block from Tlist in place of its missing $y[i]$ block, and inverting. If the result of the transform inversion equals the original plaintext message x, then A concludes that the challenge y was real (as opposed to random).

We now calculate $\text{Adv}_{\Pi'}^{\text{aon}}(A)$. For simplicity, we use $\text{Pr}_b[A=0]$ to denote Pr $[\text{Exp}_{\Pi'}^{\text{aon}}(A,b)=0]$.

$$\text{Adv}_{\Pi'}^{\text{aon}}(A) = \text{Pr}_0[A=0] - \text{Pr}_1[A=0] \tag{23}$$

Define the event $\mathbf{C}$ to be the event that the missing pseudo-message block $y[j]$ is on the $[Tlist]$. Expanding the first term in Equation (23):

$$\text{Pr}_0[A=0] = \text{Pr}_0[A=0|\mathbf{C}].\text{Pr}_0[\mathbf{C}] + \\ \text{Pr}_0[A=0|\bar{\mathbf{C}}].\text{Pr}_0[\bar{\mathbf{C}}] \tag{24}$$

From the description of $A^{\mathcal{Y}}(\text{guess})$, $\text{Pr}_0[A=0|\mathbf{C}]$ is clearly equal to unity. This implies:

$$\text{Pr}_0[A=0] \geq 1.\text{Pr}_0[\mathbf{C}] \tag{25}$$

Intuitively, one would expect $\text{Pr}_0[\mathbf{C}]$ to be lower bounded by $\text{Succ}_{\Pi}^{\text{coll}}(B)$ via:

$$\text{Pr}_0[\mathbf{C}] \geq \tfrac{1}{m} \text{Succ}_{\Pi}^{\text{coll}}(B)$$

since $\text{Succ}_{\Pi}^{\text{coll}}(B)$ gives the probability of collision with *one* of the blocks of y, and $\mathbf{C}$ implies collision with $y[j]$. However, we must also take into account that A's challenge to B is incorrectly formed, as block $z[j]$ is randomly chosen. There is a chance that B, through its queries to F/F^{-1}, will realise this, causing it to abort the game. It is in evaluating this probability that our proof differs from that of Desai.

We now examine how B could discover the anomaly. Consider the case where B queries F with a block of its choice, key k_1 and index j, and receives the block $z[j]$ in return. B can then test key k_1 on some known plaintext/ciphertext, but since $k_1 \neq a$, the known plaintext encrypted under k_1 will not equal the known ciphertext. B will realise that $z[j]$ was not the result of an encryption with key a, and abort the game.

The number of block cipher permutations in CTR mode is $m.2^k$. For each permutation, there exists some string that will encrypt to give $z[j]$, which would cause B to abort. Therefore, the maximum probability of B choosing one such query (and choosing index $= j$) is $\frac{p}{m.2^k}$ (recall p is the maximum number of queries allowed to F/F^{-1}). Taking this into account, $\text{Pr}_0[\mathbf{C}]$ is lower bounded by:

$$\text{Pr}_0[\mathbf{C}] \geq \tfrac{1}{m} \text{Succ}_{\Pi}^{\text{coll}}(B) - \tfrac{p}{m.2^k} \tag{26}$$

Combining Equations (25) and (26):

$$\text{Pr}_0[A=0] \geq \tfrac{1}{m} \text{Succ}_{\Pi}^{\text{coll}}(B) - \tfrac{p}{m.2^k} \tag{27}$$

The next step is to upper bound the second term in Equation (23), $\Pr_1[A = 0]$. This is the 'false probability' of success, i.e. the probability that A will return $d = 0$ when the challenge y was, in fact, random. From the code for $A(\text{guess})$, it is clear that this can only occur if there is (at least) one other AONT output y_1 which also decodes to x. The probability of this event is independent of the encryption mode in which the AONT mode is used, therefore we can re-use Desai's result:

$$\Pr_1[A = 0] \leq \tfrac{1}{2^l} \tag{28}$$

for $n \geq 2$. Substituting Equations (27) and (28) into Equation (23), and rearranging, gives:

$$\text{Adv}_{\Pi}^{\text{coll}}(t, m, p, q, \mu) \leq m\,\text{Adv}_{\Pi'}^{\text{aon}}(t', m) + \atop p/2^k + m/2^l \tag{29}$$

where $t' = t + (\tfrac{\mu}{l} + m - 1).T + \mathcal{O}(ml + pl + \mu)$, which is the complexity of running A.

The penultimate step is to consider an adversary A in the **IND** sense, and relate $\text{Adv}_{\Pi}^{\text{ind}}(A)$ to $\text{Succ}_{\Pi}^{\text{coll}}(A)$. Due to space restrictions, we do not present the argument here, but note that it is the same as that of [6], as it is mode-independent. We state:

$$\text{Adv}_{\Pi}^{\text{ind}}(A) \leq 2.\,\text{Succ}_{\Pi}^{\text{coll}}(A) \tag{30}$$

Finally, combining Equations (29) and (30) gives Equation (21), the theorem result. $\square$

Comparing the result of Theorem 1 with Equation (19), it can be seen that AONT-ECB mode and AONT-CTR mode achieve similar levels of security, in the indistinguishability of encryptions sense. The adversarial advantage is, in fact, smaller in AONT-CTR mode, due to the larger set of permutations opened up by the inclusion of the block index in the encryption operation. Therefore, AONT-CTR is more secure than AONT-ECB, although neither is *insecure*.

4.3   Security of Efficient AONT-CTR Encryption

We now consider the scenario where an AONT is applied to the plaintext, and r out of the m pseudo-message blocks are encrypted. Intuitively, one would assume that this scheme would somehow be less secure than if all the blocks were encrypted, but we show that this is not the case.

Theorem 2: Let $\Pi = (\mathcal{K}, \mathcal{E}, \mathcal{D})$ be an efficient all-or-nothing CTR mode in the Shannon model, using AONT $\Pi' = (\mathcal{E}', \mathcal{D}')$, and encrypting r blocks of the pseudo-message. Then, for $n \geq 2$:

$$\text{Adv}_{\Pi}^{\text{ind}}(t, m, p, q, \mu) \leq 2m\,\text{Adv}_{\Pi'}^{\text{aon}}(t', m) + \atop \left(\tfrac{r}{m}\right)\tfrac{2p}{2^k} + \tfrac{2m}{2^l} \tag{31}$$

where $t' = t + (\tfrac{\mu}{l} + m - 1).T + \mathcal{O}(ml + pl + \mu)$ and all other variables are as defined in Section 4.1. A publically known set $\mathcal{S}$ holds the indices of the pseudo-message blocks that are encrypted.

Proof: We use framework of Theorem 1, with the algorithms suitably modified. Specifically, lines 05 and 08 of $A(\text{guess})$ must be modified to:

```
04 ···
05a if i ∈ S
05b     z[i] ← y[i] ⊕ Fₐ(ctr + i);
05c else
05d     z[i] ← y[i];
06 ···
07 ···
08a if index ∈ S
08b     Elist[i] ← block ⊕ Fₐ(ctr + index);
08c else
08d     Elist[i] ← block;
09 ···
```

The proof continues in a similar manner, but $\text{Pr}_0[\mathbf{C}]$ must be re-evaluated, where $\mathbf{C}$ is the event that the missing pseudo-message block $y[j]$ is on B's Tlist. We argue that:

$$\text{Pr}_0[\mathbf{C}] \geq \frac{1}{m} \text{Succ}_{\Pi}^{\text{coll}}(B) - \left(\frac{r}{m}\right)\frac{p}{m.2^k} \tag{32}$$

Recall that the $p/(m.2^k)$ term arose in Theorem 1 as the probability that B would realise that block $z[j]$ had been fabricated. B can only come to this conclusion if $z[j]$ is one of the encrypted blocks, i.e. if $j \in S$. If $j \notin S$, B cannot perform the same check, as $z[j]$ is an AONT output block, and is not related to the other challenge blocks by the hidden key a. Therefore, the probability of $z[j] \in S$ and B aborting is $(r/m)(p/m.2^k)$, since index j is chosen at random.

Combining Equations (23), (25), (32), (28) and (30) gives Equation (31), the theorem result.   □

Note that when $r = m$, Equation (31) reduces to the result of Theorem 1, as expected. As $r \to 1$, the upper bound on the adversary's **IND** advantage gets smaller. This seems counter-intuitive, as encrypting fewer blocks would suggest a less secure scheme. However, we note that the r/m term in the theorem results from algorithm B realising that the challenge block $z[j]$ is incorrectly formed, and that this realisation should indeed be less likely when there are fewer encrypted blocks against which to compare. As $r \to 1$, the scheme's security becomes closer to the security of the AONT.

A similar encryption scheme was considered in [1], whereby an AONT is applied to a message, and the first pseudo-message block is encrypted via 'chaffing and winnowing'. The authors proved that this scheme is semantically secure, if the underlying cipher is semantically secure. Our paper provides an different proof, where we work in the Shannon model of the block cipher, encrypt using CTR-mode, and allow the number of encrypted blocks r to vary.

5 Conclusions

In this paper, we proposed a new mode of All-or-Nothing Encryption, called CTRT-CTR. In doing so, we answered an open problem from the literature regarding the speed of all-or-nothing encryption. We proposed using CTRT-CTR in an efficient AON encryption mode, to further reduce power and memory overheads. Trade-offs between on-line encryption speed and memory were identified. The scheme would be beneficial in applications such as MANETs where low-power, secure run-time encryption is required. The proposed schemes were proven secure in the Shannon model of a block cipher.

Future work will investigate if it is possible to achieve secure all-or-nothing encryption with a lower total workload (both on-line and off-line) than CTRT-CTR, whilst still maintaining low latency.

Acknowledgements

The authors would like to thank Emanuel Popovici for his helpful discussions regarding the proofs of security. This research was supported by the Embark Initiative, operated by the Irish Research Council for Science, Engineering and Technology (IRCSET).

References

1. Bellare, M., Boldyreva, A.: The Security of Chaffing and Winnowing. In: Okamoto, T. (ed.) ASIACRYPT 2000. LNCS, vol. 1976, pp. 517–530. Springer, Heidelberg (2000)
2. Bellare, M., Desai, A., Jokipii, E., Rogaway, P.: A Concrete Security Treatment of Symmetric Encryption. In: FOCS 1997, 38th Annual Symposium on Foundations of Computer Science, pp. 394–403. IEEE Computer Society Press, Los Alamitos (1997)
3. Berman, V.: Enhancing Data Security in Mobile Ad Hoc Networks via Multipath Routing and Directional Transmission. Master's thesis, University of California, Davis (2005)
4. Boyko, V.: On All-or-Nothing Transforms and Password-Authenticated Key Exchange Protocols. PhD thesis, Massachusetts Institute of Technology (2000)
5. Byers, J., Considine, J., Itkis, G., Cheng, M.C., Yeung, A.: Securing bulk content almost for free. Journal of Computer Communications, Special Issue on Internet Security 29, 290–290 (2006)
6. Desai, A.: The Security of All-or-Nothing Encryption: Protecting against Exhaustive Key Search. In: Bellare, M. (ed.) CRYPTO 2000. LNCS, vol. 1880, pp. 359–375. Springer, Heidelberg (2000), http://www.cs.ucsd.edu/users/adesai/
7. Dodis, Y.: Exposure-Resilient Cryptography. PhD thesis, Massachusetts Institute of Technology (2000)
8. Dodis, Y., Sahai, A., Smith, A.: On Perfect and Adaptive Security in Exposure-Resilient Cryptography. In: Pfitzmann, B. (ed.) EUROCRYPT 2001. LNCS, vol. 2045, pp. 301–324. Springer, Heidelberg (2001)
9. ECRYPT (2006). ECRYPT Yearly Report on Algorithms and Keysizes (2005), http://www.ecrypt.eu.org
10. Johnson, D., Matyas, S., Peyravian, M.: Encryption of Long Blocks Using a Short-Block Encryption Procedure. In: Submitted for inclusion in the IEEE P1363a standard (1996)
11. Kiong, N.C., Samsudin, A.: Incoercible Secure Electronic Voting Scheme Based on Chaffing and Winnowing. In: APCC 2003, The 9th Asia-Pacific Conference on Communications, vol. 2, pp. 838–843. IEEE, Los Alamitos (2003)
12. Lipmaa, H., Rogaway, P., Wagner, D.: CTR-Mode Encryption. Comments to NIST concerning AES Modes of Operation (2000)

13. Marnas, S.I., Angelis, L., Bleris, G.L.: All-Or-Nothing Transforms Using Quasigroups. In: Proc. of 1st Balkan Conference on Informatics, pp. 183–191 (2003)
14. Menezes, A.J., van Oorschot, P.C., Vanstone, S.A.: Handbook of Applied Cryptography. CRC Press, Boca Raton (1996), http://www.cacr.math.uwaterloo.ca/hac/
15. Peterson, Z.N.J., Burns, R.C., Herring, J., Stubblefield, A., Rubin, A.D.: Secure Deletion for a Versioning File System. In: FAST 2005 — 4th USENIX Conference on File and Storage Technologies, pp. 143–154. USENIX (2005)
16. Rivest, R.L.: All-or-Nothing Encryption and the Package Transform. In: Biham, E. (ed.) FSE 1997. LNCS, vol. 1267, pp. 210–218. Springer, Heidelberg (1997)
17. Shannon, C.E.: Communication theory of secrecy systems. Bell Systems Technical Journal 28(4), 656–715 (1949)
18. Zhang, R., Hanaoka, G., Imai, H.: On the Security of Cryptosystems with All-or-Nothing Transform. In: Jakobsson, M., Yung, M., Zhou, J. (eds.) ACNS 2004. LNCS, vol. 3089, pp. 76–90. Springer, Heidelberg (2004)
19. Zhang, R., Hanaoka, G., Shikata, J., Imai, H.: On the Security of Multiple Encryption or CCA-security+CCA-security=CCA-security? In: Bao, F., Deng, R., Zhou, J. (eds.) PKC 2004. LNCS, vol. 2947, pp. 360–374. Springer, Heidelberg (2004)

Proposals for Iterated Hash Functions

Lars R. Knudsen and Søren S. Thomsen

Technical University of Denmark, Department of Mathematics, Building 303
2800 Kgs. Lyngby, Denmark
lars@ramkilde.com, S.Thomsen@mat.dtu.dk

Abstract. The past few years have seen an increase in the number of attacks on cryptographic hash functions. These include attacks directed at specific hash functions, and generic attacks on the typical method of constructing hash functions. In this paper we discuss possible methods for protecting against some generic attacks. We also give a concrete proposal for a new hash function construction, given a secure compression function which, unlike in typical existing constructions, is not required to be resistant to all types of collisions. Finally, we show how members of the SHA-family can be turned into constructions of our proposed type.

Keywords: Cryptographic hash functions, Merkle-Damgård constructions, multi-collisions, birthday attacks.

1 Introduction

Attacks on hash functions can broadly be divided into two categories; generic attacks on hash function constructions, and so-called short-cut attacks that exploit weaknesses of specific hash functions. The last few years have seen a fairly large number of attacks of both kinds. In this paper, we particularly focus on generic attacks. We propose a new hash function construction which we believe protects against existing generic attacks, and we argue why it will also complicate short-cut attacks on existing hash functions modified to be based on this construction.

A common method of constructing hash functions taking an input of arbitrary size is to iterate a number of times over a so-called compression function $f : \{0,1\}^n \times \{0,1\}^m \to \{0,1\}^n$ taking only fixed-length input. The message d is split into a number of blocks d_i of equal size m. To do this, the message must in general be padded, and this is usually done by always appending a '1'-bit to the message, then a suitable number of '0'-bits, and finally the length of the original message is appended. When the message is split into blocks $d_1 \| d_2 \| \ldots \| d_s$, each block can be processed individually by the compression function f. An initial n-bit value h_0 is defined for the hash function, and then subsequent chaining variables are computed as $h_i = f(h_{i-1}, d_i)$, $i = 1, 2, \ldots, s$. We shall refer to this as the Merkle-Damgård construction [1,2].

In this paper, we propose a new method of constructing a hash function from a compression function. The new method has some attractive properties. For instance, it does not require the compression function to be completely collision resistant in order for the hash function to be so. It makes some generic attacks much harder to mount, and it also

J. Filipe and M.S. Obaidat (Eds.): ICETE 2006, CCIS 9, pp. 107–118, 2008.

seems to protect very well against known short-cut attacks such as recent attacks on MD5 [3] and SHA-1 [4,5]. In general, it leaves an attacker with much less freedom, and the amount of freedom that an attacker has to choose messages in existing hash functions is, we believe, a very important reason for the failure of these hash functions to achieve collision resistance. We discuss possible methods of complicating the generic attacks that our proposal in its bare form does not protect against.

In the following we denote by *the SHA-family of hash functions* the collection of hash functions of [6] and [7], i.e. SHA-1, SHA-256, SHA-512, SHA-224, and SHA-384.

2   Properties of Existing Constructions

In this section we consider some of the generic attacks on the Merkle-Damgård construction as well as on the underlying Davies-Meyer construction.

2.1   The Davies-Meyer Construction

The compression functions of most popular hash functions, including the SHA-family, in use today are of the form $f : \{0,1\}^n \times \{0,1\}^m \to \{0,1\}^n$,

$$h_i = f(h_{i-1}, d_i) = p(h_{i-1}, d_i) + h_{i-1}, \tag{1}$$

where p is a bijective mapping on n bits for fixed value of d_i. This construction was known as the Davies-Meyer construction for many years, but was since contributed to Matyas and Meyer [8]. Such functions are traditionally built from iterating a relatively weak function, say g, a number of times, $p(x,y) = g \circ g \circ \cdots \circ g(x,y)$. If the size of the range of g would be less than 2^n, then the size of p would decrease with the number of g invocations. Therefore, g is a bijection in most designs. An invertible compression function is however not always desirable which is why one adds one of the two inputs of p to the output (this is called a *feed-forward*). This design is very similar to the designs of modern block ciphers, which are typically constructed from iterating a weak function several times. Indeed the compression functions from the SHA-family can be used for encryption [9].

It is well-known [8] though that the Davies-Meyer construction has an unfortunate property, which adds to the success of the 2nd preimage attack of Section 2.2.

- Let $p_y(h_{i-1})$ denote $p(h_{i-1}, d_i)$ for a fixed value of $d_i = y$.
- Choose any m-bit value y and any n-bit value α.
- Compute $h_{i-1} = p_y^{-1}(\alpha)$.

It follows that $p(h_{i-1}, y) = \alpha$. Consequently one gets $h_i = f(h_{i-1}, d_i) = h_{i-1} + \alpha$. E.g., by choosing $\alpha = 0$ one gets $h_i = h_{i-1}$ which is called a *fixed point* for the compression function f.

2.2   The Merkle-Damgård Construction

Collision resistance of a compression function is extended to the hash function when using the Merkle-Damgård construction, as proved by the well-known Theorem 1.

Theorem 1. *Let H be a hash function based on the Merkle-Damgård construction with length padding (also known as MD-strengthening) and compression function f. Then a collision of H implies a collision of f.*

A number of attacks on the general Merkle-Damgård construction show that if the compression function fails, then the entire hash function goes down. Some of these attacks are now described.

Multi-collisions. In [10], Antoine Joux described a new method for constructing multi-collisions from a number of single collisions. A multi-collision is a set of messages, all having the same hash value. If an n-bit hash function produces random hash values, then the complexity of a multi-collision attack consisting of r messages is about $2^{(r-1)n/r}$. Joux shows that in the Merkle-Damgård construction, this complexity can be reduced to $(\log_2 r)2^{n/2}$.

The method is quite simple. It requires access to a machine $\mathcal{C}$ that finds ordinary one-block collisions of a hash function H given any initial value. Let the initial value of H be h_0, and let f be the compression function of H. f accepts two inputs, a chaining variable and a message block. Obtain a collision (d_1, d_1') from $\mathcal{C}$ with h_0 as the initial value, i.e. $f(h_0, d_1) = f(h_0, d_1')$. Call this value h_1, i.e. $h_1 = f(h_0, d_1)$. Now, obtain a second collision (d_2, d_2') from $\mathcal{C}$ with h_1 as initial value. Repeat this $t = \log_2 r$ times. We now have t pairs of messages, where for each pair we can select an arbitrary member of the pair to construct a message of t blocks, and all such messages have the same hash value. There are $r = 2^t$ ways to select such a message, an hence we have an r-way multi-collision. The complexity of the attack is t times the complexity of finding a single collision with $\mathcal{C}$, and this is at most $2^{n/2}$ for any hash function.

The Herding Attack. The herding attack [11] by Kelsey and Kohno bears some resemblance to the multi-collision attack of Joux. From a large (power of two) number $N = 2^\ell$ of chaining variables, colliding pairs of messages forming a binary collision tree are found such that by each level in the tree, the number of chaining variables is reduced by a factor two. At the root of the tree is the chaining variable h. From the N chaining variables there are N messages of length ℓ blocks, all having the hash value h. This tree of collisions can be used as follows.

Say an adversary would like to falsely claim that he is in possession of some knowledge. He constructs the collision tree described above, and publishes h. Some time later, when he acquires the knowledge, he forms a message d_I containing the information, and computes its intermediate hash. He then searches for a linking message d_L, such that the intermediate hash of $d_I \| d_L$ is among the N chaining variables at the top of the collision tree. From this chaining variable, he selects the set of message blocks that "herds" the entire message to the hash value h.

Note that the kind of collisions needed for this attack is different from the multi-collisions found using the method of Joux. In this case, the multi-collision must form a binary tree. Such multi-collisions seem harder to find than those of Joux, however, a method faster than brute force is given in [11].

2nd Preimage Attack. In [12] a second preimage attack on the general Merkle-Damgård construction was presented. This attack makes use of what the authors call expandable messages – a set of messages of *different* lengths, which all have the same intermediate hash given a certain initial value and not including MD-strengthening. In the Merkle-Damgård construction, any message of the expandable message set can be replaced with any other message from the set, without changing the intermediate hash value. To be more precise, given a hash function H with compression function f and initial value h_0, assume that $(\mu_1, \mu_2, \ldots, \mu_k)$ are k messages of lengths 1 to k, all producing the same intermediate hash value given the initial value h_0. Then $H(\mu_i\|x) = H(\mu_j\|x)$ for any x and any $0 < i, j \leq k$ *when length padding is omitted*.

Consider again the hash function H, and let its length be n. If one has produced an expandable set $\mathcal{E}$ of messages with the initial value h_0, then a second preimage attack can be performed as follows. Given a very long message M (whose second preimage we are looking for), compute a list L of all (except the first few) of the intermediate hashes of M, i.e. all the chaining variables that are produced when M is hashed. If $f(h_0, d_i) = h_e$ for all $d_i \in \mathcal{E}$, then look for a message d_L for which $f(h_e, d_L) \in L$. Since L is a very long list, this has complexity less than 2^n. Say such a d_L has been found, and it matched the jth element in L. Now, choose the message $d^* \in \mathcal{E}$ such that the number of blocks of $d^*\|d_L$ is j, meaning that the first j blocks in M can be replaced with $d^*\|d_L$ without changing the length of the message. Let M' be this new version of M. Then $H(M') = H(M)$.

The expandable message set can be quite easily produced if the hash function contains fixed points, see Section 2.1, but it is also possible in general by finding collisions between messages of lengths 1 and a for different values of a, and then concatenate messages in different ways similarly to the multi-collision attack described above.

Length-Extension Attack. The Merkle-Damgård construction is susceptible to a length-extension attack [13]: Given a hash function H, assume an attacker knows $H(d)$ and the length of d. In the Merkle-Damgård construction he can then select a suffix x, and compute $H(d\|x)$ without knowledge of d. He does this by setting the first part of x to be the padding of d (which he knows since he knows $|d|$), and he is then free to choose the remainder of x.

Discussion on the Generic Attacks. The attacks just described show that it is too simple to build messages with certain properties in the Merkle-Damgård construction. The effect of replacing a part of a message by something else, or prepending or appending some message to another message, is too modest. Moreover, recent short-cut attacks [3,4,5] on hash functions such as MD5 and SHA-1 prove that it is not as easy to construct a collision resistant compression function as once believed.

3   Possible Countermeasures

In this section we discuss some possible methods for defeating the attacks and weaknesses mentioned in the previous sections.

3.1   Alternatives to Davies-Meyer

There are twelve secure compression function constructions [14] based on a family of 2^n bijections on n bits. For eight of these, including the Davies-Meyer construction, it is relatively easy to find fixed points. One of the remaining four is the "dual mode" to the Davies-Meyer construction

$$h_i = f(h_{i-1}, d_i) = p(d_i, h_{i-1}) + d_i, \tag{2}$$

attributed to Matyas, Meyer, and Oseas [8]. Note that the problems of (1) stem from the facts that p is invertible when the second argument is fixed, and that the second argument is formed from the message block (alone), and thus the attacker has complete control over this. This is not the case in (2), where the second argument is formed from the chaining variable alone. In this light it may seem strange why (1) is more employed in practice than (2), but this is probably due to a choice of efficiency at the expense of security. One advantage of (1) compared to (2) (seen from the designer's point of view) is that the size of the data block in the former can be made larger than the size of the chaining variable, thus providing faster hashing.

3.2   Extensions and Alternatives to Merkle-Damgård

It is not as easy as it may seem to protect against the generic attacks on the Merkle-Damgård construction. The following is a discussion on what might and what might not work.

3C, a Recent Proposal.   A recent proposal named 3C [15] continuously updates an additional variable by adding (xoring) to it the chaining variable after each iteration. In the end, this additional variable is converted into a message block, which is appended to the original message. This method might complicate short-cut attacks, but it does not have any effect on the multi-collision attack, since the chaining variables are identical after each iteration.

Since 3C is just Merkle-Damgård with an extra message block derived from all intermediate chaining values, fixed points can be found in the same way as in the standard Merkle-Damgård construction. In 3C, if the fixed point is applied $2k$ times, then for any positive k the additional message block is the same. However, it seems difficult to make use of this fact, since this does not produce infinitely many collisions because of the length padding, and Kelsey and Schneier's second preimage attack is thwarted because it is hard to ensure that the additional message block has the same value as for the target message.

In the following section we analyse more general methods of appending a checksum-like value to the message. The aim is to complicate the multi-collision attack of Joux.

Appending a Checksum.   The hash function MD2 is an iterated hash function which differs from constructions of the SHA-family in several ways. One particular distinct feature is the use of a checksum function [16], which computes an additional message block as a function of all other (original) message blocks. The checksum block is appended to the original message. It shall be assumed that the checksum is computed iteratively as follows. Let $d_1, d_2, \ldots, d_s$ be the blocks to be hashed and let $c_1, c_2, \ldots, c_s$ denote the intermediate checksum, such that, $c_1 = C(d_1), c_2 = C(d_1, d_2)$, and $c_s = C(d_1, d_2, \ldots, d_s)$. We shall show that such checksums do not always provide much added security against some of the generic attacks listed above.

Consider first the simple checksum function where one computes the exclusive-or sum of all data blocks. Or more generally, consider checksum functions such that there exist invertible subfunctions $C_1, C_2, \ldots, C_s$ such that

$$c_s = C(d_1, d_2, \ldots, d_s) = \sum_{i=1}^{s} C_i(d_i). \tag{3}$$

Such checksum functions do not add much protection against the multi-collision attack. Let $\mathcal{C}$ be a collision finder of the compression function, that always returns one-block collisions where for the two messages d_i, d_i' the checksum values $C_i(d_i)$ and $C_i(d_i')$ agree on the first $m - (n/2 + \epsilon)$ bits. For positive but small ϵ, this gives enough freedom for $\mathcal{C}$ to actually find such collisions. Choose $t > n/2 + \epsilon$. Find a chain of t collisions, which form an intermediate 2^t-way multi-collision, excluding the checksum. Now choose some value S for the checksum of all blocks – of course, the first $m - (n/2 + \epsilon)$ bits of S are fixed by the messages in the multi-collision. Form two sets of checksums; the checksums of all $2^{t/2}$ combinations of the first $t/2$ blocks, and the value S subtracted the checksums of the last $t/2$ blocks. From the relation (3) one sees that this corresponds to all possible values of $c_{t/2}$ such that S is reached by the last $t/2$ blocks. Since $t > n/2 + \epsilon$ and the first $m - (n/2 + \epsilon)$ bits always match, with good probability there will be a match between the two sets. The running time of the attack which finds (roughly) a $2^{t-n/2}$-collision is the time it takes to find the t collisions, plus the time it takes to compute about $2^{t/2+1}$ checksums (or inversions). If $t = n$, for instance, then a $2^{n/2}$-collision is expected with a total running time of about $(n+2)2^{n/2}$. Note that Joux's attack on a construction without the checksum finds a $2^{n/2}$-collision in time $(n/2)2^{n/2}$.

The checksum function of MD2 is not as simple as the above. There is a rotation of the bytes in a block and applications of a nonlinear S-box, features which make it seemingly impossible to ensure that the final checksum has a number of fixed bits as above – at least when the messages are long enough. Assume, however, that a checksum function similar to the one of MD2 is used to construct a checksum of μ bits, and this checksum is appended to the message (padded, if necessary). Assume that this checksum function is invertible, that is, if $c_s = c(d_1, \ldots, d_s)$, is the checksum function value after processing the sth block, then it should be possible given d_s to compute $c_{s-1} = c(d_1, \ldots, d_{s-1})$. The MD2 checksum function is invertible under this definition. An attacker would choose some value of the checksum, say S. He would then build a, say, 2^t-way multi-collision as usual, but not considering the checksum. Similar to above, he would compute $2^{t/2}$ intermediate checksums of the first $t/2$ blocks of each message, and $2^{t/2}$ intermediate checksums of the last $t/2$ blocks in a backward direction starting from S. These last $2^{t/2}$ checksums are those from which S is reached by the last $2^{t/2}$ blocks. He would then perform a meet-in-the-middle search for matches between the two sets of checksums. One expects to get multi-collisions with

$2^{t-\mu}$ matches. The complexity of a $2^{t-\mu}$-collision attack is roughly the time it takes to find the t collisions on the compression functions, plus the time it takes to compute about $2^{t/2+1}$ checksums.

In this case the complexity of the multi-collision attack depends very much on μ, the size of the output. In the case of MD2, $\mu = n$, so multi-collisions for MD2 can be found considerably faster than by a brute-force attack. However, if μ would be much larger than n, say $\mu = 2n$, then the complexity of the (generic) attacks would be much higher.

These considerations indicate that if one wants to use a checksum to protect against the multi-collision attack, then one will have to select the checksum function carefully. At the very least the checksum value that is appended to the message must be large enough to make the attacks described at least as hard as a brute-force attack, or the checksum function must be non-invertible.

An alternative method is to insert a (simpler) checksum block for every j iterations, with e.g. $j = 8$. This would prevent an attacker from being able to choose t large enough to ensure that the 2^t-way multi-collisions would contain collisions also on the checksum.

The herding attack and the 2nd preimage attack are also complicated by appending or inserting the output of a checksum function. It becomes much more difficult to replace part of a message with something else, or to use just any of a large set of messages as in the herding attack. One would have to select a value for the checksum before the hash value is chosen, and not much freedom is left for finding the linking message in the end.

The length-extension attack is complicated by the fact that the adversary does not know the checksum of the original message.

The drawbacks of the checksum approach are that it requires both time and memory to compute and store the checksum. What's more, the resulting message length increases, and so the compression function must be invoked an additional number of times. However, the checksum function can be constructed such that it is much faster than the compression function, and the rather limited number of additional bits of message do not affect the total running time by much.

A Wide-Pipe Method. As first suggested by Lucks [17], the security of the Merkle-Damgård construction might be regained by choosing a compression function with a larger output size than the final output of the hash function. This would make each regular collision of the multi-collision attack more time-consuming, assuming the quickest method to find collisions of the compression function is the birthday attack. By doubling the internal width of the hash function, the complexity of the multi-collision attack becomes greater than the complexity of a brute-force multi-collision attack.

This method also complicates the other attacks mentioned. The herding attack and the 2nd preimage attack are complicated in that each collision is more difficult to find. The length-extension attack is complicated in that the adversary does not know the final output of the compression function, because this is not the same as the output of the hash function.

Again, the most significant drawback of this method is that it slows down the entire operation – assuming that a larger compression function is slower. In any case, an output transformation from the final output of the compression function, to the output of the hash function, is needed. This could be a narrow version of the compression function or something else, but this is an additional potential weak point of the hash function.

4   Proposals for Enhanced Security

This section gives a proposal for a variant of the Merkle-Damgård construction. This variant, which bears some resemblance to a proposal by Rivest [18], is constructed with the SHA-family in mind and it has some attractive properties, as we shall see.

Assume the existence of a (secure) compression function

$$h : \{0,1\}^n \times \{0,1\}^n \times \{0,1\}^m \rightarrow \{0,1\}^n.$$

Define a hash function H as follows.

- Let d be the data to be hashed, and append a '1'-bit to d. Now append enough '0'-bits to make the length of d a multiple of m. Now $d = d_1 \| d_2 \| \cdots \| d_s$, where $|d_i| = m, 1 \le i \le s$. It is specifically required that $s < 2^{n/2}$.
- Let iv_1 and iv_2 be given (fixed) n-bit initial values, and let $h_0 = iv_1$.
- Define

$$h_i = h(iv_1 + i, h_{i-1}, d_i) \quad \text{for } 1 \le i \le s$$

- Define $H(d) = h(iv_2, h_s, s)$ to be the output of the hash function.

The value $iv_1 + i$ is to be computed modulo 2^n. The values of iv_1 and iv_2 should be chosen such that $iv_2 \ne iv_1 + i$ for any admissible value of i. Note that this hash function can hash data strings of up to a number of blocks equal to the minimum of $2^m - 1$ and $2^{n/2} - 1$. If $m < n/2$ it is easy to extend the above construction to allow for a number of blocks up to $2^{n/2} - 1$. Simply split s into a pre-determined fixed number of blocks, say t, each of m bits for $s = s_1, s_2, \ldots, s_t$. Then modify the last step of above to $x_j = h(iv_2, x_{j-1}, s_j)$, for $1 \le j \le t$, where $x_0 = h_s$ and define $H(d) = x_t$.

Theorem 2. *Let H be a hash function as defined above. Let iv_1 and iv_2 be given. Then any collision on H implies a collision on h where the first arguments are identical. In other words, the existence of two distinct strings d and d' such that $H(d) = H(d')$ implies the existence of two distinct triples (x, y, z) and (x, y', z') such that $h(x, y, z) = h(x, y', z')$.*

Proof. Assume a collision for H, that is, $d \ne d'$, such that $H(d) = H(d')$. Let s and s' denote the number of blocks in d and d' after the padding bits. If $s \ne s'$, the result follows from $h(iv_2, h_s, s) = h(iv_2, h'_{s'}, s')$. Assume next that $s = s'$. Then if $h_s \ne h'_s$, the result follows again. If $h_s = h'_s$, then it follows that for some j, $1 \le j < s$, one gets $h(iv_1 + j, h_{j-1}, d_j) = h(iv_1 + j, h'_{j-1}, d'_j)$ and $(h_{j-1}, d_j) \ne (h'_{j-1}, d'_j)$.   ∎

Theorem 2 shows that if h is a compression function resistant to collisions where the first arguments are identical, then H is collision resistant.

4.1   Application to the SHA-Family Constructions

In the following we show how the members of the SHA-family can be turned into constructions of the above type. Given a hash function H with compression function $f : \{0,1\}^n \times \{0,1\}^m \to \{0,1\}^n$, where $m > n$, of the form

$$f(h_{i-1}, d_i) = g(h_{i-1}, d_i) + h_{i-1},$$

cf. Section 2.1. Consider the following variant $\tilde{H}$ of H. Let the compression function be

$$h : \{0,1\}^n \times \{0,1\}^n \times \{0,1\}^{m-n} \to \{0,1\}^n.$$

- Let $d = d_1 \| \cdots \| d_s$ be the data to be hashed (including padding bits), where $|d_i| = m - n$ for $1 \le i \le s$, and $s < 2^{n/2}$.
- Let iv_1, iv_2 and h_0 be given n-bit initial values (these are chosen once and for all in the specification of the hash function, and such that $iv_1 + i \neq iv_2$ for any admissible i).
- Define $h_i = h(iv_1 + i, h_{i-1}, d_i) = g(iv_1 + i, (d_i \| h_{i-1})) + h_{i-1}$ for $1 \le i \le s$.
- Define $\tilde{H}(d) = h(iv_2, h_s, s) = g(iv_2, (s \| h_s)) + h_s$.

If the compression function of SHA-n is resistant to collisions where the first input is identical for the two messages, then the construction above using SHA-n is a collision resistant hash function.

In some instantiations it might be better to omit the feed-forward. Without feed-forward, the construction would have the property that the multi-block collision techniques of e.g. [4] and [5] would be thwarted, since a near-collision after the processing of one block cannot be used to form a collision after two or more blocks; a collision in the hash function implies a collision in the compression function where the initial state is identical for the two messages. However, omitting the feed-forward might open up new doors for an attacker, so we do not recommend this in general.

Note that a pseudo-preimage for the compression function can be found in time $2^{n/2}$. Given h_i, choose arbitrary values of h_{i-1} and d_i, and invert g. This requires an expected $2^{n/2}$ work, since $2^{n/2}$ different values of i are admissible, and for each d_i, a random n-bit value corresponding to the first argument of g is found (in assumed constant time). Here, it is assumed that the fastest method to find an admissible i is by brute force. A pseudo-preimage is, however, not immediately useful since the attacker has no control over i, and it seems difficult to exploit such findings to find preimages of the hash function.

Since inverting g takes time $2^{n/2}$, this is also the time it takes to find a fixed point of the compression function. Therefore it seems that the 2nd preimage attack of Kelsey and Schneier using fixed points to produce expandable messages is no faster than a brute force attack. Furthermore, the use of a counter in the first argument means that the generic method of producing expandable messages is also not applicable: a one-block message cannot be replaced by an a-block message without changing the input to the following application of the compression function.

The length-extension attack can no longer be carried out. The padding block is processed with iv_2 as the first argument to the compression function, and when the attacker selects this block as part of the extension to the original message, $iv_1 + i$ for some i will be used as the first argument. By definition, these two values cannot be the same.

The reader may have observed that in the construction above we have not introduced any dedicated measures to try to protect against the multi-collision attack, nor against the herding attack. However, these attacks evidently require at least one collision on the compression function. Thus if the size of the compression function is large enough to make the birthday attack computationally infeasible and if one's aim is to construct a compression function resistant to collisions then this also protects against the multi-collision attacks. Nonetheless, the multi-collision attacks on the iterated hash function constructions do illustrate properties which are not inherent in a "random hashing". If one wishes a construction where the complexity of the multi-collision and the herding attacks is higher than for the birthday attack, we list two possible ways:

- Truncation of the final hash value.
- The addition of checksums.

As an example of the first item take SHA-512. Here the complexity of a birthday attack is 2^{256}, thus today, one may safely truncate the final output to less than 512 bits, say, 320 bits. Here the birthday collision attack has complexity 2^{160}, whereas a collision of a compression function (except for the final application in a hashing) requires about 2^{256} operations. For the other members of the SHA-family we do not recommend this measure.

As for the second item and applications which employ members of the SHA-family in the proposed construction; here we'd recommend to append to the original message the values of two checksums, whose outputs each has the size of one message block. These two checksums must be different in such a way as to avoid that by fixing certain bits in the message blocks one also fixes certain bits in the checksums.

4.2   Performance

There is a slowdown when a hash function uses a compression function in our new mode of operation as opposed to the Merkle-Damgård mode. If the compression function takes an $(n + m)$-bit input and produces an n-bit output, then in the traditional mode of operation, m bits of message are processed per iteration of the compression function, whereas in our new mode of operation $m - n$ bits are processed. This slows down the whole operation by a factor $m/(m - n)$. In SHA-1, $n = 160$ and $m = 512$, so the slowdown when using the compression function of SHA-1 in our new construction is by a factor of about 1.5. In SHA-256, $n = 256$ and $m = 512$, and so here the slowdown is by a factor of about 2.0 which is also the case for SHA-512.

4.3   Resistance to Short-Cut Attacks

It is clear that the above proposed construction when applied to members of the SHA-family gives the attacker less freedom, since there are fewer bits that he can choose. Currently, the best collision attack on SHA-1 is the one discovered by Wang et al. [5]. This attack produces colliding messages each formed by two blocks, with a near-collision after the first block. Such an approach is less likely to be successful against our construction used with SHA-1, because of the use of the constant iv_1 in the first argument of h.

The attacks of Wang rely heavily on message modifications [3,5], which do not leave much freedom for the attacker to choose message bits. In our construction, 160 bits of the message block in SHA-1 are reserved for the bits of the chaining variable, which makes life harder for the attacker. But clearly this is not a strong argument for our construction. The security arguments for an iterated hash function rely on the collision resistance of the compression function. If a collision is found for the latter, then there are no longer good arguments to rely on the security of the hash function. However, seen in the light of the recent developments in hash function cryptanalysis, including the SHA-1 attacks, there are good reasons to limit the freedom of the attacker in future designs. This is a central idea in our construction.

5   Conclusions

We have discussed some generic attacks on the Merkle-Damgård construction and possible countermeasures to these. It turns out that some of these attacks, notably the multi-collision and the herding attacks, seem to be more difficult to protect against than one might expect.

A new method for iterated hash function construction has been proposed. Given an n-bit compression function resistant to collisions where n bits of the two inputs to the compression function are identical, our construction ensures a completely collision resistant hash function. In its bare form our construction does not give added protection against the multi-collision nor the herding attacks, but suggestions were given for possible ways of efficiently thwarting these attacks as well.

Acknowledgements

The authors would like to thank Praveen Gauravaram and Vincent Rijmen for helpful discussions.

References

1. Damgård, I.: A Design Principle for Hash Functions. In: [19], pp. 416–427.
2. Merkle, R.C.: One Way Hash Functions and DES. In: [19], pp. 428–446.
3. Wang, X., Yu, H.: How to Break MD5 and Other Hash Functions. In: [20], pp. 19–35.
4. Biham, E., Chen, R., Joux, A., Carribault, P., Lemuet, C., Jalby, W.: Collisions of SHA-0 and Reduced SHA-1. In: [20], pp. 36–57.
5. Wang, X., Yin, Y.L., Yu, H.: Finding Collisions in the Full SHA-1. In: Shoup, V. (ed.) CRYPTO 2005. LNCS, vol. 3621, pp. 17–36. Springer, Heidelberg (2005)
6. FIPS 180-1, Secure Hash Standard. Federal Information Processing Standards Publication 180-1, U.S. Department of Commerce/NIST, National Technical Information Service, Springfield, Virginia. Supersedes FIPS 180 (1995)
7. FIPS 180-2, Secure Hash Standard. Federal Information Processing Standards Publication 180-2, U.S. Department of Commerce/NIST, National Technical Information Service, Springfield, Virginia. Supersedes FIPS 180 and FIPS 180-1 (2002)

8. Preneel, B.: Analysis and Design of Cryptographic Hash Functions. PhD thesis, Katholieke Universiteit Leuven (1993)
9. Handschuh, H., Knudsen, L., Robshaw, M.: Analysis of SHA-1 in Encryption Mode. In: Naccache, D. (ed.) CT-RSA 2001. LNCS, vol. 2020, pp. 70–83. Springer, Heidelberg (2001)
10. Joux, A.: Multicollisions in Iterated Hash Functions. Application to Cascaded Constructions. In: Franklin, M. (ed.) CRYPTO 2004. LNCS, vol. 3152, pp. 306–316. Springer, Heidelberg (2004)
11. Kelsey, J., Kohno, T.: Herding Hash Functions and the Nostradamus Attack. In: Vaudenay, S. (ed.) EUROCRYPT 2006. LNCS, vol. 4004, pp. 183–200. Springer, Heidelberg (2006)
12. Kelsey, J., Schneier, B.: Second Preimages on n-bit Hash Functions for Much Less than 2^n Work. In: [20], pp. 474–490.
13. Ferguson, N., Schneier, B.: Practical Cryptography. Wiley Publishing, Chichester (2003)
14. Preneel, B., Govaerts, R., Vandewalle, J.: Hash Functions Based on Block Ciphers: A Synthetic Approach. In: Stinson, D.R. (ed.) CRYPTO 1993. LNCS, vol. 773, pp. 368–378. Springer, Heidelberg (1994)
15. Gauravaram, P., Millan, W., Dawson, E., Viswanathan, K.: Constructing Secure Hash Functions by Enhancing Merkle-Damgård Construction. In: Batten, L.M., Safavi-Naini, R. (eds.) ACISP 2006. LNCS, vol. 4058, pp. 407–420. Springer, Heidelberg (2006)
16. Kaliski, B.: RFC 1319, The MD2 Message-Digest Algorithm. Internet Request for Comments 1319 (1992)
17. Lucks, S.: A Failure-Friendly Design Principle for Hash Functions. In: Roy, B. (ed.) ASIACRYPT 2005. LNCS, vol. 3788, pp. 474–494. Springer, Heidelberg (2005)
18. Rivest, R.L.: Abelian square-free dithering for iterated hash functions. In: NIST Cryptographic Hash Workshop (November 2005). Retrieved from,
   http://theory.lcs.mit.edu/~rivest/
19. Brassard, G. (ed.): CRYPTO 1989. LNCS, vol. 435. Springer, Heidelberg (1990)
20. Cramer, R. (ed.): EUROCRYPT 2005. LNCS, vol. 3494. Springer, Heidelberg (2005)

Secure Online English Auctions

Jarrod Trevathan and Wayne Read

School of Mathematics, Physics and Information Technology, James Cook University, Australia
{jarrod.trevathan,wayne.read}@jcu.edu.au

Abstract. Security and privacy in online auctions is a major concern as auction participants have many opportunities to cheat (e.g., repudiate bids, not deliver items, etc.). Online auctions such as those used by eBay are based on a type of auction referred to as an English auction. Dispite the English auction being the most popular type of auction, it has received less security coverage than other types of auctions (e.g., sealed-bid auctions). An existing proposal for a "secure" English auction prevents the Auctioneer from closing the auction early and from blocking bids, but does not protect a bidder's anonymity. Another proposal provides anonymity, but does not stop an Auctioneer from skewing its clock or blocking bids. This paper proposes a new scheme for conducting secure and anonymous online English auctions using a modified type of group signature. Trust is divided among three servers owned by separate companies to ensure anonymity and fairness. Our scheme solves the problems of the existing English auction schemes and has following characteristics: *unforgeability, anonymity, unlinkability, exculpability, coalition-resistance, verifiability, robustness, traceability, revocation, one-off registration, unskewability* and *unblockability*. Our scheme has comparable efficiency to the existing schemes for the enhanced security and privacy it provides.

Keywords: Online auctions, event timing, anonymity, group signature.

1 Introduction

Online auctioning is now widely accepted as one of the premiere means to do business on the web. English auctions are the most common type of online auction employed by Internet auctioneers (e.g., eBay[1] and uBid[2]). Such auctions are used to sell various items from real estate to football tickets. An English auction allows one seller to offer an item for sale. Many potential buyers then submit bids for the item attempting to outbid each other. The winner is the bidder with the highest bid after a given time-out period where no bid higher than the current highest bid has been made. The winner must pay the seller an amount equal to the winning bid.

Since the participants are not physically present in an online auction, there exist many security concerns and opportunities for people to cheat. For example, a bidder might repudiate having made a bid or the seller doesn't deliver the item. Furthermore, the Auctioneer could influence the auction in a manner inconsistent with its rules (e.g., block bids). Security and privacy in electronic auctions has been covered in [3,7,10,15,18],

---

[1] http://www.ebay.com
[2] http://www.ubid.com

J. Filipe and M.S. Obaidat (Eds.): ICETE 2006, CCIS 9, pp. 119–133, 2008.

and numerous "secure" auction schemes have been proposed. However, most of the schemes presented so far have been for *sealed bid* auctions (i.e., bids remain secret until the close of bidding). An English auction on the other hand is an *open bid* auction (i.e., everyone knows the values of the bids). This combined with the nature of the auctioning process makes English auctions more complicated than regular cryptographic auction schemes.

The timing of events in English auctions is much more critical than sealed bid auctions. As a result, this presents some unique security risks. An English auction requires a real-time link between the bidders and the Auctioneer. Frequent price quotes are issued to update bidders regarding the current highest bid. As bidders base their decisions on this information, its timeliness directly influences the auction. A corrupt Auctioneer could disadvantage certain bidders by delaying this information or by speeding up (skewing) the clock in order to close the auction early. Furthermore, the speed and ease of the bid submission process is significant, especially when an auction is nearing its end. A malicious Auctioneer could selectively block bids based on bidder identity and/or bid value.

[13] presented an English auction scheme that prevents the Auctioneer from closing the auction early and from blocking bids. However it does not protect a bidder's anonymity. Alternately, a scheme by [12] provides anonymity, but does not stop an Auctioneer from skewing its clock or blocking bids. We believe the short-comings of the existing schemes can be solved by basing the auction protocol on a modified group signature scheme.

The concept of group signatures was introduced by [6]. A group signature scheme allows members of a group to sign messages on behalf of the group, such that the resulting signature does not reveal the identity of the signer. Signatures can be verified with respect to a single group public key. Only a designated group manager is able to open signatures, and thus reveal the signer's identity. Due to these unique security characteristics, group signature schemes have recently been used as the basis for auction protocols (see [16,17]).

This paper presents a scheme for conducting online English auctions in a secure and anonymous manner. The new scheme solves the problems of the existing proposals while maintaining all of their features. The role of the Auctioneer is divided among two auction servers (owned by separate companies) to ensure that the correct timing of events is maintained and to prevent bid blocking. (see [10].) Our scheme uses a group signature that is altered so that the role of the group manager is also divided among two indepedent auction servers. This allows for bid verification and protects a bidder's identity unless the two servers collude. In the case of a dispute (e.g., a bidder repudiates a bid), a court order can be used to reveal the bidder's identity and he/she can be permanently revoked from the auction proceedings. The scheme is flexible and allows the group signature to be updated as better techniques for group signatures become available. Our scheme offers comparable efficiency trade-offs for its enhanced security and privacy characteristics.

This paper is organised as follows: the remainder of this section discusses security issues inherent in English auctions and our contribution. Existing English auction schemes and their shortcomings are discussed in Section 2. The components of our new scheme are introduced in Section 3 and the auction protocol is described in Section 4. An informal security analysis of the new scheme is given in Section 5. Section 6 presents an efficiency comparision of the new scheme and Section 7 provides some concluding remarks.

1.1   Fundamentals of Online English Auctions

There are four main activities in an online English auction:

Initialisation – The Auctioneer sets up the auction and advertises it i.e., type of good being auctioned, starting time, etc.

Registration – In order to participate in the auction, bidders must first register with the Auctioneer.

Bidding – A registered bidder computes his/her bid and submits it to the Auctioneer. The Auctioneer checks the bid received to ensure that it conforms with the auction rules.

Winner Determination – The Auctioneer determines the winner according to the auction rules. Online English auctions can terminate according to the following rules (see [8,13]):

1. *Expiration Time* - The auction closes at a predetermined expiration time.
2. *Timeout* - The auction closes when no bids higher than the current highest bid are made within a predetermined timeout interval.
3. *Combination of Expiration and Timeout* - The auction closes when there is a timeout after the expiration time.

1.2   Security Issues in Online English Auctions

The core security requirements for an English auction include:

Unforgeability - Bids must be unforgeable, otherwise a bidder can be impersonated.
Verifiability - There must be publicly available information by which all parties can be verified as having correctly followed the auction protocol. This should include evidence of registration, bidding and proof of the winner of the auction.
Exculpability - Neither the Auctioneer nor a legitimate bidder can forge a valid signature of a bidder.
Coalition-resistance - No coalition of bidders can frame an innocent bidder by fabricating a bid.
Robustness - The auction process must not be affected by invalid bids or by participants not following the correct auction protocol.
Anonymity - The bidder-bid relationship must be concealed so that no bidder can be associated or identified with the bid they submit.

One-time registration - Registration is a one-off procedure, which means that once a bidder has registered, they can participate in future auctions held by the Auctioneer.

Unlinkability - Bids are unlinkable within an auction, and also between plural auctions.

Traceability - Once a bidder has submitted a bid, they must not be able to repudiate having made it. Otherwise if a bidder wins and does not want to pay, they might deny that they submitted the winning bid. In this event the identity of the bidder who submitted the bid in question can be revealed.

Revocation - Malicious bidders can be easily revoked from all future auctions.

English auctions are open bid and the timely nature of the auction process therefore raises several further concerns. Due to the flexibility of closing rules for English auctions this introduces the following unique requirements:

Unskewability - The Auctioneer must not be able to alter the auction timing. For example, speed up its clock in an attempt to close the auction early, or slow the auction down to keep the bidding process active beyond the official timeout.

Unblockability - The Auctioneer cannot selectively block bids based on bid amount or the identity of the bidder.

Conditional bid cancellation - In online auctions using an expiration time, it is common for the auction to continue for days or weeks. In this situation a bidder might be reluctant to make such an open ended bid. Therefore depending on the closing rule and the stage of the auction it is desirable to allow bidders to conditionally cancel bids. Note that bidders should not be able to cancel bids when an auction is in a timeout stage and cancellation must only be done in strict accordance with the Auctioneer's bid cancellation policy.

2   Existing English Auction Schemes

Discussions regarding security for English auctions can be found in [8,16]. Several "secure" English auction schemes have been proposed by [9,11,12,13]. The first scheme is due to [13]. This scheme requires bidders to register with the Auctioneer. The Auctioneer must periodically timestamp the auction proceedings with a *Notary* to prove to bidders that it is not skewing its clock. Bidders submit bids using a reverse hash chain and secret bid commitments. This is done to ensure that the Auctioneer cannot block bids, and that bidders are not able to repudiate bids. The auction proceedings are recorded on a public bulletin board that is readable by everyone, but can only be written to by the Auctioneer.

We have identified the following problems with this scheme:

1. There is no anonymity for the bidders.
2. Bids are linkable, meaning that the Auctioneer can create profiles about individual bidders and their bidding strategies.
3. All parties must trust the Notary. (i.e., to ensure the correct timing is maintained.)

[12] refine a scheme by [11] that uses a form of modified group signature [1,5,6]. This scheme allows a bidder to register once and participate in any number of auctions held by the Auctioneer. Bids are claimed to be unlinkable between different auctions, but linkable within a particular auction. This is achieved by requiring the bidder to calculate a new signature generation key prior to each auction.

In this scheme there are two mangers responsible for conducting the auction. The *Registration Manager* (RM) secretly knows the correspondence of the bidder's identity and registration key. RM works as an identity escrow agency. The *Auction Manager* (AM) hosts the auction and prepares bidder's auction keys in each round.

We have identified the following problems with this scheme:

1. All bidders must update their keys between each round of auctioning, which is essentially equivalent to re-registering. Therefore, this negates the author's claims that registration is a one-off procedure.
2. AM can skew its clock and/or selectively block bids.
3. Revoking a bidder is inefficient as it requires AM to reissue new keys to all of the existing bidders.
4. [9] describe a flaw in this scheme during the winner announcement stage. Here AM is able to erroneously inform any bidder that they have won without being publicly verifiable. Lee *et al.* propose a solution. However, this introduces several more bulletin boards and requires computations that are an order of magnitude slower.
5. Bids are linkable within a current auction, but unlinkable between plural auctions. The motivation for this is stated as the auction participants gain utility in terms of entertainment from viewing the auction. For example, when there is a rally between two particular bidders, observers enjoy knowing how many bids a bidder has submitted.

With regard to the last point, it is our opinion, that in an anonymous auction scheme all bids (whether in the same auction or not) must be totally unlinkable. Observers can still see a rally, however, there is no need to know exactly whom the bids are coming from. Our scheme described in the next section, does not allow bids to be linked within the same auction or between plural auctions.

3   Components of Our Scheme

The auction has four parties:

A *Bidder*, who is interested in buying an item from a seller in an English auction.

An *Auction Manager* (AM), who organises the auction proceedings, accepts bids and determines the winner according to whoever has submitted the highest bid. To participate in an auction, a bidder presents his/her real identity to AM. AM issues the bidder with a token that allows him/her to register.

A *Registration Manager* (RM), who takes part in the protocol in order to complete the registration of a bidder, once a token has been obtained from AM. At the end of the protocol, the bidder obtains a secret key that enables him/her to generate signed bids in a proper format.

An *Auction Helper* (AH), who aids AM in accepting bids and determining the winner. AH is owned by a separate company and is tasked with ensuring that AM does not alter its clock or block bids.

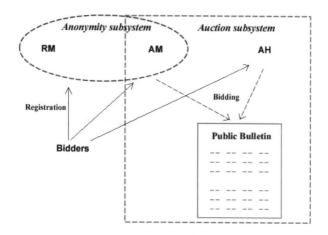

Fig. 1. The Auction Model

The scheme uses a two-server trust approach that can be broken down into two subsystems: the *anonymity subsystem* and the *auction subsystem* (see Figure 1). The anonymity subsystem protects the anonymity of the bidders provided the AM and RM do not collude. The auction subsystem ensures the correct outcome of the auction as long as AM and AH do not collude. There is no trust assumed between RM and AH.

Each bidder, AM and AH are connected to a common broadcast medium with the property that messages sent to the channel instantly reach every party connected to it. The broadcast channel is public so that everybody can listen to all information communicated via the channel, but cannot modify it. It is also assumed that there are private channels between RM and any potential bidders (who wish to join the auction proceedings).

3.1 Group Signatures

To join an auction, a bidder must first register with RM (who plays the role of a group manager in a group signature scheme). Once registered, a bidder can participate in the auction by signing bids using the group signature. Bids are submitted to an independent AM who runs the auction (with the help of AH which is explained later). AM (and AH) post the auction results on a publicly verifiable bulletin board.

One of the most efficient and popular proposals for group signature schemes is due to [1]. This is the group signature scheme that is used for the basis of our auction protocol. The [1] group signature scheme informally works as follows:

Let $n = pq$ be an RSA modulus, where p and q are two safe primes (i.e., $p = 2p' + 1$, $q = 2q' + 1$, and p', q' are also prime numbers). Denote by $QR(n)$, the set of quadratic residues - a cyclic group generated by an element of order $p'q'$. The group public key is $\mathcal{Y} = (n, a, a_0, y = g^x, g, h)$, where a, a_0, g, h are randomly selected elements from $QR(n)$. The secret key of the group manager is x.

To join the group, a user (bidder i) must engage in a protocol with the group manager (i.e., RM and AM) and receive a group certificate $[B_i, e_i]$ where $B_i = (a^{x_i}, a_0)^{1/e_i}$ mod

n with e_i and x_i chosen from two integral ranges as defined in [1]. (x_i is only known to the user/bidder).

In order to sign a message/bid, m, the user/bidder has to prove possession of his member certificate $[B_i, e_i]$ without revealing the certificate itself. More precisely, the user/bidder computes:

$$T_1 = B_i y^w \bmod n, \, T_2 = g^w \bmod n,$$

$$T_3 = g^{e_i} h^w \bmod n \, SK(m)$$

where the value $SK(m)$, computed over a message m, indicates a signature of knowledge of the secret key x_i and the e_ith root of the first part of the representation of T_3 (in the implementation of our scheme, the exact signature generation and verification procedures will be presented).

In the case of a dispute, the group manager can open a signature that reveals the identity of the signer. This is due to the fact that the pair (T_1, T_2) is an ElGamal encryption of the user's certificate (using the public key of the group manager). That is, the group manager can compute B_i, using $B_i = T_1/(T_2)^x$.

In certain circumstances users must be revoked from the group. For example, a membership expires or a user misbehaves. Reissuing keys to all existing group members is unwieldy and inefficient for a large group. Using a certificate revocation list to blacklist malicious bidders requires the verifier of the signature to check a list that is linear in the number of revoked users.

[4] propose a scheme based on a dynamic accumulator that requires a member to prove that they have not been revoked. Informally, an *accumulator* is a method to combine a set of values into one short accumulator such that there is a short witness that a given value was incorporated into the accumulator. It is infeasible to find a witness for a value that is not in the accumulator. A *dynamic accumulator* allows values to be added and deleted from the accumulator at unit cost. By incorporating dynamic accumulators into a group signature scheme, revocation can easily be performed by deleting a member's value from the accumulator.

A user must check the accumulator prior to signing. This requires an online link between the group manager and the users. In terms of an auction, a bidder must check the accumulator each time they submit a bid. This is reasonable for English auctions, as there is a real-time communication link between the Auctioneer and bidders anyway.

The [4] dynamic accumulator scheme can be defined as follows: A dynamic accumulator for a family of inputs $\{\mathcal{X}_1\}$ is a family of families of functions $\{\mathcal{F}_1\}$ with the following properties:

Efficient generation: *There is an efficient probabilistic algorithm $\mathcal{G}$ that on input 1^k produces a random element f of $\mathcal{F}_k$. Moreover, along with f, $\mathcal{G}$ also outputs some auxiliary information about f, denoted aux_f.*

Efficient evaluation: *$f \in \mathcal{F}_k$ is a polynomial-size circuit that, on input $(u, k) \in \mathcal{U}_f \times \mathcal{X}_k$, outputs a value $v \in \mathcal{U}_f$, where $\mathcal{U}_f$ is an efficiently-samplable input domain for the function f; and $\mathcal{X}_k$ is the intended input domain whose elements are to be accumulated.*

Quasi-commutative: *For all* k, *for all* $f \in \mathcal{F}_k$ *for all* $u \in \mathcal{U}_f$ *for all* $x_1, x_2 \in \mathcal{X}_k$, $f(f(u, x_1), x_2) = f(f(u, x_2), x_1)$. *If* $\mathcal{X} = \{x_1, ..., x_m\} \subset \mathcal{X}_k$, *then by* $f(u, \mathcal{X})$ *we denote* $f(f(...(u, x_1), ...), x_m)$.

Witness: *Let* $v \in \mathcal{U}_f$ *and* $x \in \mathcal{X}_k$. *A value* $w \in \mathcal{U}_f$ *is called a witness for* x *in* v *under* f *if* $v = f(w, x)$.

Addition: *Let* $f \in \mathcal{F}_1$, *and* $v = f(u, \mathcal{X})$ *be the accumulator so far. There is an efficient algorithm A to accumulate a given value* $x' \in \mathcal{X}_1$. *The algorithm outputs:*

1. $\mathcal{X}' = \mathcal{X} \cup \{x'\}$ *and* $v' = f(v, x') = f(u, \mathcal{X}')$;
2. w' *which is the witness for* $x \in \mathcal{X}$ *in* v'.

Deletion: *Let* $f \in \mathcal{F}_1$, *and* $v = f(u, \mathcal{X})$ *be the accumulator so far. There exist efficient algorithms* $\mathcal{D}, \mathcal{W}$ *to delete an accumulated value* $x' \in \mathcal{X}$. *The functionality of the algorithms includes:*

1. $\mathcal{D}(aux_f, v, x') = v'$ *such that* $v' = f(u, \mathcal{X}\{x'\})$, *and*
2. $\mathcal{W}(w, x, x', v, v') = v'$ *such that* $f(w', x) = v'$, *where* $x \in \mathcal{X}$ *and* $f(w, x) = v$.

The [4] dynamic accumulator scheme is based on the strong RSA assumption and accumulates prime numbers (i.e., the primes used for the membership certificates in [1] group signature scheme). The scheme also provides a proof that a committed value was accumulated (we will omit these details). The construction of a dynamic accumulator where the domain of accumulated values consists of prime numbers, is as follows:

- $\mathcal{F}_k$ is the family of functions that correspond to exponentiating modulo-safe prime products drawn from the integers of length k. Choosing $f \in \mathcal{F}_k$ amounts to choosing a random modulus $n = pq$ of length k, where $p = 2p' + 1$, $q = 2q' + 1$, and p, p', q, q' are all prime. We will denote f corresponding to modulus n and domain $\mathcal{X}_{A,B}$ by $f_{n,A,B}$.
- $\mathcal{X}_{A,B}$ is the set $\{e \in primes : e \neq p', q' \wedge A \leq e \leq B\}$, where A and B can be chosen with arbitrary polynomial dependence on the security parameter k, as long as $2 < A$ and $B < A^2$. $\mathcal{X}'_{A,B}$ is (any subset of) of the set of integers from $[2, A^2 - 1]$ such that $\mathcal{X}_{A,B} \subseteq \mathcal{X}'_{A,B}$.
- For $f = f_n$, the auxiliary information aux_f is the factorisation of n.
- For $f = f_n$, $\mathcal{U}_f = \{u \in QR_n : u \neq 1\}$ and $\mathcal{U}'_f = \mathbf{Z}^*_n$.
- For $f = f_n$, $f(u, x) = u^x \bmod n$. Note that $f(f(u, x_1), x_2) = f(u(x_1, x_2)) = u^{x_1 x_2} \bmod n$.
- Update of the accumulator value. Adding a value $\tilde{x}$ to the accumulator value v can be done as $v' = f(v, \tilde{x}) = v^{\tilde{x}} \bmod n$. Deleting a value $\tilde{x}$ from the accumulator is as follows: $\mathcal{D}((p, q), v, \tilde{x}) = v^{\tilde{x}^{-1} \bmod (p-1)(q-1)} \bmod n$.
- Update of a witness. Updating a witness u after $\tilde{x}$ has been added can be done by $u' = f(u, \tilde{x}) = u^{\tilde{x}}$. In case, $\tilde{x} \neq x \in \mathcal{X}_k$ has been deleted from the accumulator, the witness u can be updated as follows. By the extended GCD algorithm, one can compute the integers a, b such that $ax + b\tilde{x} = 1 \bmod n$ and then $u' = \mathcal{W}(u, x, \tilde{x}, v, v') = u^b v'^a$.

4   The Auction Protocol

This section describes the auction protocol. A high level view of the protocol is given in Figure 2. Lines dipict communication between parties while the dashed circles indicate stages in the protocol. Lines that pass through the dashed circles are communications that are performed during the particular stage.

4.1 Setup

Most activities of this stage need to be performed only once (in order to establish the auction proceedings). Let $\lambda_1, \lambda_2, \gamma_1$, and γ_2 be some lengths, Λ, Γ be some integral ranges, and $\mathcal{H}(.)$ be a collision-resistant hash function. RM sets up the group public key and his secret key by performing the following steps:

1. Chooses two safe primes p and q (i.e., $p = 2p' + 1$ and $q = 2q' + 1$, where p' and q' are prime numbers) and sets the RSA modulus $n = pq$
2. Chooses random elements $a, a_0, g, h \in QR(n)$
3. Chooses a secret element $x \in_R Z^*_{p'q'}$ and sets $y = g^x \bmod n$
4. Publishes the group public key as $\mathcal{Y} = (n, a, a_0, y, g, h)$
5. Creates the public modulus n for the accumulator, chooses a random $u \in QR_n$ and publishes (n, u)
6. Set up (empty for now) public archives E_{add} for storing values that correspond to added users and E_{delete} for storing values that correspond to deleted users

4.2 Registration

A user submits a request to AM to participate in the auction proceedings. AM verifies the identity of the requestor, and issues a token that is verifiable by RM. The user then takes part in a protocol with RM, in order to obtain his/her secret key and a certificate of membership in the auction proceedings. Note that the token does not carry the real identity of the bidder. All communication between RM and the owner of a token is authenticated and recorded. The protocol between a new bidder i, and RM is as follows (checks in which values are chosen from proper intervals, the user knows discrete logarithms of values, etc. are omitted):

1. Bidder i selects random exponents x'_i, r and sends $C_1 = g^{x'_i} h^r \bmod n$ to the RM
2. RM checks that $C_1 \in QR(n)$. If this is the case, RM selects random values α_i, β_i and sends them to bidder i
3. Bidder i computes $x_i = 2^{\lambda_1} + (\alpha_i x'_i + \beta_i \bmod 2^{\lambda_2})$ and sends to RM the value $C_2 = a^{x_i} \bmod n$
4. RM checks that $C_2 \in QR(n)$. If this is the case, RM selects a random $e_i \in \Gamma$ and computes $B_i = (C_2 a_0)^{1/e_i} \bmod n$ then sends the membership certificate $[B_i, e_i]$ to bidder i (note that $B_i = (a^{x_i} a_0)^{1/e_i} \bmod n$)
5. Bidder i verifies that $a^{x_i} a_0 = B_i^{e_i} \bmod n$
6. Add the current u to the bidder's membership certificate. Update u: $u = f_n(u, e_i)$. Update E_{add}: store e_i there
7. Verify that $f_n(u_i, e_i) = u_i^{e_i} = u$

RM creates a new entry in the membership table and stores bidder i's membership certificate $[B_i, e_i]$ and a transcript of the registration process in this location.

4.3 Setup - Before Each Auction

AM organises the auction (i.e., advertising and calls for auction). AM posts information to the bulletin board regarding the auction including the auction id (which uniquely identifies the auction), the reserve price (minimum winning price that will be accepted), the auction starting time and the auction closing rules.

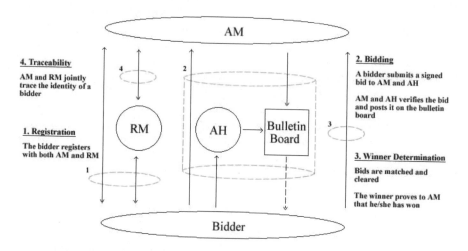

Fig. 2. The Auction Protocol

4.4 Bidding

Using a membership certificate $[B_i, e_i]$, a bidder can generate anonymous and unlinkable group signatures on a bid m. m contains the auction id and the amount of the bid (i.e., $m = id \parallel$ bid value). Bidder i submits a bid m to both AM and AH signed using his/her secret key.

Update Membership - Prior to submitting a bid, a bidder must check if there have been any changes to the group (i.e., new bidders have been added, or other bidders have been revoked). If this is the case, a bidder must perform a membership update. This is done as follows:

An entry in the archive is called "new" if it was entered after the last time bidder i performed an update.

1. Let y denote the old value of u
2. For all new $e_j \in E_{add}$, $u_i = f(u_i, \prod e_j) = u_i^{\prod e_j}$ and $y = y^{\prod e_j}$
3. For all new $e_j \in E_{delete}$, $u_i = W(u_i, e_i, \prod e_j, y, u)$ (Note that as a result $u = f(u_i, e_i)$)

Sign Bid - In order to generate a signature on a message/bid, m, bidder i performs the following:

1. Chooses a random value w and computes:

$$T_1 = B_i y^w \bmod n, \quad T_2 = g^w \bmod n,$$

$$T_3 = g^{e_i} h^w \bmod n$$

2. Chooses r_1, r_2, r_3, r_4 (randomly) from predetermined intervals and computes:

   (a) $d_1 = T_1^{r_1}/(a^{r_2} y^{r_3})$, $\quad d_2 = T_2^{r_1}/(g^{r_3})$, $\quad d_3 = g^{r_4}$, $\quad$ and $d_4 = g^{r_1} h^{r_4}$ (all in mod n),
   (b) $c = \mathcal{H}(g \parallel h \parallel y \parallel a_0 \parallel a \parallel T_1 \parallel T_2 \parallel T_3 \parallel d_1 \parallel d_2 \parallel d_3 \parallel d_4 \parallel m)$,
   (c) $s_1 = r_1 - c(e_i - 2^{\xi_1})$, $\quad s_2 = r_2 - c(x_i - 2^{\lambda_1})$, $\quad s_3 = r_3 - c e_i w$, $\quad$ and $s_4 = r_4 - cw$ (all in Z).

3. In addition to T_1, T_2, and T_3 the bidder computes the values $C_e = g^e h^{r_1}$, $C_u = u h^{r_2}$, and $C_r = g^{r_2} h^{r_3}$ and sends them to AM, with random choices $r_1, r_2, r_3 \in_R Z_{[n/4]}$

4. The output is

$$(c, s_1, s_2, s_3, s_4, r_1, r_2, r_3, r_4, T_1, T_2, T_3, C_e, C_u, C_r)$$

Prove Membership/Verify Bid - AM and AH check the validity of the bidder's signature using the group's public key $\mathcal{Y}$. A bid of the correct form is considered to be valid and is included in the auction (i.e., posted on the bulletin board). An invalid bid is discarded. There are two copies of the bid on the bulletin, one posted by AM and the other posted by AH. AM and AH verify the signature on the bid as follows:

1. Compute (all in mod n):

   $c' = \mathcal{H}(g \parallel h \parallel y \parallel a_0 \parallel a \parallel T_1 \parallel T_2 \parallel T_3 \parallel (a_0^c\, T_1^{(s_1 - c 2^{\xi_1})})/(a^{s_2 - c 2^{\lambda_1}} y^{s_3}) \parallel$
   $(T_2^{s_1 - c 2^{\xi_1}})/(g^{s_3}) \parallel T_2^c g^{s_4} \parallel T_3^c g^{s_1 - c 2^{\xi_1}} h^{s_4} \parallel m)$
2. AM, AH and the bidder engage in a protocol to prove membership (see [4] for details)
3. Accept the signature if and only if $c = c'$, and the parameters s_1, s_2, s_3, s_4 lie in the proper intervals

Bid Cancellation - If a bidder desires to cancel a bid, they must send a copy of the bid they wish to cancel and a CANCEL message signed using his/her group key to both AM and AH. Upon receiving the CANCEL message, AM and AH check the bidder's signature on the message using the group's public key $\mathcal{Y}$. If the signature is valid, AM and AH then check what stage the auction is in. If the auction close rule is currently in an expiration time stage, AM and AH each post a message to the bulletin stating that the particular bid has been cancelled. If the auction is currently in a timeout stage, the CANCEL message is discarded and the bid remains in effect.

4.5 Winner Determination

Once the auction has closed, AM and AH then determine the auction outcome according to which bidder has made the highest bid. The winning bidder can produce a copy of the signed bid as evidence that they have won.

4.6 Traceability

In the event of a dispute, RM (with the help of AM) can open the signature on a bid to reveal which bidder is the original signer. This process is as follows:

1. Check the signature's validity via the verification procedure
2. Recover B_i (and thus the identity of bidder i) as $B_i = T_1/T_2^x \bmod n$

RM then checks the registration transcripts, and determines the token associated with this certificate. AM, who knows the relation between tokens and real identities, can determine the identity of the bidder. Note that in our scheme, revealing the identity of a bidder does not reveal any information about his/her past bids.

4.7 Revocation

When a bidder has been caught breaking the auction rules, they can be permanently revoked from the auction proceedings by cancelling the bidder's ability to sign future bids. To achieve this, the bidder's prime number used in his/her membership certificate is not included when the dynamic accumulator is updated. This can be done as follows: Retrieve e_i which is the prime number corresponding to the bidder's membership certificate. Update u: $u = \mathcal{D}(\psi(n), u, e_i)$. Update E_{delete}: store e_i there.

5 Security

This section provides an informal security analysis of the online English auction scheme presented in this paper based on the characteristics described in Section 1.2.

Unforgeability - Only bidders that are members of the group are able to sign messages on behalf of the group. This is due to the unforgeability of the underlying group signature.

Anonymity - Given a valid signature $(c, s_1, s_2, s_3, s_4, T_1, T_2, T_3)$ identifying the actual signer is computationally difficult. Determining which bidder with certificate $[B_i, e_i]$ has signed a bid, requires deciding whether the three discrete logarithms $\log_y T_1/B_i$, $\log_g T_2$, and $\log_g T_3/g^{e_i}$ are equal. This is assumed to be infeasible under the decisional Diffie-Hellman assumption, and thus anonymity is guaranteed. Note that in our auction, RM can figure out the certificate associated with each signature, but cannot determine the identity of the bidder associated with this certificate.

Table 1. Comparison of English auction schemes

	SS99	OM001	Our Scheme	TX03
Registration	1 exp.	480 mul.	30 exp.	2 exp.
Signing	1 exp.	240 mul.	25 exp.	17 exp.
Verification	1 exp.	320 mul.	21 exp.	16 exp.
Revocation	N/A	$O(\ell)$	$O(1)$	$O(1)$

Unlinkability - Deciding if two signatures $(c, s_1, s_2, s_3, s_4, T_1, T_2, T_3)$ and $(\widetilde{c}, \widetilde{s}_1, \widetilde{s}_2, \widetilde{s}_3, \widetilde{s}_4, \widetilde{T}_1, \widetilde{T}_2, \widetilde{T}_3)$ were computed by the same bidder is computationally hard (with the same argument as for anonymity).

Exculpability - Neither a bidder nor AM, AH and/or RM can sign on behalf of another bidder. This is because the secret key x_i, associated to user i is computationally hidden from RM. RM, at most, can learn $a^{x_i} \bmod n$, which cannot help him to learn the exponent x_i (since the discrete logarithm over the safe composite modulo n, is difficult).

Coalition-resistance - This is due to the following theorem: [1] Under the strong RSA assumption, a group certificate $[B_i = (a^{x_i} a_0)^{1/e_i} \bmod n, e_i]$ with $x_i \in \Lambda$ and $e_i \in \Gamma$ can be generated only by the group manager provided that the number K of certificates the group manager issues is polynomially bounded.

Verifiability - All bids (including signatures) are posted to the public bulletin, therefore all parties can verify the auction outcome.

Robustness - Invalid bids will not be posted to the bulletin board. Moreover, malicious bidders will be revoked from the system, and thus cannot affect the auction outcome.

Traceability - RM is always able to open a valid signature and, with the help of AM, identify the signer of the bid.

Revocation - Bidders can be easily revoked from the future auctions if they have broken the auction rules. See theorem 2 in [4].

One-time registration - Once a bidder has received a signature generation key, they are free to participate in future auctions.

Unskewability - AH observes AM's clock (and vice versa) therefore any clock skews will not go unnoticed. AM's clock can be trusted as long as both AM and AH do not collude.

Unblockability - A bidder must submit his/her bids to both AM and AH, who post the bid on the bulletin board. If either tries to block a bid, then only one confirmation of the bid will be posted to the bulletin board which will indicate that one of the parties has blocked a bid. Bids cannot be blocked unless AM and AH collude.

Conditional bid cancellation - Bidders can conditionally cancel bids by sending a CANCEL message to AM and AH as long as the auction is not in a timeout stage.

6   Efficiency

This section discusses the efficiency considerations of the new scheme. We contrast our approach with the existing English auction schemes. Table 1 shows the amount of work performed during each major stage of the auction in terms of the number of modular exponentiations (exp) or multiplications (mul) required. The schemes compared include: [13] (SS99), [12] (OM01), our scheme, and [14] (TX03). ([14] is an alternate implementation of our approach.)

The registration, signing and verification procedures for SS99 are relatively efficient. However, SS99 do not protect a bidder's identity, nor do they discuss revocation issues. To incorporate revocation into this scheme, it is likely that the registration procedure would have to be repeated between auctions. Furthermore, SS99 do not address the issue of one-time registration. Once again bidders would have to repeat the registration process for each auction they want to participate in.

OM01 is significantly less efficient than SS99. OM01 does not address bid cancellation whereas SS99 does. Furthermore, OM01 does not prevent the Auctioneer from skewing its clock. However, OM01 protects a bidders identity and addresses one-time registration. The cost of one-time registration in OM01 is issuing new keys to bidders between auctions, which is essentially equivalent to re-registering. The revocation method in OM01 is tied in with the one-time registration mechanism and therefore must also be repeated between each auction. To revoke a bidder requires the Auctioneer to perform work proportional to $O(\ell)$ where ℓ is the number of bidders.

In contrast, our scheme has the most practical one-time registration procedure. That is, once a bidder has registered, there is no work required to retain membership other than regularly checking the accumulator. We address bid cancellation, clock-skewing and privacy concerns. To revoke a bidder, the Auctioneer only has to update the accumulator. Bidders must check the accumulator value prior to each bid which is a constant operation. Our auction scheme can also be implemented using TX03 which has significant efficiency gains.

The efficiency of our scheme is comparable to the existing proposals. First of all our scheme has an enhanced set of security requirements that are much more comprehensive. Furthermore, our scheme clearly has the most efficient revocation method. In addition, we have the most practical one-time registration procedure.

7 Conclusions

This paper presented a scheme for conducting secure and anonymous online English auctions. Such a scheme is vital for protecting the security and anonymity of participants who engage in online auctioning. The timeliness of information and verifiability of the Auctioneer's actions is critical in an online English auction. We have shown that the existing "secure" English auction schemes are inadequate for the task. The scheme by [13] does not provide anonymity for the bidders and requires all parties to trust a public Notary. The scheme by [12] does not prevent an Auctioneer from skewing his/her clock or from blocking bids.

In direct contrast, our scheme solves all of the problems of the existing schemes and has a more comprehensive set of security requirements. We use a group signature to provide verification of bids and to protect the identities of bidders. The group signature is modified so that the identity of a bidder is divided among two separate parties (i.e., the anonymity subsystem). The role of the Auctioneer is also divided among two parties to prevent clock-skewing and bid-blocking (i.e., the auction subsystem). The scheme has comparable efficiency to the existing proposal for its enhanced security and privacy characteristics. The efficiency and security of the scheme rests with the underlying group signature scheme used. Our approach offers the client flexibility in choosing from any group signature scheme. The scheme offers efficient one-time registration and revocation procedures that are clearly better suited to handling multiple auctions than existing proposals.

References

1. Ateniese, G., Camenisch, J., Joye, M., Tsudik, G.: A Practical and Provably Secure Coalition-Resistant Group Signature Scheme. In: Bellare, M. (ed.) CRYPTO 2000. LNCS, vol. 1880, pp. 255–270. Springer, Heidelberg (2000)
2. Ateniese, G., Song, D., Tsudik, G.: Quasi-Efficient Revocation of Group Signatures. In: FC 2002. LNCS, vol. 2357, pp. 183–197. Springer-Verlag, Heidelberg (2002)
3. Boyd, C., Mao, W.: Security Issues for Electronic Auctions, Technical Report, Hewlett Packard, TR-HPL-2000-90 (2000)
4. Camenisch, J., Lysyanskaya, A.: Dynamic Accumulators and Application to Efficient Revocation of Anonymous Credentials. In: Yung, M. (ed.) CRYPTO 2002. LNCS, vol. 2442, pp. 61–76. Springer, Heidelberg (2002)
5. Camenisch, J., Stadler, M.: Efficient Group Signature Schemes for Large Groups. In: Kaliski Jr., B.S. (ed.) CRYPTO 1997. LNCS, vol. 1294, pp. 410–424. Springer, Heidelberg (1997)
6. Chaum, D., van Heyst, E.: Group Signatures. In: Davies, D.W. (ed.) EUROCRYPT 1991. LNCS, vol. 547, pp. 257–265. Springer, Heidelberg (1991)
7. Franklin, M., Reiter, M.: The Design and Implementation of a Secure Auction Service. IEEE Transactions on Software Engineering 22, 302–312 (1996)
8. Kumar, M., Feldman, S.: Internet Auctions. In: Proceedings of the Third USENIX Workshop on Electronic Commerce, pp. 49–60 (1998)
9. Lee, B., Kim, K., Ma, J.: Efficient Public Auction with One-Time Registration and Public Verifiability. In: Pandu Rangan, C., Ding, C. (eds.) INDOCRYPT 2001. LNCS, vol. 2247, pp. 162–174. Springer, Heidelberg (2001)
10. Naor, M., Pinkas, B., Sumner, R.: Privacy Preserving Auctions and Mechanism Design. In: The 1st ACM Conference on Electronic Commerce, pp. 129–139 (1999)
11. Nguyen, K., Traore, J.: An On-line Public Auction Protocol Protecting Bidder Privacy. In: Clark, A., Boyd, C., Dawson, E.P. (eds.) ACISP 2000. LNCS, vol. 1841, pp. 427–442. Springer, Heidelberg (2000)
12. Omote, K., Miyaji, A.: A Practical English Auction with One-Time Registration. In: Varadharajan, V., Mu, Y. (eds.) ACISP 2001. LNCS, vol. 2119, pp. 221–234. Springer, Heidelberg (2001)
13. Stubblebine, S., Syverson, P.: Fair On-Line Auctions without Special Trusted Parties. In: Franklin, M.K. (ed.) FC 1999. LNCS, vol. 1648, pp. 230–240. Springer, Heidelberg (1999)
14. Tsudik, G., Xu, S.: Accumulating Composites and Improved Group Signing. In: Laih, C.-S. (ed.) ASIACRYPT 2003. LNCS, vol. 2894, pp. 269–286. Springer, Heidelberg (2003)
15. Trevathan, J.: Security, Anonymity and Trust in Electronic Auctions. Association for Computing Machinery Crossroads, Spring Edition, 11(3), 3–9 (2005)
16. Trevathan, J., Ghodosi, H., Read, W.: Design Issues for Electronic Auctions. In: 2nd International Conference on E-Business and Telecommunication Networks, pp. 340–347 (2005)
17. Trevathan, J., Ghodosi, H., Read, W.: An Anonymous and Secure Continuous Double Auction Scheme. In: 39th International Hawaii Conference on System Sciences, vol. 125, pp. 1–12 (2006)
18. Viswanathan, K., Boyd, C., Dawson, E.: A Three Phased Schema for Sealed Bid Auction System Design. In: Clark, A., Boyd, C., Dawson, E.P. (eds.) ACISP 2000. LNCS, vol. 1841, pp. 412–426. Springer, Heidelberg (2000)

Using Microsoft Office InfoPath to Generate XACML Policies

Manuel Sanchez[1], Gabriel Lopez[1], Antonio F. Gomez-Skarmeta[1], and Oscar Canovas[2]

[1] Department of Information Engineering and Communications
University of Murcia, Spain
{msc,gabilm,skarmeta}@dif.um.es
[2] Department of Computer Engineering
University of Murcia, Spain
ocanovas@ditec.um.es

Abstract. Today, when organizations perform access control over their resources they are not only interested in the user's identity, but in other data such as user's attributes or contextual information. These requirements can be found, for example, in a network access control scenario where end users pay for a specific access level and depending on it, they can get different network quality of service. The network provider has to check, not only the user identity, but the user's attributes to make sure that he can access to the specified resource. These systems are based on the use of policy languages to define the authorization process. However, due to the increasing complexity of current systems, policies are becoming more and more complex to be managed by system administrators. Therefore, in this paper we present an user friendly approach to policy specification, based on the use of high level templates and common desktop applications. These templates are easily built from XML schemas, and once they have been filled, a XACML policy is automatically generated using a XML transformation.

Keywords: Policy editor, XACML, XSLT, access control.

1 Introduction

Access control management is a main concern for domain administrators since target resources have to be protected against unauthorized accesses from malicious attackers. One of the main scenarios is the network access control and several mechanisms have been proposed recently for that, such as 802.1X [9] or PANA [7]. Initially, these mechanisms were only based on user authentication, mainly using shared secrets or public key cryptography. However, they are evolving to more sophisticated proposals performing user authorization based on user attributes, such as NAS-SAML [12]. Usually, the authorization process is guided by a set of rules, that is, the access control policy, which has been usually described by means of specific, and technology dependent, policy languages, such as PERMIS [4] or Akenti [14].

Due to the existence of different proprietary and application specific access control policy languages, policies can not be easily shared between different organizational domains, as described in [6], which involves a serious interoperability drawback. Besides,

J. Filipe and M.S. Obaidat (Eds.): ICETE 2006, CCIS 9, pp. 134–145, 2008.

it makes difficult the development of good editing tools for access control policies. This situation has motivated the creation of a standard access control policy language, named XACML [2], by the OASIS consortium. XACML, which was proposed to become a common framework for defining access control policies, addresses all the requirements of an access control environment and is currently used to represent and evaluate policies in a wide range of authorization scenarios, such as NAS-SAML [11] or systems described in [10] (Cardea and PRIMA). However, this versatility implies a high level of complexity in the policy language definition. Therefore, administrators should have a depth knowledge of XACML in order to define an accurate medium-sized access control policy. For example, in a medium or large organization which needs to protect a high number of resources, policy management may become a very complex task.

Therefore, it would be desirable the existence of software tools to facilitate the development of access control policies from the point of view of the domain administrator, especially when they cannot be considered XACML or security experts. At the moment there are several alternatives to deal with XACML policies, such as general XML editors or even specific XACML editors, but as explained below, all of them present any deficiency. This paper presents a framework to generate XACML policies from user friendly templates that can be filled in by a domain administrator in the same way they write a document in natural language, using the Microsoft®Office InfoPath™utility [8]. Finally, the resulting high level policy files are transformed into the final low level XACML policies by means of XSL transformations [5].

In this way, as Figure 1 shows, to obtain a new XACML policy, the administrator writes the initial document. Then, the security expert of the organization applies the XML transformation to generate the policy. Finally, this policy is added to the XACML repository containing the rest of policies.

The rest of this paper is structured as follows. Section 2 introduces the XACML standard. Section 3 explains the features of the tool used to design user friendly forms

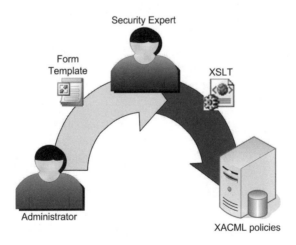

Fig. 1. Policy life cycle

for administrators. The policy life cycle is shown in Section 4. To clarify the policy generation process, Section 5 presents a specific example. Related work is shown in Section 6. Finally, conclusions and future work are presented in Section 7.

2   XACML Policy Language

XACML (eXtensible Access Control Markup Language) [2], the OASIS proposal for a standard access control language, was defined to represent access control policies in a standard way. XACML is XML-based and includes two different specifications: the first one is an access control policy language, which defines the set of subjects that can perform particular actions on a subset of resources; the second one is a representation format to encode access control requests and responses, that is, a way to express queries about whether a particular access should be allowed and the related answers.

As Figure 2 shows, the main element of all XACML policies is a *Policy* or *Policy-Set* element. A PolicySet is a container that can hold other Policies or PolicySets, as well as references to other policies (*PolicyIDReference*). A Policy represents a single access control policy, expressed by a set of *Rules*. A Policy or PolicySet may contain multiple policies or Rules, each of which may evaluate to different access control decisions. XACML needs some way of reconciling the decisions each makes, and this is done through a collection of *Combining Algorithms*. An example of those is the *Permit Overrides Algorithm*, which says that if at least an evaluation returns Permit, then the final result is also Permit. A Policy or PolicySet element may also specify a set of *Obligation Attributes*, that is, a set of actions to be performed if the request has been approved.

XACML provides another feature called *Target*. It is a set of simplified conditions for the Subject, Resource and Action that must be met for a PolicySet, Policy or Rule to apply to a given request. If all the conditions of a Target are met, then its associated PolicySet, Policy, or Rule are applied to the request. Once a Policy is found, the included

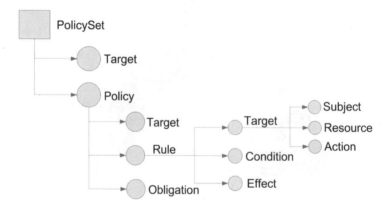

Fig. 2. XACML policy structure

rules are evaluated. The main element of a rule is the *Condition*. If the evaluation of the Condition results true, then the Rule's Effect (Permit or Deny) is returned.

The main object that XACML deals with is attributes. Attributes are named values of known types. Specifically, attributes are characteristics of the Subject, Resource, Action or Environment in which the access request is made.

3   Microsoft Office Infopath

InfoPath [8] is a desktop application which allows organizations to efficiently gather the needed information using dynamic forms. This architecture includes design character-istics which make easy the structured creation and flexible viewing of XML documents. This tool has the following architectural features and design objectives:

- Build an hybrid tool which combines document editing experience with the data capture ability of forms. Users can view and modify abstract data structures using a traditional word-processing environment.
- The use of XML documents belonging to user defined schemas for the input and output. InfoPath uses and produces XML schemas and XSL transformations, and it is integrated with XML Web services standards. When editing an XML document, InfoPath enables adding and deleting valid attributes and XML elements which belong to a XML schema defined by the user. Then, when the XML document is saved or submitted, it remains valid following the XML schema.
- Provide structural editing. InfoPath enables gathering structured and validated XML information which can be reused. Structural editing in InfoPath provides an easy and natural user's interface which allows to normal users add and delete valid XML attributes and elements.
- Provide flexible views to present XML documents in a coherent way to the user. InfoPath uses XSLT to enable the content of the editing views to be organized in a different way that the XML data structure.

Three different validation levels exist in InfoPath: schema based validation, XPath val-idation rules and script based validation. The first validation level helps users to create structured XML documents which are ready to be reused by XML based systems. The second level allows to check conditions, e.g. the value of some field must be greater than a particular minimum. And the third level may define additional validations in the XML document or define other business logic.

Form templates can be designed in several ways, ranging from an existing XML schema or document to defining an XML schema from scratch.

4   Using Templates to Generate Policies

Complexity in policy definition languages makes difficult the specification of the poli-cies governing the access control system. Therefore, a methodology to simplify this task is proposed in this document. The main idea, shown in Figure 3, is that the administrator

Fig. 3. Policy generation

writes a document in natural language expressing what the system must enforce, that is, the set of access control rules. Later, by means of XSL transformations, this document is translated into an XACML policy. Specifically, a set of templates are available to the system administrator, each one for every specific policy existing in the system. These templates define documents that can be used to describe a specific feature of the access control system, such as the roles assigned to each user or the set of roles enabled to access to a specific resource.

Microsoft Word might be used as text editor to design the required templates, but InfoPath has been selected since this tool was specifically designed to work with templates. The design of a policy template is based on a XML schema defining the information elements which can be specified by the administrator. This schema should be designed by an XACML expert, since it has to contain the more relevant elements of the XACML policy.

Once the initial document is written, a XSL transformation must be applied to transform it into the final XACML policy. This can be done either using a XSLT compiler, such as XALAN [3], or some XML editor implementing the XSLT standard, such as XMLSpy [1]. The XSL transform generates the XACML policy completing the required sections using the information from the initial document. As the initial XML schema, the design of the XSLT implies a deep knowledge about the XACML standard, because it is necessary to know how to generate a complete policy fulfilling the XACML specifications.

Consequently, the *"security expert"* is responsible for developing the XML schemas, the policy templates and the XSL transformations for each policy in the organization. On the other hand, specific system administrator, for example administrators who are in charge of the role assignment to users, are able to specify the security policy without any knowledge of XACML. All they have to do is to complete the policy template, expressed in natural language, and this will be automatically transformed into the target XACML policy by means of the XSL transformations. Finally, policies are stored in the XACML repository to make them available to the system.

This kind of policies doesn't have real time requirements, therefore it is not necessary for administrators to apply the XSLT transformation and to store the XACML policy in the repository directly. In this way, administrators only have to fill in the template due to the security expert can perform all the related technical tasks.

```
<xs:element name="Condition">
 <xs:complexType>
  <xs:sequence>
   <xs:element ref="SelectCondition"/>
   <xs:element ref="BooleanCondition"
     minOccurs="0" minOccurs="unbounded">
  </xs:sequence>
 </xs:complexType>
</xs:element>
<xs:element name="BooleanCondition">
 <xs:complexType>
  <xs:sequence>
   <xs:element name="BooleanOperator"/>
   <xs:element ref="SelectCondition"/>
  </xs:sequence>
 </xs:complexType>
</xs:element>
<xs:element name="SimpleCondition">
 <xs:complexType>
  <xs:sequence>
   <xs:element name="LeftElement" type="xs:string"/>
```

```
    <xs:element name="RelationalOperator"/>
    <xs:element name="RightElement" type="xs:string"/>
   </xs:sequence>
  </xs:complexType>
 </xs:element>
 <xs:element name="DoubleCondition">
  <xs:complexType>
   <xs:sequence>
    <xs:element ref="SimpleCondition"/>
    <xs:element name="BooleanOperator"/>
    <xs:element ref="SimpleCondition"/>
   </xs:sequence>
  </xs:complexType>
 </xs:element>
 <xs:element name="SelectCondition">
  <xs:complexType>
   <xs:choice>
    <xs:element ref="SimpleCondition"/>
    <xs:element ref="DoubleCondition"/>
   </xs:choice>
  </xs:complexType>
 </xs:element>
```

Fig. 4. Simplified Condition Element XML Schema

The conversion of the XML document into the XACML policy depends mostly on the specific policy being generated, therefore transformation details are given next using some examples.

4.1 Translating Policy Elements

Definition of the XML schema containing the elements managed by the administrator can be made using the string data type, for attributes, subjects, etc. However, there are special cases needing special attention. For example, obligations commonly express the assignment of a value to an attribute, so they need to be represented as a pair of strings.

A more complicated example is related to *conditions*, because they can be expressed in a variety of ways. For example, $((: current - time \geq 9h)and(: current - time \leq 21h))and((: dayOfWeek \geq Monday)and(: dayOfWeek \leq Friday))$ needs to be represented in a recursive way, but InfoPath does not allow recursive schemas.

Therefore an iterative approach must be taken, where simple relational checks are joined using boolean operators, and new checks are joined to the previous relation as a whole. For example, the condition stated before could be expressed as $((((: current - time \geq 9h)and(: current - time \leq 21h))and(: dayOfWeek \geq Monday))and(: dayOfWeek \leq Friday)$. Moreover, since the most common condition in policies implies two relational comparison in the form of $(x > A)and(x < B)$, this structure can be introduced in the schema to make easy the design of the *Condition* element. Figure 4 shows a simplified view of the *Condition* element schema.

Finally, the basic XML document must be transformed into the complete XACML policy by means of a XSL transformation. Therefore, elements from the basic XML document must be translated into XACML elements, obeying the specific structure, formats and namespaces. The XSL transformation generates the specific policy structure using the *xsl:element* and *xsl:attribute* operators in a fixed way, and then it uses the input XML document generated before to fill in the specific gaps in the final XACML policy. Once the transformation is designed, it has only to be applied to every InfoPath-generated document.

5   Policy Generation for a Network Access Control Authorization Scenario

This section depicts how to generate one of the required policies for the NAS-SAML system, where the main resource to be protected is the communication network.

5.1   NAS-SAML: A Network Access Control Approach Based on SAML and XACML

NAS-SAML [12] is a network access control approach based on X.509 identity certificates and authorization attributes. This proposal is based on the SAML and the XACML standards, which will be used for expressing access control policies based on attributes, authorization statements and authorization protocols. Authorization is mainly based on the definition of access control policies including the sets of users pertaining to different subject domains which will be able to be assigned to different roles in order to gain access to the network of a service provider, under specific circumstances. The starting point is a network scenario based on the 802.1X standard and the AAA (Authentication, Authorization and Accounting) architecture, where processes related to authentication, authorization, and accounting are centralized.

The system operates as follows. Every end user belongs to a home domain, where he was given a set of attributes stating the roles he plays. When the end user requests a network connection in a particular domain by means of a 802.1X connection, the request is obtained by the AAA server, and it makes a query to obtain the attributes linked to the user from an authority responsible for managing them, based on a *Role Assignment Policy*. In case the user's home domain is based on a different authorization system, the AAA server uses a credential conversion service, as defined in [6], to translate the user's authorization credentials into internal format, based on a *Conversion Policy*. Finally, the AAA server sends an authorization query to a policy decision point (PDP), which consults a *Resource Access Policy*. The PDP firsty recognizes if the user belongs to well known source domain, by means of the *Role Allocation Policy* sub-policy. Then, it checks if the user is allowed or not to use the target resource, by means of the *Target Access Policy* sub-policy. Furthermore, it also establishes the set of obligations derived from the given decision, for example some QoS properties, security options, etc. This general scheme works both in single and inter-domain scenarios, and using both push an pull based communications.

5.2   Editing the Target Access Policy

This section shows an example of how one of the policies introduced in NAS-SAML (*Target Access Policy*), can be defined by means of the proposed policy editor. First, the *Target Access Policy* is described, and next the policy template is generated step by step.

Target XACML Policy. As described in [11], the *Target Access Policy* comprises a set of *target access* elements. Each of them grants a user playing a specified set of roles the permission to carry out the specified actions on the specified list of targets, but only if the are satisfied conditions. Every *target access* element has the following elements:

- *Attributes:* Set of allowed attributes or enabled roles to execute the actions on the resource.
- *Resources:* Set of controlled resources.
- *Actions:* Set of allowed actions over the resource.
- *Conditions:* Users holding some of the attributes have permission to execute some actions on the specified resources only if the conditions are fulfilled. Otherwise, the permission will be denied. These conditions can establish time constraints or other constraints related to contextual information.
- *Obligations:* Once the action has been granted, some obligations defining network properties might be applied. Obligations can specify options related to network addressing, security or QoS properties that must be enforced.

Figure 6 shows an example of the *Target Access Policy*. In this figure we can see a *PolicySet* element, where *Target* defines the role type and value, in this case *role-id* and *Student*. Besides, it contains a *Policy* to define that the *wireless-network* resource, can be *used* by the users playing that role. This example also shows the set of obligations derived from this decision. That is, if a user holding the *Student* role, requests *wireless-network* connection, it should obtain an IPv6 address from the range *2001:720:1710:100::/64* and the network must guarantee a quality of service established by *Class1*.

Definition of the XML Schema. To define the initial XML schema, we have to identify first the policy elements the administrator needs to complete in order to create a new policy instance. In this example, as described above, these elements are the attributes, the rights which are going to be granted, the resource/access pair, the conditions which have to be fulfilled to apply the policy decision and the obligations which may be derived. In this way, we can define an XML schema where an *Attribute* and several *Resource/Action* pairs are specified. Besides, *Condition* and *Obligation* need to be stated as optional elements. Figure 5 clarifies this structure.

Definition of the XSL Transformation. The next step in the policy template generation process is the definition of the XSL transformation, which has to translate the document in natural language written by the system administrator into the final XACML policy. The resulting XACML policy is structured using a *PolicySet* to specify the *Attribute*. Then, for each resource/action pair, a new *Policy* is added with the *Resource*, *Action*, *Condition* and *Obligation* elements. The XSL transformation creates the XACML policy in a fixed way and then fills in some specific gaps using the information contained in the initial document.

Figure 8 shows a fragment of the XSL transformation used to generate the target access policy in this example. It is interesting to see how the XACML police structure is generated in a fixed way using the *xsl:element* and *xsl:attribute* operators, while the suitable gaps are completed using the sentence *xsl:value-of select="text()"* to extract the information from the initial XML document.

Design of the InfoPath Form Template. The final step in this process lies in the design of the InfoPath template to enable the system administrator an easy way to create

Fig. 5. XML schema representation

```
<PolicySet PolicySetId="TargetAccessPolicy">                    <Actions>
  <Target>                                                        <Action>
    <Subjects>                                                      <ActionMatch>
      <Subject>                                                       <AttributeValue>enable</AttributeValue>
        <SubjectMatch>                                                <ActionAttributeDesignator AttributeId="action-id"/>
          <AttributeValue>Student</AttributeValue>                  </ActionMatch>
          <SubjectAttributeDesignator AttributeId="role-id"/>     </Action>
        </SubjectMatch>                                           </Actions>
      </Subject>                                                </Target>
    </Subjects>                                                </Rule>
  </Target>                                                    <Obligations>
  <Policy PolicyId="WirelessPermission">                         <Obligation ObligationId="obligation-id" FulfillOn="Permit">
    <Target/>                                                      <AttributeAssignment AttributeId="Framed-IPv6-Prefix">
    <Rule RuleId="ruleid" Effect="Permit">                           2001:720:1710:100::/64</AttributeAssignment>
      <Target>                                                     </Obligation>
        <Resources>                                                <Obligation ObligationId="obligation-id" FulfillOn="Permit">
          <Resource>                                                 <AttributeAssignment AttributeId="QoS-Filter-Rule">
            <ResourceMatch>                                            Class1</AttributeAssignment>
              <AttributeValue>wireless-network</AttributeValue>     </Obligation>
              <ResourceAttributeDesignator AttributeId=":resource-id"/>  </Obligations>
            </ResourceMatch>                                      </Policy>
          </Resource>                                          </PolicySet>
        </Resources>
```

Fig. 6. Target Access Policy example

new policies without XACML knowledge. This is done with the InfoPath editor, which allows to import the XML schema defining the template. Figure 7 shows an example of template designed using this editor.

6   Related Work

This section analyzes two main tools which are currently used to manage XACML policies, XMLSpy[1] and UMU-XACML-Editor [15]. The first one is a powerful and commercial generic XML editor, the second one is a specific XACML editor developed by the University of Murcia.

XMLSpy is an IDE designed to work with XML documents in general, which allows users to enter data into XML documents as they would into a word processor-type application. It allows the definition of XML documents in multiple editing formats, well-formedness checking and built-in validator, intelligent editing, definition of XSLT documents, code generation, etc. These characteristics enable users to specify the XACML schema in the IDE and thus generate XACML policies from scratch in a fast way. The user builds the policy adding each element step by step and checking that it is well formed.

UMU-XACML-Editor is a XACML policy definition open source software, developed using Java, which fulfills the XACML 2.0 standard. This editor is specifically

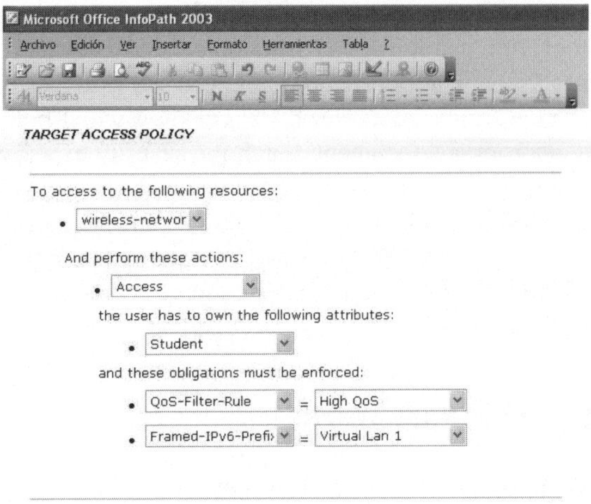

Fig. 7. Target access policy form template

```
<xsl:stylesheet>
  <xsl:output method="xml"/>
  <xsl:template match="WordTargetAccessPolicy">
    <xsl:element name="PolicySet">
      <xsl:attribute name="PolicySetId">
        GeneratedAccessPolicySet
      </xsl:attribute>
      <xsl:attribute name="RuleCombiningAlgId">
        permit-overrides
      </xsl:attribute>
      <xsl:element name="Description">
        Descritpion of the policy
      </xsl:element>
      <xsl:element name="Target">
        <xsl:element name="Subjects">
          <xsl:apply-templates select="Attribute"/>
        </xsl:element>
        <xsl:element name="Resources">
          <xsl:element name="AnyResource"/>
        </xsl:element>
        <xsl:element name="Actions">
          <xsl:element name="AnyAction"/>
        </xsl:element>
      </xsl:element>
      <xsl:apply-templates select="ResourcePolicy"/>
    </xsl:element>
  </xsl:template>
  <xsl:template match="WordTargetAccessPolicy/Attribute">
    <xsl:element name="Subject">
      <xsl:element name="SubjectMatch">
        <xsl:attribute name="MatchId">
          urn:oasis:names:tc:xacml:1.0:function:string-equal
        </xsl:attribute>
        <xsl:element name="AttributeValue">
          <xsl:attribute name="DataType">
            http://www.w3.org/2001/XMLSchema#string
          </xsl:attribute>
          <xsl:value-of select="text()"/>
        </xsl:element>
        <xsl:element name="SubjectAttributeDesignator">
          <xsl:attribute name="AttributeId">
            role-id
          </xsl:attribute>
          <xsl:attribute name="DataType">
            http://www.w3.org/2001/XMLSchema#string
          </xsl:attribute>
        </xsl:element>
      </xsl:element>
    </xsl:element>
  </xsl:template>
  ...
  </xsl:template>
...
</xsl:stylesheet>
```

Fig. 8. XSL transformation fragment

designed to create and modify XACML policies, providing facilities to manage these policies. It is free and can be downloaded from the OASIS's XACML Home Page [13].

Although both solutions deals with XACML in a proper way, the main problem is that they work directly with XACML policies. In this way, the system administrator has to known the XACML standard to create a new policy. But also, he has to decide how to organize the elements in the XACML structure to express correctly the meaning of the policy. With our proposal, this work is made only once for each kind of policy. Besides, only one person, the security expert, has to deal with the XACML related work.

Furthermore, each XACML editor has its own editing interface and its own characteristics, so the system administrator has to learn how to use these programs before start editing policies. However, we provide standard templates to create the XACML policies. Therefore, the system administrator opens the template and completes it as he was writing a natural language specification. He does not need any previous knowledge to start editing the policies of the organization. He only has to know which policy wants to define and then writes the appropriate document. Later, the security expert will deal with the automatic translation from the natural language document to the XACML policy.

Finally, related to modifications in policy format, when using a generic XML editor we have to specify the new XACML schema to generate new policies. On the other hand, with the specific UMU-XACML editor, the source code has to be modified to add the new elements and relations.

7   Conclusions and Future Work

XACML has appeared to cover the need of the current authorization systems to represent in a standard language the access control policies used to control critical resources. Most of those current systems are migrating their specific policies to XACML in order to offer a more scalable and extensible solution.

The fact that XACML is a very helpful tool for secure domain administrator does not imply that it is easy to use. In a typical access control scenario, during a routine policy creation or update, the domain administrator does not have to deal with complex XML schemes and documents but only with the fulfillment of the set of permissions assigned to users under specific circumstances. In fact, the domain administrator could not even understand the XACML language.

It shows the need of tools able to help domain administrators to deal with complex XML documents in a natural language. Moreover, this paper shows that current generic XML or specific XACML editors do not fulfill these requirements.

We have defined a way to manage those XML documents in a transparent way for the domain administrator, making use of a word-processing style editor such as Microsoft InfoPath. In this way, once the necessary XML templates and transformations are created by a XACML expert, the domain administrator can define low level XACML policies using human readable forms.

The sample scenario we have used to test the proposed solution is the NAS-SAML infrastructure. This paper shows how the *Target Access Policy* template and its associated XSL transformation can be generated by a security expert to make easy the administration tasks to the network administrator. The rest of policies used in this scenario can be defined in a similar way.

Finally, the solution proposed in this work can be also used to define other kind of documents based on other XML specification, such as [14,4].

References

1. Altova (2006), XMLSpy®http://www.altova.com/xmlspy
2. Anderson, A., Parducci, B., Adams, C., Flinn, D., Brose, G., Lockhart, H., Beznosov, K., Kudo, M., Humenn, P., Godik, S., Andersen, S., Crocker, S., Moses, T.: EXtensible Access Control Markup Language (XACML) Version 1.0. OASIS Standard (2003)

3. Apache Software Foundation. The apache xalan project (2006),
   `http://xalan.apache.org`
4. Chadwick, D., Otenko, O., Ball, E.: Implementing role based access controls using x.509 attribute certificates. IEEE Internet Computing, 62–69 (2003)
5. Clark, J.: XSL Transformation (XSLT). W3C Recommendation (1999)
6. Canovas, O., Lopez, G., Gómez-Skarmeta, A.: A Credential Conversion Service for SAML-based Scenarios. In: Katsikas, S.K., Gritzalis, S., López, J. (eds.) EuroPKI 2004. LNCS, vol. 3093, pp. 297–305. Springer, Heidelberg (2004)
7. Forsberg, D., Ohba, Y., Patil, B., Tschofenig, H., Yegin, A.: Protocol for Carrying Authentication for Network Access (PANA). Internet Draft (2005)
8. Hoffman, M.: Architecture of Microsoft Office InfoPath 2003. Microsoft Technical Report (2003)
9. IEEE Computer Society, P802.1x/d11: Standard for port based network access control. IEEE Draft (2001)
10. Lorch, M., Proctor, S., Lepro, R., Kafura, D., Shah, S.: First Experiences Using XACML for Access Control in Distributed Systems. In: ACM Workshop on XML Security (2002)
11. Lopez, G., Canovas, O., Gomez, A.F.: Use of xacml policies for a network access control service. In: Proceedings 4th International Workshop for Applied PKI, IWAP 2005, pp. 111–122. IOS Press, Amsterdam (2005)
12. Lopez, G., Canovas, O., Gomez, A.F., Jimenez, J.D., Marin, R.: A network access control approach based on the aaa architecture and authorzation attributes. Journal of Network and Computer Applications JNCA (to be published, 2006)
13. OASIS (2006). OASIS eXtensible Access Control Markup Language (XACML)TC,
    `http://www.oasis-open.org/committees/tc_home.php?wg_abbrev=xacml`
14. Thompson, M., Essiari, A., Mudumbai, S.: Certificate-based authorization policy in a PKI environment. ACM Transactions on Information and System Security (TISSEC) 6, 566–588 (2003)
15. University of Murcia, UMU XACML editor. (2006), `http://xacml.dif.um.es`

Least Privilege in Separation Kernels

Timothy E. Levin, Cynthia E. Irvine, and Thuy D. Nguyen

Department of Computer Science, Naval Postgraduate School
833 Dyer Rd., Monterey, CA USA
{Levin,irvine,tdnguyen}@nps.edu

Abstract. We extend the separation kernel abstraction to represent the enforcement of the principle of least privilege. In addition to the inter-block flow control policy prescribed by the traditional separation kernel paradigm, we describe an orthogonal, finer-grained flow control policy by extending the protection of elements to subjects and resources, as well as blocks, within a partitioned system. We show how least privilege applied to the actions of subjects provides enhanced protection for secure systems.

Keywords: Assurance, Computer Security, Least Privilege, Separation Kernel.

1 Introduction

The Sisyphean purgatory of penetrate and patch to which users of commodity systems are currently subjected has lead to increasing recognition that platforms with assurance of penetration resistance and non-bypassability are required for certain critical functions. This need for high assurance calls for a layered system architecture where enforcement mechanisms of the most critical policies themselves depend upon layers of no less assurance. For many high assurance systems currently being planned or developed, a general-purpose security kernel may provide more functionality than necessary, which has resulted in increased interest in the use of separation kernels to support real-time embedded systems and virtual machine monitors (VMM). Many of these separation kernels are minimized to have both static policies and static allocation of resources, such as is suitable for certain fixed-configuration or embedded environments.

Despite a resurgence of interest in the separation kernel approach, the principle of least privilege (PoLP) [19] is often overlooked in the design of traditional separation kernels due to the belief that a separation kernel should only be concerned with resource isolation. A principal consequence of this omission is that problems relating to all-or-nothing security and over-privileged programs are left for application designers (and security evaluators) to resolve. For systems that must protect highly sensitive or highly valuable resources, formal verification of the ability of the system to enforce its security policy is required. Recent advances in the assurance requirements for high assurance systems [14] have included verification of the target system's conformance to the principle of least privilege. To provide vendors and integrators with tools to formally describe least privilege in separation kernels, a least privilege separation model is presented.

J. Filipe and M.S. Obaidat (Eds.): ICETE 2006, CCIS 9, pp. 146–157, 2008.
© Springer-Verlag Berlin Heidelberg 2008

1.1 A Least Privileged Separation Kernel

In the context of a research project to build a high assurance separation kernel [10] we have extended the separation kernel abstraction so that the principle of least privilege can be examined at the model level and can be verified to be enforced by systems that conform to that model.

The traditional separation kernel paradigm describes a security policy in which activities in different blocks of a partitioned system are not visible to other blocks, except perhaps for certain specified flows allowed between blocks. (Here, "block" is defined in the traditional mathematical sense as a member of the non-intersecting set of elements that comprise the partition 0). If information flow is described only at the block level, then everything in a block can flow to everything in another block. This is contrary to the principle of least privilege required in high assurance systems. The least privilege separation model builds on the traditional separation abstraction by extending the granularity of described elements to the subjects [9] and resources within the partition. An orthogonal flow control policy can then be expressed relative to subjects and resources, thus providing all of the functionality and protection of the traditional separation kernel, combined with a high level of confidence that the effects of subjects' activities may be minimized to their intended scope.

In the sections that follow we will elaborate on the concept of separation kernels and the need for least privilege in such systems. In particular, the granularity of inter-block flows will be discussed in terms of "subject" and "resource" abstractions. A formalization of the least privilege separation model is presented and several aspects of secure system design and verification are discussed with respect to the model. The last sections of the paper review related work, and summarize our results.

2 Concepts

2.1 The Separation Kernel

The term separation kernel was introduced by Rushby, who originally proposed, in the context of a distributed system, that a separation kernel creates "within a single shared machine, an environment which supports the various components of the system, and provides the communications channels between them, in such a way that individual components of the system cannot distinguish this shared environment from a physically distributed one" [18]. A separation kernel divides all resources under its control into blocks such that the actions of an active entity (i.e., a subject) in one block are isolated from (viz., cannot be detected by or communicated to) an active entity in another block, unless an explicit means for that communication has been established (e.g., via configuration data).

A separation kernel achieves isolation of subjects in different blocks by virtualization of shared resources: each block encompasses a resource set that appears to be entirely its own. To achieve this objective for resources that can only be utilized by one subject at a time, such as the CPU, the ideal separation kernel must ensure that the temporal usage patterns of subjects from different blocks are not apparent to each other. Other resources, such as memory, may be accessed by different blocks simultaneously, while preserving idealized isolation, if the separation kernel ensures, for example, that blocks are allocated different and non-interacting portions of the resource. Furthermore, kernel utilization of its own internal resources must also preserve the desired isolation properties.

Separation kernels differ from virtual machine monitors, in that support for communication between blocks is required in the former, whereas a functional replication of the hardware interface is required in the latter. Specific implementations may, however, provide both kinds of support.

2.2 The Principle of Least Privilege

Saltzer and Schroeder concluded that least privilege is one of the eight design principles that can reduce design flaws [19]. They defined least privilege by stating "every program and every user of the system should operate using the least set of privileges necessary to complete the job. Primarily, this principle limits the damage that can result from an accident or error. It also reduces the number of potential interactions among privileged programs to the minimum for correct operation, so that unintentional, unwanted, or improper uses of privilege are less likely to occur."

A decade later, the U.S. Department of Defense included a similar definition of least privilege in the Trusted Computer System Evaluation Criteria (TCSEC) [6]. Layering, modularity and information hiding are constructive techniques for least privilege that can be applied to the internal architecture of the underlying trusted foundation (e.g., separation kernel) to improve the system's resistance to penetration. The kernel can also be configured to utilize protection mechanisms such as access control and fine-grained execution domains to limit the abilities of a subject so that it is constrained to perform only the tasks for which it is authorized.

2.3 High Assurance Criteria and Least Privilege

The TCSEC refers to the principle of Least Privilege in two different contexts: the internal structure of the "trusted computing base" (TCB), and the ability of the TCB to grant to subjects a minimal set of authorizations or privileges. Despite the lack of an explicit reference to the principle of least privilege, the Common Criteria (CC) [5] provides the groundwork for it in several ways. It defines assurance as "grounds for confidence that an entity meets its security objectives." The CC explains that the correctness and effectiveness of the security functions are the primary factors for establishing the assurance that security objectives are met. A high assurance separation kernel must be proven to correctly implement the security functions defined in its specifications and effectively mitigate risks to a level commensurate with the value of the assets it protects. To complement the formal proof, a constructive analysis is used to demonstrate that the implementation maps to the specification. Thus, a focus on resource separation and the structured allotment of privileges affords simplicity to the separation kernel, and enables a high assurance analysis of the correctness of its implementation.

If a system cannot restrict individual users and programs to have only the access authorizations that they require to complete their functions, the accountability mechanisms (e.g., audit) will likely be less able to accurately discern the cause of various actions. A securely deployed system must be capable of supporting least privilege, and must have been administratively configured such that any programs that might execute will be accorded access to the minimal set of resources required to complete their jobs. To provide high assurance of policy enforcement, a system should be able to apply least privilege at the same granularity as the resource abstractions that it exports (e.g., individual files and processes).

2.4 Practical Considerations

In the commercial security community, the use of the principle of least privilege has taken on the primary meaning, over time, of placing limits on the set of simultaneous policy-exemption privileges that a single user or application program can hold, such as may be associated with a 'root' process on a UNIX system. The commercial use of "least privilege" is not concerned with internal TCB structure or with the limitation of normal file-access authorizations for non-privileged processes. Note however, that a separation kernel has no notion of policy-exemption privileges or of privileged processes -- if the SK does not provide individual authorizations to the resources available at its interface, it cannot be used provide least privilege protection in the application domain. It is also noted that commercial product vendors have long ignored the assurance benefits of well-structured code. Thus, commercial product development experience and precedence in the area of PoLP is not germane to the construction of high robustness separation kernels, wherein both contexts of PoLP must be applied.

In practice, a separation kernel providing strict isolation is of little value. Controlled relaxation of strict separation allows applications to interact in useful ways, including participation in the enforcement of application-level policies. In the latter case, applications hosted on a separation kernel will need to be examined and evaluated to ensure that the overall system security policies are enforced. A monolithic application that runs with the same set of privileges throughout all of its modules and processes is hard to evaluate. In order to reason about the assurance properties of the system, the applications should be decomposed into components requiring varying levels of privilege. Such decomposition is more meaningful if the privilege boundaries are enforced by the separation kernel, rather than relying on, for example, error-prone ad hoc agreements between programmers or integrators. The principle of least privilege affords a greater degree of scrutiny to the evaluation of both the kernel and the application, resulting in a higher level of assurance that the overall system security objectives are met.

To better understand the use of least privilege in a separation kernel, we now turn to a closer examination of isolation and flows in these systems.

3 Inter-block Flows

The first-order goal of a separation kernel is to provide absolute separation of the (effects of) activities occurring in different blocks. In practice, however, separation kernels are often used to share hardware among kindred activities that have reason to communicate in some controllable fashion. Therefore, we include in the separation kernel a policy and mechanism for the controlled sharing of information between blocks.

The control of information flow between blocks can be expressed abstractly in an access matrix, as shown in the example of Table 1. This allows arbitrary sharing to be defined, establishing the inter-block flow policy to be enforced on the separation kernel applications.

Table 1. Block-to-Block Flow Matrix

	Block A	**Block B**	**Block C**
Block A	RWX	W	-
Block B	-	RWX	W
Block C	-	-	RWX

Notice that an inter-block flow policy in which the flow relationships partially order the blocks, such as in Table 1, may be suitable for the enforcement by the separation kernel of a *multilevel* confidentiality or integrity policy if meaningful sensitivity labels are immutable attributes of the blocks. Under the conditions that a static separation kernel does not change the policy or resource allocation during execution, and that the policy is not changed while the separation kernel is shut down, the policy may be considered to be global and persistent, viz. non-discretionary. In this example, information flows (represented by $\Rightarrow$) form the following ordering: Block A $\Rightarrow$ Block B $\Rightarrow$ Block C. An assignment of labels to these blocks in conjunction with the rules defined in Table 1 results in a recognizable multilevel security policy:

```
Block A := Unclassified
Block B := Secret
Block C := Top Secret
```

The block-to-block flow policy allows all of the information in a "source" block (e.g., Block A, above) to flow to every element of a "target" block (e.g., Block B, above). Extending the Table 1 scenario, if block B is also allowed to write to block A, for example to implement a downgrade function with respect to the assigned labels, then all of the code or program(s) in block B would need to be examined to ensure that their activities correspond to the intended downgrading semantics. If this assurance of correct behavior cannot be provided, such a circular flow ($A \Rightarrow B \Rightarrow A$) would create, in effect, one large policy equivalence class consisting of all of the information in blocks A and B.

To limit the effects of block-to-block flows, we next introduce the notion of controlling how much information is to be allowed to flow between and within blocks.

4 Least Privilege Flow Control

The implementation of a separation kernel results in the creation of active entities (subjects) that execute under the control of the separation kernel and the virtualization of system resources exported at the kernel interface (see Figure 1). Historically, many security models have utilized the abstraction of an object [10]. Because objects have been classified in various ways, we decided to avoid this nomenclature issue by simply modeling "resources." Similarly, as the definition of "resources" includes the abstractions that are exported by the separation kernel, "subjects" are defined to be a type of resource.

Resources are defined as the totality of all hardware, firmware and software and data that are executed, utilized, created, protected or exported by the separation kernel. Exported resources are those resources (including subjects) to which an explicit reference is possible via the separation kernel interface. That interface may include programming, administrative, and other interfaces. In contrast, internal resources are those resources for which no explicit reference is possible via the kernel interface.

Various implementations of separation kernels have elected to describe the system only in terms of blocks without describing the active system entities that cause information flow. Since the concept of subjects [10] is a term of art – and for good reason – we will use it to describe the active entities exported by in the separation kernel.

We have found the use of the subject abstraction to be indispensable for reasoning about security in secure systems. Without the subject abstraction, it may be difficult to understand, for example, which block in a partitioned system is the cause of a flow between blocks [1] (e.g., the flow could have been caused by the receiving block as a reader or by the sending block as a writer), which application programs within a block need to be trusted (e.g., evaluated with respect to the security policy), and how to minimally configure the programs and resources of such a system to achieve the principle of least privilege. Just as when writing prose, if actions are described *passively* (i.e., not attributable to the subject of a sentence) the cause of the action can be ambiguous. In addition, use of subjects permits construction of a resource-to-block allocation that provides a minimal configuration for least privilege (see Section 4.3). Modeling of subjects within a partition also allows the representation and examination of more complex architectures such as multiple rings of execution, as well as multithreaded and multi-process approaches.

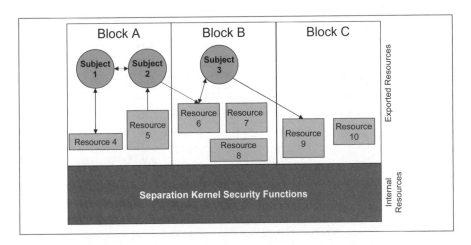

Fig. 1. Example Separation Kernel Configuration

Figure 1 shows an example separation kernel system with three blocks, three subjects, a set of other resources, and some designated flows.

An allocation of subjects and other exported resources to blocks is illustrated in Table 2, i.e., a "tagging" of each subject and resource with its partition (per Figure 1). Of the resources described in this table, the first three are subjects and the remaining exported resources are passive. Every resource is allocated to one and only one block. Consequently, we can state that the blocks of the separation kernel constitute a partition (in the mathematical sense) where: R is the nonempty set of resources and B is a nonempty set of subsets of R such that each element of R belongs to exactly one of the elements of B. From elementary set theory, it is known that a partition, B, can be used to create an equivalence relation on R. Thus we may induce that the allocation of resources to partitions creates equivalence classes.

Table 2. Resource to Block Allocation

	Resources									
	1	2	3	4	5	6	7	8	9	10
Blocks	A	A	B	A	A	B	B	B	C	C

The principle of least privilege requires that each subject be given only the privileges required to do its particular task and no more. The separation kernel can support this objective by assigning access rights appropriately to the subjects within the block. Rules can be defined for accessing different resources within a block. Table 3 illustrates how allocations to support the principle of least privilege are possible when the separation kernel supports per-subject and per-resource flow-control granularity: no subject is given more access than what is required to allow the desired flows (only the resources that are part of a flow are shown in this table).

Table 3. Subject-to-Resource Flow Matrix

		Resources					
		1	2	4	5	6	9
Subjects	1	-	RW	RW	-	-	-
	2	RW	-	-	R	W	-
	3	-	-	-	-	RW	W

Together, Tables 2 and 3 show abstract structures which allow only the flows illustrated in Figure 1. It is clear that the corresponding Block-to-Block flow matrix in Table 1, by itself, would allow many more flows than those illustrated in Figure 1.

5 Applications of Least Privilege

5.1 Kernel-Controlled Interference

In practical MLS system policies, several cases arise in which the normal information flow rules are enhanced. For example, (1) a high confidentiality user may need to downgrade a file and send it to a low confidentiality user, and (2) a high integrity user may need to read a low integrity executable file (viz., a program). In both cases, the system may allow the transfer if the file passes through an appropriate filter: in the former, the filter must ensure that the file does not include any high-confidentiality information; in the latter case, the filter must ensure that the file does not include any Trojan Horses. These system policies allow a "controlled" interference of the low sensitivity domain (sometimes called "intransitive noninterference" [18]). That is, a flow connecting two endpoint processes is prohibited except when going through an intermediate filter process.

A typical implementation of these policies in separation kernel and security kernel architectures is to use a "trusted subject," in which the filter process is assigned a security range that spans the confidentiality or integrity range of the endpoint processes. However, this solution has the drawback that the kernel allows the filter process to access all information in both domains. With a Least Privilege Separation Kernel, the kernel can be configured to restrict the interference to a specific subset of the information in each domain, thereby requiring less trust in to be placed the filter process, as shown in Figure 2.

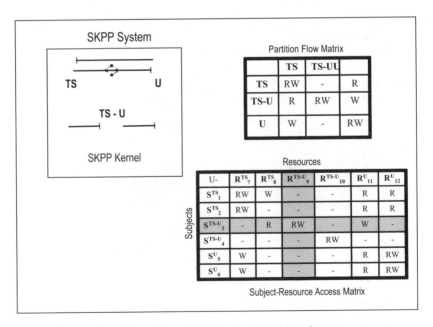

Fig. 2. Kernel-based Strictly-Controlled Interference

5.2 Regraders

Within a block, it may be necessary to perform certain transformations on information that change its security attributes. For example, a guard [3] performs information review and downgrading functions; and a quality assurance manager transforms prototype code into production code by re-grading it in terms of reliability. For each of these transformations there may be several subjects within a block performing various aspects of the task at hand. The principle of least privilege requires that each of these subjects be given only the privileges required to do its particular task and no more.

An example of the application of least privilege separation is that of a "downgrader," (see Figure 3) for re-grading selected information from classified to unclassified. An initiator (UInit) process in A writes selected classified information to a classified holder buffer in Block A. An untrusted copier process moves the contents of the holder to the dirty-word search workspace in Block B. An untrusted dirty-word search process (UDWS) in B provides advisory confirmation that the information is "suitable" for downgrading and copies the information into the clean results buffer (note that this process's actions should be considered "advisory" since it is fully constrained by the mandatory policy enforcement mechanism). Then the trusted downgrader (TDG) program in C reads the information from the clean results buffer and writes it to an unclassified receiver buffer in D where it may be accessed by an unclassified end-point process (UEnd). As constrained by least privilege as encoded in the subject-to-resource flow matrix, the downgrader process in Block C cannot read from any resource other than the clean results and cannot write to any resource in D other than the receiver.

This limits damage in the event of errors, for example in the downgrader, initiator or search processes, and contributes to a substantive argument that only the downgrader program needs to be *trusted* with respect to the application-level multilevel policy (viz., *depended* on to write down only when appropriate), and thus requires security verification with respect to that policy.

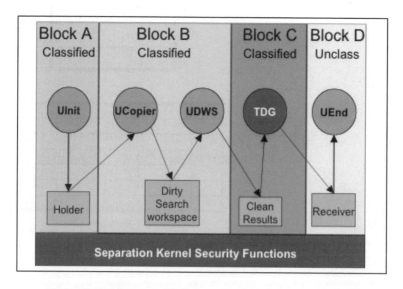

Fig. 3. Trusted Downgrader. Dark areas with white text are trusted.

6 Related Work

6.1 Protection Profiles for Separation Kernels

The Common Criteria security evaluation paradigm includes a document called a *protection profile* that specifies the security functionality and assurance for an entire class of IT products, as well as a document called a *security target*, which provides a similar specification for a specific IT product. The protection profile is evaluated for consistency with the Common Criteria requirements for protection profiles; the security target is evaluated for consistency with the Common Criteria requirements for security targets, as well as for consistency with an identified protection profile (if any); and finally the product is evaluated against the security target.

A forthcoming high robustness protection profile for separation kernels [11]; [15] includes least privilege requirements regarding subjects as well as kernel-internal mechanisms. Several commercial efforts are underway to develop separation kernels to meet this profile, include those at Greenhills, and LinuxWorks [2].

6.2 Trusted Computing Exemplar Project

Separation kernel technology is being applied in our *Trusted Computing Exemplar* project [7]. This ongoing effort is intended to produce a high assurance least privilege separation kernel. The kernel will have a static runtime resource configuration and its security policy regarding access to resources will be based on process/resource access bindings, via offline configuration (e.g., via an access matrix, such as are shown in Figures 1, 2 and 4). The static nature of resource allotment will provide predictable processing behavior, as well as limit the *covert channels* based on shared resource utilization [10]; [9]; [13]. Simple process synchronization primitives will also be provided, that can be implemented to be demonstrably free of covert channels (Reed, 1979). This kernel is also used as the security foundation for the SecureCore architecture [7].

6.3 Type Enforcement Architectures

Bobert and Kain [4] described a "type enforcement architecture" with the capability to provide least privilege at a fine granularity, a form of which is used in the SELinux project [12]. There are currently no high assurance instances of such systems today.

7 Conclusions

The separation kernel abstraction and the principle of least privilege are significant tools for the protection of critical system resources. In this paper, we described a fusion of the separation abstraction with the least privilege principle. In addition to the inter-block flow control policy prescribed by the traditional separation kernels, this approach supports an orthogonal, finer-grained flow control policy by extending the granularity of protected elements to subjects and resources, as well as blocks, in a partitioned system. We showed how least privilege provides assurance that the effects of subjects' activities may be minimized to their intended scope.

In summary, application of the principle of least privilege, resource separation and controlled sharing are synergistic security properties in a separation kernel. Each subject is only given a minimum set of logically separated resources necessary to perform its assigned task, and the sharing of resources between subjects is rigorously controlled by the kernel. A separation kernel that correctly implements these properties can meet the objective to minimize and confine damage with a high level of assurance.

Acknowledgements

We like to thank Michael McEvilley for his helpful comments regarding the history of the principle of least privilege.

References

1. Alves-Foss, J., Taylor, C.: An Analysis of the GWV Security Policy. In: Proc. of Fifth International Workshop on the ACL2 Theorem Prover and its Applications (ACL2-2004) (November 2004)
2. Ames, B.: Real-Time Software Goes Modular. Military & Aerospace Electronics 14(9), 24–29 (2003)
3. Anderson, J.P.: On the Feasibility of Connecting RECON to an External Network. Tech. Report, James P. Anderson Co. (March 1981)
4. Boebert, W.E., Kain, R.Y.: A Practical Alternative to Hierarchical Integrity Policies. In: Proc. of the National Computer Security Conference, vol. 8(18) (1985)
5. Common Criteria Project Sponsoring Organizations (CCPSO). Common Criteria for Information Technology Security Evaluation. Version 3.0 Revision 2, CCIMB-2005-07-[001, 002, 003] (June 2005)
6. Department of Defense (DOD). Trusted Computer System Evaluation Criteria. DoD 5200.28-STD (December 1985)
7. Irvine, C.E., Levin, T.E., Nguyen, T.D., Dinolt, G.W.: The Trusted Computing Exemplar Project. In: Proc. of the 2004 IEEE Systems, Man and Cybernetics Information Assurance Workshop, West Point, NY, June 2004, pp. 109–115 (2004)
8. Irvine, C. E., SecureCore Project. (last accessed April 8, 2006) (last modified April 5, 2006), http://cisr.nps.edu/projects/securecore.html
9. Kemmerer, R.A.: A Practical Approach to Identifying Storage and Timing Channels. In: Proc. of the 1982 IEEE Symposium on Security and Privacy, Oakland, CA, April 1982, pp. 66–73 (1982)
10. Lampson, B.: Protection. In: Proc. of 5th Princeton Conference on Information Sciences, Princeton, NJ, pp. 18–24 (1971), Reprinted in Operating Systems Reviews 8(1), 18-24 (1974)
11. Levin, T.E., Irvine, C.E., Nguyen, T.D.: A Note on High Robustness Requirements for Separation Kernels. In: 6th International Common Criteria Conference (ICCC 2005), September 28-29 (2005)
12. Loscocco, P.A., Smalley, S.D.: Meeting critical security objectives with Security-Enhanced Linux. In: Proc. of the 2001 Ottawa Linux Symposium (2001)
13. Millen, J.K.: Covert Channel Capacity. In: Proc of the IEEE Symposium on Research in Security and Privacy, Oakland, CA, April 1987, pp. 60–66 (1987)

14. National Security Agency (NSA). U.S. Government Protection Profile for Separation Kernels in Environments Requiring High Robustness (July 1, 2004), `http://niap.nist.gov/pp/draft_pps/pp_draft_skpp_hr_v0.621.html`
15. Nguyen, T.D., Levin, T.E., Irvine, C.E.: High Robustness Requirements in a Common Criteria Protection Profile. In: Proceedings of the Fourth IEEE International Information Assurance Workshop, Royal Holloway, UK (April 2006)
16. Preparata, F.P., Yeh, R.T.: Introduction to Discrete Structures for Computer Science and Engineering. Addison-Wesley, Reading (1973)
17. Reed, D.P., Kanodia, R.K.: Synchronization with Eventcounts and Sequencers. Communications of the ACM 22(2), 115–123 (1979)
18. Rushby., J.: Design And Verification Of Secure Systems. Operating Systems Review 15(5) (1981)
19. Saltzer, J.H., Schroeder, M.D.: The Protection of Information in Operating Systems. In: Proceedings of the IEEE, vol. 63(9), pp. 1278–1308 (1975)

Inter-node Relationship Labeling: A Fine-Grained XML Access Control Implementation Using Generic Security Labels

Zheng Zhang[1] and Walid Rjaibi[2]

[1] University of Toronto, Toronto, Ontario, Canada
[2] IBM Toronto Software Laboratory, Markham, Ontario, Canada
zhzhang@cs.toronto.edu, wrjaibi@ca.ibm.com

Abstract. Most work on XML access control considers XML nodes as the smallest protection unit. This paper shows the limitation of this approach and introduces an XML access control mechanism that protects inter-node relationships. Our approach provides a finer granularity of access control than the node-based approaches(*i.e.*, more expressive). Moreover, our approach helps achieve the "need-to-know" security principle and the "choice" privacy principle. This paper also shows how our approach can be implemented using a generic label infrastructure and suggests algorithms to create/check a secure set of labeled relationships in an XML document.

Keywords: Authorization-transparent, fine-grained access control, label-based access control, XML relationship labeling.

1 Introduction

XML has rapidly emerged as the standard for the representation and interchange of business and other sensitive data on the Web. The current trend of adding XML support to database systems poses new security challenges for an environment in which both relational and XML data coexist. In particular, fine-grained access control is even more necessary for XML than for relational data, given the more flexible and less homogeneous structure of XML data compared to relational tables and rows. The additional difficulty of controlling access over XML data compared to relational data can be summarized as follows.

- The semi-structured nature of XML data, where a schema may be absent, or, even if it is present, may allow much more flexibility and variability in the structure of the document than what is allowed by a relational schema.
- The hierarchical structure of XML, which requires specifying, for example, how access privileges to a certain node propagate from/to the node's ancestors and descendants.

In almost all of the work on XML access control [1,2,3], the smallest unit of protection is the XML node of an XML document, which are specified by XPath fragments.

J. Filipe and M.S. Obaidat (Eds.): ICETE 2006, CCIS 9, pp. 158–170, 2008.

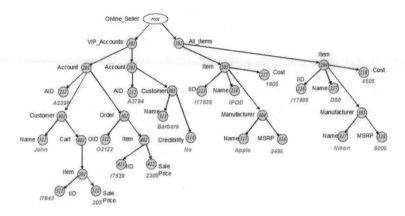

Fig. 1. A document that contains information on accounts, orders and items for an online seller

Access to ancestor-descendant and sibling relationships among nodes has not been considered. An access control policy consists of positive (resp. negative) authorization rules that grant (resp. deny) access to some nodes of an XML document. The main difference between XML access control models lies in privilege propagation. Some [1,4] forbid access to the complete subtree rooted at an inaccessible node. Alternatively, if a node is granted access while one of its ancestor nodes is inaccessible, the ancestor node would be masked as an empty node in the XML document [2]. However, this makes visible the literal of the forbidden ancestor in the path from the root to that authorized node. This can be improved by replacing the ancestor node literal by a dummy value [3]. However, this still does not solve the problem that different descendant nodes may require their ancestor's literal to be visible or invisible differently. From the differences among the above models, it is clear that defining a view that precisely describes the path leading to an authorized node is difficult. The question that begs to be asked is therefore the following: Is a node the most fine-grained entity within an XML document upon which a fine-grained access control model for XML is to be built?

We believe that the answer to this question is an unequivocal NO. We contend that the path between nodes is a better alternative upon which a fine-grained access control model for XML is to be built [5]. In other words, we contend that ancestor-descendent relationships and sibling relationships should be considered as legitimate elements to be protected. The main advantages of our approach are as follows.

First of all, blocking access to a node can be addressed by blocking access to all the relationships relating to the node. For example, in Figure 1, if we want to block all access to the Account Node "202", we could simply block access to all the paths from that node's ancestors to the node and all the paths from the node to its sibling and descendants.

Second, blocking access to relationships helps achieve the "need-to-know" principle, one of the most fundamental security principles. This principle requires information to be accessed by only those who strictly need the information to carry out their assignments. The practice of "need-to-know" limits the damage that can be done by a trusted insider who betrays our trust. The hierarchical structure of an XML document often reveals classification information. For example, in Figure 1, the root of the left subtree of the document represents a special account type "VIP_Accounts". Knowing an account node, say Node "201", belongs to that subtree reveals the account type. If the smallest protection unit is a node, once we let the root of the subtree accessible, we may leak unnecessary information. For example, suppose that the relationship between the Account Node "202" and the account type "VIP_Accounts" at the root of the subtree should be protected, knowing the account type of Node "201" in the subtree reveals the account type of Node "202". With relationship protection, we identify that the ancestor-descendant relationship between Node "101" and Node "202", and the sibling relationship between Node "201" and Node "202" should be protected while we let the ancestor-descendant relationship between Node "101" and Node "201" be accessible.

Third, blocking access to relationships helps achieve the "choice" principle, one of the most fundamental privacy principles. At its simplest, the principle means giving clients options as to how any personal information collected from them may be used. If the smallest protection element is a node, access control over one node is propagated to its ancestor/descendant nodes [6], *i.e.*, whenever access is denied to a node, access is denied to its descendants; whenever access is granted to a node, access is granted to all its ancestors. Hence, negative access control policies over ancestor nodes give a common authorized view of the paths leading to their descendants. This violates the "choice" principle: in Figure 1, a client may want to hide the account type but not the other account information for the account with AID "A2398". If the smallest protection element is a relationship between nodes in an XML document, we could protect the relationships between Node "101" and the nodes in the subtree rooted at Node "201", and the sibling relationship between Node "201" and Node "202". Then all the account information except the account type is still accessible from the root of the document tree. Moreover, there is no way to know that the subtree rooted at Node "201" is a subtree of Node "101".

Last but not least, protecting relationships between nodes in an XML document is more expressible in terms of access control policy translation.

Contributions: The contributions made in this paper can be summarized as follows:

1. We propose an authorization-transparent fine-grained access control model that protects the ancestor-descendant and sibling relationships in an XML document. Our model distinguishes two levels of access to relationships, namely the *existence access* and the *value access*.

2. We propose a new semantics for concealing relationships in an XML document where a relationship is defined by a path in the document.

3. We propose a generic and flexible label-based access control mechanism to protect relationships. Our mechanism allows DBAs to define label-based access control policies.

4. We propose a new query evaluation mechanism to enforce our access control model.

5. We develop algorithms to check/create a secure set of labeled relationships of an XML document.

2 Related Work

XML access control has been studied on issues such as granularity of access, access-control inheritance, default semantics, overriding, and conflict resolutions [1,2,4,6]. In particular, a useful survey of these proposals is given in [7], which uses XPath to give formal semantics to a number of different models in a uniform way, making it possible to compare and contrast them. Almost all the recent models [1,2,4] propose to restrict the user's view of a document by access control policies. In particular, authors in [2,4] mark each node as "accessible" or "inaccessible" in an XML document and apply conflict resolution policies to compute an authorized pruned view of the document. An alternative approach [8] defines access control policies as XQuery expressions. A user is given a modified document with encrypted data and queries are posed on this modified document. They present a new query semantics that permits a user to see only authorized data. In [3], security is specified by extending the document DTD with annotations and publishing a modified DTD. Similarly, work by Bertino *et al.* [9] and Finance *et al.* [10] provides XML-based specification languages for publishing secure XML document content, and for specifying role-based access control on XML data [11,12]. Restricting access to nodes has also been used in XACL [13] and XACML [14], two proposed industrial standards. Kanza *et al.* propose to restrict access to ancestor-descendant relationships [5] and introduce authorization-transparent access control for XML data under the Non-Truman model [15].

3 Data Model and Queries

We consider an XML document as a rooted directed tree over a finite set of node literals L with a finite set of values A attached to atomic nodes (*i.e.*, nodes with no outgoing edges). Formally, a document D is a 5-tuple $(N_D, E_D, root_D, literal\_of_D, value\_of_D)$, where N_D is a set of nodes, E_D is a set of directed edges, $root_D$ is the root of a directed tree, $literal\_of_D$ is a function that maps each node of N_D to a literal of L, and $value\_of_D$ is a function that maps each atomic node to a value of A. In order to simplify the data model, we do not distinguish between elements and attributes of an XML document. We also assume that all the values on atomic nodes are of type *PCDATA* (*i.e.*, *String*).

Example 1. Figure 1 shows a document that contains information on accounts, orders, and items for an online seller. Nodes are represented by circles with ID's for easy reference. Values in A appear below the atomic nodes and are written in bold font.

In this paper, we use XPath [16] for formulating queries and specifying relationships. XPath is a simple language for navigation in an XML document. In XPath, there are thirteen types of axes that are used for navigation. Our focus is on the *child* axis ($/$), the *descendant-or-self* axis ($//$), the *preceding-sibling* axis and the *following-sibling* axis that are the most commonly used axes in XPath. Our model, however, can also be applied to queries that include the other axes.

4   Relationship Access

First, we consider what it means to conceal a relationship. In general, a *relationship* is an undirected path between two nodes in an XML document. A set of *relationships* is represented by two sets of nodes. For example, the pair (C, N), where C is the set of all Customer Nodes and N is the set of all Name Nodes in Figure 1, represents the set of relationships between customers and their names. Concealing the relationships (C, N) means that for every customer c and name n in the document, a user will not be able to infer (with certainty), from any query answers, whether n is the name for c. We want this to be true for all authorized query results. Note that we are concealing the presence or absence of relationships, so we are concealing whether any of the set of pairs in (C, N) exists in the document.

Definition 1 (Concealing a Relationship). *Given an XML document D and a pair of nodes n_1 and n_2 in D, the relationship (n_1, n_2) is concealed if there exists a document D' over the node set of D, such that the following is true.*

1. *Exactly one of D and D' has a path from n_1 to n_2.*
2. *For any XPath query Q, the authorized answer set of Q over D is equal to that of Q over D'.*

We consider two kinds of relationships in an XML document, namely the ancestor-descendant relationships and the sibling relationships. Kanza *et al.* consider ancestor-descendant relationships only [5]. Sibling relationships are inferred by the ancestor-descendant relationships. Hence, when access to an ancestor-descendant relationship is blocked in their model, access to the related sibling relationships is automatically blocked.

Example 2. In Figure 1, suppose the relationship between VIP_Accounts Node "101" and Account Node "201" is inaccessible, then the sibling relationship between Node "201" and Node "202" is lost.

It could be necessary to preserve such sibling relationship information. For example, one policy may want to block access to the ancestor-descendant relationships between VIP_Accounts Node and Account Nodes while maintain access to the sibling relationships between the Account Nodes.

On the other hand, it might be desirable to block access to sibling relationships only. For example, one policy may want to block access to the sibling relationship between Customer and his Order.

In order to express such access control policies, we consider sibling relationships as well as ancestor-descendant relationships.

We distinguish two levels of access to relationships, namely the *existence access* and the *value access*. In value access, information about a relationship indicates a node whose ID is "v_a" and whose literal is "A" is related to a node whose ID is "v_b" and whose literal is "B". For example, the pair (C, N) is a value access to the relationships between Customer Nodes and Name Nodes. In existence access, information about a relationship is basically the same as information of value access but lacks at least one of the values "v_a" and "v_b". In other words, existence access to a relationship returns whether a node of some literal is related to some node. For example, existence access could indicate a node whose literal is "A" is related to a node whose literal is "B". Obviously, if a relationship is not accessible under existence access, then the relationship is not accessible under value access.

Example 3. Consider the relationship between the account with AID "A2398" and its customer name in Figure 1. The value access to this relationship returns that Node "201" whose literal is "Account" is related to Node "311" whose literal is "Name" and whose value is "John". The typical queries that will return this information are:

Q_1: *//Account[AID= "A2398"]*,
Q_2: *//Account[AID= "A2398"]/Customer/Name*.

Now consider an existence access to this relationship: a query Q_3 wants to return all the accounts' AID's that have a customer name. The fact that "A2398" is returned tells us that there exists a customer with name under the account with AID "A2398", but it does not tell us what the customer's name is, nor the Node ID "311". In other words, Q_1 and Q_3 reveal that Node "201" whose literal is "Account" is related to some node n whose literal is "Name", where n is a child of some node whose literal is "Customer" and which is a child of Node "201".

Q_3: *//Account[Customer/Name]/AID*.

In the next section, we show how to specify ancestor-descendant and sibling relationships and attach access labels to them.

5   Access Control Policy Specification

Our access control model uses a generic, flexible label infrastructure [17] where a label has only one component "access level". The value of the component can be "EXISTENCE", "VALUE", or "NULL". The ranks of these values are as follows: "EXISTENCE" > "VALUE" > "NULL". We distinguish two types of labels: *Access labels* and *Path labels*. Access labels are created and assigned to database users, roles, or groups along with the type of access for which the access label is granted (*i.e.*, Read/Write). For simplicity, we consider only users in this paper. We call *read (resp. write) access label* an access label associated with the Read (resp. Write) access type. Path labels are created and attached to paths of an XML document. When a user or a path is not associated with a label, the "NULL" label is assumed for that user or path.

Example 4. The following statement creates and grants the "EXISTENCE" access label to a database user Mike for the Read access type.

GRANT ACCESS LABEL EXISTENCE
TO USER Mike FOR READ ACCESS

The following statement revokes the "EXISTENCE" read access label from Mike.

REVOKE ACCESS LABEL EXISTENCE
FROM USER Mike FOR READ ACCESS

Access to an XML document is based upon the labels associated with the paths of the XML document and the label associated with the user accessing the document via the paths. A label access policy consists of label access rules that the database system evaluates to determine whether a database user is allowed access to an XML document. Access rules can be categorized as Read Access rules and Write Access rules. The former is applied by the database system when a user attempts to read a path in an XML document; the latter is applied when a user attempts to insert, update or delete a path in an XML document. In both cases, a label access rule is as follows:

Access Label ⟨operator⟩ Path Label

where the operator is one of the arithmetic comparison operators $\{=, \leq, <, >, \geq, \neq\}$.

Example 5. The following statement creates a label access policy that *(1)* does not allow a user to read a path unless his read access label is larger than or equal to the path label, *(2)* does not allow a user to write a path unless his write access label is equal to the path label.

CREATE LABEL POLICY XML-FGAC
READ ACCESS RULE rule
  READ ACCESS LABEL $\geq$ Path LABEL
WRITE ACCESS RULE rule
  WRITE ACCESS LABEL $=$ Path LABEL

Recall value access to a relationship returns more information than existence access. An "EXISTENCE" label protects existence and value access. A "VALUE" label protects value access only. Therefore, if a user with a "NULL" read access label wants to existence access a path with a "VALUE" path label, access should be allowed since this existence access does not return the complete relationship information from value access. We call this the DEFAULT policy. This policy only applies to Read Access since any Write Access involves real node ID's (*i.e.*, existence access is impossible). This policy could coexist with other policies such as XML-FGAC to give a more complete authorized answer set of a query.

Example 6. Assume the relationship in Example 3 has a "VALUE" path label. If a user with a "NULL" read access label asks query Q_3, the existence access to the relationship should be allowed.

Next, we introduce how the labels are attached to paths in an XML document. First, attaching a label to ancestor-descendant paths are specified by an SQL statement in the following form:

ATTACH *path_label* ANCS *path$_1$* DESC *path$_2$*,

where *path$_1$* and *path$_2$* are two XPath expressions. Notice expression *path$_2$* is a relative XPath expression w.r.t. *path$_1$*. The two expressions specify pairs of ancestor nodes (*i.e.*, *path$_1$*) and descendent nodes (*i.e.*, *path$_1$*/*path$_2$*). Expression *path_label* is a label.

Example 7. The following expression attaches "EXISTENCE" path labels to the relationships between Account Nodes and their Customers' Name Nodes in Figure 1.

ATTACH EXISTENCE ANCS *//Account*
DESC */Customer/Name*

The following expression attaches a "VALUE" path label to the relationship between the Item Node with Name "IPOD" and its Cost Node in Figure 1.

ATTACH VALUE ANCS *//Item[Name = "IPOD"]*
DESC *//Cost*

For sibling relationships, we consider the *preceding-sibling axis* and *the following-sibling axis* in XPath. Thus, attaching a label to sibling paths are specified by XPath expressions in the following form:

    ATTACH *path_label*
    NODE *path$_1$* PRECEDING-SIBLING *path$_2$*
    FOLLOWING-SIBLING *path$_3$*,

where *path$_1$*, *path$_2$* and *path$_3$* are three XPath expressions. Notice expressions *path$_2$* and *path$_3$* are two relative XPath expressions w.r.t. *path$_1$*. The expressions specify relationships between some nodes (*i.e.*, *path$_1$*), and their preceding siblings (*i.e.*, *path$_1$/preceding-sibling* :: *path$_2$*) as well as the relationships between the nodes and their following siblings (*i.e.*, *path$_1$/following-sibling* :: *path$_3$*). Notice the *PRECEDING-SIBLING* expression and the *FOLLOWING-SIBLING* expression do not have to appear at the same time.

Example 8. The following expression attaches a "VALUE" path label to the relationship between the Account whose Customer has Name "Barbara" and its preceding sibling.

ATTACH VALUE
NODE *//Account[Customer/Name = "Barbara"]*
PRECEDING-SIBLING *Account*

Note that the SQL statement to detach a label from an ancestor-descendant path or a sibling path is similar to the SQL statement to attach a label to those paths except that ATTACH is replaced by DETACH.

6   Query Evaluation

In authorization-transparent access control, users formulate their queries against the original database rather than against authorization views that transform and hide data [18]. In [15], authorization transparent access control is categorized into two basic classes, the *Truman model* and the *Non-Truman model*. In the Truman model, an access control language (often a view language) is used to specify what data is accessible to a user. User queries are modified by the system so that the answer includes only accessible data. Let Q be a user query, D be a database and D_u be the part of D that the user is permitted to see, then query Q is modified to a safe query Q_s such that $Q_s(D) = Q(D_u)$. We call $Q_s(D)$ the *authorized answer set* of Q over D. In contrast, in the Non-Truman model, a query that violates access control specifications is rejected, rather than modified. Only *valid* queries are answered.

Our model is an authorization-transparent Truman model. We allow users to pose XPath queries against the original labeled XML document. The evaluation of an XPath query over a labeled XML document has two parts. First, we change the usual XPath query semantics as follows. If a child axis occurs, the evaluation follows a parent-child path; if a descendant-or-self axis occurs, the evaluation follows an ancestor-descendant path; if a preceding-sibling axis occurs, the evaluation follows a preceding-sibling path; if a following-sibling axis occurs, the evaluation follows a following-sibling path.

Second, we need to make sure that for each path accessed, a user is allowed access to that path based on the path label and the user's access label. Suppose a path P has a path label L_1 and a user Mike has a read access label L_2. According to the XML-FGAC policy, *(1)* if L_2 is "EXISTENCE", Mike could read the path P regardless of the value of label L_1; *(2)* if L_2 is "VALUE", Mike could read the path P if L_1 is not "EXISTENCE"; *(3)* if L_2 is "NULL", Mike can only access paths with "NULL" labels; if the DEFAULT policy coexists, Mike could ask queries to existence access the path P if L_1 is "VALUE". The discussion for Write Access is similar. The above logic is inserted into the query access plan. When the access plan is executed, the access rules from the label access policy associated with the labeled XML document are evaluated for each path accessed in the document. This approach allows the cached access plan to be reused because the access labels of the user who issued the query are acquired during runtime.

For an XML document, there is an ordering, *document order* [16], defined on all the nodes in the document corresponding to the order in which the first character of the XML representation of each node occurs in the XML representation of the document. This ordering information may leak information as shown in the following example.

Example 9. Let us look at Figure 1 again. Suppose one security policy wants to block public access to the sibling relationships between the Customer Nodes and their Order Nodes. Suppose the following queries are allowed to return their answers in document order: *//Customer* and *//Order*. Then the order of Customer output might match the order of Order output, hence leaks secret information. The situation becomes worse if the document has a registered schema and the schema shows publicly that each customer has a fixed number, say 2, of orders. In this case, the association between a Customer and his Orders is completely leaked.

To prevent an information leak based on document order, we shuffle the output as follows. Each node in the output will receive a random number. And the nodes will be output based on the order of their assigned random numbers.

In sum, the processing algorithm to be inserted in the access plan for a labeled XML document with XML-FGAC and DEFAULT policies is as follows.

Algorithm: Insert Read and Write Access logic into a query access plan for a labeled XML document.

1. Fetch the user's Access Labels for Read and Write actions (*e.g.*, from a system catalog table).
2. For all paths accessed, do the following.
   (a) If it is a Read Access and READ Access rules do not permit access, skip the path unless *(1)* the Read Access Label is "NULL", *(2)* the Path Label is "VALUE", and *(3)* it is an existence access.
   (b) If it is a Write Access and Write Access rules do not permit access, skip the path.
3. Shuffle output.

Example 10. Suppose the document in Figure 1 has two labels attached to its paths as specified in Example 7 and the label access policies are XML-FGAC and DEFAULT. Suppose a database user Mike with a read access label "EXISTENCE" asks the query Q_1: *//Account[Customer/Name]*. The query access plan checks the following paths:

1. the paths P_1 from the root of the document to Account Nodes, *i.e.*, *//Account*,
2. the paths P_2 from Account Nodes to their descendant Name Nodes via Customer Nodes, *i.e.*,
   ANCS *//Account* DESC */Customer/Name*,
3. the paths P_3 from Customer Nodes to their children Name Nodes, *i.e.*, *Customer/ Name*.

Paths P_1 and P_3 have "NULL" labels, hence, access is allowed. Paths P_2 have "EXISTENCE" labels. Mike could read them since his read access label is "EXISTENCE". Read access to P_2 is denied for any other labels and the authorized answer set is empty. Next, suppose another user John with a read access label "VALUE" asks the query Q_2: *//Item//Cost*. The query access plan checks the following paths:

1. the paths P_1 from the root of the document to the Item Nodes, *i.e.*, *//Item*,
2. the paths P_2 from the Item Nodes to their descendant Cost Nodes, *i.e.*, ANCS *//Item* DESC *//Cost*.

Paths P_1 have "NULL" labels, hence, access is allowed. For P_2, one path P_{21} has a "NULL" label; the other path P_{22} has a "VALUE" label as it is ANCS *//Item [Name= "IPOD"]* DESC *//Cost*. John could read P_2 if his read access label is "VALUE". John could read P_{21} but not P_{22} if his read access label is "NULL". Hence, the authorized answer set is "450$". However, even if John's read access label is "NULL", the following query from John will still return the complete answer to Q_3: *//Item[Cost]*. This is because Q_3 only existence accesses the paths P_2, *i.e.*, the authorized answer set only indicates there exist Cost children Nodes for the Item Nodes "203" and "204", but no information about the values and node ID's of the Cost Nodes is leaked.

7   Create a Secure Set of Labeled Relationships

Our goal is to allow users to label node relationships and let them be sure that what they want to conceal is truly concealed from the users whose access labels do not satisfy the label access policy with the path labels. Unfortunately, it is impossible to guarantee concealment for any arbitrary set of relationships. Sometimes, it is possible to infer a concealed relationship from the relationships that are not concealed.

Let us see an example of four cases where a relationship could be inferred from a pair of non-concealed relationship.

Example 11. In Figure 1, suppose it is known that Account Node "201" is a descendant of VIP_Accounts Node "101" and Customer Node "301" is a descendant of Account Node "201". Then, there is no point to conceal the ancestor-descendant relationship between VIP_Accounts Node "101" and Customer Node "301". Suppose it is known that Customer Node "301" is a descendant of VIP_Accounts Node "101" as well as

Account Node "201". Since there is only one path from the root of the document to Account Node "201", there is no point to conceal the ancestor-descendant relationship between VIP-Accounts Node "101" and Account Node "201". Suppose it is known that Account Node "201" and Account Node "202" are the children of VIP-Accounts Node "101", then there is no point to conceal the sibling relationship between Account Node "201" and Account Node "202".

Suppose it is known that VIP-Accounts Node "101" has a descendant Customer Node "301" and the customer has a sibling Order Node "302", then there is no point to conceal the ancestor-descendant relationship between VIP-Accounts Node "101" and Order Node "302".

We say a set of labeled relationships/paths in an XML document D is *not secure* w.r.t. a path label L if one of the following four cases happens.

1. Case 1: D has three nodes, n_1, n_2 and n_3 s.t. the ancestor-descendant path from n_1 to n_2 and the ancestor-descendant path from n_2 to n_3 have labels $L_{12} < L$ and $L_{23} < L$. The ancestor-descendant path from n_1 to n_3 has a label $L_{13} \geq L$.
2. Case 2: D has three nodes, n_1, n_2 and n_3 s.t. the ancestor-descendant path from n_1 to n_3 and the ancestor-descendant path from n_2 to n_3 have labels $L_{13} < L$ and $L_{23} < L$. The ancestor-descendant path from n_1 to n_2 has a label $L_{12} \geq L$.
3. Case 3: D has three nodes, n_1, n_2 and n_3 s.t. n_1 is the parent of n_2 and n_3, the parent-child path from n_1 to n_2 and the parent-child path from n_1 to n_3 have labels $L_{12} < L$ and $L_{13} < L$. The sibling path from n_2 to n_3 has a label $L_{23} \geq L$ or the sibling path from n_3 to n_2 has a label $L_{32} \geq L$.
4. Case 4: D has three nodes, n_1, n_2 and n_3 s.t. the ancestor-descendant path from n_1 to n_2 has a label $L_{12} < L$, and either the sibling path from n_2 to n_3 has a label $L_{23} < L$ or the sibling path from n_3 to n_2 has a label $L_{32} < L$. The ancestor-descendant path from n_1 to n_3 has a label $L_{13} \geq L$.

There is a simple test to verify that a set of labeled relationships/paths in an XML document D is not secure w.r.t. a path label L. The test starts by computing three ternary relations R_1, R_2 and R_3. The first two columns store the start/end nodes of paths. The third column stores the label associated with paths (if a label is missing, then it is a NULL value). In particular, R_1 stores all ancestor-descendant paths in D, R_2 stores all parent-child paths in D, and R_3 stores all sibling paths in D.

1. Case 1 is true for a path label L iff the expression $\pi_{\$1,\$5}(R_{1,L} \bowtie_{\$2=\$1} R_{1,L}) - R_{1,L}$ is not empty where $R_{1,L}$ is $\sigma_{\$3<L}(R_1)$.
2. Case 2 is true for a path label L iff the expression $\pi_{\$1,\$4}(R_{1,L} \bowtie_{\$2=\$2} R_{1,L}) - R_{1,L}$ is not empty where $R_{1,L}$ is $\sigma_{\$3<L}(R_1)$.
3. Case 3 is true for a path label L iff the expression $\pi_{\$2,\$5}(R_{2,L} \bowtie_{\$1=\$1} R_{2,L}) - R_{3,L}$ is not empty where $R_{2,L}$ is $\sigma_{\$3<L}(R_2)$ and $R_{3,L}$ is $\sigma_{\$3<L}(R_3)$.
4. Case 4 is true for a path label L iff the expression $\pi_{\$1,\$5}(R_{1,L} \bowtie_{\$2=\$1} R_{3,L}) - R_{1,L}$ is not empty where $R_{1,L}$ is $\sigma_{\$3<L}(R_1)$ and $R_{3,L}$ is $\sigma_{\$3<L}(R_3)$.

Furthermore, we give intuitive conditions to construct a secure set of labeled relationships for an XML document. If we ignore the directions of ancestor-descendant and sibling paths, all these paths form cycles in an XML document. To assign a path label L

to a relationship between two nodes n_1 and n_2 in an XML document D, we must make sure, for every cycle that includes the path from n_1 to n_2, either there is another path whose label $L' \geq L$, or n_1 and n_2 are descendants of some nodes in the cycle and n_1, n_2 are not children of the same parent. Both cases ensure there is uncertainty whether a relationship between two nodes n_1 and n_2 exists: the first case by having another path missing in the cycle, while in the second case, the fact that n_1 and n_2 are descendants of some nodes in the cycle introduces uncertainty except when they are children of the same parent, in which case the sibling relationship between n_1 and n_2 is leaked.

There is another possible information leak due to *singleton-source disclosure* [5]. In short, a user can infer that two nodes n_1 and n_2 are related in a document D when *(1)* the path from the root of document D to node n_2 must go through a node whose literal is A, *(2)* the only node with literal A in document D is node n_1.

An algorithm to test singleton-source disclosure has been proposed in [5] and we will not repeat it here.

8   Conclusions

This paper has introduced a fine-grained access control model for XML data using generic security labels. Our model is based on inter-node relationship labeling and provides finer-grained access control than traditional node labeling approaches, hence helps achieve the "need-to-know" security principle and the "choice" privacy principle. We propose a new semantics for concealing relationships in an XML document under the Truman model. To enforce our model, we provide a new query evaluation algorithm and suggest algorithms to check/create a set of secure labeled paths for an XML document. Our future work includes implementing our model and validating its effectiveness and performance using real-life XML access control user cases. An important challenge is adapting our mechanism to XQuery, general XML document graphs and XML schemas.

Acknowledgements

We thank NSERC and IBM Toronto CAS for their support, and Renée J. Miller for her careful comments.

Trademark: IBM is a trademark or registered trademark of International Business Machines Corporation in the United States, other countries, or both.

Disclaimer: The views expressed in this paper are those of the authors and not necessarily of IBM Canada Ltd. or IBM Corporation.

References

1. Bertino, E., Ferrari, E.: Secure and selective dissemination of xml documents. ACM Trans. Inf. Syst. Secur. 5, 290–331 (2002)
2. Damiani, E., de C. di Vimercati, S., Paraboschi, S., Samarati, P.: A fine-grained access control system for xml documents. ACM Trans. Inf. Syst. Secur. 5, 169–202 (2002)

3. Fan, W.F., Chan, C.Y., Garofalakis, M.N.: Secure xml querying with security views. In: SIG-MOD, pp. 587–598 (2004)
4. Gabillon, A., Bruno, E.: Regulating access to xml documents. In: Working Conference on Database and Application Security, pp. 311–328 (2001)
5. Kanza, Y., Mendelzon, A.O., Miller, R., Zhang, Z.: Authorization-transparent access control for xml under the non-truman model. In: EDBT, pp. 222–239 (2006)
6. Murata, M., Tozawa, A., Kudo, M., Hada, S.: Xml access control using static analysis. In: CCS, pp. 73–84. ACM Press, New York (2003)
7. Fundulaki, I., Marx, M.: Specifying access control policies for xml documents with xpath. In: SACMAT, pp. 61–69 (2004)
8. Miklau, G., Suciu, D.: Controlling access to published data using cryptography. In: VLDB, pp. 898–909 (2003)
9. Bertino, E., Castano, S., Ferrari, E.: On specifying security policies for web documents with an xml-based language. In: SACMAT, pp. 57–65 (2001)
10. Finance, B., Medjdoub, S., Pucheral, P.: The case for access control on xml relationships. Technical report, INRIA (2005), http://www-smis.inria.fr/dataFiles/FMP05a.pdf
11. Bhatti, R., Bertino, E., Ghafoor, A., Joshi, J.: Xml-based specification for web services document security. IEEE Computer 4(37), 41–49 (2004)
12. Wang, J.Z., Osborn, S.L.: A role-based approach to access control for xml databases. In: SACMAT, pp. 70–77 (2004)
13. IBM: Xml access control (2001), http://xml.coverpages.org/xacl.html
14. Oasis.: Oasis exensible access control markup language (xacml 2.0) (2005), http://www.oasis-open.org/committees/xacml
15. Rizvi, S., Mendelzon, A., Sudarshan, S., Roy, P.: Extending query rewriting techniques for fine-grained access control. In: SIGMOD, pp. 551–562 (2004)
16. Clark, J., DeRose, S.: XML Path Language (XPath) version 1.0 (1999), http://www.w3.org/TR/xpath
17. Rjaibi, W., Bird, P.: A multi-purpose implementation of mandatory access control in relational database management systems. In: VLDB, pp. 1010–1020 (2004)
18. Motro, A.: An access authorization model for relational databases based on algebraic manipulation of view definitions. In: ICDE, 1989, pp. 339–347 (1989)

PART III
SIGMAP

Using Placeholder Slices and MPEG-21 BSDL for ROI Extraction in H.264/AVC FMO-Encoded Bitstreams

Peter Lambert, Wesley De Neve, Davy De Schrijver,
Yves Dhondt, and Rik Van de Walle

Department of Electronics and Information Systems – Multimedia Lab
Ghent University – IBBT
Gaston Crommenlaan 8/201, B-9050 Ledeberg-Ghent, Belgium
{peter.lambert,wesley.deneve,davy.deschrijver,yves.dhondt
rik.vandewalle}@ugent.be

Abstract. The concept of Regions of Interest (ROIs) within a video sequence is useful for many application scenarios. This paper concentrates on the exploitation of ROI coding within the H.264/AVC specification by making use of Flexible Macroblock Ordering. It shows how ROIs can be coded in an H.264/AVC compliant bitstream and how the MPEG-21 BSDL framework can be used for the extraction of the ROIs.

The first type of ROI extraction that is described, is simply dropping the slices that are not part of one of the ROIs. The second type is the replacement of these slices with so-called placeholder slices, the latter being implemented as P slices containing only macroblocks that are marked as 'skipped'. The exploitation of ROI scalability, as achieved by the presented methodology, illustrates the possibilities that are offered by the single-layered H.264/AVC specification for content adaptation.

The results show that the bit rate needed to transmit the adapted bitstreams can be reduced significantly. Especially in the case of a static camera and a fixed background, this bit rate reduction has very little impact on the visual quality. Another advantage of the adaptation process is the fact that the execution speed of the receiving decoder fairly increases.

Keywords: Content adaptation, FMO, H.264/AVC, MPEG-21 BSDL, placeholder slices, ROI, video coding.

1   Introduction

The concept of Regions of Interest (ROIs) within a video sequence is useful for many application scenarios. A ROI is an area within the video pane that usually contains visual information that is more important or interesting than the other parts of the video image. If one or more ROIs are defined in a video sequence, they can be used to steer the bit allocation algorithm in such way that the ROIs are coded with a higher quality than the 'background'. This functionality is part of the JPEG2000 standard for still images [14]. The Fine Granularity Scalability (FGS) profile of MPEG-4 Visual [12] also has provisions to support the coding of a ROI at a higher quality level.

J. Filipe and M.S. Obaidat (Eds.): ICETE 2006, CCIS 9, pp. 173–185, 2008.
© Springer-Verlag Berlin Heidelberg 2008

Besides the fact that the idea of ROIs is adopted by various (standardized) coding schemes to provide different levels of quality within one picture, there are many applications that can benefit from the clever use of ROI coding. In the domain of video surveillance for instance, cameras are developed that capture 360 degrees of video footage resulting in high resolution pictures. Within these large pictures, a ROI is defined and only a coded representation of that area is transmitted over the network in order to reduce the required bandwith. The relative location of the ROI and its size can often be adjusted by an operator in real time. This technique was developed to avoid the delays that are introduced by traditional Pan Tilt Zoom (PTZ) cameras.

The domain of video conferencing is another domain where the use of ROIs can have advantages. In these scenarios, the ROI itself is easy to detect and its position is rather fixed in time. Next to this, the background is virtually always fixed and semantically unimportant; this is in contrast with video surveillance where the background can contain a lot of motion. For instance, such a video conferencing system is deployed in the European Parliament where every speaker is recorded in close-up.

With the emergence of standardization efforts by the Joint Video Team (JVT) regarding Scalable Video Coding (SVC) [13], it has become clear that there is a broad interest in ROI coding and ROI-based scalability [8,18,15]. Applications that are often mentioned in this context include video surveillance (real-time monitoring) and multipoint video conference. More details about ROI coding and scalability can be found in the requirements document of SVC [9].

This paper concentrates on the exploitation of ROI coding within the H.264/AVC specification [17]. Notwithstanding the fact that the H.264/AVC standard does not explicitly define a system for ROI coding, the authors have shown that the use of *slice groups* (often called Flexible Macroblock Ordering or FMO) enables an encoder to perform ROI coding [11]. Furthermore, it was illustrated that this approach can form the basis for content adaptation [6]. The exploitation of ROI scalability, as well as the exploitation of multi-layered temporal scalability [3], illustrates the possibilities that are offered by the single-layered H.264/AVC specification for content adaptation. The way the MPEG-21 BSDL framework can be used for this content adaptation process, is elaborated in later sections.

In this paper, the authors show how H.264/AVC FMO is to be used to encode one or more ROIs; how the MPEG-21 BSDL framework can be applied to extract the coded ROIs from a given bitstream; how placeholder slices can be used for the replacement of the background slices (not belonging to a ROI); and what the benefits are of this approach by means of some experimental results.

The rest of the paper is organized as follows. The two main enabling technologies, FMO and MPEG-21 BSDL, are described in Section 2 and 3. Section 4 describes the actual ROI extraction process. The concept of placeholder slices is introduced in Section 5. The experimental results are presented in Section 6 while Section 7 draws the conclusion of this paper.

2   ROI-Coding with FMO

Flexible Macroblock Ordering is one of the new error resilience tools that is defined within the H.264/AVC standard. Conceptually, it creates an additional level in the

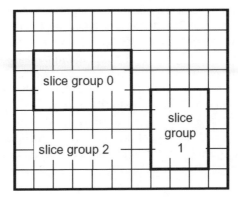

Fig. 1. H.264/AVC FMO type 2

hierarchy from picture to macroblock. When applying FMO, a picture is made up of maximally 8 *slice groups*, and every slice group contains one or more slices. Finally, a slice is a collection of macroblocks. The most important aspect of FMO is the fact that every macroblock can be assigned individually to one of the slice groups of a picture, in contrast with the default raster scan order. This results in a so-called *MacroBlock Allocation map* (MBAmap) which is coded in a Picture Parameter Set (PPS). When this map is constructed, an encoder will code the macroblocks of a slice group in raster scan order (within that particular slice group), and they can be further grouped into slices.

Besides the coding of the entire MBAmap, the H.264/AVC standard has specified 6 predefined types of FMO. For these types, the MBAmap has a specific pattern that can be coded much more efficiently. In this paper, we focus on FMO type 2 (this only requires two numbers to be coded for each slice group – see later). This means that the slice groups of a picture are rectangular regions within the video pane, as shown in Figure 1. We will consider these regions as Regions of Interest. A more in-depth overview of FMO is given in [11].

While many applications would implement automatic ways to define ROIs (e.g., by using image processing techniques), the ROIs in the context of this paper were defined manually. To be more precise, an in-house defined syntax for a configuration file was developed that is parsed by the encoder; the latter being a modification of the H.264/AVC reference encoder (JM 9.5). This configuration file contains the macroblock numbers of the top left and the bottom right macroblock of the ROIs. These macroblock numbers are obtained by using a self-developed application that allows one to graphically select one or more rectangular regions within a video sequence on a picture-by-picture basis.

Since the slice group configuration is coded in a Picture Parameter Set, a PPS is inserted into the bitstream before every picture in which the ROI configuration changes (e.g., a ROI is moving across the video pane, a ROI is appearing or disappearing). Every slice has a reference to the PPS that is applicable for the picture the slice belongs to. Note that this may cause some overhead, especially if the ROI configuration changes every picture. In this paper, the size of a PPS mainly depends on the number of slice groups and on the magnitude of the macroblock numbers that are coded within. The biggest PPS in our test set was 21 bytes long (without the 4-byte start code). At 30 Hz, this results in a worst case overhead of 5040 bits per second, which is still reasonable.

There are four syntax elements of a PPS that are important in the context of this paper. The syntax element `num_slice_groups_minus1` indicates the number of slice groups. In this paper, the number of ROIs is equal to the number of slice groups minus one (the 'background' also is a slice group). Because we only discuss FMO type 2, the syntax element `slice_group_map_type` is always equal to 2. Finally, for every slice group, the macroblock numbers of the top left and the bottom right macroblock of that slice group are coded by means of the syntax elements `top_left_iGroup` and `bottom_right_iGroup`.

3   MPEG-21 BSDL

In order to be able to deliver (scalable) video in a heterogeneous environment, it is important to be aware of the need of complementary logic that makes it possible to adapt the bitstream or to exploit the scalability properties of the bitstream. This bitstream adaptation process typically involves the removal of certain data blocks and the modification of the value of certain syntax elements.

One way to realize this, is to rely on automatically generated XML-based descriptions that contain information about the high-level structure of (scalable) bitstreams. These descriptions can subsequently be the subject of transformations, reflecting the desired adaptations of the bitstream. Lastly, they can then be used for the automatic generation of an adapted version of the bitstream in question.

The Bitstream Syntax Description Language (BSDL), part of the Digital Item Adaptation standard (DIA) of MPEG-21 [16], is a language that provides solutions for discovering the structure of a multimedia resource resulting in an XML description (called a Bitstream Syntax Description, or BSD) and for the generation of an adapted multimedia resource using a transformed description. In Figure 2, the entire chain of actions within the BSDL framework is given.

As illustrated by the figure, one starts from a given bitstream that is encoded with a certain codec. Dependent on the codec, a Bitstream Syntax (BS) Schema is developed that represents the high-level structure of bitstreams generated by the codec in question. Note that the granularity can be chosen freely, often dependent on the application. The language of a BS Schema is standardized in the MPEG-21 DIA specification, as is the functioning of the BintoBSD tool. Once a bitstream description is available in XML, it can be transformed based on, for instance, the characteristics of the network or the consuming terminal.

The way the BSD transformation is to be realized is, however, not defined by the BSDL specification. For instance, one can use Extensible Stylesheet Language Transformations (XSLT, [10]); Streaming Transformations for XML (STX, [1]) or an implementation based on an XML API (such as Simple API for XML, SAX, or Document Object Model, DOM).

The final step in the framework for media resource adaptation is the regeneration of the adapted bitstream. This is realized by the BSDtoBin tool, taking as input the adapted

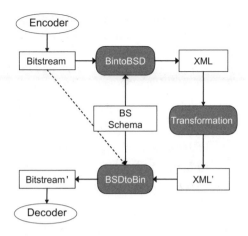

Fig. 2. The MPEG-21 BSDL framework

description, the BS Schema, and the original bitstream. The latter is needed because the coded data is not part of the BSDs. The functioning of this tool is also standardized within the BSDL specification.

As such, the BSDL framework provides all necessary ingredients for the construction of a generic (i.e., format-agnostic) and modular content adaptation engine: a BSD transformation engine and the format-agnostic bitstream generation by means of the BSDtoBin Parser. In practice, this is supplemented with an Adaptation Decision Taking Engine (ADTE) to steer and control the adaptation process. If such a framework is to support a new coding format, then only a new BS Schema is to be uploaded, accompanied by some transformations. The actual software (the BintoBSD Parser and the BSDtoBin Parser) does not have to be modified.

4   ROI Extraction

In this paper, the extraction of ROIs that are defined within a coded video sequence goes together with the deletion of the 'background' or the replacement thereof by other coded data. When a bitstream is disposed of its non-ROI coded parts, the required bandwidth to transmit the bitstream will be much lower. Next to this, the use of placeholder slices (see Section 5) results in a speed-up of the decoder, a decrease of the decoder complexity, and an easing of the decoder's memory management (e.g., cache behavior). As will be shown in later sections, this extraction, replacement, and adjustment process can even be used to transform a bitstream conforming to the H.264/AVC Extended Profile to a bitstream that is compliant with the H.264/AVC Baseline Profile.

In order to extract the ROIs from an FMO type 2 coded H.264/AVC bitstream, one has to decide for every slice if that particular slice is part of one of the rectangular slice groups. Every slice header contains the syntax element `first_mb_in_slice`. This number can be used to determine whether or not this slice is part of one of the rectangular slice groups. This can be done in the following manner.

Let S be a slice of a picture containing a number of ROIs R_i and let FMB_S be the macroblock number of the first macroblock of slice S (first_mb_in_slice). Further, let TL_i and BR_i be the macroblock numbers of the top left and bottom right macrobock of ROI R_i. Finally, let W be the width of a picture in terms of macroblocks (pic_width_in_mbs_minus1, coded in a Sequence Parameter Set). Then, S is part of R_i if

$$(TL_i \bmod W \leq FMB_S \bmod W)$$
$$\wedge (FMB_S \bmod W \leq BR_i \bmod W)$$
$$\wedge (TL_i \operatorname{div} W \leq FMB_S \operatorname{div} W)$$
$$\wedge (FMB_S \operatorname{div} W \leq BR_i \operatorname{div} W)$$

Note that the div operator denotes the integer devision with truncation and the mod operator denotes the traditional modulo operation. In other words, S is part of R_i if its first macroblock is located inside the rectangular region defined by R_i. After a BSD is generated by the BSDL framework, the above calculation can be performed by means of an XPath expression within an XSL Transformation. The result of such a transformation is a BSD in which the descriptions of non-ROI slices are removed. The BSDtoBin Parser can then generate the adapted bitstream.

It should be noted that I slices are not removed from the bitstream in the context of this paper. This is to prevent major drift errors due to the fact that the inter prediction of macroblocks in a given ROI can be based on macroblocks outside the ROI in question. In other words, the ROIs that are used here are no *isolated regions*, as described in [7]. If *all* background slices would be dropped (including I slices), then prediction errors would continuously build up at the inner boundaries of the ROI.

It is also important to note, however, that a bitstream obtained in this way is not compliant with the H.264/AVC standard because the latter specifies that all slice groups need to be present in an H.264/AVC bitstream. This means that an H.264/AVC compliant decoder will not guarantee the correct decoding of such a bitstream. Notwithstanding the fact that only minor modifications of an H.264/AVC decoder are needed for the correct decoding of the adapted bitstream (thanks to the independent nature of slices in H.264/AVC), this may be considered a disadvantage or gracelessness of the procedure described above. It should also be noted that the requirement that all slice groups need to be coded is proposed to be relaxed in the currently developed SVC specification [13].

5   Placeholder Slices

In order to avert any deviation of the H.264/AVC specification, as explained in the previous section, the authors propose the use of placeholder slices. A placeholder slice can be defined as a slice that is identical to the corresponding area of a certain reference picture, or that is reconstructed by relying on a well-defined interpolation process between different reference pictures [2]. This implies that only a very limited amount of information has to be stored or transmitted. In this paper, placeholder slices are used to fill up the gaps that are created in a bitstream due to the removal of certain background slices. Taking into account the appropriate provisions of the H.264/AVC specification,

```
------------------ original description ------------------
<coded_slice_of_a_non_IDR_picture>
  <slice_layer_without_partitioning_rbsp>
    <slice_header>
      <first_mb_in_slice>0</first_mb_in_slice>
      <slice_type>5</slice_type>
      <pic_parameter_set_id>0</pic_parameter_set_id>
      <frame_num xsi:type="b4">1</frame_num>
      <!-- ... -->
    </slice_header>
    <slice_data>
      <bit_stuffing>7</bit_stuffing>
      <slice_payload>7875 1177</slice_payload>
    </slice_data>
  </slice_layer_without_partitioning_rbsp>
</coded_slice_of_a_non_IDR_picture>

------------------ adapted description ------------------
<coded_slice_of_a_skipped_non_IDR_picture>
  <skipped_slice_layer_without_partitioning_rbsp>
    <slice_header>
      <first_mb_in_slice>0</first_mb_in_slice>
      <slice_type>5</slice_type>
      <pic_parameter_set_id>0</pic_parameter_set_id>
      <frame_num xsi:type="b4">1</frame_num>
      <!-- ... -->
    </slice_header>
    <skipped_slice_data>
      <mb_skip_run>108</mb_skip_run>
    </skipped_slice_data>
    <rbsp_trailing_bits>
      <rbsp_stop_one_bit>1</rbsp_stop_one_bit>
      <rbsp_alignment_zero_bit>0</rbsp_alignment_zero_bit>
    </rbsp_trailing_bits>
  </skipped_slice_layer_without_partitioning_rbsp>
</coded_slice_of_a_skipped_non_IDR_picture>
```

Fig. 3. P slice replaced by a skipped P slice

these placeholder slices are in this paper implemented by means of P slices in which all macroblocks are marked as skipped (skipped P slices).

How the XML-driven content adaptation approach can be exerted for the substitution of coded background P or B slices by skipped P slices, is embroidered here. We first focus on background P slices (both reference and non-reference), as this is the most straightforward case. In this situation, there is no need to change any of the syntax elements of the NAL unit header or the slice header: only the actual slice data are to be substituted. The necessary slice data for the definition of a skipped P slice is the number of skipped macroblocks in that slice (by means of the syntax element mb_skip_run). Additionally, the slice layer has to be filled with a number of trailing bits (by means of the syntax element rbsp_slice_trailing_bits) in order to get byte-aligned in the bitstream. The XML descriptions of both the original and the adapted P slice are given in Figure 3. Note that some simplifications were introduced in the code in order to meet the place constraints and to improve the readability.

Regarding the syntax element mb_skip_run, it should be noted that the value of this element depends on the size of the slice being replaced. Since the ROIs are varying in time, the number of macroblocks in the slices of the background is not the same for every picture. Without loss of generality, consider the case that there is only one slice in the background slice group. The number of macroblocks in this slice is equal to the total number of macroblocks in a picture (denoted by PicSizeInMbs) minus the number of macroblocks that are contained by the various ROIs in that picture. Using the notation of Section 4, it is rather straighforward to calculate this number using TL_i, BR_i and W (taking into account the fact that ROIs may overlap each other). If there are multiple slices in the background slice group, then they can all be substituted by a single skipped P slice containing the same number of skipped macroblocks as in the case of a single background slice.

If the background slice group also contains B slices, then several changes have to be made to the slice header if one wants to substitute that particular slice with a skipped P slice. First, the slice type (indicated by the syntax element `slice_type`) has to be changed from 1 or 6 (B slice) to 0 (P slice). Changing `slice_type` to 5 (also indicating a P slice) would not be correct since this would imply that all other slices of the current picture are P slices, which is not always the case since the ROI in the current picture can contain B slices. Next to changing the slice type, B slices contain some slice header syntax elements that cannot appear in the slice header of a P slice. These syntax elements are related to the specific nature of B slices (associated with, for instance, reference picture list L1 or weighted prediction), and need to be removed. To be more specific, the following elements (and the syntax elements that are implied by these syntax elements) are removed by the XSL Transformation in the XML domain:

- `direct_spatial_mv_pred_flag`;
- `num_ref_idx_l1_active_minus1`;
- `ref_pic_list_reordering_flag_l1`;
- `luma_weight_l1_flag` (if applicable);
- `chroma_weight_l1_flag` (if applicable).

The actual slice data is replaced by a serie of skipped macroblocks in the same way as described above. Note that in all cases, the value of the syntax element `slice_qp_delta` can be set to zero to save some aditional bits during the adaptation process. An example of a B slice and a corresponding skipped P slice, as generated by the adaptation process, is given in Figure 4.

One could argue that the use of the MPEG-21 BSDL framework for the substitution process is somehow too complicated because the encoder could simply be instructed *directly* to code the background slices as skipped P slices. This would surely reduce the overall complexity, but if the bitstream is delivered to multiple receivers, each one would receive an adapted version, whereas the method using MPEG-21 BSDL could be applied only in those network nodes where an adaptation is needed or wanted.

6 Results

In this section, the experimental results of a series of tests are presented. These results give some insight into the implications of the approaches that are described in the previous sections. An overview will be given of the impact on the properties of the bitstreams and on the decoder. Next to this, some performance measurements will be presented regarding the content adaptation process (the BSDL framework). While most of the results demonstrate the benefits of the proposed methods, certain results indicate some drawbacks and the need for further research.

Four well-known video sequences were used in the experiments: Hall Monitor, News, Stefan, and Crew. The latter sequence has a resolution of 1280×720 pixels whereas the former three have a CIF resolution (352×288). Within these sequences, some ROIs

```
------------------ original description ------------------
<coded_slice_of_a_non_IDR_picture>
  <slice_layer_without_partitioning_rbsp>
    <slice_header>
      <first_mb_in_slice>0</first_mb_in_slice>
      <slice_type>6</slice_type>
      <pic_parameter_set_id>1</pic_parameter_set_id>
      <frame_num>2</frame_num>
      <pic_order_cnt_lsb>2</pic_order_cnt_lsb>
      <direct_spatial_mv_pred_flag>1</direct...>
      <num_ref_idx_active_override_flag>1</num...>
      <num_ref_idx_l0_active_minus1>1</num...>
      <num_ref_idx_l1_active_minus1>0</num...>
      <ref_pic_list_reordering_flag_l0>0</ref...>
      <ref_pic_list_reordering_flag_l1>0</ref...>
      <slice_qp_delta>2</slice_qp_delta>
    </slice_header>
    <slice_data>
      <bit_stuffing>6</bit_stuffing>
      <slice_payload>9543 851</slice_payload>
    </slice_data>
  </slice_layer_without_partitioning_rbsp>
</coded_slice_of_a_non_IDR_picture>

------------------ adapted description -------------------
<coded_slice_of_a_skipped_non_IDR_picture>
  <skipped_slice_layer_without_partitioning_rbsp>
    <slice_header>
      <first_mb_in_slice>0</first_mb_in_slice>
      <slice_type>0</slice_type>
      <pic_parameter_set_id>1</pic_parameter_set_id>
      <frame_num>2</frame_num>
      <pic_order_cnt_lsb>2</pic_order_cnt_lsb>
      <num_ref_idx_active_override_flag>1</num...>
      <num_ref_idx_l0_active_minus1>1</num...>
      <ref_pic_list_reordering_flag_l0>0</ref...>
      <slice_qp_delta>0</slice_qp_delta>
    </slice_header>
    <skipped_slice_data>
      <mb_skip_run>264</mb_skip_run>
    </skipped_slice_data>
    <rbsp_trailing_bits>
      <rbsp_stop_one_bit>1</rbsp_stop_one_bit>
      <rbsp_alignment_zero_bit>0</rbsp...>
    </rbsp_trailing_bits>
  </skipped_slice_layer_without_partitioning_rbsp>
</coded_slice_of_a_skipped_non_IDR_picture>
```

Fig. 4. B slice replaced by a skipped P slice

were identified: the moving persons in Hall Monitor and the little bag that is left behind by one of these persons; the heads of the two speakers in News; the tennis player in Stefan; the first two persons of the crew and a separate ROI for the rest of the crew in the sequence Crew. Note that these ROIs have changing positions, as well as sizes in the course of time, and that some ROIs are disappearing at certain points in time.

The sequences were encoded with a modified version of the reference software (based on JM 9.5), once conform to the Baseline Profile and once conform to the Extended Profile (the only difference being the use of B slices). A constant Quantization Parameter (QP) of 28 was used, every slice group contains only one slice, and the GOP size was 16. Table 1 summarizes some other properties of the resulting bitstreams, as well as the impact of the adaptation process on the bit rate. In the table, br_p stands for the bit rate of the bitstream in which all background P and/or B slices were replaced by skipped P slices and br_d stands for the bit rate of the bitstream in which all background P and/or B slices were dropped (leading to bitstreams that are no longer compliant with the H.264/AVC specification – see also Section 4). Also note that the number of slice groups is one more than the number of ROIs.

It is clear from the numbers in Table 1 that the bit rate is reduced significantly when performing the adaptation (up to 64%). Of course, this usually has a profound impact

Table 1. Bitstream characteristics (bit rate in kbit/s)

sequence		# ROIs	# PPSs	# slices	br	br_p	br_d
IP	crew	1–3	48	2020	3856	1379	1376
	hall monitor	1–3	26	924	457	274	272
	news	2	3	904	382	193	190
	stefan	1	31	632	1657	758	756
IBBP	crew	1–3	48	2020	3725	1403	1400
	hall monitor	1–3	26	924	444	277	274
	news	2	3	904	402	193	190
	stefan	1	31	632	1829	819	817

on the resulting visual quality (also because the ROIs are not coded as isolated regions). However, in the case of a static background (as for instance in Hall Monitor), the visual quality is almost not affected at all: the resulting average PSNR-Y is 36.7 dB whereas the unadapted version has an average PSNR-Y of 37.7 dB (or 38.0 dB for the Extended Profile). Subjectively, even an expert viewer can scarcely notice that the bitstream has undergone any content adaptation. This also indicates that the encoder could have coded the bitstream much more efficiently if a minor decrease in quality was allowed. This opens up exciting new possibilities for video conferencing applications. Indeed, when the video feeds are to be sent over unreliable networks (as is more and more the case), rather big decreases in available bandwidth can be sustained easily without jeopardizing the visual quality, provided that the network has some Quality of Service (QoS) implemented so that if packets are to be dropped, only the background is affected.

Another important consequence of replacing coded background slices with skipped slices is the impact thereof on the decoding speed of the receiving decoder. Since a considerable amount of macroblocks within a picture are marked as skipped when placeholder slices were inserted into the bitstream, it is expected that this is reflected on the behavior of the decoder because the latter can rely directly on its decoded picture buffer in order to decode the current skipped macroblock without the need for additional computations. To get some more insight, the decoding speed of the reference decoder (JM 10.2) was measured when decoding the various bitstreams several times. The averages of these measurements are summed up in Table 2.

As one can see from this table, the decoding speed increases significantly when placeholder slices are inserted into the bitstreams compared to the decoding speed for the original bitstream. The decoding speeds of the decoder, when decoding bitstreams in which the background was dropped, are merely given for completeness. These speeds

Table 2. Impact on decoding speed (frames per second)

sequence		original	placeholders	dropping
IP	crew	1.5	2.0	1.8
	hall monitor	15.6	16.9	17.9
	news	16.7	18.9	18.2
	stefan	10.4	14.9	13.9
IBBP	crew	1.1	1.3	-
	hall monitor	13.8	17.0	17.2
	news	14.3	17.5	17.2
	stefan	9.5	14.4	13.3

are comparable to the case of the inserted placeholder slices, but it is important to note that the reference decoder applies a spatial interpolation algorithm to conceal the apparent transmission errors in the background slices by default, rendering a comparison with these numbers unjustified. It should also be noted that, to the best of the authors' knowledge, the reference decoder is the only implementation of the H.264/AVC specification that supports FMO. As a result, measurements for other decoders (having real-time behavior) could not be performed.

Another important observation is that, as mentioned earlier, when replacing coded B slices with skipped P slices, one actually performs 'profile scalability'. Indeed, the bitstreams that are conform to the Extended Profile can be adapted in such way that the resulting bitstreams are conform to the Baseline Profile if *all* coded B slices are replaced by skipped P slices.

The final part of this results section deals with some measurements related to the BSDL framework. It is reported in literature that most performance issues of the BSDL framework are related to the BintoBSD Parser [5,4]. The results of this paper also lead to the same conclusion. As an illustration, Figure 5 shows the execution speed of the BintoBSD Parser in function of the number of PPSs that are present in a bitstream. All measurements were done on an Intel Pentium 4 2.8 GHz system running a 2.4.19 Linux kernel by making use of the `time` command. The execution speed is given in terms of slices per second as slices are the basic units of parsing for the BintoBSD Parser in the context of this paper.

As one can clearly see from this figure, only when very few PPSs are present in the bitstream, the BintoBSD Parser achieves reasonable execution speeds. The fundamental reason for this, however, lies in the fact that the reference encoder puts all PPSs in the beginning of the bitstream. If the PPSs would appear scattered in the bitstream (at places where the ROI configuration changes), the execution speed would be independent of the number of PPSs, provided that a PPS is never referenced again once another PPS appears in the bitstream. Nevertheless, the fact that the BintoBSD Parser cannot cope with this can be considered a disadvantage.

The transformation of the BSDs (embodying the actual content adaptation) is currently implemented in XSLT. The execution speeds of the transformations barely reach

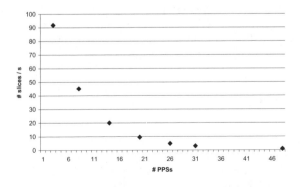

Fig. 5. Decreasing execution speed of the BintoBSD Parser

Table 3. Execution times of XSLT (seconds)

sequence		placeholders	dropping
IP	crew	50.0	48.4
	hall monitor	13.5	13.1
	news	12.9	12.5
	stefan	5.7	5.5
IBBP	crew	49.0	49.2
	hall monitor	13.3	13.3
	news	12.9	12.8
	stefan	5.8	5.4

real-time performance, which is caused by the fact that the XSLT engine (Saxon 8) needs the entire DOM tree in memory in order to perform the transformation. The execution times are summarized in Table 3. Therefore, future research will concentrate on the implementation of the transformations by making use of STX. This should dramatically improve the performance.

7   Conclusions and Future Work

In this paper, it is shown how Regions of Interest can be defined within the H.264/AVC specification and how these ROIs can be coded by making use of Flexible Macroblock Ordering. For the adaptation of the bitstreams, the MPEG-21 BSDL framework was applied for the extraction of the ROIs and for the replacement of the coded background slices with placeholder slices (skipped P slices).

By doing so, the bit rate needed to transmit the bitstream can be reduced significantly. Especially in the case of a static camera and a fixed background, this bit rate reduction has very little impact on the visual quality. This opens up interesting new possibilities for certain video applications such as video conferencing where the proposed approach can be seen as the basis for QoS. Another advantage of the adaptation process is the fact that the execution speeds of the receiving decoder fairly increase. Next to this, the concept of placeholder insertion can be used to switch from one Profile to another; for instance going from the Extended Profile to the Baseline Profile.

The XML-driven content adaptation process, as described in this paper, is elegant and generic by design, but the results indicate that there are some performance issues. These shortcomings will be examined in future research aiming to achieve a content adaptation engine that is employable in real-life use cases.

Acknowledgements

The research activities as described in this paper were funded by Ghent University, the Interdisciplinary Institute for Broadband Technology (IBBT), the Institute for the Promotion of Innovation by Science and Technology in Flanders (IWT), the Fund for Scientific Research-Flanders (FWO-Flanders), the Belgian Federal Science Policy Office (BFSPO), and the European Union.

References

1. Cimprich, P.: Streaming transformations for XML (STX) version 1.0 working draft (2004), http://stx.sourceforge.net/documents/spec-stx-20040701.html
2. De Neve, W., De Schrijver, D., Van de Walle, D., Lambert, P., Van de Walle, R.: Description-based substitution methods for emulating temporal scalability in state-of-the-art video coding formats. In: Proceedings of the 7th International Workshop on Image Analysis for Multimedia Interactive Services, Korea (accepted, 2006)
3. De Neve, W., Van Deursen, D., De Schrijver, D., De Wolf, K., Van de Walle, R.: Using Bitstream Structure Descriptions for the Exploitation of Multi-layered Temporal Scalability in H.264/AVC's Base Specification. In: Ho, Y.-S., Kim, H.J. (eds.) PCM 2005. LNCS, vol. 3767, pp. 641–652. Springer, Heidelberg (2005)
4. De Schrijver, D., Poppe, C., Lerouge, S., Neve, W.D., Walle, R.V.d.: MPEG-21 bitstream syntax descriptions for scalable video codecs (article in press). Multimedia Systems (2006), http://dx.doi.org/10.1007/s00530-006-0021-5
5. Devillers, S., Timmerer, C., Heuer, J., Hellwagner, H.: Bitstream syntax description-based adaptation in streaming and constrained environments. IEEE Trans. Multimedia 7(3), 463–470 (2005)
6. Dhondt, Y., Lambert, P., Notebaert, S., Van de Walle, R.: Flexible macroblock ordering as a content adaptation tool in H.264/AVC. In: Proceedings of the SPIE/Optics East conference, Boston (2005)
7. Hannuksela, M.M., Wang, Y.-K., Gabbouj, M.: Isolated regions in video coding. IEEE Transactions on Multimedia 6(2), 259–267 (2004)
8. Ichimura, D., Honda, Y., Sun, H., Lee, M., Shen, S.: A tool for interactive ROI scalability. In: JVT-Q020 (2005), http://ftp3.itu.ch/av-arch/jvt-site/2005_10_Nice/JVT-Q020.doc
9. ISO/IEC JTC1/SC29/WG11 : Applications and requirements for scalable video coding. ISO/IEC JTC1/SC29/WG11 N6880 (2005), http://www.chiariglione.org/mpeg/working_documents/mpeg-04/svc/requirements.zip
10. Kay, M.: XSLT Programmer's Reference, 2nd edn. Wrox Press Ltd., Birmingham, UK (2001)
11. Lambert, P., De Neve, W., Dhondt, Y., Van de Walle, R.: Flexible macroblock ordering in H.264/AVC. Journal of Visual Communication and Image Representation 17(2), 358–375 (2006)
12. Li, W.: Overview of fine granularity scalability in MPEG-4 video standard. IEEE Trans. Circuits Syst. Video Technol. 11(3), 301–317 (2001)
13. Reichel, J., Schwarz, H., Wien, M.: Joint scalable video model JSVM-4. JVT-Q202 (2005), http://ftp3.itu.ch/av-arch/jvt-site/2005_10_Nice/JVT-Q202.zip
14. Taubman, D., Marcellin, M.: JPEG 2000: Image Compression Fundamentals, Standards and Practice. Kluwer Academic Publishers, Dordrecht (2002)
15. Thang, T.C., Kim, D., Bae, T.M., Kang, J.W., Ro, Y.M., Kim, J.G.: Show case of ROI extraction using scalability information SEI message. JVT-Q077 (2005), http://ftp3.itu.ch/av-arch/jvt-site/2005_10_Nice/JVT-Q077.doc
16. Vetro, A., Timmerer, C.: Text of ISO/IEC 21000-7 FCD - part 7: Digital item adaptation. ISO/IEC JTC1/SC29/WG11 N5845 (2003), http://www.chiariglione.org/mpeg/working_documents/mpeg-21/dia/dia_fcd.zip
17. Wiegand, T., Sullivan, G.J., Bjøntegaard, G., Luthra, A.: Overview of the H.264/AVC video coding standard. IEEE Trans. Circuits Syst. Video Technol. 13(7), 560–576 (2003)
18. Yin, P., Boyce, J., Pandit, P.: FMO and ROI scalability. JVT-Q029 (2005), http://ftp3.itu.ch/av-arch/jvt-site/2005_10_Nice/JVT-Q029.doc

Design and Implementation of Video on Demand Services over a Peer-to-Peer Multioverlay Network

Jia-Ming Chen, Jenq-Shiou Leu, Hsin-Wen Wei, Li-Ping Tung,
Yen-Ting Chou, and Wei-Kuan Shih

Department of Computer Science, National Tsing Hua University, Hsinchu, Taiwan
{jonathan,jerry_leu,bertha,lptung,corey,
wshih}@rtlab.cs.nthu.edu.tw

Abstract. Video-on-Demand (VoD) services using peer-to-peer (P2P) technologies benefit by balancing load among clients and maximizing their bandwidth utilization to reduce the burden on central video servers with the single
point of failure. Conventional P2P techniques for realizing VoD services only
consider data between active peers in the same VoD session. They never consider those inactive peers that have left the session but may still hold partial
media content in their local storage. In this article, we propose a novel architecture to construct a fully decentralized P2P overlay network for VoD streaming
services based on a multioverlay concept. The architecture is referred to as
MegaDrop. It not only takes the types of peers into consideration but also provides mechanisms for discovering nodes that may contain desired media objects. Such a P2P-based scheme can distribute media among peers, allow peers
to search for a specific media object over the entire network efficiently, and
stream the media object from a group of the peers. We employ a layered architecture consisting of four major tiers: Peer Discovery Layer, Content Lookup
Layer, Media Streaming Layer, and Playback Control Layer. The evaluation results show that our architecture is particularly efficient for huge media delivery
and multiuser streaming sessions.

Keywords: Peer-to-Peer, Video-on-Demand, Overlay Network.

1 Introduction

Video-on-demand (VoD) services generally rely on one or only a small number of
video servers to deliver video content. This topology places a heavy processing load
on video servers, with the client–server paths representing a heavy network burden.
Conventional techniques such as batching, patching [12], broadcasting, IP multicast-
ing, proxy caching, and content distribution networks rely on centralized servers for
delivering media. Peer-to-peer (P2P) computing represents another possible solution
to such problems in media streaming.

The peers in P2P communications interact with others without the use of intermediar-
ies, and can thereby reduce the burden on the servers delivering the media and increase
bandwidth utilization. To the best of our knowledge, the Chaining technique [14] is the
first to apply the P2P concept to VoD streaming. Each client in Chaining has a fixed-size

J. Filipe and M.S. Obaidat (Eds.): ICETE 2006, CCIS 9, pp. 186–198, 2008.
© Springer-Verlag Berlin Heidelberg 2008

buffer to cache the most recent content of the video stream it has received, but this scheme does not provide a recovery protocol in case of failures. DirectStream [15] constructs tree structures to deliver video based on an interval-caching scheme similar to Chaining. However, the directory server in DirectStream represents a possible single point of failure. P2Cast [16] is derived from the traditional patching technique with unicast connections among peers, but it is vulnerable to disruption due to server bottlenecks at the source. P2VoD [17] works similarly to P2Cast, and makes a late client obtain the initial missing part of a video (namely, a patch) not only from the server but also from other clients, and handles failures locally without the involvement of the source. The major disadvantage of P2VoD is a possible long recovery time due to a client having an out-of-date list of its siblings' IP addresses.

The aforementioned schemes do not consider those inactive peers that have left the session but may still hold some of the media content in their local storage. Involving these inactive users in a VoD session for streaming the video content they still hold will provide peers with more potential resources in the same session, which could increase the effectiveness and efficiency of the VoD system. This scheme requires a mechanism for a requesting user to find video objects among both active and inactive users, which may be possible using generic P2P architectures with efficient lookup algorithms.

Based on the above, we aimed to design a new architecture supporting VoD streaming services. The proposed architecture, referred to as MegaDrop, is based on a multioverlay network. The first overlay network is used to find a specific object, and the second overlay network is used to stream media data. The architecture is fully decentralized without any central administrative points. To define the service boundary at different levels, we further partition the architecture into four tiers: Peer Discovery Layer (PDL), Content Lookup Layer (CLL), Media Streaming Layer (MSL), and Playback Control Layer (PCL). The PDL is responsible for finding peers and constructing the first overlay network. The CLL generates a unique identifier for a media object and provides a content-matching capability. The MSL transmits media between peers and constructs the second overlay network. The PCL interacts with end users by providing the interface of control operations. Finally, we performed a series of experiments on the MegaDrop system to evaluate the startup delay, efficiency of bandwidth utilization, and effectiveness of peer bandwidth aggregation. The result shows that the aggregate bandwidth available to peers increases with the number of peers participating in a session, which thereby reduces the average streaming time.

The remainder of this paper is organized as follows. Section 2 introduces the media representations to properly fulfill the characteristics of a VoD streaming environment stated above. Section 3 provides an overview of the MegaDrop system, and the detailed design and implementation of the various components in the architecture are described in Section 4. Section 5 presents a performance evaluation of the MegaDrop system, and Section 6 proposes some ideas about how to consolidate this system. Finally, concluding remarks are made in Section 7.

2 Media Representations

According to the aforementioned characteristics, we devise a media representation that breaks the content of a typical media object (usually a media file) into media blocks based on a group of pictures (or frames). It allows both active and inactive peers to potentially share their (incomplete) media content to form media streaming, or each peer to only hold some of the media data and gather the remaining required media data from multiple peers. The proposed media representation provides several advantages: (i) the loss of some of the media blocks during media transmission would not damage the media object or make it undecodable, (ii) the amount of data involved in the error recovery or retransmission of the media data under certain conditions of unreliability can be reduced to the unit of a media block, and (iii) it is easy to implement certain VCR-like interactions (e.g., fast forward, fast rewind, and jump forward/backward) at multiples of the normal playback speed by skipping media data on the basis of multiple media blocks.

A single media object may be spread over multiple peers, and hence the receiving peer must know how to gather multiple portions of the media blocks from other peers. We therefore introduced an original structure, called *media-info*, to provide a unique identifier for a specific media object that allows it to be located and restored by a receiving peer. Basically, *media-info* provides the global information of a media object, such as the frame rate, video codec, media title, creation time, author information, and copyright information, and is followed by hashed information. In the following subsections, we first describe the hashing procedure to generate the hashed information, called *media-hash*, and then use this to construct the original *media-info*.

2.1 Media-Hash

As depicted in Figure 1, *media-hash* is produced by a two-step hash scheme. First, a specific hash function $H(x)$ (e.g., SHA1, CRC32, or MD5) is applied to each media block to produce a hashed block. Then, those hashed blocks together with *media size*, *hash scheme*, and *hash size* are hashed again by $H(x)$ to generate the *media-hash*, which uniquely represents a media object. In Figure 1, B_n denotes the n-th media block, where $1 \leq n \leq B_N$. B_{len} represents the length of a media block, which generally would be chosen as 128, 256, 512, or 1024 kB. Thus B_N can be computed as $\lceil M_{len}/B_{len} \rceil$, where M_{len} is the size of the media object (in bytes) and $\lceil \; \rceil$ denotes the ceiling operation. Furthermore, HB_n, and H_{len} (in bytes) indicate the value and length

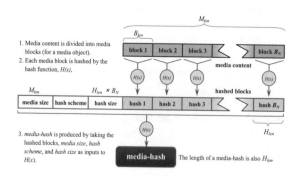

Fig. 1. The flow for generating hashed blocks and *media-hash*

of the hashed data for media block B_n, respectively (i.e., $HB_n = H(B_n)$ and $H_{len} =$ length of HB_n). Note that zero values are padded to the last media block if its size is less than B_{len}. Obviously, before applying the second step of hashing, the hash size could be calculated as $H_{len} \times B_N$, the media size equals to M_{len}, and the field of hash scheme merely specifies the hash function used in this procedure. In particular, since we only choose one hash function in this two-step hash scheme procedure, the size of produced *media-hash* also equals H_{len}.

2.2 Media-Info

Media-info is created to provide not only the unique identifier for a specific media object through *media-hash*, but also the sufficient information for a receiving peer to know (i) where the media object is stored; (ii) how to gather and stream the media object; (iii) what characteristics of a media object owns for decoding and rendering. Consequently, a *media-info* should be retrieved before a streaming session starts. Figure 2 shows the structure of a *media-info*. The fields of *media title*, *date time*, *creator*, and *comments* are extracted from original header of a media object, which are provided by *media-info* optionally. Note that *media-info* contains hashed blocks as well, which could be used to verify the correctness of each retrieved media block for the purpose of error recovery. Additionally, the field of brokers informs the receiving peer how to gather and stream the media blocks, which may probably spread among multiple peers. The detailed usage of this field is described in Section 3.3.

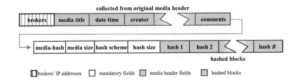

Fig. 2. The structure of a *media-info*

Especially, the size of the *media-info* highly depends on the choice of the size for each media block. Equation (1) expresses this relation, where M_{len}, B_{len}, H_{len} are the symbols as stated in Section 2.1, I_{len} is the size of *media-info*, and NF_{len}, OF_{len} represent the size of mandatory fields (including brokers field) and media header fields in Figure 2, respectively. Compact size of *media-info* tends toward larger B_{len}. However, larger B_{len} produces smaller amount of media blocks, which potentially reduces the degree of concurrence for media transmission among multiple peers.

$$I_{len} = \left\lceil \frac{M_{len}}{B_{len}} \right\rceil \times H_{len} + NF_{len} + OF_{len} \tag{1}$$

Based on the designed media representation, we now present the proposed architecture for providing VoD streaming services in a P2P environment.

3 MultiOverlay Architecture

In order to make VoD functions such as locate, stream, and control-playback for a media object behave smoothly with the abovementioned media representations, we devise the MegaDrop system, which has a multioverlay architecture with the four layers mentioned in Section 1, as shown in Figure 3.

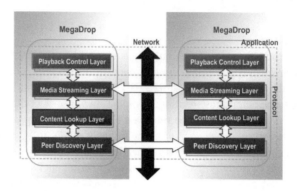

Fig. 3. MegaDrop architecture

3.1 Peer Discovery Layer

The PDL, as its name implies, provides an efficient peer lookup service such that upper layers can search for desired media objects propitiously. It contains several major functions: routing messages between peers, filtering out unnecessary messages, caching queries within peers, and maintaining peer information. Especially, The PDL is not restricted to a specific P2P network, that is, any typical P2P overlay networks such as Gnutella [11], Pastry [18], Chord [8], and CAN [9] can be adopted and wrapped in this layer as well.

3.2 Content Lookup Layer

The CLL plays the mediator for the PDL and the MSL. At least, two basic operations should be handled in this layer: (i) when a peer is willing to share a media object, a corresponding *media-info* has to be generated by the CLL, e.g., the CLL keeps a media pool for maintaining the *media-info*s of shared media objects; (ii) it should help content search for queries received by the PDL, so as to allow the PDL to focus on routing messages/queries to ignore processing the media content at all. Optionally, a mechanism for error recovery to ensure the completeness of received media blocks could be designed in this layer.

3.3 Media Streaming Layer

Media transmissions between peers are handled by this layer. Since the MSL has no idea of which peers media objects are located in, it must rely on the cooperation between the CLL and the PDL to find out these peers. In the MegaDrop system, over-all peers could be classified as three types: suppliers, brokers, and droppers. A sup-plier is a peer that has a complete media object. A dropper, in contrast, is a peer that has an incomplete media object and still needs to retrieve missing media blocks from other peers. Therefore, for a specific media object, a supplier is always capable of providing any portions of media blocks, while a dropper only provide partial media blocks. Furthermore, a broker is an intermediate peer that assists suppliers and drop-pers in exchanging peer information (via the field of brokers in a *media-info* as men-tioned in Section 2.2).

As Figure 4 displayed, during a media session in the MSL, several peers can form a cluster virtually, where some peers act as suppliers and the others act as droppers. Among these peers, one peer would be treated as a broker, which is connected by other peers to periodically maintain the list of sending peers. Note that in this virtual cluster, there should be existed at least either one supplier or several droppers contain-ing exclusive media blocks to restore an entire media object.

Furthermore, providing buffer management for caching the most up-to-date media blocks of a media object is also necessary. In addition, concerning problems of fair-ness, or freeriding that exists in common P2P environments due to unequal contribu-tion among peers, it is better to equip a bartering technique to raise incentive of contributing media objects by each peer.

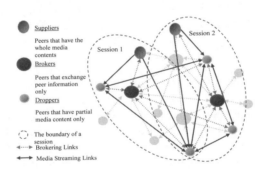

Fig. 4. The Media Streaming Layer

3.4 Playback Control Layer

In VoD streaming services, the PCL is designed to directly interact with end users and exposes a user interface for administrating and controlling operations, e.g., providing VCR-like interactions, such as playing, pausing, stopping, seeking, fast-forwarding, and so on. Depending on users' behaviors, the PCL cooperates with the MSL to change cach-ing policy (via buffer management). For example, when a user issue a seeking operation to change current play point, the PCL needs to notify the MSL to acquire the media blocks starting at the new play point first because the MSL never knows the occurrence of such an event without this notification. Besides, for the convenience of controlling playback, the PCL should apparently provide the status of monitoring and operational statistics for users to manage the overall system performance.

4 Implementation

In this section, we present the comprehensive implementation of crucial operations in eac layer to realize the MegaDrop system.

4.1 Peer Discovery Layer

The PDL is implemented from modifying an LGPL library, GnucDNA [4], which is based on Gnutella2 [5] overlay network. Figure 5 shows the topology. In experience, this topology benefits from minimizing searching and routing traffic to reserve network bandwidth for media transmission. Theoretically, the adequate amount of trunks could maintain the ability for a peer to find desired media blocks located anywhere on the network.

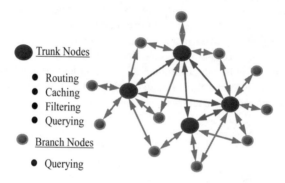

Fig. 5. Overlay network with tree-like topology

The following major operations are implemented in the PDL. First, bootstrapping allows a peer to participate in the MegaDrop system. We utilized GWebCache [6] to allow a peer to discover which active peers are currently available for connection. Second, after obtaining several IP addresses via a bootstrapping procedure, a peer becomes a trunk or branch by handshaking with these IP addresses. We adopt a common three-way handshaking mechanism to develop this protocol. Third, the communications between peers are unified by replicating a subset of the messaging system in the Gnutella2 protocol [5]. Likewise, query hash tables are utilized to facilitate the query-routing protocol, which is implemented by modifying Prinkey's scheme [19].

4.2 Content Lookup Layer

Any behaviors reliant on the media content could be implemented in the CLL. Here we have implemented three major operations. The first is generating *media-info*. We used the SHA1 algorithm as our hash scheme, which generated each hashed block in 20 bytes. The construction methodology is detailed in Section 2. Second, the CLL implements content searching/matching based on the media content rather than keyword searching by the PDL. Providing content searches in advance can complement keyword searches because media objects are usually not uniquely identified by keywords. Third, data integrity is ensured by hashing and comparing a received media

according to the information provided by *media-info*. Thereafter, the CLL can cooperate with the MSL to decide whether to drop or retransmit a received media block
that is corrupted.

4.3 Media Streaming Layer

Within a media session, the MSL performs media transmission across multiple sending peers. We employ a variant of BitTorrent protocol [1], [2] to accomplish the most
parts of this layer, and several operations are implemented: (i) *Media-info* requesting:
the MSL needs this information before establishing a media session; (ii) Brokering:
due to versatile status of active peers in P2P environment, a receiving peer can periodically update the list of sending peers from the broker through brokering mechanism. (Remind that a broker maintains a global view to aggregate a media object).
This protocol is simply realized by HTTP conventions; (iii) Media streaming: this
procedure enables a receiving peer maintaining TCP/IP connections to sending peers.
In our implementation, this procedure contains three sub-functions, (a) handshaking,
which is designed to ensure that whether a sending peer is serving the desired media
object or not before a TCP/IP connection is established, (b) connection state guarding,
which tracks remote peers' states (in three modes: chocking, unchoking, or interesting) to monitor this connection, and (c) message/media data communication, which
delivers control or media data between both peers; (iv) Buffer management: in order
to deliver media blocks efficiently, in the MSL, every media block can further de-
compose into a bunch of smaller units called media piece, such that a media piece
could be treated as the smallest transmission unit during a media session. Therefore, a
buffer space provided by sending and receiving peers could act as a cache to manage
these media pieces. However, because media pieces of a media block may not always
delivered in order or the play point of video may jump randomly due to users' behaviors, we used a request-on-demand policy to handle this issue; We omit the detail explanations here due to limit space; and last, (v) Bartering: a variant of tit-for-tat
scheme is used to implement this technique. Finally, a typical access flow of the MSL
is shown in Figure 6.

4.4 Playback Control Layer

We implemented the PCL via the Microsoft™ DirectShow media framework [13].
DirectShow is essentially built on a group of filters, each of which performs a specific
operation for streaming a media file. Connecting several filters via input/output ports
results in a filter graph. In this implementation, we additionally introduce a high-level
component, called the *Filter Graph Manager*, to control the flow of a filter graph.
Figure 7 displays the topology, where a source filter directs the media data that may
come from local storage, the network, or capture devices to the transform filter, which
could be decoders, encoders, splitters, or multiplexers. Then, the media data are output to display devices via rendering filters. This topology can make the MegaDrop
system suitable for a variety of codecs (e.g., MPEG series, H.264, WMV series),
thereby increasing its flexibility.

Instead of implementing these filters from scratch, we based them on filters provided by Microsoft™ SDK. Actually, we merely design a customized source filter to
collaborate with the MSL, such that buffer management with a request-on-demand

policy could be seamlessly connected to the source filter. A transform filter was added to aid the MSL in gathering or splitting the media pieces. Finally, the overall VCR-like operations were implemented through the *IMediaControl* interface in DirectShow. Our implementation of PCL not only supports playback operations within the MegaDrop system, but also could be executed as a purely local media player.

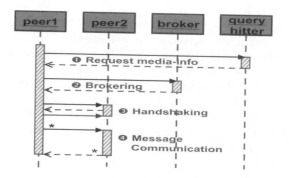

Fig. 6. Access flows of the Media Streaming

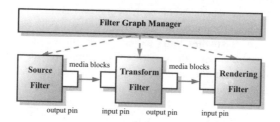

Fig. 7. Topology of a DirectShow filter graph

5   Evaluation

In this section, we show that the MegaDrop system is particularly efficient of huge amount of media data and multiuser streaming sessions by evaluating it from three essential metrics: (i) the startup delay versus the size of the *media-info* before starting a media transmission; (ii) efficiency of bandwidth utilizations by measuring the overheads induced from network traffics other than real transmitted media blocks; and (iii) effectiveness of bandwidth aggregations among multiple peers.

5.1   Startup Delay

Delivering *media-info* merely relies on communication between a broker peer and the receiving peer, making it easy to measure the startup transmission delay. Assume that the maximum startup delay for a media session is D (in seconds) and the average network speed is BS (in bytes/second), from equation (1) listed in Section 2.2 we can derive the minimal size of the media block, B_{len}, required to satisfy the maximum tolerable startup delay D:

$$B_{len} \geq \frac{M_{len} \times H_{len}}{BS \times D - NF_{len} - OF_{len}} \qquad (2)$$

Figure 8 illustrates the relationship between the number of media blocks, the size of *media-info*, and media size for various media objects, and reveals that the length of media block should be carefully chosen based on the media size.

5.2 Efficiency of Bandwidth Utilization

The transmission of data in the system other than media blocks is treated as traffic overhead, such as that for *media-info* structures, messages for brokering, and other control messages within the PDL. We can use this criterion to evaluate the efficiency of the MegaDrop system. The results shown in Figure 9 indicate that the overhead ratio arises significantly only when the media object is smaller than 10 kB, but even then is still very low at less than 2.4%. Given that almost all media objects are significantly larger than 10 kB, the MegaDrop system exhibits high bandwidth utilization.

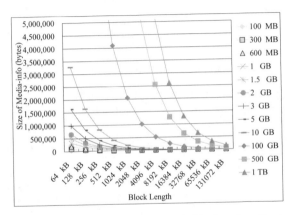

Fig. 8. Size of *media-info* versus media block and media size

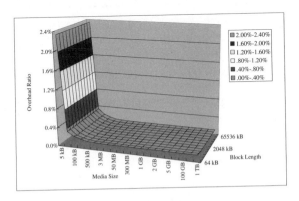

Fig. 9. Overheads versus media size

5.3 Effectiveness of Bandwidth Aggregation

To investigate effectiveness of bandwidth aggregating among peers, we setup an environment with four PCs in different specifications as shown in Table 1. Moreover, in this simulation, there are five video clips with various sizes, ranging from 200 MB to 1000 MB, and the length of each media block is fixed at 256 kB for each video clips. During the simulation, up to 16 peers are constructed to join a media session by selecting PCs in sequence order of Table 1. That is, if a media session contains 11 peers, then PCA6, PCA1, and PCP4 acts as three peers, individually while NBP3 only acts as two peers. We select PCA6 as the broker in all scenarios due to its superior equipments. Besides, to approach the reality of the scenario, we have limited the total uplink bandwidth to 1000 kB and uplink bandwidth to 200 kB per media connection for each peer, such that bartering mechanism will be triggered while bandwidth is running out. Therefore, during a media session, the join time of a peer, denoted as TJ_i, can be determined by equation (3), where N is the total number of peers in each test case.

$$TJ_i = \begin{cases} 0 & \text{, when } i = 1,2 \\ \dfrac{MLen \times (i-2)}{200 \times 1024 \times (N-1)} & \text{, when } 3 \leq i \leq N \end{cases} \quad (3)$$

Table 1. Specifications of the simulation environment

Name	PCA6	PCA1	PCP4	NBP3
Platform	Desktop PC	Desktop PC	Desktop PC	Notebook
CPU	AMD Athlon XP 1.6 GHz	AMD Athlon XP 1 GHz	Intel P4 1.5 GHz	Intel P3 Mobile 1.06 GHz
RAM	DDR 512 MB	DDR 256 MB	DDR 384 MB	SD 256 MB
OS	Microsoft Windows XP Professional SP2	Microsoft Windows XP Professional SP1	Microsoft Windows 2000 Workstation SP4	Microsoft Windows XP Home SP2
Network	Ethernet 100 Mb	Ethernet 100 Mb	Ethernet 100 Mb	Ethernet 100 Mb

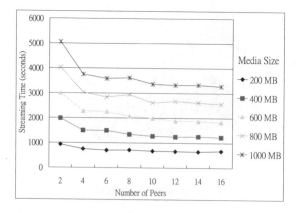

Fig. 10. Average transmission time versus number of joined peers with various media size

Figure 10 shows the results of the simulations. As we expected, the average transmission time per media session is reduced when more peers participated in it since this enlarged the degree of bandwidth aggregation. Especially for a large media object, the descending slope is more significantly but is retarded at a certain constant level, indicating that the effects of bandwidth aggregation are limited by the uplink bandwidth setting in the simulation scenario.

6 Extensions to the MegaDrop System

Error recovery is implemented in the current MegaDrop system by simply dropping or retransmitting a received media block that is corrupted. As mentioned in Section 2, this simple scheme does prevent a video from being undecodable or damaged, but it may induce video glitches or longer transmission delay. To solve this problem, path diversity with *Multiple Description Coding* (MDC) technique [7], [10] can be adopted to combine with the originated media representations in the MegaDrop system. Basic idea is that, for a media object, every media block can be further decomposed into two or more sub media blocks based on MDC technique. For example, each media block can be divided into two sub media blocks, consisting even and odd video frames separately. Then in the MSL, every original media session can be split into multiple sub media sessions to deliver these sub media blocks accordingly through path diversity technique. Therefore, through this methodology, the probability of the occurrence in video glitches and longer transmission delay can greatly reduce by conceding to video quality. Besides, we leave several challenges such as security and QoS management for the readers, as the further researches to extend and consolidate the MegaDrop system.

7 Conclusions

In this paper we propose a novel layered architecture to realize VoD streaming services in a P2P environment. The proposed architecture implements a fully decentralized system running on a P2P multioverlay network. Unlike existing mechanisms in which certain video servers must be deployed in advance, the proposed architecture does not rely on any centralized resource allocation. Instead, every media object is delivered and propagated over the network, and every peer in the network retrieves media content from as well as forwards it to other peers, thereby acting as a miniserver. The processing and sharing of the same media objects by multiple peers results in the formation of virtual server clusters. Major advantages of the proposed architecture are that it can balance the load among peers and efficiently utilize the network bandwidth.

The experimental results revealed that our approach is appropriate for serving VoD streaming, especially in the delivery of huge amounts of media data. Moreover, the participation of more peers in a media session can result in higher bandwidth aggregation, result in a decrease in the average time required to stream a given media object.

Finally, we have presented methods for reducing the probabilities of video glitches and longer transmission delays by combining our original media representations with the promising MDC and path-diversity techniques. These concepts are recommended as topics for future research to extend and consolidate the MegaDrop system.

References

1. Cohen, B.: BitTorrent Protocol (2001),
   `http://www.bittorrent.com/protocol.html`
2. Cohen, B.: Incentives build robustness in BitTorrent. In: Proceedings of the First Work-shop on the Economics of Peer-to-Peer Systems, Berkeley, CA (2003)
3. Rohrs, C.: Query routing for the Gnutella network (2001), `http://rfc-gnutella.sourceforge.net/`
4. GnucDNA (2000), `http://www.gnucleus.com/GnucDNA/`
5. Gnutella2 (2005), `http://www.gnutella2.com/`
6. GWebCache (2003), Gnutella Web Caching System, [Online], available,
   `http://www.gnucleus.com/gwebcache/`
7. Frank., H.P., Fitzek, B.C., Prasad, R., Katz, M.: Traffic analysis and video quality evalua-tion of multiple description coded video services for fourth generation wireless IP net-works. Special Issue of the International Journal on Wireless Personal Communications (2005)
8. Stoica, I., Morris, R., Karger, D., Kaashoek, M.F., Balakrishnan, H.: Chord: A scalable Peer-to-peer Lookup Service for Internet Applications. In: Proceedings of ACM SIG-COMM 2001, San Diego, CA, USA (2001a)
9. Stoica, I., Morris, R., Karger, D., Kaashoek, F., Balakrishnan, H.: Chord: A scalable con-tentaddressable network. In: Proceedings of the ACM SIGCOMM 2001, San Diego, CA, USA (2001b)
10. Lee, I., Guan, L.: Reliable Video Communication with Multi-Path Stream-ing Using MDC. In: Proceedings of the IEEE International Conference on Multimedia & Expo, pp. 711–714 (2005)
11. Frankel, J., Pepper, T.: Gnutella (2000), `http://www.gnutella.com/`
12. Hua, K.A., Tantaoui, M.: Cost effective and scalable video streaming techniques. In: Furht, B., Marques, O. (eds.) Handbook of Video Databases, CRC Press, Abingdon (2003)
13. Microsoft Corporation (2006), Microsoft Developer Network (MSDN),
   `http://msdn.microsoft.com/`
14. Sheu, S., Hua, K.A., Tavanapong, W.: Chaining: A generalized batching technique for Video-on-Demand Systems. In: Proceedings of the IEEE International Conference on Mul-timedia Computing and System, Ottawa, Canada, pp. 110–117 (1997)
15. Guo, Y., Suh, K., Kurose, J., Towsley, D.: A Peer-to-peer On-Demand streaming service and its performance evaluation. In: Proceedings of the IEEE International Conference on Multimedia & Expo., Baltimore, MD, pp. II-649-652 (2003a)
16. Guo, Y., Suh, K., Kurose, J., Towsley, D.: P2Cast: Peer-to-Peer patching scheme for VoD service. In: Proceeding of the 12th International World Wide Web Conference, Budapest, Hungary, pp. 301–309 (2003b)
17. Do, T.T., Hua, K.A., Tantaoui, M.: P2VoD: Providing fault tolerant Video-on-Demand streaming in Peer-to-peer environment. In: Proceedings of IEEE International Conference on Communications, Paris, pp. 1467–1472 (2004)
18. Rowstron, A., Druschel, P.: Pastry: scalable, decentralized object location and routing for large-scale Peer-to-peer systems. In: Guerraoui, R. (ed.) Middleware 2001. LNCS, vol. 2218. Springer, Heidelberg (2001)
19. Prinkey, M.T.: 'An efficient scheme for query processing on peer-to-peer networks (2001),
   `http://aeolusres.homestead.com/files/index.html`

Traffic Trunk Parameters for Voice Transport over MPLS⋆

A. Estepa, R. Estepa, and J. Vozmediano

University of Sevilla, C/ Camino de los descubrimientos s/n, Spain
{aestepa,rafa,jvt}@trajano.us.es

Abstract. Access nodes in NGN are likely to transport voice traffic using MPLS Traffic Trunks. The traffic parameters describing a Traffic Trunk are basic to calculate the network resources to be allocated along the nodes belonging to its corresponding Label-Switched-Path (LSP).

This paper provides an analytical model to estimate the lower limit of the bandwidth that needs to be allocated to a TT loaded with a heterogeneous set of voice connections. Our model considers the effect of the Silence Insertion Descriptor (SID) frames that a number of VoIP codecs currently use. Additionally, two transport schemes are considered: VoIP and VoMPLS. The results, experimentally validated, quantify the benefits of VoMPLS over VoIP.

Keywords: Voice transport, MPLS Traffic Engineering, VoMPLS, VoIP.

1 Introduction

Voice transport over New Generation Networks (NGN) will likely make use of QoS-supporting packet-switching networks. Multi-Protocol-Label Switching [2](MPLS) is a packet forwarding technique that facilitates the creation of Label-Switched-Paths (LSPs) and allows the use of traffic engineering needed to support the provision of QoS at an optimal cost.

The traffic engineering [1] inherent capability of MPLS allows to dynamically route a set of forwarding equivalence classes over a so-called Traffic Trunk (TT) which follows the most adequate path according to its traffic characteristics, available resources in the network and administrative criteria. For the remainder of this paper, a TT will be used to transport a set of voice streams which demand the same QoS and follow the same LSP between two Label-Edge Routers (LERs) as indicated in figure 1.

In order to provide a TT with traffic engineering capabilities, the source LER needs to be aware of a number of its characteristics. Among them, we are interested in the traffic parameters (e.g. mean and peak bit-rates), which can be calculated from the traffic characterization of each voice stream belonging to the TT. These traffic parameters are required to calculate the capacity to be reserved for the TT in each link of the MPLS network and to develop a faithful map of the overall capacity remaining free in the network. Consequently the traffic parameters are a basic input to any constrained-routing algorithm.

⋆ This work was supported in part by the Spanish *Secretaría de Estado de Universidades y Educación* under the project number TIC2003-04784-C02-02.

J. Filipe and M.S. Obaidat (Eds.): ICETE 2006, CCIS 9, pp. 199–210, 2008.

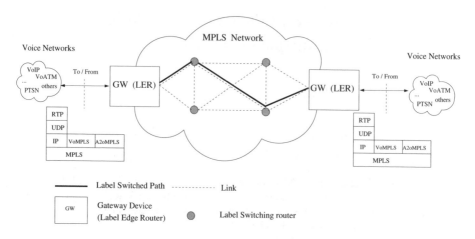

Fig. 1. Sample scenario

The methods used to calculate the optimal capacity to be reserved are usually based in complex analytical models [8] and are out of the scope of this paper. However, the bandwidth reservation should range from the sum of the conversation's mean bit-rates (stability condition) to the sum of its peak bit-rates[1]. A common and simple approach to calculate the actual bandwidth reservation is to use the sum of the conversation's peak bit-rates and take this upper limit as the allocation to be requested for the TT. This guarantees that no packet loss occurs at the cost of some over-provisioning of network resources. However, this conservative peak bit-rate approach could potentially cause the rejection of a new TT in the LER's admission procedure (CAC,) in spite of having enough capacity.

As the number of multiplexed sources in the TT increases, the traffic burstiness is smoothed and the capacity to be reserved should gradually change from the peak bit-rate approach to the mean bit-rate approach, thus making a more effective use of the network resources. However, the current calculus [4] of the mean-bit rate of the TT is inaccurate, since it is based in the ON-OFF model which does not consider the generation of Silence Insertion Descriptor (SID) frames that a number of voice codecs generate during voice inactivity periods [5]. These SID frames mark the end of talkspurts and update the Comfort Noise Generation parameters at the receiver.

Starting from the previous results in [5], we find a more accurate analytical expressions for the traffic parameters of a TT (i.e. mean and peak bit-rates) transporting a set of heterogeneous voice sources when SID-capable codecs are used. We apply them to two possible voice transport schemes: VoIP over MPLS and VoMPLS [2]. This would facilitate the use of the mean bit-rate value as a reference for a effective resource allocation in traffic engineering. In addition, the comparison between these different transport

---

[1] Within that range, the capacity selected represents a balance between the maximum burst size and the probability of out-of-profile.

[2] The case of A2oMPLS is not addressed in detail because the current implementation agreement does not specify the packetization scheme for the SID frames. However, the findings presented for VoMPLS are still valid for A2oMPLS with some minimum changes.

schemes (i.e. VoIP and VoMPLS as observed in figure 1) will let us to assess the bandwidth savings of VoMPLS over VoIP. Our results could be also applied to optimize the off-line analysis of packet loss and delay by using the analytical models to provide a desired QoS level as a function of both the TT mean bit-rate and the number of sources to be multiplexed.

The rest of the paper is structured as follows: section 2 sets the basic models to transport voice over an MPLS cloud and establishes the TT model used throughout the paper. Section 3 calculates the maximum and minimum capacity allocation for a voice TT in a VoIP over MPLS and VoMPLS scenario. Section 4 presents the main results and finally, section 5 concludes the paper.

2   Models for Voice Transport in MPLS

This section addresses two subjects: the characterization of a voice source traffic a in a digital environment, and the means of transporting a set of those conversations belonging to a TT over an MPLS network. Conversely to previous studies, we will not use the ON-OFF model but the more general ON-SID model presented in [6]. The main reason for this is the inadequacy of the ON-OFF model to capture the effect of the SID frames in the conversation's mean bit-rate.

2.1   Single Voice Source Model: The ON-SID Model

Low bit-rate codecs are commonly used in the transport of voice over packet-switched networks. Typically, these type of codecs analyze the speech samples generated during a period of time T and generate a information data-unit termed *frame* that can be used at the receiver to faithfully restore the original sequence of speech samples. Low bit-rate codecs are usually equipped with a voice activity detection (VAD) feature which pursues bandwidth savings by avoiding the generation of frames during voice inactivity periods.

Additionally, some audio codecs like G.729, G.723.1 or AMR are also featured with an algorithm which allows, at the beginning of each voice inactivity period, to send SID frames. Reception of a SID frame after a voice frame can be interpreted as an explicit indication of the end of the talk-spurt. In addition, SID frames may be also transmitted at any time during the silence interval to update comfort noise generation parameters. This allows a faithful reproduction of the background noise at the receiver's side, increasing the quality of the conversation at the cost of some additional bandwith [5].

Thus, the voice traffic model to be used in the remainder of this paper will not be limited to the traditional ON-OFF model, but the more general ON-SID model. This model assumes that in the discrete time space $t_i = i \cdot T$ (where T is the codec's frame generation period), the codecs continuously generate frames which can be either of type: ACT (compressed voice), SID (background noise) or NoTX. The latter corresponds to a zero-length frame used to model instants when no frames (ACT nor SID) are being generated. ON and SID periods are exponentially distributed. During voice activity periods ACT frames are generated every T seconds. During voice inactivity periods, SID frames are generated randomly according to the codec's specific algorithm and to changes in

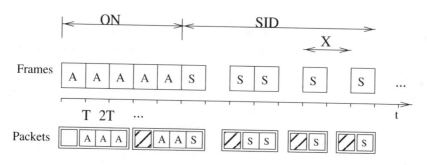

Fig. 2. ON-SID frame generation model for VoIP and $N_{fpp}=3$

the background-noise signal. Since SID frames generation is a random process, we can use a discrete random variable, X, to indicate the inter-arrival time (in number of periods T) between SID frames as expressed in figure 2. Moreover, we assume that SID frame generation is a renewal process.

Additionally, we also assume that during voice activity periods, to compensate the excess of overhead of layer protocols (H), ACT frames are usually sent to the network in groups of N_{fpp} consecutive frames per packet. Note that this also causes a packetization delay that limits the maximum acceptable value of N_{fpp}.

Mean Bit-Rate of a Single Voice Source. According to the ON-SID model, a packetized voice stream transmitted with VAD capable codecs which transmit SID frames exhibits a mean bit rate of:

$$r = \rho \cdot p + (1 - \rho) \cdot r_{SID} \qquad (1)$$

where ρ is the conversation mean activity rate, p is the peak rate and r_{SID} is the mean rate during voice inactivity periods caused by the transmission of SID frames. For those codecs which do not generate SID frames, obviously $r_{SID} = 0$.

The factors of equation 1 depend on the transport scheme used (i.e. VoIP and VoMPLS,) and will be addressed in next subsections.

2.2 Alternatives for Voice Transport in MPLS

This paper addresses two possible ways of voice transport over an MPLS TT, depending on whether the tributary conversations come from VoIP or are directly taken from the payload of the VoIP packets; that is, the transport of codec frames directly over MPLS or VoMPLS.

VoMPLS. The implementation agreement defined by the MPLS-FrameRelay Alliance [3] describes how to transport voice directly over MPLS. The method is illustrated in figure 3 and can be summarized in the following ideas:

- A number of voice calls may be transported over an LSP. The multiplexing structure consists of a mandatory Outer Label, zero or more Inner Labels, and one or more

VoMPLS Primary Subframes consisting of a 4-octet Header (HDR) and variable length Primary Payload each, as shown in figure 3.

- Each Primary Subframe may be associated with a different voice connection. A Primary Payload is either a sequence of encoded ACT voice frame(s) or a single SID frame.
- Within the header of a Primary Subframe, the length field is indicated in multiples of 4 octets. Thus, up to three padding octets may be inserted in each subframe depending on the codec's frame size and the number of codec's frames carried in the Primary Subframe.
- A Primary Payload contains the traffic that is fundamental to the operation of a connection identified by a Channel Identifier (CID). It includes ACT and SID frames. Primary Payloads are variable-length subframes.
- Control Subframes may be sent to support the Primary Payload (e.g., dialled digits for a primary payload of encoded voice) and other control functions (like RTP-timestamps). Control and Primary Subframes are not mixed together in the same multiplexing frame. Thus, Control Subframes will not be considered in the present study since they belong to the signalling plane.

The header's Channel ID (CID) allows up to 248 VoMPLS calls to be multiplexed within a single LSP so the Inner Labels will not be considered in the rest of the paper.

The aforementioned implementation agreement also establishes the maximum N_{fpp} allowed value for each codec (e.g. in VoMPLS there is a maximum value of $N_{fpp}=6$ for the G.729B codec, while for the G.723.1 codec N_{fpp} is forced to be 1).

VoIP over MPLS. The protocols involved in the transport of IP packets are the Real Time Protocol (RTP) and the UDP protocol, resulting in a RTP/UDP/IP header of 40 octets per each IP packet.

Packets are generated every $T \cdot N_{fpp}$ seconds during voice activity periods. During voice inactivity periods, SID frames are packed according to the RFC 3551 packetization scheme, where only those SID frames consecutively generated may be carried in the same packet, up to the maximum of N_{fpp}.

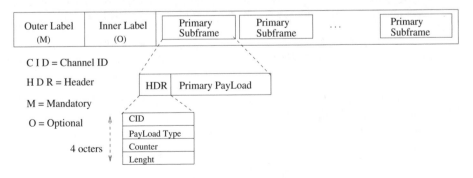

Fig. 3. VoMPLS traffic trunk format

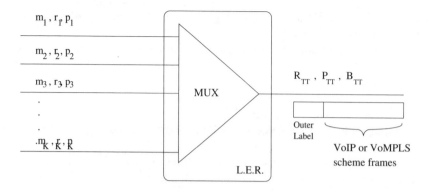

Fig. 4. Voice multiplexing model

Each VoIP stream is multiplexed in a Subframe of the MPLS TT multi-frame structure. A new TT multi-frame is sent whenever any conversation of the TT needs to send a new IP packet. The multi-frame has an Outer Label as indicated in next section.

2.3 Aggregation of Heterogeneous Voice Sources in a Traffic Trunk

For the aggregation of the voice sources in a single TT we consider the multiplexing model illustrated in Figure 4, where a set of K classes of m_i homogeneous ON-SID sources feed a multiplexer (which can be a LER) where a TT of real-time voice sources is created. Each one of the m_i voice streams belonging to the same class i will have a common value of N_{fpp} and codec, and consequently, the same ON-SID parameters; namely, the peak bit-rate (p_i) and mean bit-rate (r_i).

According to figure 4, the traffic characterization should include the Outer Label of the TT. Therefore, traffic parameters defining the traffic profile are:

- Traffic Trunk's Mean Bit-rate: this parameter is the minimum service rate that guarantees stability in the system and thus, is the minimum capacity that should be allocated for the TT. It includes the sum of all the conversations mean bit-rate for the class i plus the mean bit-rate caused by the Outer Label of the TT (R_{OL}).

$$R_{TT} = \sum_{i=1}^{K} m_i \cdot r_i + R_{OL} \qquad (2)$$

- Traffic Trunk's Peak bit-rate: is the sum of all the peak rates plus the peak bit-rate of the Outer Label of the trunk supposed that all sources are ON (P_{OL}). This is the maximum capacity that should be allocated to the TT to avoid packet loss.

$$P_{TT} = \sum_{i=1}^{K} m_i \cdot p_i + P_{OL} \qquad (3)$$

– Traffic Trunk burst-size: this parameter can be considered to be free. The reason for this is that the allocated capacity (C) for the TT must be a value greater than R_{TT} (to be stable) and smaller than P_{TT} (to take advantage of statistical multiplexing). For C=P_{TT}, the buffer size (B) needs to be only big enough to store one voice packet from each conversation, while for C=R_{TT}, B should be large enough in order to queue all the instant traffic in order to bound the potential packet loss. An excellent paper reviewing this tradeoff is [7].

Since the relation between B and the QoS depends on the multiplexing analytical model used in the study (i.e. either fluid model or MMPP), our goal is to find the values of P_{TT} and R_{TT} for VoMPLS and VoIP trunks. The next section is devoted to this task.

To account the Outer Label influence in the TT mean bit rate, we make the following assumption: a new MPLS frame is generated every $T_{min}=min\{i = 1, ..k; Ti\}$ whenever there is any source generating a new frame (i.e. voice frames or SID frames). For the peak bit-rate calculation, we assume that a new trunking frame is generated every T_{min}. Thus, the values of P_{OL} and R_{OL} result as follow:

$$P_{OL} = \frac{H_{OL}}{T_{min}} \tag{4}$$

$$R_{OL} = \frac{H_{OL}}{T_{min}} \cdot G_{TX} \tag{5}$$

where G_{TX} is the probability of having at least one voice source generating a new frame at T_{min}.

3   New Value of the Traffic Parameters for MPLS Transport

This section is devoted to finding out the analytical expression for the traffic parameters as indicated in equations 3 and 2 of previous subsection. In our approach, we first find analytical expressions for p_i and r_i for both transport schemes under study: VoIP over MPLS, and VoMPLS.

3.1   Mean and Peak Bit-Rate for VoIP

The peak rate of a VoIP conversation depends upon both the codec characteristics and the number of frames per packet (N_{fpp}). Thus, it is clearly given by:

$$p_i = \frac{H + N_{fpp}L_{ACT}}{N_{fpp}T} \tag{6}$$

where H is the header size of the protocol layers involved in the transport service (i.e. 40 octets), L_{ACT} is the voice frame size and T is the frame generation period of a given codec. Table 1 shows the characteristics of some VoIP codecs.

Regarding the r_{SID} member of equation 1, an analytical expression for the VoIP transport may be found in [6]. The deduction was based in the separation of the contribution of the header and the SID frames to the mean bit-rate so $r_{SID} = R_H + R_{fr}$.

Table 1. Codec characteristics

Codec	Mode	L_{ACT}	L_{SID}	T (ms)	$E[X]$	P_1
G.729	-	10	2	10	7.33	0
G.723.1	6.3	24	4	30	13.05	0.27
	5.3	20	4	30		
AMR	4.75	12	5	20	7.47	0
	12.2	31	5	29	7.47	0

The contribution of the SID frames can be obtained by application of the Elementary Renewal Theorem (ERT) which states that the SID frames arrival long-term rate is the inverse of the expected inter-arrival time $(E[X] \cdot T)$.

$$R_{fr} = \frac{L_{SID}}{T \cdot E[X]} \tag{7}$$

where L_{SID} is the size of a SID frame.

In VoIP, the contribution of the packet header generated during inactive periods follows the packet generation pattern imposed by the RFC 3551, where one packet header is sent every non-consecutive SID frame ($X = x > 1$). For consecutive SID frames, one packet header is sent every N_{fpp} frames, so both cases must be considered. Since the mean time between SID frames is given by $(E[X] \cdot T)$, the header contribution (R_H) can be expressed as:

$$R_H = P_1 \cdot \frac{H}{N_{fpp} \cdot T \cdot E[X]} + (1 - P_1)\frac{H}{T \cdot E[X]} \tag{8}$$

where P_1 stands for the probability of having two time-consecutive SID frames (i.e. $P(X = 1)$).

Thus, for the VoIP case we have an overall mean bit-rate of:

$$r_i = \rho \cdot p_i + \frac{1 - \rho}{T \cdot E[X]}$$
$$\cdot \left(L_{SID} + H \cdot \left(1 + \frac{P_1(1 - N_{fpp})}{N_{fpp}} \right) \right) \tag{9}$$

3.2 Mean and Peak Bit-Rate for VoMPLS

When compared to the VoIP case introduced above, VoMPLS transportation shows three main changes:

1. The header size (H) only accounts for one HDR header, with a size of 4 octets instead of the VoIP header of 40 octets.
2. The padding phenomenon may add extra octets to the packets generated during voice activity periods or SID periods.
3. The packetization scheme forces that one primary subframe may carry only one SID frame. This implies changes in R_H when compared to the VoIP case.

According to the first and second items, an extra load of $(N_{fpp}L_{ACT})$ mod 4 octets needs to be added in the ON periods. Thus, p_i is:

$$p_i = \frac{H + N_{fpp}L_{ACT} + (N_{fpp}L_{ACT}) \mod 4}{N_{fpp} \cdot T} \tag{10}$$

On SID periods, an extra load of L_{SID} mod 4 octets needs to be added to equation R_{fr}. Applying again the renewal theorem and taking into account that only one SID frame can travel in the subframe, we can redefine:

$$R_{fr} = \frac{L_{SID} + (L_{SID} \mod 4)}{T \cdot E[X]} \tag{11}$$

and,

$$R_H = \frac{H}{T \cdot E[X]} \tag{12}$$

So the mean bit-rate for VoMPLS will be:

$$r_i = \rho \cdot p_i + (1 - \rho) \cdot \frac{H + L_{SID} + (L_{SID} \mod 4)}{T \cdot E[X]} \tag{13}$$

where all the information units are measured in octets.

3.3 Traffic Trunk Parameters

According to equations 2 and 3, the lower and upper limits of the bandwidth reservation for the TT can be readily calculated, since p_i and r_i have been deduced in sections 3.1 and 3.2 for VoMPLS and for VoIP over MPLS respectively.

However, the traffic parameters of the TT should also include the effect of the MPLS Outer Label in the mean and peak bit-rates. To do this, we have to compute the probability of having at least one voice source generating a new frame at T_{min} (G_{TX}). This can be calculated from the probability that no source from any class generates a packet.

In the VoIP over MPLS case, and according to equation 8, it is given by:

$$G_{TX} = 1 - \prod_{i=1}^{K} \left(1 - \frac{\rho \cdot T_{min}}{N_{fpp} \cdot T_i} \right.$$
$$\left. - \frac{T_{min}(1 - \rho)}{E[X_i] \cdot T_i} \left(1 + \frac{P_1 \cdot (1 - N_{fpp})}{N_{fpp}} \right) \right)^{m_i} \tag{14}$$

In the VoMPLS case, we should consider that packetization scheme forces that one primary subframe may only carry one SID frame. Thus, G_{TX} results into:

$$G_{TX} = 1 - \prod_{i=1}^{K} \left(1 - \frac{\rho \cdot T_{min}}{N_{fpp} \cdot T_i} \right.$$
$$\left. - \frac{(1 - \rho) \cdot T_{min}}{E[X_i] \cdot T_i} \right)^{m_i} \tag{15}$$

Experimental values show that, when more than 5 sources are multiplexed, G_{TX} is greater than 0.95, and for more than 10 sources, the probability increases up to 0.99. Thus, we may assume $G_{TX}=1$ for a large number of multiplexed sources (i.e. more than 10).

4 Validation and Numerical Results

This section presents the results of a comparative study between VoIP over MPLS and VoMPLS. This allows to quantify the benefits of VoMPLS, and validates the equations presented in the previous section.

4.1 Experiment Setup

Following the methodology found in [5], both edges of 14 conversations which took place between males and females speakers, were recorded from an ISDN line in a low-noise office environment (i.e SNR > 20dB.) The 600 minutes of PCM audio files obtained were encoded using the G.729B codec. This codec, highly available in any VoIP environment, holds the capability of generating SID frames and is widely referenced in the literature, so it will let us to compare our results with previous studies. The output of the codec was processed to obtain the sequence of types of frames generated (ACT, SID or NoTXN for none.) This information was stored in a file -*ftype* files- for each conversation, and all of them were processed to experimentally find the proper parameters to be used in the models (i.e. activity rate ρ, $E[X]$, P_1.)

The *ftype* files were also split into 120 pieces of five-minutes-long conversations. This database of five-minute pieces of speech conformed a pool from which N were randomly chosen to feed a simulator. Each simulation was repeated 40 times to provide accurate measures of the TT mean bit-rate at the output of the LER.

The mean bit-rate obtained in our simulations is then compared to those provided by the analytical expressions of R_{TT}, for both VoIP over MPLS and VoMPLS, respectively.

4.2 Numerical Results

A total of N=20 homogeneous voice sources were multiplexed following the procedure explained above. Figure 5 plots R_{TT} as obtained from simulations and from our analytical ON-SID model for both VoIP and MPLS TTs. Additionally, it shows R_{TT} when $r_{SID}=0$, as is traditionally assumed by the one-source ON-OFF model.

In the VoIP over MPLS case the differences between our analytical ON-SID model prediction and the simulation results, measured at the LER's output, range between 1% ($N_{fpp}=1$) and 4% ($N_{fpp}=6$). For VoMPLS those differences vary from 0%($N_{fpp}=1$) to 5% ($N_{fpp}=6$). This validates the analytical results in both cases.

When using the traditional ON-OFF model, the VoIP over MPLS case shows differences ranging from 11% to 31%, at the same measuring point. In the VoMPLS case, with the same frame-generation model, the differences range between 11% and 19%. This means that the SID-frames effect, known to be non-negligible in VoIP, should also be taken into account in the VoMPLS case.

Note that, due to the padding phenomenon in VoMPLS, at $N_{fpp}=2$ R_{TT} is smaller than at $N_{fpp}=3$. It also demonstrates that $N_{fpp}=2$ is an interesting working point for the G.729 codec, achieving less delay with lower bandwidth consumption than $N_{fpp}=3$.

Figure 6 reveals that using VoMPLS instead of VoIP over MPLS yields bandwidth savings ranging from 69% ($N_{fpp}=1$) to 48% ($N_{fpp}=6$).

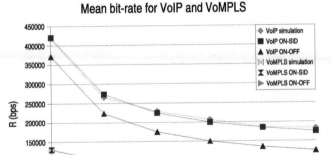

Fig. 5. Experimental and analytical values of R_{TT}

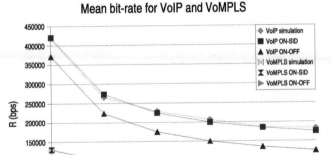

Fig. 6. Bandwidth saving and ON-OFF error

5   Conclusions

Traffic engineering needs accurate traffic parameters in order to calculate the optimal capacity allocation for a Traffic Trunk. We have provided analytical expressions for the mean and peak bit-rate of a Traffic Trunk loaded with a mix of heterogeneous voice sources for both the VoIP and VoMPLS transport models. Conversely to the ON-OFF based models, the model used for voice sources captures the effect of the SID frames generated by a number of modern voice codecs. We show that the SID-frames effect has to be considered in the VoMPLS case, too. This conveys an improvement in the accuracy of results, which show a quantitative gain in the bandwidth necessary to transport voice trunks when compared to VoIP.

The calculation of required bandwidth to be allocated for a voice TT with QoS commitments is in progress at the time of writing this paper. This subject as well as the A2oMPLS transport case are left for further study.

References

1. Requirements for traffic engineering over mpls. RFC 2702 (1999)
2. Multiprotocol label switching architecture. RFC 3031 (2001)
3. Voice over mpls- bearer transport implementation agreement. MPLS Forum I.A.1.0 (2001)
4. B, G.: Voice over internet protocol (voip). In: Proceedings of the IEEE, IEEE Press, Los Alamitos (2002)
5. Estepa, A., Estepa, R., Vozmediano, J.: Packetization and Silence Influence on VoIP Traffic Profiles. In: Ventre, G., Canonico, R. (eds.) MIPS 2003. LNCS, vol. 2899, pp. 331–339. Springer, Heidelberg (2003)
6. Estepa, A., Estepa, R., Vozmediano, J.: Accurate prediction of voip traffic mean bit rate. IEE Electronic Letters 8(10), 644–647 (2005)
7. Procissi, G., Garg, A., Gerla, M., Sanadidi, M.: Token bucket characterization of long-range dependent traffic. Computer Communications. Ed. Elsevier 25, 1009–1017 (2002)
8. Guérin, H.A.R., Naghshineh, M.: Equivalent capacity and its application to bandwith allocation in high-speed networks. JSAC. IEEE 9 (1991)

On-the-Fly Time Scaling for Compressed Audio Streams

Suzana Maranhão, Rogério Rodrigues, and Luiz Soares

TeleMídia Lab, PUC-Rio University, P.O. Box 38.097
Rio de Janeiro, Brazil
{smbm,rogerio,lfgs}@telemidia.puc-rio.br

Abstract. Time scaling is a technique used to modify media-object presentation duration. This paper proposes an audio time-scaling algorithm focused on supporting applications that need: to maintain the original data format for storage or immediate presentation on any legacy audio player; to perform linear time scaling in real time, allowing the adjustment factor to vary along the audio presentation; and to perform time mark-up maintenance, that is, to compute new time values for original marked audio time instants. The proposed algorithm is appropriate for those applications that do not need a great adjustment factor variation. The integration with content rendering tools is presented in the paper and also an example of using these tools in a hypermedia presentation formatter.

Keywords: Time scaling; High-Quality Compressed Audio; MPEG-2 Audio; MPEG-4 Audio, MPEG-2 Systems; Inter-media Synchronization; Hypermedia Document Presentation.

1   Introduction

Time scaling and elastic time adjustment are usual names given to the technique of modifying media-object playing duration. The adjustment can be quantified by a (tuning or adjustment) factor, expressed by a real number greater than zero. A media exhibition speed up is expressed by a tuning factor $f<1$ and a media exhibition slow down by a factor $f>1$.

Time-scale modifications are useful in many applications [2], [15], [18]. The next paragraphs give some examples that raised the goals of the algorithm proposed in this paper. As will become evident, hypermedia (or interactive multimedia) systems are our main target, reason why the proposed algorithm is called *HyperAudioScaling*.

The first example comes from the temporal synchronization consistency of hypermedia document presentations. In such presentations, all media-objects should be exhibited in proper times taking into account time restrictions specified by authors, including interactive actions. Time-scaling processing should be applied before document presentation (at compile time) trying to solve all temporal inconsistencies. However, the temporal synchronized media-objects can lose their synchronization due to several factors in their route to the presentation machine (from now on called *formatter*). For example, network delays, user interactions and unpredictable end of media exhibitions (as in live streams) can cause synchronization loss. In all theses cases, time scaling will play an important role in the synchronization maintenance and

J. Filipe and M.S. Obaidat (Eds.): ICETE 2006, CCIS 9, pp. 211–223, 2008.
© Springer-Verlag Berlin Heidelberg 2008

must be performed in presentation time (on-the-fly). Moreover, to track the synchronization, the adjustment factor may also vary in real time. The fidelity of the processed media must be high and, thus, adjustments must be performed as smoothly as
possible, in order to be imperceptible to users.

The adjustment mechanism should not depend on which audio presentation tool (i.e.
audio player) will be used by a hypermedia formatter. As a consequence, time-scale modifications must be independent of the stream decoding process that takes place in presentation tools. Moreover, since hypermedia applications usually manipulate compressed media
formats, and since real-time time-scale modifications are needed, the adjustments should
be performed in the compressed data, without needing to decode them.

Finally, hypermedia documents use anchors (defined in this paper as time periods
in the stream) to specify synchronization points. So, the time- scaling algorithm
should also be able to track new anchor values during the adjustment computation.

Other multimedia applications also demand time-scaling processing. For example,
time scaling can be useful to allow TV or radio stations to speed its scheduling up or
down. Time scaling can also be used to optimize channel allocation for multiple users
in a Video (or audio)-On-Demand (VOD) system. Media streams of the same content
can be transmitted with different speeds until the same piece of information is reached
in the flows. At this time, the streams can be unified in one multicast flow.

The HyperAudioScaling algorithm, proposed in this paper, focuses on supporting
audio time scaling for those applications that need: i) to maintain the original data
format aiming at the storage or immediate presentation on any legacy audio player; ii)
to perform time-scale modifications in real time (presentation time) but allowing to
vary the adjustment factor during the audio presentation; iii) high fidelity, that is,
given an adjustment factor, the time-scaling processing should be performed as
smoothly as possible in order that speed variation in the resultant media is imperceptible to users; and iv) time mark-up maintenance, that is, time scaling must be able to
compute new time values for original marked time instants. In addition, the HyperAudioScaling algorithm focuses only on those applications that do not need a great
tuning-factor variation ($0.9 \leq f \leq 1.1$).

This paper is organized as follows. Section 2 discusses some related work. Section 3
introduces the HyperAudioScaling algorithm for audio-only streams. Section 4 briefly
discusses how the algorithm can also be applied in multiplexed audio and video (system)
streams. Section 5 presents the time-scaling tool (library) developed based on the proposed algorithm. In order to illustrate the use of the time-scaling tool in a hypermedia
document presentation system, Section 6 describes its integration with a hypermedia
formatter. To conclude, Section 7 presents the final remarks.

2 Related Work

Audio time-scaling algorithms can be classified in three categories [5], [15], presented
in increasing order of quality and computational complexity.

Time-based algorithms assume signal segmentation in time domain in order to
perform adjustments by segment manipulations (for example, through discarding,
duplication or interpolation of segments). They usually reach good quality for adjustment factor between *0.8* and *1.2*.

Frequency-based algorithms perform time scaling, modifying frequencies of the original audio signal. They can produce high quality output over a wide range of stretching factors.

Analysis-based algorithms make an examination of the audio signal and then perform time-scaling mechanisms specifics for that audio type, in order to create an adjusted high-quality audio.

Most of the commercial tools use time or frequency-based algorithms for adjustments on generic audio, once the computational complexity of algorithms based on detailed analysis is usually too high.

Independent of the time-scaling algorithm category, there are, at least, tree ways to perform adjustments in compressed audio. The first possibility is to decode, process, and recode the stream. The advantage of this solution is that there are many good time-scaling algorithms proposed for uncompressed audio [15]. However, this option can be very time-consuming, making it difficult to be used in real-time. Furthermore, there is a loss of quality associated with the recompression process.

When audio streams must be processed while they keep playing, originating new streams without perceptible delay, there are two other different solutions to perform time-scale modifications.

The first one is carrying out time scaling soon after the decompression and before the presentation. The advantage in this case is the possibility of manipulating non-compressed streams using the aforementioned good algorithms already defined in the literature. However, it may be difficult to intercept the decoder output before sending it to exhibition. Even when this interception is possible, it may require a particular implementation for each decoder.

The second solution is performing time scaling before decompression, straight on compressed streams. This option gives to the time-scaling algorithm independency from the decoder. However, time scaling must consider the syntax rules specified by the media format. Note that, for the requirements stated in Section 1, this is the approach to be followed.

Sound Forge [19] allows professional audio recording and editing. It supports several audio formats, but always applies a pre-processing procedure when opening compressed files. Time-scaling processing can be performed in presentation time, however, probably using the pre-processed stream. Nevertheless, the generation of the resultant (recompressed) file is not performed in real time. The user can choose among *19* different ways of applying time-scale modifications according to his/her needs. The adjustment factor varies between *0.5* and *5*. The tool has an excellent audio output stream quality, but introduces an intolerable delay for real time processing. Sound Forge is used for comparison with this paper proposal in Section 7.

Windows Media Player 10 [16] supports many audiovisual formats, such as MP3 and WMA. The tool allows choosing the adjustment factor to be used during media exhibition and to change this factor in presentation time. Although the adjustment factor can assume values between *0.06* and *16*, the program specification suggests a range between *0.5* and *2.0* to keep media quality high. Although not mentioned, it is almost assured that the time-scaling processing takes place after the decoding, due to two reasons: it is not possible to save the processed audio in a compressed format; and, since the algorithm is done for a specific player, it is better to apply time scaling just before presentation.

The MPEG-4 audio specification defines a presentation tool called PICOLA (Pointer Interval Controlled OverLap Add), which can make time-based adjustments after decompression, in mono audio with sample rate of 8kHz or 16kHz [13].

FastMPEG [7] is a time-scaling proposal that explores the partial decoding/encoding strategy. It describes three time-based algorithms for MP2 format on-the-fly adjustments. The algorithms are performed after a partial decoding of the audio stream and followed by a partial re-encoding. The adjustment factor varies between 2/3 and 2.0.

All aforementioned time-scaling algorithms are not applied straight on the compressed stream. Instead, streams are decoded (at least partially), processed, and, eventually, encoded again. The solutions are complex and decoder dependent. The algorithms allow a large range for the tuning factor f, perhaps one of the reasons that guided their implementation. However, this is reached by the dependence of the presentation tool, or by the use of non-real-time computation.

Different from all mentioned work, this paper proposes a time-scaling algorithm for compressed audio streams, simple enough to be executed in presentation time. The algorithm is performed straight on the compressed data, supporting tuning-factor variation, and being independent of the decoder (and thus the player) implementation. Due to the intentional simplicity of the proposed algorithm, its tuning-factor is limited to the range $[0.90, 1.10]$.

Indeed, this paper proposes a framework for a class of algorithms, that is, a meta algorithm. The framework is instantiated for a set of format-dependent algorithms, described in the paper, and implemented as a library, called HyperAudioScaling tool, which can be easily integrated with third-party applications. The media formats handled by the library are MPEG-1 audio [9], MPEG-2 systems [12] and audio [11], [10], MPEG-4 AAC audio [13], and AC-3 [3]. These standards were chosen because they have been largely used in commercial applications, such as those for digital and interactive TV, and also in different audiovisual formats, like VCD, SVCD and DVD.

3   Audio Time-Scaling Algorithm

Many high-quality audio formats deal with audio streams as a sequence of frames (or segments). Every *frame* has a *header* and a *data field*, and is associated with a *logical data unit (LDU)*. A set of coded audio samples, gathered during a small time interval (typically, about 30ms), concatenated with auxiliary bits (called PAD) compose a logical data unit. The number of PAD bits is not limited and are generally used to carry metadata.

Although associated with a specific frame, the LDU does not need to be carried in the data field of this frame. Alternatively, the LDU can borrow bits from data fields of previous frames (the *bit reservoir* in MPEG nomenclature) and be transported partially or entirely in previous frames. The maximum size of the bit reservoir is limited. Thus, data fields can contain one, several or part of an LDU. Fig. 1 shows an audio stream with frames separated by vertical lines. In each frame, the header bytes are stripped. They are located in the beginning of the frame and are followed by a data field. The figure also depicts the LDU of each frame.

The HyperAudioScaling algorithm is based on a well-known time-based algorithm called *Granular synthesis* [8]. However, an important difference must be pointed out.

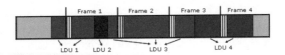

Fig. 1. Frame representation of a compressed audio stream

Once time scaling must be executed without decoding the compressed audio (to recover the audio samples), and because an LDU can be coded in frequency domain, the chosen adjustment unit is the LDU (and not samples, as in the Gabor's proposal). Thus, HyperAudioScaling time scaling is performed by removing or duplicating LDUs when the stream must be speed up or slowed down, respectively.

Nevertheless, removing an LDU is not that simple, since the associated frame must also be removed. As a frame may contain LDUs associated with frames that are ahead, these LDUs cannot simply be taken out of the stream, and must be respread into previously scheduled frames.

Similar care must also be taken when duplicating an LDU, since the associated frame must also be duplicated. If a frame has its associated LDU spread into other previous frames, the duplicated frame may also have to distribute part of its LDU. Furthermore, bits of other LDUs within the frame must not be duplicated.

As in both the removing and the duplicating processes there could not be enough room for the LDUs that have to be distributed, HyperAudioScaling tries to avoid using frames where the problem may happen. So, the following rules are adopted:

1. First try to remove only the frames that have their associated LDUs larger than the frame data fields.
2. Similarly, first try to duplicate only frames that have their associated LDUs smaller than their data fields.

The rules ensure that there will always be place to process the selected frame. Note also that new PAD bits may have to be added to previous frames after removal, or to the processed frame in the case of duplication. Fig. 2 illustrates the removing process after dropping frame 3 in Fig. 1 example. The duplicating process is illustrated in Fig. 3 after the duplication of frame 2 in the same Fig. 1 example. The figures consider that there are no PAD bits in the LDUs of frames 3 and 2, before removal and duplication, respectively.

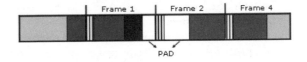

Fig. 2. Dropping frame 3 in the stream of Fig. 1

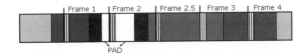

Fig. 3. Duplication of frame 2 in the stream of Fig. 1

The added auxiliary bits when rules 1 and 2 are applied can now be used to refine the proposed algorithm. In order to use these PAD bits in future processing, they can be transferred frame by frame, till the next LDU to be processed, using the following algorithm:

- Compute the number X of PAD bits which can be transferred from one frame to the next. In this case, the X value must be limited to the *bit reservoir* maximum size.
- Transfer X bits of the next-frame LDU to the PAD field and insert new X PAD bits into the end of the transferred LDU.

Fig. 4 shows PAD transference from frame 2 to frame 4 in the stream of Fig. 3.

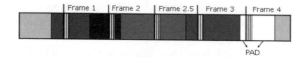

Fig. 4. Frames of Fig. 3 after PAD transference

Using this mechanism, new rules can be defined to process frames:

3. If a frame does not satisfy rule *1*, it can still be removed if the length of its associated LDU added to the transferred PAD length is greater than or equal to the frame data field length.
4. If a frame does not satisfy rule *2*, it can still be duplicated if the length of its associated LDU is smaller than or equal to the frame data field length plus the transferred PAD length.

Since there are frames that still cannot be processed, the elastic time adjustments may not be uniformly distributed. However, with the new added rules, more frames can be processed and closer to linear the time scaling can be. A linearity measure of this algorithm will be presented in Section 7. Note also that the non-linearity prevents marked time instants in the original audio to be estimated using a linear equation based on the adjustment factor (see requirement (iv) in Section 1). Therefore, the time-scaling mechanism should track particular time instants and indicates their new values during time-scaling processing.

HyperAudioScaling operation does not require a frame of fixed length. The frame extractor algorithm, instantiated for each audio format, must be responsible for recognizing and creating frames from the stream.

During the audio time scaling, a frame must be properly selected and analyzed to verify if it can be processed. The frame selector processing algorithm is responsible for this task and can be summarized as follows:

a. Compute the effective adjustment factor applied until this moment. This calculus must take into account the number of frames already processed divided by the number of frames analyzed;
b. Compare this result with the original adjustment factor to decide whether the frame should be processed, then verify if the frame can be processed considering rules 1 to 4, described previously. If it cannot be processed, take the next frame, and return to step (a).

When changes are made in the adjustment factor, the frame selector processing algorithm must recalculate the effective adjustment factor from the moment of the change on.

HyperAudioScaling preserves bytes before the first frame and after the last frame of the stream, because they may represent important metadata, like ID3 standard [17] on MP3 streams. Moreover, HyperAudioScaling also maintains metadata inside non-processed frames. Unfortunately, the metadata of the processed frames cannot be always preserved. As some audio formats (MP2, for example) have their LDUs coinciding with their data fields, it is impossible to discard or duplicate frames without their PAD fields. In addition, in other format types, it is difficult to discover where the PAD bits begin without decoding. Fortunately, PAD bits of LDUs usually just carry stuffing bits for length alignment and can be discarded or duplicated without compromising metadata information.

The HyperAudioScaling algorithm was instantiated to MPEG-1 and MPEG-2 BC Audio (MP1, MP2, MP3), AC-3 and MPEG-2/4 AAC. Since there is no *bit reservoir* in MP1, MP2 and AC-3 streams, the instantiations assume that the number of borrowed bytes is always zero, that is, the frame associated LDU is always inside the frame data field. In MP3 streams there is a *bit reservoir* and the algorithm was applied straightly. MP1, MP2 and MP3 have equal-size frames (using constant bit and sampling rate) and auxiliary bytes (PAD) at the end of each LDU, while AC-3 streams have frames with variable length. As previously discussed, this does not affect the algorithm.

The current algorithm implementation for MPEG-2/4 AAC streams uses the ADTS transport protocol. Similarly to MP3, MPEG-2/4 AAC streams provide the *bit reservoir* facility and have frames with both audio and auxiliary data. However, this format introduces some new challenges, since its encoder may use sample values of previous frames to predict sample values of the current frame. Since this encoder facility is optional, it was left to be treated in a future work.

4   Time Scaling in System Flows

Some media formats can multiplex video, audio and metadata in a unique flow called system stream. System streams are usually composed by PACKETs, each one containing one, several or part of an elementary-stream frame.

System time-scale modifications are performed by adjusting each elementary stream and recalculating some metadata within the PACKET header. System time-scaling algorithms usually consist of the following steps:

1. Identify PACKETs from the original stream and demultiplex the input stream into its elementary streams;
2. Convert PACKETs into frames of the corresponding elementary stream.
3. Execute elementary time-scaling algorithms.
4. Recreate system PACKETs using the processed bits and multiplex them creating the new system stream.

The algorithm proposed in Section 3 can be used to adjust elementary audio streams. Another algorithm should be used to process the video stream. However, some changes must be made in the audio time-scaling algorithm. First, time scaling on elementary streams needs to cope with system and elementary stream metadata, since some of the metadata can be affected by the time-scaling processing, such as clock timestamps, etc. Second, time scaling on elementary streams must provide information for adjustment control and inter-media synchronism verification.

Since time-scaling algorithms do not necessarily make linear adjustments, a synchronization mismatch among elementary streams may occur and must be detected by the intermedia synchronism verification function. If the mismatch crosses a specific upper bound[1], the intermedia synchronism verification function must call the services of the adjustment control function to change the tuning-factors of each individual media, in order to correct the problem.

Fig. 5 resumes the proposed time scaling for system streams.

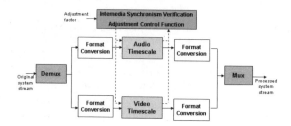

Fig. 5. Time scaling for system streams

The system time-scaling algorithm was instantiated to MPEG-2 system program stream, together with the audio time-scaling algorithm described in Section 3 and the video time-scaling algorithm proposed in [6]. In this instantiation, the metadata that must be considered for updating are the timestamps PTS (Presentation Time Stamp) and DTS (Decoding Time Stamp), inserted in the elementary streams, and SCR (System Clock Reference), in the system stream. Also, it may be necessary to update the PES_packet_length field in the PACKETs that had their frames processed for elastic time adjustments.

5   Audio Time-Scaling Tool

The audio time-scaling tool was implemented using the Java language. The time-scaling tool receives requests from client applications (adjustment API). The audio input can be retrieved (pull applications) or received as a stream (push applications). The adjusted stream can be stored in a file or returned to the client application.

Time-scale modifications can be performed at *compile-time* or during *execution-time*. Since these approaches have different characteristics, one API was developed for each one. Table 1 describes the API to request compile-time adjustments. The *config* method receives the original audio content, a tuning-factor for each specified audio section (set of samples), and the URI of the output file.

---

[1] Reference [1] discusses the audio and video mismatch problem and states that the loss of quality can only be perceived when adjustments cause a synchronization mismatch higher than 160ms.

The *start* and *stop* methods begin and stop the time-scaling processing, respectively. The *addTimeScalingListener* method allows client applications to register themselves to be notified when the time-scaling processing finishes.

After time scaling finishes, client applications can use the *getTimeScalingInstant* method to discover new time values for marked time intervals; the *getOutputTools* method to get the output file URI; and the *getReport* method to retrieve statistics about time-scaling processing (such as number of frames processed, processing time, etc).

Table 1. Compile-time adjustment API

Method	Description
config (originalMedia, {tuningFactor, audioSection}, outputFileURI)	Configures the time-scaling tool.
start()	Starts processing.
stop()	Stops processing.
addTimeScalingListener (observer)	Adds a new observer to the time-scaling finish event.
getTimeScalingInstant (timeInstant)	Gets the new time value after adjustments for an original time instant.
getOutputTools()	Gets the output file URI.
getReport()	Gets statistics about the adjustment processing.

Table 2 describes the API for requesting time scaling on the fly. The *config* method receives the original audio, the tuning-factor, and, optionally, a set of time intervals to track. The *setFactor* method can be invoked during time-scaling processing to modify the tuning-factor. If client applications want to be warned when new values of marked time intervals are found, they need to register themselves as observers using *addTimeScalingIntervalListener* method. The *getOutputTools* method must be called by the client application to get the processed stream. The other methods have the same meaning of their compile-time counterparts.

Table 2. Execution-time adjustment API

Method	Description
config (originalMedia, tuningFactor, {timeInterval})	Configures the time-scaling tool.
setFactor (tuningFactor)	Modifies the tuning-factor.
start()	Starts processing.
stop()	Stops processing.
addTimeScalingIntervalListener (observer)	Adds a new observer to track new values of a marked time interval.
getOutputTools()	Gets the processed stream.
getReport()	Gets statistics about adjustment processing.

6 Integrating HyperAudioScaling with a Hypermedia Formatter

In order to illustrate the time-scaling package usage in hypermedia document presentations, the HyperAudioScaling tool was integrated with the HyperProp formatter [4].

When controlling document presentations, the HyperProp may need to change media durations in order to maintain the document temporal consistency. The HyperProp formatter delegates to media players the task of content rendering. To enable incorporation of third-party content players, HyperProp defines an API specifying the methods that media players should implement and how media players should notify presentation events (e.g. user interaction, start/end of a content fragment presentation, etc.). Media players that do not implement the required methods, or do not know how to signalize presentation events, should be plugged to the formatter through adapters.

Based on this approach, the time-scaling package implementation has been used to implement a set of HyperProp time-scaling audio players, as shown in Fig. 6. Each audio player is composed by an adapter, the time-scaling tool (Section 5), and a legacy audio player. The adapter receives commands from the HyperProp formatter, executes its tasks and requests the services of the time-scaling tool. The package returns the processed audio stream and dispatches events like the conclusion of time-scaling computation and the discovery of a new time instant. The adapter sends the processed audio stream to the legacy audio players. This legacy player exhibits the processed audio and can dispatch presentation events. These steps can take place both at compile or execution-time.

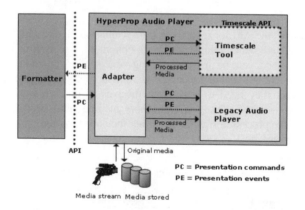

Fig. 6. Time-scaling player integrated with the HyperProp formatter

Two versions of audio presentation tools were implemented using JMF (Java Media Framework) [20]. One version works only for compile-time adjustments, using the file generation facility of HyperAudioScaling. The time-scaling tool saves the processed audio in a new file that may be sent to a JMF player after the complete adjustment. To support runtime time-scale modifications another version of audio presentation tool was developed extending the JMF data source. An instance of this new class of data source receives data from the stream returned by HyperAudioScaling and feeds the JMF player for content playing. Since JMF players run as threads of the client application process, it is possible to monitor player events (like user interactions, pause, resume, stop, finish, etc.). One drawback of using JMF is that the set of available codecs are still limited to a few audio formats.

In order to play a wider variety of audio formats, VLC [21] player was also integrated with the audio time-scaling tool. Unlike JMF, VLC runs as an external process fired from the client application. As a consequence, it is difficult for the adapter (Fig. 6) to interact with VLC players, for example, to monitor events like pause and resume during the audio playing.

7 Final Remarks

This paper discussed time-scaling issues considering specific requirements found in some applications that demand runtime elastic-time short adjustments, in particular the hypermedia presentation systems. From related work analysis, the authors could not find any existing solution that fulfills all the raised requirements.

The proposed time-scaling algorithm was implemented as a library in order to be used by third-party applications. Since, for the purpose of this paper, time-scale modifications are used to manage inter-media synchronization, it normally runs on small stream segments and with a tuning-factor close to 1, what usually brings imperceptible effects to users.

Some subjective and objective simple tests have been performed to measure the algorithm quality and to compare it with the time-scaling algorithm of Sound Forge 8.0. Sound Forge was chosen because of its high quality obtained with the expenses of high processing.

Four tuning factors were used to compare the tools: 0.90, 0.95, 1.05 and 1.10. MP3 44.1 kHz files were used with a compressed audio rate of 128kbps. Ten listeners participated on the test analyzing five audio types.

Subjective notes were assigned by comparing the original file with a processed one. Figure 7 and Figure 8 illustrate the notes obtained. In the pictures, notes are given in MOS (Mean Opinion Score) units [14]. The audios processed by the HyperAudioScaling algorithm and by the Sound Forge best algorithm are marked, respectively, by "h" and "s", followed by the used tuning factor (in %).

Although, as expected, the audio quality of the proposed algorithm is worse than the audio quality of Sound Forge, the subjective results showed that they are very close.

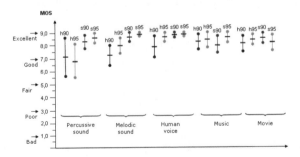

Fig. 7. MOS for each media type using 0.90 and 0.95 tuning factors and confidence level of 95%

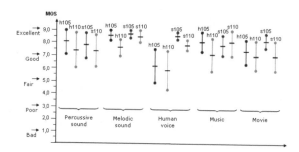

Fig. 8. MOS for each media type using 1.05 and 1.10 tuning factors and confidence level of 95%

On the other hand, the processing rate for MP3 files was about 8-times faster than Sound Forge (2640 frames/sec, using factor 1.1 in a Pentium 4 2.4GHz 1GB-RAM machine). The precision of the proposed algorithm, the reached (actual) audio duration minus the corresponding expected (ideal) audio duration, was always better than, or equal to, the Sound Forge precision for the five different types of audio files. Furthermore, the same tests demonstrated that the audio adjustment algorithm runs almost uniformly along the stream. The worst standard deviation was smaller than half of the distance between two processed frames.

Some media files, processed using HyperAudioScaling algorithm, are available in http://www.telemidia.puc-rio.br/~smbm/ajusteaudio. As future work, we intend to make tests considering different compressed-audio bit rates and also different audio compression standards.

References

1. Aly, S., Youssef, A.: Synchronization-Sensitive Frame Estimation: Video Quality Enhancement. In: Multimedia Tools and Applications (2002)
2. Arons, B.: Techniques, Perception, and Applications of Time-Compressed Speech. In: Proc. of American Voice I/O Society (1992)
3. ATSC, Digital Audio Compression Standard (AC-3) (1995)
4. Bachelet, B., Mahey, P., Rodrigues, R.F., Soares, L.F.G.: Elastic Time Computation in QoS-Driven Hypermedia Presentations. Research Report RR-04-16, Blaise-Pascal University, Clermont-Ferrand (2004)
5. Bonada, J.: Audio Time-Scale Modification in the Context of Professional Post-Production. Doctoral Pre-Thesis Work. UPF. Barcelona. Retrieved (June 3, 2006) (2002), from http://www.iua.upf.edu/mtg/publicacions.php?lng=eng&aul=3&did=219
6. Cavendish, S.A.: Ferramenta de Adaptação de Ajuste Elástico em Fluxos MPEG2. Master Dissertation, Departamento de Informática – PUC-Rio, Rio de Janeiro, Brazil (in portuguese) (2005)
7. Covell, M., Slaney, M., Rothstein, A.: FastMPEG: Time-Scale Modification of Bit-Compressed Audio Information. In: Proceedings of the Int. Conference on Acoustics, IEEE-ICASSP, Los Alamitos (2001)
8. Gabor, D.: Theory of Communication. Journal of Institution of Electrical Engineers (1946)

9. ISO. Coding of Moving Pictures and Associated Audio for Digital Storage Media at up to about 1.5 Mbit/s - Part 3: Audio, 11172-3 (1993)
10. ISO. Information technology - Generic coding of moving pictures and associated audio information - Part 7: Advanced Audio Coding (AAC), 13818-7 (1997)
11. ISO. Information technology - Generic coding of moving pictures associated audio information - Part 3: Audio, 13818-3 (1998)
12. ISO. Information technology - Generic coding of moving pictures and associated audio information: Systems, 13818-1 (2000)
13. ISO. Information technology - Coding of audio-visual objects - Part 3: Audio, 14496-3 (2001)
14. ITU-T. Subjective audiovisual quality assessment methods for multimedia applications, P.911 (1998)
15. Lee, E., Nakra, T.M., Borchers, J.: You're The Conductor: a Realistic Interactive Conducting System for Children. In: Proc. of the NIME 2004 Int. Conference on New Interfaces for Musical Expression, Japan (2004)
16. Microsoft. Windows Media Player. Retrieved March 20, 2006, from http://www.microsoft.com/
17. Nilsson, M.: ID3v2. Retrieved (March 20, 2006), from http://www.id3.org/
18. Omoigui, N., He, L., Gupta, A., Grudin, J., Sanacki, E.: Time-Compression: Systems Concerns, Usage, and Benefits. In: Proc. of the SIGCHI Conference on Human Factors in Computing Systems, USA (1999)
19. Sony, The Sound Forge Product Family. Retrieved March 20, (2006), from http://www.soundforge.com
20. Sun. Java Media Framework v2.0 API Specification. Retrieved March 20 (2006), from http://java.sun.com/
21. VideoLan Project. VLC media player. Retrieved March 20 (2006), from http://www.videolan.org/vlc/

Improving Multiscale Recurrent Pattern Image Coding with Deblocking Filtering

Nuno M.M. Rodrigues[1,2], Eduardo A.B. da Silva[3], Murilo B. de Carvalho[4], Sérgio M.M. de Faria[1,2], and Vitor M.M. da Silva[1,5]

[1] Instituto de Telecomunicações, Portugal
[2] ESTG, Instituto Politécnico Leiria, Portugal
[3] PEE/COPPE/DEL/Poli, Univ. Fed. Rio de Janeiro, Brazil
[4] TET/CTC, Univ. Fed. Fluminense, Brazil
[5] DEEC, Universidade de Coimbra, Portugal
nuno.rodrigues@co.it.pt, eduardo@lps.ufrj.br
murilo@telecom.uff.br, sergio.faria@co.it.pt,
vitor.silva@co.it.pt

Abstract. The Multidimensional Multiscale Parser (MMP) algorithm is an image encoder that approximates the image blocks by using recurrent patterns, from an adaptive dictionary, at different scales. This encoder performs well for a large range of image data. However, images encoded with MMP suffer from blocking artifacts. This paper presents the design of a deblocking filter that improves the performance the MMP. We present the results of our research, that aims to increase the performance of MMP, particularly for smooth images, without causing quality losses for other image types, where its performance is already up to 5 dB better than that of top transform based encoders. For smooth images, the proposed filter introduces relevant perceptual quality gains by efficiently eliminating the blocking effects, without introducing the usual blurring artifacts. Besides this, we show that, unlike traditional deblocking algorithms, the proposed method also improves the objective quality of the decoded image, achieving PSNR gains of up to about 0.3 dB. With such gains, MMP reaches an almost equivalent performance to that of the state-of-the-art image encoders (equal to that of JPEG2000 for higher compression ratios), for smooth images, while maintaining its gains for non-smooth images. In fact, for all image types, the proposed method provides significant perceptual improvements, without sacrificing the PSNR performance.

Keywords: Multidimensional Multiscale Parser, MMP-Intra, Deblocking Filter, Image Coding.

1 Introduction

The success of the current state-of-the-art transform-quantisation based encoders results from their excellent performance in the compression of natural images. Nevertheless, the relative performance of these encoders decreases noticeably when we deviate from the smoothness assumption, as is the case for images like text, compound (text and graphics), computer generated, texture, medical, among others. Indeed, it is a well known fact that most of the encoders that achieve top results for these image classes have poor performances for smooth images.

J. Filipe and M.S. Obaidat (Eds.): ICETE 2006, CCIS 9, pp. 224–236, 2008.

The Multidimensional Multiscale Parser (MMP) [1] is a lossy multidimensional signal encoder, that, unlike most state-of-the-art image encoders, is not based on the transform-quantisation paradigm. It is a multiscale recurrent pattern matching method, that uses an adaptive dictionary for approximating blocks of the original signal.

Using the same pattern matching paradigm, a new image encoding method, that combines MMP with the prediction techniques of H.264/AVC [3], was proposed in [4]. MMP-Intra is able to achieve quality gains over the original MMP algorithm for all image types, but particularly for smooth images, where the performance of MMP is inferior to that of the top transform-quantisation based encoders. Experimental results show that, when combined with convenient dictionary design techniques, the rate distortion (RD) performance of MMP-Intra becomes only marginally inferior (about 0.2 to 0.5 dB) to that of the JPEG2000 [6] and H.264/AVC *high* profile [3] image encoders, for the coding of smooth images [5]. For other types of images, MMP-Intra consistently maintains its excellent performance, achieving gains over standardised state-of-the-art encoders that range from 1 to 5 dB.

MMP-Intra, as MMP, uses the concatenation of the approximations of the original image blocks, at different scales. This process introduces blocking artifacts in the decoded image, that are particularly evident for higher compression ratios.

This paper presents a new deblocking scheme for MMP-Intra, that improves the performance of this image encoder for smooth images, without compromising its compression performance for other image types. The proposed method is based on a deblocking method, originally proposed for MMP and a matching pursuit based multiscale algorithm [1][2], but introduces new adaptive features, that allow it to optimise the perceptual results, as well as the objective performance of the encoded image.

The experimental results presented in this paper demonstrate that when the new method is combined with proper strategies to control the deblocking filter's parameters, it is able to consistently improve the objective results for smooth images, achieving gains that go up to about 0.3 dB. For smooth images, these gains in PSNR correspond to obvious improvements in the perceptual quality, resulting from the reduction of the blocking effects introduced by the encoding process. For non smooth images, like text and compound images, the new filtering strength control procedure is able to attenuate, or even eliminate, the smoothing effects of the deblocking process, that result in a loss of objective quality.

In the next section we briefly present the MMP and MMP-Intra image encoding methods. Section 3 describes a recently proposed dictionary design technique and explains its importance in increasing the performance of the MMP-Intra encoder. Section 4 presents the new deblocking strategies proposed in this paper and is followed by section 5 where the experimental results of this method are presented . Section 6 ends the paper with some closing remarks and conclusions.

2   Image Coding with MMP

A brief discussion of the application of the MMP and MMP-Intra algorithms to image coding is presented in this section. More information about these methods can be found respectively in [1] and [4].

2.1　The MMP Algorithm

MMP is an multiscale approximate pattern matching algorithm. It approximates an original square image block, or its successive binary segmentations, using a vector from an
adaptive dictionary $\mathcal{D}$. Scale transformations are used to adapt the dimensions of blocks
with different sizes. The successively segmented blocks, $\mathbf{X}^l$, are represented by a binary
segmentation tree, where each original square block is segmented first in the vertical,
then in the horizontal direction. The superscript l means that the block $\mathbf{X}^l$ belongs to
scale l or *level l* of the segmentation tree (with dimensions $(2^{\lfloor \frac{l+1}{2} \rfloor} \times 2^{\lfloor \frac{l}{2} \rfloor})$).

A simple definition of the MMP algorithm can be given by the following main steps.
For each block of the original image, $\mathbf{X}^l$:

1. find the dictionary element $\mathbf{S}_i^l$ that minimises the Lagrangian cost function of the
   approximation, given by: $J(\mathcal{T}) = D(\mathbf{X}^l, \mathbf{S}_i^l) + \lambda R(\mathbf{S}_i^l)$, where $D(.)$ is the sum
   of square differences (SSD) function and $R(.)$ is the rate needed to encode the
   approximation;
2. parse the original block into two blocks, $\mathbf{X}_1^{l-1}$ and $\mathbf{X}_2^{l-1}$, with half the pixels of the
   original block;
3. apply the algorithm recursively to $\mathbf{X}_1^{l-1}$ and $\mathbf{X}_2^{l-1}$, until level 0 is reached;
4. based on the values of the cost functions determined in the previous steps, decide
   whether to segment the original block or not;
5. if the block should not be segmented, use vector $\mathbf{S}_i^l$ of the dictionary to approximate
   $\mathbf{X}^l$;
6. else
   (a) create a new vector $\mathbf{S}_{new}^l$ from the *concatenation* of the vectors used to ap-
       proximate each half of the original block: $\mathbf{X}_1^{l-1}$ and $\mathbf{X}_2^{l-1}$;
   (b) use $\mathbf{S}_{new}^l$ to approximate $\mathbf{S}^l$;
   (c) use $\mathbf{S}_{new}^l$ to *update* the dictionary, making it available to encode future blocks
       of the image.

This algorithm results in a binary segmentation tree that represents each original
image block. This tree, represented in figure 1, is encoded using a top-bottom preorder
approach. In the final bit-stream, each leaf is encoded using a binary symbol '1' and
followed by an index, that identifies the vector of the dictionary that should be used to
approximate the corresponding sub-block. Each tree node is encoded using the binary
symbol '0'. The string of symbols that represents the segmentation tree is encoded using
an adaptive arithmetic encoder.

Unlike conventional vector quantisation (VQ) algorithms, MMP uses *approximate
block matching with scales* and an *adaptive dictionary*.

Every concatenation of two dictionary blocks of level $l - 1$ results in a new block,
that corresponds to a pattern that did not exist in the dictionary and is used to update it,
becoming available to encode future blocks of the image, independently of their size.
This updating procedure efficiently adapts the dictionary, by using only information that
can be inferred by the decoder, since it is based exclusively in the encoded segmentation
flags and dictionary indexes.

MMP uses a separable scale transformation T_N^M to adjust the vectors' sizes before
attempting to match them, allowing for the matching of vectors of different dimensions.

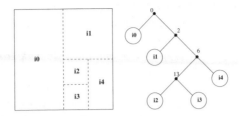

Fig. 1. Segmentation of a block and corresponding binary tree: the root corresponds to a original 4×4 block (level 4), while nodes i_2 and i_3 (1×1 blocks) belong to level 0

For example, in order to approximate an original block $\mathbf{X}^l$ using one block $\mathbf{S}^k$ of a different scale of the dictionary, MMP first determines $\mathbf{S}^l = T_k^l[\mathbf{S}]$. Detailed information about the use of scale transformations in MMP is presented in [1].

2.2   The MMP-Intra Algorithm

MMP-Intra combines the original MMP algorithm with predictive coding. For each original block, $\mathbf{X}^l$, MMP-Intra determines a prediction block, $\mathbf{P}_m^l$, using previously encoded image pixels and then it determines a residue block, given by $\mathbf{R}_m^l = \mathbf{X}^l - \mathbf{P}_m^l$. This residue block is then encoded using MMP.

MMP-Intra uses essentially the same prediction modes defined by H.264/AVC for Intra coded blocks [3][4]. Intra prediction is also used *hierarchically* for blocks of dimensions 16×16 down to 4×4 (corresponding to levels 8 to 4 of the segmentation tree). By the use of the Lagrangian RD cost function, the encoder jointly optimises the block prediction and the MMP residue encoding, determining the best trade-off between the prediction accuracy and the additional overhead introduced by the prediction data.

MMP-Intra encodes some additional information for the block prediction, namely the used prediction mode, m, and the block size used for the prediction step. This information is used by the decoder to determine the same prediction block, $\mathbf{P}_m^l$, that was used in the encoder. This block is added to the decoded residual block, $\hat{\mathbf{R}}_m^l$, in order to reconstruct the decoded image block, given by $\hat{\mathbf{X}}^l = \mathbf{P}_m^l + \hat{\mathbf{R}}_m^l$. Details about MMP-Intra can be found in [4].

3   Efficient Dictionary Design for MMP-Intra

MMP-Intra, as MMP, uses an initial dictionary consisting of a few blocks with constant value. This highly sparse initial dictionary is very inefficient, but the updating procedure quickly adapts its blocks to the original images' patterns, by introducing new blocks, $\mathbf{S}_{new}^l$, created by the concatenation of two vectors of level $l - 1$ of the dictionary.

Experimental studies have shown that the final number of blocks for each level of the dictionary is, by far, much larger than the total number of blocks that are actually used. This difference grows with the target bit-rate, but can be observed for different image types and target compression ratios. The exaggerate growth of the dictionary has the disadvantage of increasing the dictionary's indexes' entropy, compromising the method's performance.

In [5], a new algorithm was proposed to limit the dictionary growth, that introduces a "minimum distance condition" between any two vectors of each level of the dictionary. This process avoids that new vectors, very close to those already available in the dictionary space, are used to update the dictionary, by using a new test condition in the dictionary update procedure. With this new algorithm, a new block of level l, $\mathbf{S}^l_{new}$, is only used to update the dictionary if its minimum distortion, in relation to the blocks already available in the dictionary, is not inferior to a given threshold d.

The optimum value for d is a function of the target bit-rate and therefore of the parameter λ, and must be carefully chosen. If this value is too small, the aim of controlling the dictionary growth will not be achieved, and if it is too large, the dictionary will lose its efficiency in approximating the images' patterns. A simple expression for $d(\lambda)$ (see eq. 1) was determined by the use of a test image set, and allows the encoder to automatically achieve a close to optimum RD relation, for any given target bit-rate. Further details on how this equation was determined can be found in [5].

$$d(\lambda) = \begin{cases} 5 & if \quad \lambda \le 15; \\ 10 & if \quad 15 < \lambda \le 50; \\ 20 & otherwise. \end{cases} \tag{1}$$

In [5], the authors also show that the dictionary's indexes can be more efficiently encoded by using a context adaptive arithmetic encoder. The dictionary indexes are divided into groups, according to a context criterion, that, for MMP-Intra, is the original scale of the block. Instead of using just one symbol to encode a dictionary index, each index is transmitted using one context symbol followed by an index, that chooses among the elements of the corresponding segment. This carefully chosen segmentation criterion further explores the statistical dependencies of the MMP symbols, generating gains in the arithmetic coding module.

4   The Deblocking Filter

The MMP-Intra algorithm uses the concatenation of several approximations of the image blocks, at different scales. For each approximation, $\hat{\mathbf{X}}^l$, the RD control algorithm only controls the distortion for the image block and makes no consideration regarding the continuity in the border of the blocks. This introduces blocking artifacts in the reconstructed image, that originate from the discontinuities in the block boundaries.

In this work we present the results of our investigation in deblocking techniques that increase both the objective as the perceptual quality of the MMP-Intra's reconstructed image. We use an adaptive space-variant finite impulse response (FIR) filter to attenuate the blocks' borders discontinuities.

Let $\hat{\mathbf{X}}$ be the reconstructed signal. $\hat{\mathbf{X}}$ can be regarded as the concatenation of several blocks, $\hat{\mathbf{X}}^{l_k}_k$, that represent the algorithm's approximation of the various adjacent areas of the image. The K blocks $\hat{\mathbf{X}}^{l_k}_k$, used in the approximation, have no overlapping areas and different block sizes, given by $(2^{\lfloor\frac{l_k+1}{2}\rfloor} \times 2^{\lfloor\frac{l_k}{2}\rfloor})$. The decoded image can thus be represented as

$$\hat{\mathbf{X}} = \sum_{k=0}^{K-1} \hat{\mathbf{X}}_k^{l_k}(x - x_k, y - y_k). \tag{2}$$

In equation 2, each block $\hat{\mathbf{X}}_k^{l_k}$ corresponds to a dictionary block, of scale l_k, that was created by the MMP dictionary update process. This means that each of these blocks can be further decomposed into their basic components, $\mathcal{D}_0$, each belonging to the original dictionary, i.e.

$$\hat{\mathbf{X}}_k^{l_k} = \sum_{j=0}^{J-1} \mathcal{D}_{0j}^{l_j}. \tag{3}$$

The blocks $\mathcal{D}_{0j}^{l_j}$ can be regarded as the basic "building units" that were used by the MMP-Intra encoder and the l_j values represent the scale that was used by the encoder to represent each area of the image. The border points between each of these blocks correspond to the most probable areas for discontinuities in the decoded image.

In this work we apply a running bi-dimensional FIR filter to the reconstructed image, $\hat{\mathbf{X}}$. The filter's kernel dimensions are successively adapted to the scale of the original dictionary block that was used to approximate the area of the image that is currently being deblocked.

Blocks $\mathcal{D}_{0j}^{l_j}$ of large scales have larger support regions, meaning that the corresponding area of the image is smoother, while blocks with small values of l_j are used in more detailed image areas. The used space-variant filter has the ability to adapt its support, and smoothing strength, to the dimensions of each image segment, $\mathcal{D}_{0j}^{l_j}$, being considered.

Figure 2 has a unidimensional representation of a reconstructed portion of the image, that was approximated by the concatenation of three basic blocks, $(\mathcal{D}_0^{l_0} \quad \mathcal{D}_1^{l_1} \quad \mathcal{D}_2^{l_2})$, with different scales: l_0, l_1 and l_2. At each filtered pixel, represented in the figure by the arrow, the kernel support of the deblocking filter is set according to the scale l_k.

This process is similar to the one proposed in [2], that uses a running average filter and sets the kernel support at each point to $l_k + 1$. This filter is known for its highly smoothing effect, but the support adaptation process controls its strength according to

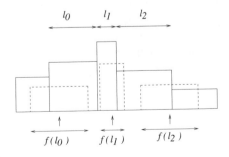

Fig. 2. The deblocking process uses an adaptive support for the FIR of the filters used in the deblocking

the detail level of the region that is being deblocked. This prevents some of the blurring artifacts that are usually caused by the use of too powerful deblocking techniques, but the original filtering process still results in a reduction in objective quality for smooth images. Another disadvantage of the original process is that it introduces highly disturbing blurring artifacts in non smooth images, resulting in a severe decrease in the final values of PSNR. This fact limits the applicability of this filter, because there is no practical way of avoiding the blurring of images that do not need deblocking.

In our work, we have adapted this deblocking process to MMP-Intra and developed it. This investigation resulted in a more efficient, highly adaptive, deblocking filter, that has some important advantages over the original method, namely:

- it uses a Gaussian kernel with optimised shape and support for each image, that adapts the deblocking strength to the image features resulting in perceptual, as well as, *objective* quality gains;
- the kernel shape optimisation means that the filtering strength is automatically adjusted and can be set to an arbitrarily low power. This means that, for non low-pass images, the new process automatically eliminates the highly annoying blurring effects and the corresponding PSNR losses;
- the new method considers the dimensions of the neighbouring blocks as well as those of the block being filtered, eliminating some artifacts that were introduced by the original method;
- the proposed algorithm monitors the differences in the frontiers' pixels' intensities, in order to avoid smoothing steep variations that were present in the original image and do not correspond to blocking artifacts.

4.1 Adapting Shape and Support for the Deblocking Kernel

In our investigation we tested different kernels with various support regions for the deblocking filter. Experimental results showed that the use of Gaussian kernels, instead of the original rectangular filter, produces gains in the PSNR value of the decoded image, as well as the desired effect of eliminating the blocking artifacts.

These tests also demonstrated that the quality of the deblocked image strongly depends on the dimensions of the support region of the used filter. In the original method, this support is set to $l_k + 1$. We varied this value and discovered that it is optimal for the running average filter, but that this is not the case when we use a Gaussian kernel.

Instead of adjusting the support region of the Gaussian kernel, we set the filter length at the same $l_k + 1$ samples used in the original method, but adjust the Gaussian's variance, producing filter kernels with different shapes. Consider a Gaussian filter, with variance σ^2 and length L, with an impulse response (IR) given by:

$$g_L(n) = e^{-\frac{\left(n - \frac{L-1}{2}\right)^2}{2.\sigma^2}}, \tag{4}$$

with $n = 0, 1, ..., L - 1$. We controlled the shape of the filter by changing a filter parameter α, that controls the variance of the Gaussian, by using the expression:

$$g_L(n) = e^{-\frac{\left(n - \frac{L-1}{2}\right)^2}{2.(\alpha.L)^2}}, \tag{5}$$

to determine the filters' IR.

Figure 3 represents the shape of a 17 tap filter for the several values of parameter α represented in the legend. This figure clearly demonstrates the explored relation between the filters' shape and their approximate support. By varying the value of the filter's α parameter, one is able to efficiently adjust its IR from an almost rectangular filter, with a support region $l_k + 1$, to a Gaussian filter with different lengths. In the limit, when α tends to zero, the IR of the filter becomes a simple impulse, deactivating the deblocking effect for those cases were it is not beneficial.

The value of the parameter α is controlled by the MMP-Intra encoder. At the end of the encoding process, the MMP-Intra encoder tests the deblocking process using different values for the α parameter. It is then able to determine the value that maximises the PSNR of the reconstructed image. The value of α is then appended at the end of the encoded bit-stream, by using a 3 bit code, that corresponds respectively to the 8 possible values for α: $\{0, 0.05, 0.10, 0.15, 0.20, 0.25, 0.30, 0.40\}$. This introduces a marginal additional computational cost in the encoder, as well as an additional rate overhead, that is equally negligible.

4.2   Eliminating the Artifacts Introduced by Deblocking

The original method only considers the dimensions of the block currently being filtered to set the filter support. In our investigation we noticed that this fact introduces an unexpected artifact, when there exists the concatenation of wide and short blocks, with very different intensity values.

This case is represented in figure 4, where a wide dark block A is concatenated with two bright blocks: one narrow block B followed by one wide block C. When we filter blocks A and B, a smooth transition appears, that eliminates the blocking effect in the AB border. When the block C is filtered, because the used filter has a very wide support region, the pixels near the BC border will suffer from the influence of some of the dark pixels of block A. This causes a dark "valley" to appear in the BC border, that introduces a visible artifact in the deblocked image.

In order to avoid these artifacts, the new method controls the filter length so that the deblocking filter never takes in consideration pixels that are not from the present block

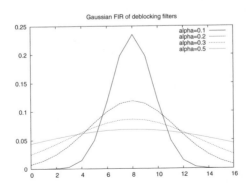

Fig. 3. Adaptive FIR of the filters used in the deblocking

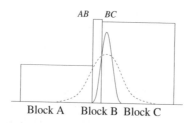

Fig. 4. A case were the concatenation of blocks with different supports and pixel intensities causes the appearance of an image artifact, after the deblocking filtering

or its adjacent neighbours. In the example of figure 4, the length of the filter used in the C block's pixels that are near the BC border is controlled, so that the left most pixel that is used in the deblocking is always the first (left most) pixel of block B, eliminating the described artifact. In figure 4, this means that the new method uses the filter represented by the solid line, instead of the original one, represented by the dashed line.

Another artifact caused by the original method is the introduction of smooth transitions in regions of the image that originally have very steep transitions from low to high pixel intensity values (or vice versa). The proposed algorithm monitors the differences in the frontiers' pixels' intensities, in order to avoid filtering steep variations that do not correspond to blocking artifacts. This is again controlled by the encoder, using an adaptive method.

The proposed method uses a step intensity threshold, s, that corresponds to the maximum intensity difference between the two border pixels, that still allows for the filtering to occur. This process is represented in figure 5, where two blocks A and B with very different intensity values are concatenated. In this case, the AB border is only filtered if the absolute difference between the border pixels is inferior to the defined value for s, i.e., $|A_k - B_0| < s$.

The value of s is again chosen in order to maximise the PSNR value for the particular image that is being deblocked. The encoder tests a set of different step values and transmits the code corresponding to the chosen value. A three bit code is again used to represent the eight possible values for s, belonging to the set $\{0, 16, 32, 64, 96, 128, 192, 255\}$, where $s = 0$ corresponds to never filtering the borders and $s = 255$ corresponds to the case where all blocks are filtered.

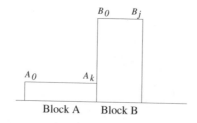

Fig. 5. A case where a steep variation in pixel intensities is a feature of the original image

5   Experimental Results

Experimental tests were performed using the proposed and original deblocking methods. Figure 6 presents a detail of image LENA 512, encoded using the described MMP-Intra algorithm without using any deblocking technique and compares it with the results of using the the deblocking technique from [2], and the new deblocking technique, proposed in this paper.

Perceptually, we can observe that the new deblocking filter is able to efficiently eliminate the blocking artifacts in Lena's face and hat, without compromising the image quality at regions with high detail, like Lena's hair and her hat's feathers. In this case, the used filter has $\alpha = 0.10$ and $s = 255$.

When compared with the original deblocking method, we can observe that the smoothing effect introduced by the proposed method is not as strong, avoiding the introduction of some blurring artifacts that are noticeable in the image of figure 6 b), specially in the areas with finer details.

In figure 6 b) we can also observe the first type of artifacts, explained in section 4.2. They appear in Lena's shoulder, where the previously described "dark valleys" are easy to observe. We can see that the proposed method efficiently eliminates these artifacts.

Figure 6 b) also shows that the original method, developed originally for the MMP encoder, suffers from a unexpectedly high performance loss, when used with MMP-Intra. Because MMP-Intra uses predictive coding, the used dictionary blocks approximate *residue* patterns. In some cases, where the prediction step is particularly efficient, some detailed areas are approximated by large, smooth, residue blocks added with detailed prediction blocks. In this case, the deblocking process uses a wide filter to deblock an image area that is not necessarily smooth. When this happens, the use of the original deblocking method originates serious artifacts, like the one observed in Lena's lip. Even when this fact is not as obvious as in the presented case, we can generally say that this factor seriously compromises the performance of the original method, when applied to MMP-Intra, resulting in a severe reduction in the PSNR results. However, due to its adaptability, the proposed method does not seem to suffer from this disturbing factor.

(a) No deblocking (30.92 dB)

(b) Original deblocking (28.93 dB)

(c) New deblocking (31.21 dB)

Fig. 6. A detail of image Lena 512, encoded with MMP-Intra at 0.135 bpp

Figure 7 a) shows the objective quality results for image Lena 512, for the MMP-Intra method with no deblocking and with the two tested deblocking techniques. Figure 7 b) highlights the PSNR quality gains introduced by the deblocking filter, that are more relevant for higher compression ratios, where the blocking artifacts are more notice-able. These gains go up to more than 0.3 dB, allowing for the PSNR results of MMP-Intra for image Lena to come even closer to the ones of top state-of-the-art transform-quantisation based encoders, like JPEG2000 [6] and H.264/AVC, [3], shown in figure 7 a). In fact, we can see that, for low bit-rates, the proposed method allows for MMP-Intra to achieve equivalent results to those of the JPEG2000 algorithm.

We also performed experimental tests using non smooth images, like text image PP1205 and compound (text and grayscale) image PP1209. Images PP1205 and PP1209 were scanned, respectively, from pages 1205 and 1209 of the *IEEE Transactions on Image Processing*, volume 9, number 7, July 2000 and are available for download at *http://www.estg.ipleiria.pt/~nuno/MMP/*. These tests showed that the proposed kernel adaptation algorithm eliminates the highly disturbing blurring artifacts introduced when

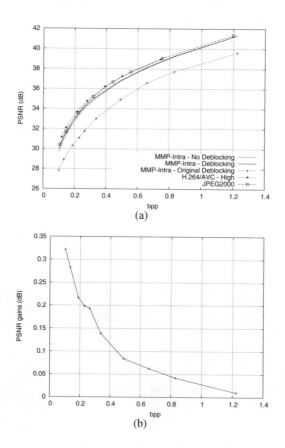

Fig. 7. a) Objective quality results for image Lena; b) PSNR gains of the new method, when compared with MMP-Intra with no deblocking, using $\alpha = 0.10$, $s = 255$

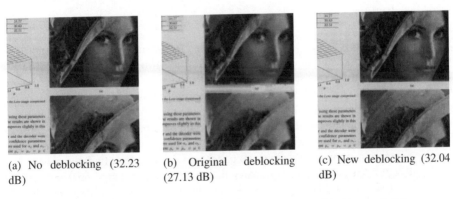

(a) No deblocking (32.23 dB)

(b) Original deblocking (27.13 dB)

(c) New deblocking (32.04 dB)

Fig. 8. A detail of compound image PP1209, encoded with MMP-Intra at 0.61 bpp

the original deblocking techniques are applied to these images. This can be confirmed in figure 8, where the perceptual results for compound image PP1209 are presented.

Figure 8 c) also shows that the use of the new strategies as a simple post processing deblocking algorithm, allows for a deblocking effect that improves the subjective quality of the decoded image, at the cost of a slight reduction in the PSNR value. In addition, it shows that the second type of artifacts introduced by the original method, that introduce a smoothing ramp in areas of the image that originally had an abrupt variation, is efficiently eliminated by the proposed algorithm (in this example, the value of s was set to 32).

Figure 9 shows the PSNR results for compound image PP1209, for the case presented in figure 8, where the deblocking process allows for an increased perceptual image quality, at the cost of a small reduction of the PSNR value. As we can see, even in this case the objective quality achived by the MMP-Intra encoder is still about 1 dB better than that of the H.264/AVC encoder and 2 dB better than that of the JPEG2000 encoder.

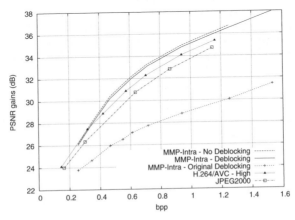

Fig. 9. Objective quality results for image PP1209 (adaptive deblocking filter used $\alpha = 0.10$ and $s = 32$)

6 Conclusions

In this paper we present a new adaptive deblocking technique that allows for improvements in both perceptual and objective quality, for the MMP-Intra image encoding algorithm. This method uses a space-variant FIR filter with an adaptive shape and support Gaussian impulse response. The filter parameters are automatically controlled in order to maximise the objective quality for smooth images and eliminate the disturbing blurring artifacts for non smooth images, like text and graphics.

The use of the new deblocking techniques achieves one of the main objectives in the on going research of multiscale recurrent pattern image encoders: finding ways to improve the algorithm's performance for smooth images, without compromising its excellent performance for non low-pass images, like text and graphics. Experimental results have shown that, for smooth images, the proposed techniques allows for coding gains that go up to 0.3 dB for low bit-rates, where the blocking artifacts are more noticeable, achieving the same objective quality as the JPEG2000 algorithm. Nevertheless, for non low-pass images, like text and graphics, the proposed method introduces no losses, allowing MMP-Intra to maintain its 1 to 5 db advantage over the state-of-the-art image encoders.

References

1. de Carvalho, M., da Silva, E., Finamore, W.: Multidimensional signal compression using multiscale recurrent patterns. Elsevier Signal Processing (82), 1559–1580 (2002)
2. de Carvalho, M., Lima, D.M., da Silva, E., Finamore, W.: Universal multi-scale matching pursuits algorithm with reduced blocking effect. In: IEEE International Conference on Image Processing (2000)
3. Joint Video Team (JVT), ISO/IEC MPEG & ITU-T VCEG, I.J..I.T.S.Q.: Draft of Version 4 of H.264/AVC (ITU-T Recommendation H.264 and ISO/IEC 14496-10 (MPEG-4 part 10) Advanced Video Coding) (2005)
4. Rodrigues, N.M.M., da Silva, E.A.B., de Carvalho, M.B., de Faria, S.M.M., Silva, V.M.M.: Universal image coding using multiscale recurrent patterns and prediction. In: IEEE International Conference on Image Processing (2005)
5. Rodrigues, N.M.M., da Silva, E.A.B., de Carvalho, M.B., de Faria, S.M.M., Silva, V.M.M., Pinagé, F.: Efficient dictionary design for multiscale recurrent patterns image coding. In: IS-CAS 2006 IEEE International Symposium on Circuits and Systems (2006)
6. Taubman, D.S., Marcelin, M.: JPEG2000: Image Compression Fundamentals, Standards and Practice. Kluwer Academic Publishers, Dordrecht (2001)

A Network Scheduler for an Adaptive VoD Server*

Javier Balladini, Leandro Souza, and Remo Suppi

Computer Architecture & Operating System Department
Universitat Autonoma of Barcelona, Spain
{javier,leandro}@aomail.uab.es, remo.suppi@uab.es

Abstract. Most of the Video on Demand (VoD) systems were designed to work in dedicated networks. However, there are some approaches that provide VoD service in nondedicated and best effort networks, but they adapt the media's quality according to the available network bandwidth. Our research activities focus on VoD systems with high quality service on nondedicated networks. Currently, we have designed and developed, to integrate in the VoD server, a network manager that provides: total network control, network state information, and adaptation of the transmission rate in a TCP-Friendly way. The present work describes this network manager, named Network Traffic Scheduler (NTS), which incorporates a congestion control algorithm named "Enhanced Rate Adaptation Protocol" (ERAP). ERAP is an optimization of the well-known protocol denominated "Rate Adaptation Protocol" (RAP). Maintaining the basic behavior of RAP, ERAP increases the efficiency of the NTS by reducing the resources usage (of the server and the network). These components has been extensively evaluated by simulations and real tests in which the resource consumption and the performance were measured. This paper presents the advantages of using ERAP instead of RAP in a VoD server, and its viability to be integrated within the NTS in a VoD server on nondedicated networks.

Keywords: Video on demand, media streaming, internet congestion control protocol, network scheduler.

1 Introduction

Our research group have designed a distributed Video on Demand (VoD) system architecture for dedicated networks [1]. This platform works very well in Local Area Network (LAN) environments, but many problems appear that need to be solved whilst trying to provide a service in nondedicated Wide Area Network (WAN) environments.

Therefore, our investigation must be lead to solve other kinds of problems that arise when the VoD system works in a nondedicated network such as the Internet. It is necessary to adapt the main component of the platform, the Video Proxy Server (VPS), to a set of restrictions imposed by the type of communication that is possible to make on this type of networks.

Since at the moment the Internet does not offer a multicast service (in a general form), the first change that must be made is that the VoD service will be made solely on unicast channels (instead of a combination of multicast and unicast).

---

* This research is supported by the MEyC-Spain under contract TIN 2004-03388.

J. Filipe and M.S. Obaidat (Eds.): ICETE 2006, CCIS 9, pp. 237–251, 2008.
© Springer-Verlag Berlin Heidelberg 2008

Another problem is that on the Internet all the packets are treated in the same way, without discrimination or explicit delivery guarantees, known as the "best-effort service model". The quality of service and the resources are not guarantees in terms of bandwidth, transfer delay, delay variation (jitter), and packet losses. The packet losses can be due to physical reasons and droppings. In the first case, the noise that affects the transmission of the signals or the putting out of service of active communication devices (links, routers, etc.) are included. The dropping of packets is due to the congestion that takes place because the network is overloaded by the demand of network resources and this demand is close or exceeds the network capacity [2].

When the transmission is made within the network capacity, the packets arrive at their destination (except for a few that are affected by noise in general) and the number of received packets is proportional to the number of sent packets. However, when increasing the traffic, the network cannot handle it, and begins to lose packets. The result is a state of congestion which continues to build up and get worse. When a packet loss exists (for example if any router has dropped it), the retransmission timer will expire and the sender will possibly retransmit the packet. More packets in the network make the situation worse, and as the capacity of delivery of the network continues to be the same, the proportion of received packets against the sent packets declines even more. [3,2]

In order to adapt to congestion states, the VoD server must decreases the traffic sent by the network, allowing the possibility to identify two types of strategies for this aim: *Dynamic Rate Control* and *Anticipation*.

The Dynamic Rate Control strategy, allows the transmission rate to adapt dynamically according to the network conditions, but to reduce the transmission rate, the media quality must be lowered [4]. The solutions based on Anticipation are applicable only to prerecorded continuous media, that is to say, the whole multimedia file that can be sent to the client already exists. This strategy, takes advantage of the periods of low use of the server and the network bandwidth, to send media in advance that the client will consume later. In this way, it is possible to tolerate moments in which the network or the server are overloaded.

The algorithm developed in our VPS is named *Credit Based Media Delivery Algorithm* (Cb-Mda), and belongs to the Anticipation category. This type of algorithm, from a general point of view, is a *Logical Channel Scheduler* (LCS), or is also known as *Streams Scheduler*.

The main function of the LCS is to plan the different streams in order to make use of the server exit bandwidth. However, the LCS does not have the capacity to manage the communications at the network level. This capacity, necessary to guarantee the QoS, is assigned to a new module that we named *Network Traffic Scheduler* (NTS). The NTS works together with the LCS (Cb-Mda in our case), and a feedback from NTS to LCS is provided to inform of the communication state between the server and clients. When the NTS detects congestion, in the path of communication with a client, it must warn the LCS so that it takes the suitable measures to reduce the transmission rate of the logical channel or stream. For that reason, it is necessary that the NTS and the LCS work coordinately and cooperatively to obtain the best solution to the problem raised. Without information of the real transmissions and the state of the network, the LCS will not be able to work accordingly.

The investigation has been centered in the development of a NTS based on User Datagram Protocol (UDP) packets and with congestion management so that the VPS can be used on the Internet with total guarantees and quality of service. The use of UDP, instead of TCP, has significant advantages with respect to the overload that implies TCP in the transmission. Furthermore, TCP does not give any of the information required by the LCS, and it does not allow that this capacity can be added to it.

The rest of this paper is organized as follows: in section 2 the related works to this article are described. In section 3, the NTS and its interaction with the rest of the components of the VPS are explained. Furthermore, the characteristics that must have their algorithm of congestion control in order to adapt it to the new necessities of the VPS are indicated. The "Rate Adaptation Protocol" (RAP) [5,6], a well-known congestion control protocol, whose basic characteristics are suitable in order to adapt to the NTS, is described in section 4. This protocol is optimized to be introduced in the NTS, giving origin to the new protocol "Enhanced Rate Adaptation Protocol" (ERAP), which is presented in section 5. In section 6, the RAP and ERAP behaviours are compared, and the advantages to using ERAP instead of RAP as congestion control algorithm of the NTS are analyzed. Finally, in section 7 the conclusions and future works are described.

2   Related Works

Congestion control has been studied for many years, nevertheless, the existing protocols are not many if we are restricted to TCP-Friendly protocols for multimedia transmission on the Internet.

Jacob et al. [7] presents a congestion control algorithm similar to TCP except that this one does not make retransmissions.

Cen et al. [8] proposes the "Streaming Control Protocol" (SCP) for real-time streaming of continuous multimedia data across the Internet. Dorgham Sisalem et al. presents the "Loss-Delay Adjustment Algorithm" (LDA) in [9] and their variant "LDA+" in [10]. Sally Floyd et al. exposes the protocol "TCP-Friendly Rate Control" (TFRC) in [11], and later M. Handley et al. describes this protocol in the RFC 3448 [12].

Reza Rejaie et al. presents the "Rate Adaptation Protocol" (RAP), and a mechanism of layered quality adaptation for Internet video streaming in the context of unicast congestion control are described in [13].

Between the commercial players of video streaming on the Internet we can include: RealPlayer, Windows Media Player, and QuickTime. Although their algorithms of congestion control have not been revealed, there exists publications ([14] and [15] among others) that show studies on the performance and its behaviours with respect to if they are or not TCP-Friendly according to the answers that they offer in congestion cases in real networks.

3   Network Traffic Scheduler

The NTS is the component of the VPS in charge to manage the communications at the network level guaranteeing a video transport with QoS to the LCS. The NTS will inform the LCS about the state of communication with each client, in such a way that the

LCS can carry out their tasks with real and updated information of the network. If the NTS finds that the communication of a certain connection has improved, then the LCS will be able to increase the transmission rate of that channel. In case the communication gets worse, the LCS will have to reduce the transmission rate immediately.

The NTS must be equipped with a congestion control algorithm to fulfill their responsibilities. All congestion control algorithm that is used on the Internet must have the property of being TCP-Friendly, that is to say, the use of bandwidth (in a stable state) does not have to be greater than that required by TCP under similar circumstances [16]. If irresponsible users capture more bandwidth than corresponds to them, the delivery service of the users that cooperate for the good operation of the network could be degraded. Furthermore, the stability and operation of the whole system would be threatened [17].

Different strategies for the congestion control exist, but the NTS must make use of a strategy of type *Black-Box* (this scheme sees the network as a black or closed box) since there is no feedback from the interconnection devices (routers) and the feedback from the receiver is the only one available. The streaming applications generally have better behaviour (and therefore they require it) when the traffic flows in continuous forms and with few throughput variations in the time. This property is known as Smooth Sending Rate. Although it is a characteristic that our LCS does not use, it is good that the congestion control protocol of the NTS includes it for versatility purposes.

Furthermore, it has been decided for a line of work of *rate-based* protocols (instead of *window-based*) because they have the advantage of not transmitting packets in bursts. If a sender has the transmission capacity of b packets/second, is better to send a packet each $1/b$ seconds and not a sequence of b packets every second. A sequence of b packets could be unacceptable for an interconnection device that does not have the sufficient amount of memory to store it temporarily. On the other hand, if it does have the sufficient amount of memory, long queues in routers will increase the end-to-end delay. This can cause retransmissions (when expiring the time of the packets) that produces an increase of the congestion state.

Several rate-based congestion control protocols exist in the literature, between which are LDA, RAP, TFRC, and SCP (see section 2). Many of the existing protocols are proposed by investigators, and in many cases a real implementation does not exist, or this does not adapt to the NTS. Thus, our investigation has been oriented in taking the specifications of the most open of them, and the most suitable to our objectives.

We have chosen the RAP specification because this has the expected properties of black-box, rate-based, and smooth sending rate, and also because it is simple, well documented, and well known as the Network Simulator - NS2 [18,19] includes an implementation of them. Nevertheless, in the official site of RAP no real implementation of this protocol is provided.

The RAP protocol was adapted and optimized to fulfill the requirements of the NTS, giving origin to a new RAP version named *Enhanced Rate Adaptation Protocol* (ERAP).

4   The RAP Protocol

As their authors explain in [5,6], the RAP is an end-to-end rate-based congestion control mechanism that utilizes an Additive Increase Multiplicative Decrease (AIMD) algorithm for rate adaptation to achieve TCP-friendliness. The AIMD rate adaptation algorithm can have non TCP-friendly behaviour when a heavy load produces the reduction of TCP's performance. Therefore, a fine-grain rate-adaptation mechanism is added to assist RAP in becoming more stable and reacting to temporary congestion while realizing the AIMD algorithm at a coarser granularity. Basic RAP has a TCP-Friendly behaviour in many situations, and the fine-grain rate-adaptation mechanism expands this behaviour to more circumstances.

The RAP protocol is mainly implemented in the sender. A RAP sender sends data packets with a sequence number, and a RAP receiver sends an acknowledgment (ACK) for each packet. Using this feedback, the RAP sender can detect losses and sample the round-trip-time (RTT). Timeouts and gaps in the sequence space are used to detect packet losses. This protocol only considers the packet losses as a congestion symptom. Unlike TCP, a RAP sender may send many packets before receiving a new ACK.

In principle, an ACK packet includes the sequence number of the delivered data packet, but in order to provide robustness against single ACKs losses, the following redundant information is added to them:

- *lastRecv*: the sequence number of the last received packet
- *lastMiss*: the sequence number of the last missed packet previous to *lastRecv*, or 0 if no packet was missing
- *prevRecv*: the sequence number of the received packet previous to *lastMiss*, or 0 if *lastRecv* was the first packet

For example, if the pattern of packet losses was "1 _ _ 4 _ _ 7", the values are: *lastRecv* = 7, *lastMiss* = 6, and *prevRecv* = 4. A packet with sequence number Seq_i will be considered received if $((lastRecv \geq Seq_i)and(Seq_i > lastMiss))or(Seq_i = prevRecv)$.

Basically, the algorithm is conformed to by two timers, the *ipgTimer* and the *rttTimer*, that along with the reception of ACKs are the triggers of the three events that direct the algorithm.

Furthermore, the following important variables are included: *IPG* (inter packet gap, used to control the transmission rate), *SRTT* (smoothed - or estimated - round trip time, defines the periodicity of the transmission rate increment), and *Timeout* (defines the time to live or expiration of the packet); and a list named *transmissionHistory*. This list stores the sent packets but not the acknowledged packets, which change to the *ignored* state when the loss of a packet is detected. Thus, the algorithm only reacts once, at the most, when a burst of packet losses occurs, related to the same congestion case. The *SRTT* and *Timeout* variables are updated based on the last sample RTT using the Jacobson/Karels algorithm [20].

The diagram of the figure 1 describes the operation of the RAP, where the arrows represent the events that direct it, and the boxes represent their main procedures. To start the algorithm, initially, the *IpgTimeout* and the *RttTimeout* procedures are invoked.

The algorithm uses an adaptation scheme (AIMD) so that if does not detect congestion, the transmission rate is periodically and additively increased, and if it detects congestion, the transmission rate is immediately and multiplicatively decreased.

When no packet losses are detected, the transmission rate, S_i, is increased by a certain value α (i.e. $S_{i+1} = S_i + \alpha$) updating the value of the IPG (inter packet gap) based on equation (1).

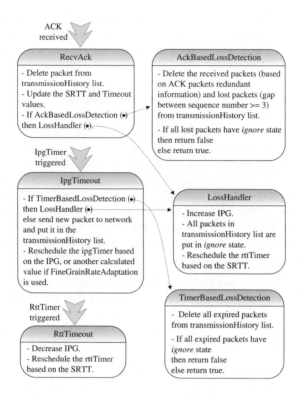

Fig. 1. The RAP algorithm

$$S_i = \frac{PacketSize}{IPG_i} \qquad IPG_{i+1} = \frac{IPG_i * C}{IPG_i + C} \qquad (1)$$

In this equation, C has the dimension of time and determines the value of α. RAP assigns to C the value of *SRTT* to emulate the TCP window adjustment mechanism in the steady state. At any rate, α represents the increment of one packet in each adjusting point. When packet losses are detected, the transmission rate is multiplicatively decreased by a certain value β (i.e. $S_{i+1} = \beta * S_i$), updating the value of the IPG based on equation (2).

$$IPG_{i+1} = IPG_i/\beta \qquad \beta = 0.5 \qquad (2)$$

RAP gives a value of $\beta = 0.5$ in order to follow the behaviour adopted by TCP.

The expected behaviour would be of a progressive increase of the transmission rate in absence of congestion and a abrupt decrement of this upon congestion (tooth of mountain range) as can be observed in the figure 2.

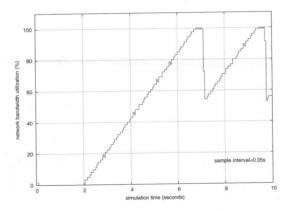

Fig. 2. Characteristic RAP behaviour

5   The ERAP Protocol

The Enhanced Rate Adaptation Protocol (ERAP) is an adaptation and optimization of
the RAP protocol to be introduced in the NTS. The NTS must work with a lot of connections in order to utilize the maximum possible of the available bandwidth and to
serve the greater amount of possible requests.

With the purpose of diminishing the use of resources and increasing the efficiency of
the NTS, the ERAP protocol was designed with the following particular characteristics:

1. **Encapsulation:** A ERAP packet is encapsulated within a UDP packet to be transmitted by the Internet.
2. **Reliability:** as our system does not analyze streams of video, making a separation
   in frames, it is impossible to determine if certain packets contain data of low or
   high relevance. Therefore, all lost packets must be retransmitted. Is not possible to
   retransmit a lost packet with its initial sequence number, because of the fact that a
   packet with an old sequence number (smaller or equal to the last sequence number
   minus 3) immediately will be considered as lost and retransmitted.
   In order to solve this problem, the packets that need to be retransmitted, are transmitted as if they were new packets (i.e. with a sequence number equal to the last,
   plus one). However, a new sequence number is added to each packet, named *ap-
   plication_sequence_number*, that the receiver uses to maintain the real sequence of
   packets, and to identify the duplicated packets.
3. **Centralized ACKs' Reception:** The decentralized ACKs' reception does not work
   well when it is used in a server with many active sessions. According to the model
   proposed by RAP, each Sender must handle his own packets' reception. In this
   manner, in a real implementation that uses sockets (to transmit the packets), each
   Sender would have a thread in charge of packets' reception. Therefore, by each active video or established session a thread would be used.
   However, ERAP centralizes the reception of ACKs from multiple destinations, and
   in this way, only a single thread is necessary instead of so many threads as con-

nections as the server has. Thus, when a packet arrives at the server, it is received by a central module named RapManager and later it is given to the corresponding ErapSender.

The RAP and ERAP architectures are showed in the figure 3 (a) and the figure 3 (b), respectively, where *RS* is a RapSender agent, *RM* is a RapManager agent, *RR* is a RapReceiver agent, and *ART* is a Acks Reception Thread.

4. **Centralized Packets' Sending:** The decentralized data packets' sending used by RAP presents different problems depending if the UDP packet sending (in a specific operating system) is blocking or not. In blocking sending, several RapSender will try to send packets to the network at the same time. Then, the operating system will block the packets' sending until the Network Interface Card (NIC) accepts them. During this time, the threads executing the sending operation will remain blocked producing waste of resources. In the non-blocking sending, the length of the transmit queue of the device must be increased in order to tolerate the traffic fluctuations and diminish packet drops. However, the packets will have an incorrect timestamp because of the large gap between the sending operation run time and the packet exit time.

All these problems are solved by ERAP. This protocol centralizes the packets' sending of all connections, and adds a queue named readyToSendQueue, in which each RapSender agent will deposit packets that already can leave to the network. The

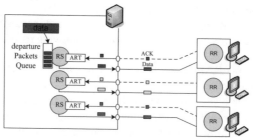

(a) RAP architecture with decentralized ACKs' reception

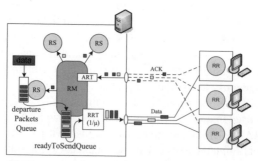

(b) ERAP architecture with centralized ACKs' reception

Fig. 3. RAP and ERAP architectures

ERAP architecture with centralized packets' sending is showed in the figure 3 (b). A new thread named Rate Regulator Thread (RRT) is included in the RapManager agent and is in charge to take packets from the readyToSendQueue and transmit them to a regulated rate. The RRT will never try to transmit more data than accepted by the network, and therefore the packets will not remain for a long time in the device's queue. In this way, the problem that occurs in non-blocking sending of UDP packets is solved. Furthermore, in ERAP, the RapSender agents put packets to send in the readyToSendQueue, instead of send packets directly to the network. Consequently, the problem of blocking sending of UDP packets is solved because the send operation is executed by only one thread, releasing occupied resources by other threads.

5. **Header Size Reduction:** so that the protocol is versatile and it does not overload the network, a minimum set of information has been defined to the data and ACK packets. RAP has only one header used for data packets and ACKs packets, that contain the following integer data: *seqno*, *size*, *rap_flags*, *lastRecv*, *lastMiss*, and *prevRecv*. *Seqno* is the sequence number, *size* is the packet size, *rap_flags* identify the type (ACK or DATA) of packet, and the rest of the fields are only used when the packet is of ACK type.

On the other hand, ERAP determines two types of headers, the *data header* and the *ACK header*, avoiding the unnecessary data transport in the headers. The *data header* has only two integer data: *seqno*, and *appSeq*. The first field is the sequence number, and the second field is the application sequence number added to manage the retransmissions. As the packets are received by different ports, ERAP automatically identifies the type of them (ACK or DATA) and, therefore, the *rap_flags* field is not used. The rest of the fields (*lastRecv*, *lastMiss*, and *prevRecv*) are specifics of the *ACK header*. The *size* field is not necessary because each ERAP packet is encapsulated in only one UDP packet.

The *ACK header* has the following fields of integer type: *port*, *seq*, *lastRecv*, *lastMiss*, and *prevRecv*. The port field is added so that the centralized ACKs' reception module (RapManager) can distinguish to what connection the ACK belongs. If the Receiver wants to send ACK packets to the Sender with a source IP (Internet Protocol) address different to the IP address by which receives the data packets, then the ACK header will contain an extra field named *IP* that will have the IP address of the Receiver by which it receives the data packets, allowing it to identify the session correctly.

6. **Optimized Events Management:** When in a session, the transmission of packets is suspended temporarily, and later this is re-initiated, the protocol would have to continue the transmission supposing that the network state has not changed. In this way, the network state information, learnt during the previous course (of use of connection) would be wasted. At this moment of inactivity (i.e. when there are no more packets to send) it does not make sense to continue shooting events of the protocol for that session. Then, ERAP deactivates the timers and maintains the state of the session so that when the transmission is resumed, the timers will be reactivated and the transmission rate will be continued from the previous point.

On the other hand, RAP stops only the *ipgTimer* and the *rttTimmer* continues being triggered, that will invoke the *RttTimeout* procedure repeatedly, with the consequent

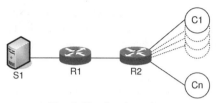

Fig. 4. Simulated topology

CPU cost. This procedure will only decrease the *IPG* if during the past *SRTT* time, a certain percentage (modifiable) of the *SRTT/IPG* packets were sent. If RAP sent less than that, the rate is not increased.

7. **Generation of Information Required by the LCS:** as it were explained in section 1, it is necessary that the NTS and the LCS work coordinately and cooperatively in order to optimize the transmission. The information that the NTS must give to the LCS and that ERAP must generate is: total server exit bandwidth (Mbps), available bandwidth (Mbps) for each connection at each moment, and the number of enqueued Mbits in the queue of the NTS that waits to be transmitted (considering all the packets of all the connections). All these measures only include the length of the Application Data Unit (ADU) without counting the overhead of the protocols, that is to say, the bits corresponding to the headers of the own ERAP or any used protocol of the Internet protocol stack (link, network, transport). RapManager is the central module in charge of collecting information from all ERAP connections and the network to generate this data.

6 RAP vs. ERAP

The NTS-ERAP and the RAP have been extensively evaluated by simulations and real tests in which the consumption of resources and the performance are measured. The simulator used is the NS2 version 2.29 released on October 19, 2005. This version of the NS2 includes the implementation of the RAP protocol that we used to compare with ERAP. The results presented in this section show the advantages of using ERAP instead of RAP in a VoD server.

Figure 4 shows the topology used for the simulations, where *R1* and *R2* are routers, *C1...Cn* are clients, and *S1* is the VPS.

The link *R1-R2* is the bottleneck and *R1* is the bottleneck point. The routers are simulated as elements with FIFO scheduling and drop-tail queuing. When the NTS-ERAP is simulated, *S1* is composed of a RapManager and *n* RapSender, whereas, when the RAP is simulated, *S1* only has *n* RapSender.

The simulation parameters used are shown in table 1.

Because of the fact that ERAP does not try to modify the basic behaviour presented by the RAP protocol, one of the objectives of the simulations was to show that both protocols act in a similar way reducing or increasing the transmission rate, upon detection of congestion or in absence of it, respectively.

Table 1. Simulation parameters

Packet Size	100, 512, 1024 bytes
Data Header Size	RAP: 24 bytes ERAP: 8 bytes
ACK Size	RAP: 24 bytes ERAP: 20 bytes
Links Bandwidth	R1-R2: 1 MB/s Others: 2 MB/s
Links Delay	10 ms
Queue Size R1-R2	10 packets

RAP and ERAP have presented almost the same performance as far as the use of network bandwidth, the small difference that is observed is because RAP uses greater ACK packets (4 bytes) than ERAP.

Figure 5 (a) shows the percentage of network bandwidth usage for a total simulation time of 120 seconds, with a data packet size of 100 bytes, and with a continuous data sending by only one active connection.

The transmission rate is increased until the maximum transmission capacity (100%) of the R1-R2 link is used, so that the router R1 begins to drop packets, and, upon detection of packet losses, the transmission rate is decreased immediately. These two phases, the increase and decrease of the transmission rate, are continuously repeated.

As described in item 6 of section 5, ERAP and RAP solve the inactivity problem in different ways. Nevertheless, for our specific environment, in which the packets will be given in a form of burst by the LCS, behaviour differences practically do not exist. This can be observed in the figure 5 (b), corresponding to a simulation with an inactivity period between time 4 and 6, and a data packet size of 100 bytes. Also, the deactivation of both timers at inactivity moments that ERAP carries out has two advantages, the saving of CPU and memory resources. The queue of event scheduler will be much smaller. Instead of having $X + N$ timers, N being the total number of connections, and X the number of connections that have been selected by the LCS to be served at certain moment or slot of time, will only have $X * 2$ timers. In this way, when reducing the events queue, the used memory is reduced and the useless triggering of timers is avoided saving CPU cycles.

ERAP makes better use of the resources when the ACKs' reception is centralized (item 3 of section 5). In this approach, a single thread is necessary in order to receive the ACK packets corresponding to all connections. In this way, a great amount of memory and CPU resources are saved. Each empty thread (i.e. without data and code) occupies approximately 10 MB of memory. If a decentralized ACK packet reception is used, N active sessions (therefore, with N threads) will require $N * 10$ MB of memory, and the system will quickly begin to start swapping.

With respect to the CPU usage, when having many threads, the scheduling and context changes will be more expensive. In order to verify this affirmation, tests were made in which a sender application sends an UDP traffic load, equitably distributed between N destination ports of another computer. And, in this other computer, N threads (one by port) were waiting to receive the corresponding packets.

The graph in figure 6 shows the sum of the times consumed in user and system mode for each set of receiving threads (1, 50, 100, 150, 200, and 250 threads), with a load of 10^6 pack-

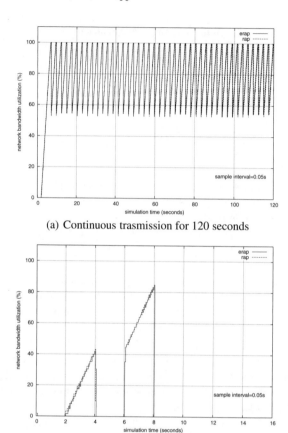

(a) Continuous trasmission for 120 seconds

(b) Inactivity times behaviour

Fig. 5. RAP and ERAP network utilization

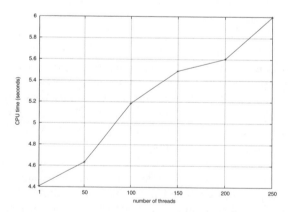

Fig. 6. CPU usage according to the number of packets receiving threads

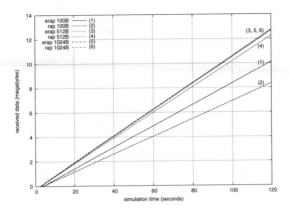

Fig. 7. Amount of application data received by the client in the time

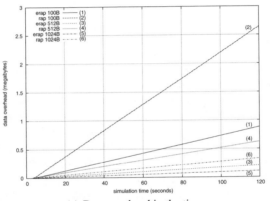

(a) Data overhead in the time

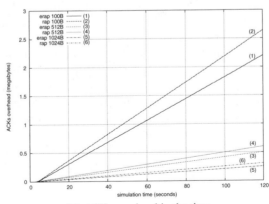

(b) ACKs overhead in the time

Fig. 8. RAP and ERAP protocols overheads

ets uniformly distributed between participants threads (i.e. 1 thread: 10^6 packets/thread, 200 threads: 5000 packets/thread). A clear increase of the consumption of CPU time is observed when the number of threads are increased. Another disadvantage, is that the number of threads that each process can have is limited by the operating system, therefore the number of sessions that the server can support will be restricted.

The header size reduction (item 5 of section 5), using different headers to data and ACK packets, improves the performance of the protocol. Simulations were made of 120 seconds in length with continuous transmission through only one active connection and sizes of data packet of 100, 512, and 1024 bytes.

In figure 7 it is observed that when the ERAP protocol is used, the amount of application data received by the client is increased, this is because ERAP has a smaller data header.

The overhead decrease in the network, that presents the ERAP protocol as opposed to RAP, can be observed in figure 8, where the bandwidth consumption caused by data and ACK headers at each moment of the simulation time, are presented in the figure 8 (a) and 8 (b), respectively.

7   Conclusions and Future Works

This paper is part of an innovative investigation line focus on VoD systems that guarantee a high quality of service in the Internet domain, or another nondedicated and best effort network. We present a Network Traffic Scheduler (NTS) to be included in a Video Proxy Server (VPS). The VPS must support a high workload, therefore, the NTS was designed to maximize the performance and minimize the resource consumption.

To achieve the better system perform of the VPS, the NTS must cooperate with it, and also must cooperate with the Internet's operation. Therefore, the NTS must include a congestion control protocol that is TCP-Friendly. Based on the specification of the RAP congestion control protocol, the ERAP has been developed to be included in the NTS module. The results presented in this paper show that ERAP improves the RAP protocol, not from the point of view of the behaviour in the adjustment of the transmission rate (that is practically the same), but from the point of view of the resource usage as much of the server as of the network. This improvement also allow to conclude that the ERAP protocol avoid the limitant factors arising on RAP protocol, giving to the video server more flexibility and opportunity to attend the client's petitions. The optimized events management, the header size reduction, the centralized ACKs' reception, and the centralized packets' sending, were the strategies to obtain such resource usage diminution.

The NTS has been developed and evaluated extensively by means of simulations. The future works are centered mainly in the integration of the NTS module with the rest of the VPS architecture. The benefits of this new platform, in contrast to the pre-existing platform that does not include the NTS, will be evaluated.

References

1. Qazzaz, B., Suppi, R., Cores, F., Ripoll, A., Hernandez, P., Luque, E.: Providing interactive video on demand services in distributed architecture. In: Proceedings 29th Euromicro Conference, vol. CL - I, pp. 215–222 (2003), ISBN: 1089-6503-03

2. Tanenbaum, A.: Computer Networks. Prentice Hall PTR, Englewood Cliffs (2002)
3. Kurose, J.F., Ross, K.W.: Computer Networking: A top down approach featuring the Internet. Addison-Wesley, Reading (2004)
4. Wang, X., Schulzrinne, H.: Comparison of adaptive internet multimedia applications. IEEE TRANS. COMMUN. E82-B(6) (1999)
5. Rejaie, R., Handley, M., Estrin, D.: RAP: An end-to-end rate-based congestion control mechanism for realtime streams in the internet. INFOCOM 3, 1337–1345 (1999)
6. Rejaie, R., Handley, M., Estrin, D.: RAP: An end-to-end rate-based congestion control mechanism for realtime streams in the internet. In: Technical report 98-681, CS-USC (August 1998), http://netweb.usc.edu/reza/papers/rap.html
7. Jacobs, S., Eleftheriadis, A.: Real-time dynamic rate shaping and control for internet video applications (1997)
8. Cen, S., Pu, C., Walpole, J.: Flow and congestion control for internet media streaming applications. Technical Report CSE-97-003 (1997)
9. Sisalem, D., Schulzrinne, H.: The loss-delay based adjustment algorithm: A TCP-friendly adaptation scheme. In: Proceedings of NOSSDAV, Cambridge, UK (1998)
10. Sisalem, D., Wolisz, A.: LDA+: A TCP-friendly adaptation scheme for multimedia communication. In: IEEE International Conference on Multimedia and Expo (III), pp. 1619–1622 (2000)
11. Floyd, S., Handley, M., Padhye, J., Widmer, J.: Equation-based congestion control for unicast applications. In: SIGCOMM 2000, Stockholm, Sweden, August 2000, pp. 43–56 (2000)
12. Handley, M., Pahdye, J., Floyd, S., Widmer, J.: TCP Friendly Rate Control (TFRC): Protocol specification, RFC 3448 (2003)
13. Rejaie, R., Handley, M., Estrin, D.: Layered quality adaptation for internet video streaming (2000)
14. Hessler, S., Welzl, M.: An empirical study of the congestion response of realplayer, windows mediaplayer and quicktime (2005)
15. Chung, J., Zhu, Y., Claypool, M.: FairPlayer or FoulPlayer? - Head to Head Performance of RealPlayer Streaming Video Over UDP versus TCP (2002)
16. Floyd, S., Fall, K.: Promoting the use of end-to-end congestion control in the Internet. IEEE slash ACM Transactions on Networking 7, 458–472 (1999)
17. Gevros, P., Crowcroft, J., Kirstein, P., Bhatti, S.: Congestion control mechanisms and the best effort service model. IEEE Network 15, 16–25 (2001)
18. McCanne, S., Floyd, S.: Ns - Network Simulator (2005), http://www.isi.edu/nsnam/ns/
19. Breslau, L., et al.: Advances in network simulation. IEEE Computer 33, 59–67 (2000)
20. Jacobson, V., Karels, M.J.: Congestion avoidance and control. In: ACM Computer Communication Review; Proceedings of the Sigcomm 1988 Symposium in Stanford, CA, August 1988, vol. 18(4), pp. 314–329 (1988)

Enhanced Interaction for Streaming Media

Wolfgang Hürst[1], Tobias Lauer[1], and Rainer Müller[2]

[1]Institute of Computer Science, University of Freiburg, D-79098 Freiburg, Germany
huerst@acm.org, lauer@informatik.uni-freiburg.de
[2]imc AG, Office Freiburg, Georges-Köhler-Allee 106, D-79110 Freiburg, Germany
rainer.mueller@im-c.de

Abstract. Streaming is a popular and efficient way of web-based on-demand multimedia delivery. However, flexible methods of interaction and navigation, as required, for example, in learning applications, are very restricted with streamed contents. Using the example of recorded lectures, we point out the importance of such advanced interaction which is not possible with purely streamed media. A new delivery method based on a combination of streaming and download is proposed which can be realized with Rich Internet Applications. It combines the advantages of streaming delivery with navigational and interactive features that are usually known only from locally available media.

Keywords: Media delivery, multimedia streaming, lecture recording, interfaces, interaction, navigation.

1 Introduction

Generally, multimedia content is delivered to the users either via streaming or by download and local replay of the respective files. The decision which of these two approaches for media delivery is offered by the providers usually depends on the application and the data. However, there are situations where it is not obvious which approach should be used. Examples are teaching materials such as recorded lectures. Some institutions offer such recordings online as Webcasts where learners can access and review them via streaming. This has the advantage of giving the providers more control over the contents, and it does not require from the users to download huge amounts of data prior to viewing. However, many universities also allow students to download their lecture recordings as a whole for local replay (exclusively or in addition to streaming). Users sometimes prefer download over replay because it makes them less dependent on the provided service and online connection after a file has been downloaded once. In addition, manipulation of replay such as fast forward at different speeds, flexible navigation such as real-time scrolling along any direction of the time line, etc. are often cumbersome or even impossible to do with streamed data. However, such possibilities for an advanced navigation and interaction are particular important in learning applications.

In this paper, the delivery and access of recorded lectures is used as an example scenario for multimedia applications that require a high degree of user interaction.

J. Filipe and M.S. Obaidat (Eds.): ICETE 2006, CCIS 9, pp. 252–263, 2008.

First, we describe the necessary basics for lecture recording and delivery. We identify enhanced interaction functionality as a key requirement in such a scenario (*Section 2*). Then, we present a synchronization model for lecture replay whose standard implementation offers this required interaction but lacks the possibility for streaming (*Section 3.1*). Motivated by this issue, we present a new method for the delivery of multimedia data which is based on a combination of streaming and download (*Section 3.2*). The proposed solution combines the advantages of streaming with interactive and navigational features that are usually only known from media replayed locally after they have been downloaded before.

2 Download vs. Streaming

Automatic lecture recording and delivery via Web casting has become a common trend at many universities: Live lectures and presentations are captured and the recordings are automatically post-processed and published on the Web [1], [2]. Initially originating from educational institutions, this approach is gaining increasing popularity in the industries as well. Users access and use these documents, for example, to review content, to look up specific information, or even as a substitute of the corresponding live event [4], [10].

One important issue for lecture Web casting is the final delivery of the documents, i.e. the question whether the respective data is sent to the viewers online via streaming-servers or if it has to be downloaded as a whole to the user's local machine. When comparing local replay vs. streaming, no absolute answer can be given as to which approach is generally preferable. For example, when asked about the importance of streaming vs. local availability (after downloading), the participating students of the study in Lauer et al. [10] rated local availability much higher on a scale from 1 to 5 (Mean = 1.31, SD = 0.50) than streaming (Mean = 3.48, SD = 1.14). These subjective ratings were backed up by the server statistics: In all cases where both documents for local download and identical versions of the lecture in some streaming format were available, the overwhelming majority accessed (i.e. downloaded) the former one. However, the situation is different for corporate learners, who often do not have authorization for large downloads at all at their workstations. Since those computers are usually connected permanently to the corporate intranet, streaming is considered a better way of delivering the contents. This is especially true for companies with pre-configured client configurations, where the widespread "de-facto standards" (such as RealMedia [11] or Windows Media [14]) are often the only accepted formats, because no additional installation of software (such as a proprietary multimedia player) is permitted.

In addition, there are general arguments in favor of streaming, not only in corporations but also for the distribution of online lectures at universities. For the learners, having to download large files (a 45-minute lecture including video may well amount to 500 MB or more) results in enormous preload times and may quickly fill up the local hard drives. Moreover, streaming servers provide solutions to handle large numbers of concurrent users and to adjust to changing bandwidth conditions.

In addition, streaming technologies offer a certain degree of content protection. Since the streamed data are not stored permanently on the end user's system, the danger of unauthorized copies and their distribution is reduced.

On the other hand, local download and replay of the files has some significant advantages over streaming approaches. One of the reasons why students often prefer the former over the latter one is the pure desire to possess the files. Students often do not have a permanent high speed connection to the internet. Therefore, a long but one-time download is often accepted for the sake of complete independence of any network connection afterwards. The second and probably most important advantage of local replay is the ability to provide advanced features for interaction and navigation. In a survey [10], we evaluated the importance of different interaction features which are illustrated in Figure 1. The results confirmed the assumption that advanced browsing and navigation functionality is essential when learning with lecture recordings. This observation is consistent with other studies, for example the one of Li et al. [9], which evaluated different kinds of browsing approaches for digital video recordings (including but not limited to lecture recordings). Such subjective user ratings are also confirmed by studies observing the actual usage of different features in real-world situations. For example, Zupancic and Horz [13] present a log file analysis indicating that users of recorded lectures make intensive use of such advanced browsing and navigation functionality when reviewing these documents.

It is obvious that the efficient use of the mechanisms presented in Figure 1 crucially depends on their responsiveness, i.e. the speed at which the resulting jumps in the document can be carried out. Even simple interactions, such as a slide-based navigation through a document, often result in a significant time delay when contents are streamed, thus disrupting the learning process and limiting the interaction with the data. Certain features, such as *random visible scrolling* (cf. (a) in Fig. 1) which was found to be very important according to Lauer et al. [10], cannot be realized with streaming at all, because the ability to navigate along the timeline at any speed directly conflicts with the basic concept of streaming, as this feature requires real-time random access to any position within a document.

3   Models for Delivery

Based on the discussion in the previous section, we see ourselves confronted with two contradicting demands: On the one hand, there are good reasons why the recordings should be kept centrally and delivered to the users with streaming technologies. On the other hand, advanced interaction, which is a key requirement in order to achieve high acceptance and successful learning, usually requires local availability of the data. In the following, we first describe our established replay model which offers this requested interactivity but whose previous implementation relies on local replay (*Section 3.1*). Then we introduce a new realization of this concept which makes use of the underlying replay and synchronization model in a distributed scenario, thus enabling streaming as well as interactive navigation (*Section 3.2*).

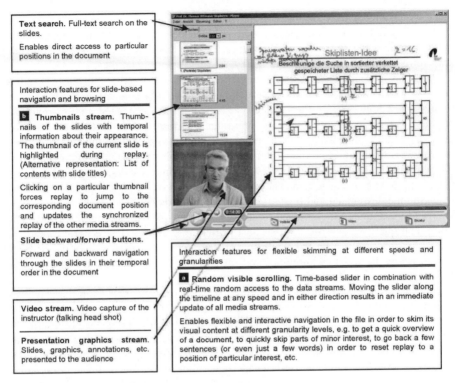

Fig. 1. Different interaction functionalities of a media player replaying a recorded lecture

3.1 Generic Model for Local Replay

Multi-stream Recording and Delivery. Most approaches for automatic lecture re-cording use a *multi-stream capturing* approach, i.e. they capture each media stream sepa-rately and later synchronize them during replay or in an additional post-processing step. This way, each stream can be provided in the best possible quality. In addition, the final delivery can be adapted to the available resources (bandwidth, storage, etc.) depending on the relevance of the respective media channel. For example, the less critical, but very data intensive video of the instructor is often downsized, replaced with a few snapshots, or even removed completely in environments with limited resources. Often, only the critical media streams of a (tele-)presentation [7], i.e. the audio with the lecturer's narra-tion and the presentation graphics (slides, annotations, etc.) are delivered. On the other hand, additional but less data intensive streams containing meta-information about the content and structure may also be synchronized with the recordings (cf. the thumbnails stream depicted in (b) in Fig. 1). As discussed in Section 2, such meta-information can be very important for navigation and interaction.

Synchronized Replay. In order to realize a reliable *synchronized replay* of such an arbi-trary number of streams we need a generic synchronization model. In addition, we have to support advanced navigation functionality in order to provide high *interactivity* to the users, as specified above. For this reason, we introduced a multi-stream synchronization model in [8]. In the following, we summarize this model insofar as it is important for the understanding of the remainder of this paper. Readers interested in the technical details are referred to [8].

The basis for our *synchronization model* is an open intermediate format where the different media streams are kept separately, only implicitly coupled by the time. The streams are structured in a flat hierarchy oriented at one designated audio stream. In our case, the audio stream covers the presenter's narration. This flexible structure of the individual documents (i.e. audio stream, presentation graphics, and any other media channels that should be integrated for the final replay) is mapped to a generic replay architecture with separate processes, threads, or instances (*slaves*), each replaying one particular media stream. They are coupled with the particular process (*master*) replaying the designated audio stream. The master sends out timestamps to the slaves in order to guarantee synchronized replay. This allows for a tight temporal synchronization and quality assurance for the most critical media type. The generic replay architecture does not restrict the flexibility of the document structure and can be realized in nearly all target technologies and formats (including standard formats such as Flash, QuickTime, or SMIL).

Navigation in the document is supported through backchannels from the slaves to the process replaying the master stream. For example, if a user navigates through the slides by clicking on an icon in the thumbnail stream (cf. (b) in Fig. 1), a timestamp is sent over its backchannel to the master which synchronizes its own replay and guarantees an alignment of the other slaves. When a user is dragging a slider along the timeline, basically the same activity takes place but at a much finer granularity: Timestamps indicating the current position of the slider thumb on the timeline are continuously sent to the master stream which guarantees the synchronization of all other slaves for visual media and thus realizes the random visible scrolling feature (cf. (a) in Fig. 1). As with common media players, audio replay is paused while a user is dragging the slider thumb but starts replay at the corresponding position as soon as the slider is released. The content of raster-based visual streams, such as videos, is updated immediately if the respective data is encoded in a format which supports real-time random access to each frame. If the respective content is not considered important for browsing, the video stream can alternatively be paused during scrolling similarly to the audio feedback. This synchronization model guarantees high flexibility and quality because it enables the synchronized replay of arbitrary streams and it supports advanced navigation and browsing of the respective files.

Implementation. In our implementation, the stream containing the presentation graphics is captured in a symbolic representation and stored in an XML-like format. Such *object-* or *vector-based* recording has several advantages over *raster-based* capturing (i.e. a stream of bitmap-based frames). For example, the recordings can be scaled to fit any window size during replay without significant loss of quality thus enabling high quality replay on different platforms and devices. In addition, an object-based representation can easily be transferred to other data formats, while the transformation of raster graphics into a non-bitmap format may lead to a decreased quality (or might not be possible at all without unreasonable effort). Other advantages include a (usually) smaller data volume, the option to post-edit the contents if necessary (e.g. to remove errors, misspellings etc. from slides), easier analysis and index generation, (e.g. to enable full-text

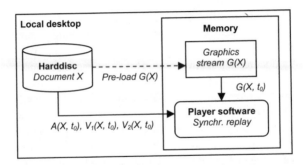

Fig. 2. Illustration of the implementation of the replay model (example with audio stream A, presentation graphics G, and two video streams V_1 and V_2)

search on the slides), or the possibility to implement better, advanced interaction functionalities, such as the ones described above.

Figure 2 illustrates the standard implementation. All vector graphics of the document (slides, annotations, etc. as well as metadata such as thumbnails and content lists) are kept in the system's main memory due to their reasonable size even for long documents. Media channels such as audio and raster-based streams are played as streams from the hard drive (or other local storage), using a buffer which only stores the data to be displayed next. The central player module replays the master stream (audio), guarantees the synchronization of the other media streams, and handles the graphical user interface which offers different functionalities for document browsing. Hence, the player software is realized as a standalone desktop application that relies on the local availability of the respective documents. This stands in direct conflict with our aim discussed in Section 2: to support streaming media as well.

3.2 Integration of Streamed Replay

The synchronization model described above enables generic integration and processing of different media streams, guarantees a high quality, synchronized replay, and supports advanced features for navigation and browsing. The experience and feedback we gained with the usage of its different implementations since we originally introduced it, confirm these statements. For example, our evaluations showed that students strongly prefer the respective recordings over the ones provided with standard streaming technologies, although this involved the installation of proprietary player software and large file downloads [10].

On the other hand, as discussed before, there are various reasons for document delivery via streaming technologies. The recent trend of so called *Rich Internet Applications* (RIAs) now enables us to combine the best of both approaches. RIAs run in a Web browser but resemble traditional desktop applications by providing a similar look and feel as well as functionalities comparable to local desktop applications. This is achieved by transferring some of the processing from the server to the client side (i.e. the Web browser) using Ajax (Asynchronous JavaScript and XML) technologies, such as Dynamic HTML, XML, Cascading style sheets, DOM, and JavaScript.

Distributed Implementation for Streamed Replay. The basic idea of our new approach is to transfer our synchronization model to a distributed client-server architecture that enables us to access the data- intensive streams (i.e. the raster-based and acoustic data) of a document via streaming. However, less data-intensive streams (i.e. the presentation graphics as well as some potential metadata streams) are stored and managed on the local client application. The realization of this distributed implementation is a direct transfer of the local architecture as it is illustrated in Figure 2. Figure 3 shows the respective example for the distributed case. It should be noted that the actual synchronization model is still the master-slave synchronization where the audio with the instructor's voice is the designated master stream and synchronization of all other media streams is controlled by the RIA implementation.

This approach is based on the observation that the most important media stream for browsing and navigating, i.e. the presentation graphics stream has a relatively low data volume (especially if the recording was done in a vector-based description as described above). Additional streams for navigation, for example, the thumbnail stream or any other stream featuring metadata for navigation purposes, are normally even smaller. They can easily be transmitted as a whole when the user starts to view a lecture and will then be available locally on the client throughout the session. Thus, navigation within the graphics stream can be carried out with all the desired features mentioned above, including visible scrolling. Locating a certain part of the talk in the slides stream is very quick and requires no buffering, since none of the streamed media is involved. Once the position has been found, replay resumes there: the audio and video streams are requested from the streaming server and delivered via the respective streaming protocols. Hence, the situation is similar to the local case with the exception that the video stream is not updated during scrolling. However, this is not a problem for our application scenario, since the video recording is not considered critical [7]. During normal replay, the streamed audio signal is still used as the master stream synchronizing all other media channels. Thus, the best possible replay quality of the two critical media (i.e. audio and presentation graphics) is still guaranteed.

Client-server Communication. Figures 4 till 6 visualize the event traces for the communication between user, RIA, and server. The grey area marks the data stored

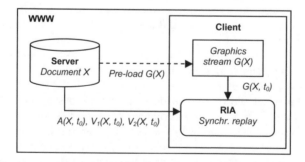

Fig. 3. Illustration of the distributed implementation of the model (cf. Fig. 2) using RIA technology

and the RIA application running on the client machine. When the user accesses the URL of a lecture document X (Fig. 4), the RIA is transmitted to the client. The RIA's program logic then downloads the document description, which contains information about the different streams in X (in our example, one audio stream A, the graphics stream G, and two video streams V_1 and V_2). The RIA requests the graphics stream $G(X)$ (i.e. slide and annotations). $G(X)$ is transmitted completely and managed locally in a database that is part of the RIA. Upon completion of this step, the lecture document X is ready for replay.

When replay is started at t_0 (e.g. by the user pressing the "play" button in the application, cf. Fig 5), the audio stream $A(X, t_0)$ and video streams $V_j(X, t_0)$ are requested from the streaming server. The appropriate part of the graphics stream $G(X, t_0)$ is retrieved from the local database and synchronized with the continuous streams. Note that all synchronization is done by the RIA program logic on the client. Thereby, the RIA takes buffering and pausing into account, and the server is not involved in the synchronization process. In each synchronization cycle (at time-stamp t_i of the master stream A), the respective part $G(X, t_i)$ of the graphics stream is requested locally, synchronized with the streamed media and displayed to the user.

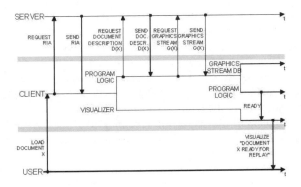

Fig. 4. Event traces at startup of the RIA

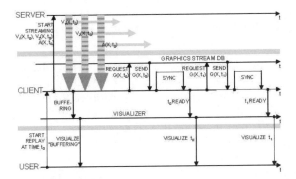

Fig. 5. Event traces during replay

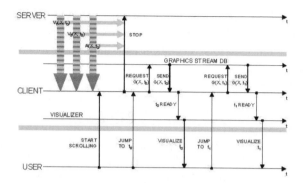

Fig. 6. Event traces during random visible scrolling

The most interesting cases in our scenario are the different forms of user interaction, e.g. dragging the slider in order to locate some specific part of the document (cf. Fig. 6). When the user starts scrolling (by holding down the mouse button on the slider), the server is notified to stop streaming the continuous media. As long as the user is scrolling, every new position on the slider is mapped to the corresponding time-stamp t_i in document X and the respective part of the graphics stream $G(X, t_i)$ is retrieved and displayed immediately. Note that no server access is required since the complete graphics stream is available locally and no synchronization with other streams is necessary. Thus, we can achieve real-time visible scrolling on the most important streams for browsing, i.e. slides and annotations as well as meta data. Thereby, the RIA enables the user to get a quick overview of the contents and to easily locate known sections in the recorded document without any network latency. The RIA does not reconnect to the server for streaming until the user releases the slider. Then, replay is resumed with all involved streams just as described above and shown in Fig. 5.

All other forms of navigation (such as slide forward/backward, clicking a thumbnail in the table of contents, etc.) use the same basic mechanism. The contents of all object-based streams are pre-loaded at startup to the client. Any interaction that forces the player to jump to a new position within the document is displayed in those streams without any delay by the respective slaves. Streaming of all other media streams (usually audio and video) is resumed at this new position as soon as normal replay continues.

Object- vs. Raster-Based Recording. It is important to note that the individual presentation streams must be available separately in order to permit this type of media delivery. In addition, the visual graphics streams required for navigation (most importantly the presentation graphics) must be small enough to allow for a quick transmission to the client at the start-up of the RIA. It now becomes obvious that presentation recording approaches producing integrated documents cannot support the proposed distributed replay architecture. This is especially true for the two extreme approaches, streaming-only and download-only. Screen grabbers (e.g. [5]) generate videos, which can be streamed from the server. There is no further interaction or functionality provided on the client side except the usual start, pause and stop of streaming video. The other extreme are approaches producing, e.g., Flash or QuickTime documents [3]. These documents often provide convenient interaction facilities client-side, but have to be preloaded in a progressive download mode from the server without any later client-server communication. Hence, our claim that an object-based recording should be preferred is not only motivated by the arguments given in Section 3.1 but also to support better interaction with the documents. With massive binary information involved in the preloaded streams (as is the case for sampled audio and video), transmission time increases sharply, which quickly turns the advantage of the approach into the opposite. Thus, if such data is to be used, the compression rate and, consequently, the quality of the represented contents, is a crucial factor.

Implementation. Although the implementation of the proposed method is not trivial and involves a lot of small technical difficulties it can be done with common internet technologies usually applied for the realization of Rich Web Applications. A browser-based implementation can be realized using (D)HTML, JavaScript, and streaming technologies such as Windows Media [14] or RealMedia [11]. In the latter case, synchronization can also be done using SMIL. Our own implementation, for example, produces Windows Media-, Flash-, and RealMedia-based RIAs. These can be executed in any common web browser. Figure 7 shows an example of the RealMedia implementation which provides the same look and feel as the desktop player illustrated in Figure 1. Further examples can be accessed from our website [6].

Providing Desktop Look and Feel Via Templates. For reasons of recognition and convenience, a RIA's graphical user interface is normally adapted to the desktop counterpart, i.e., the stand-alone media player. Most of the GUI components should behave as expected from "normal" applications, following common desktop interaction paradigms. This allows the users to switch seamlessly between desktop and Web-based applications. For example, assume a student who uses a desktop player in combination with previously downloaded lecture recordings at home but a Web browser to access these recordings on a laptop via wireless LAN while on campus. From the user's perspective, these two applications should look and feel almost identical. When comparing the local desktop media player and its Web-based counterpart shown in Figure 1 and 7, respectively, it can be seen that this demand is clearly fulfilled by our implementation.

In order to support a convenient production process and to guarantee a similar look and feel, we developed and implemented a template-based approach (illustrated in Figure 8) which enables document authors to choose from a variety of basic templates (or create new custom templates). These specify the interaction, layout, and design of the RIA. An example would be the choice whether a table of contents should be included, what it should look like, and where it should be placed. The selected template can then be customized further, for example, to include corporate logos. Authors or producers can also customize the quality of the individual media streams, i.e. audio and video encoding, screen resolution, supported bandwidths, the versions of the supported player plug-in and streaming server, or choose to include metadata required for compatibility with document exchange standards such as SCORM [12]. A complete automation of the production process can be achieved if all the above selections (the fields connected with "Author" in Fig. 8) are stored in a profile that is processed by the RIA generator. The realized generation and publishing component uses XML as description language.

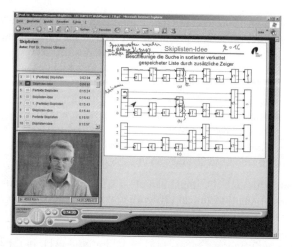

Fig. 7. RIA implementation of a media player similar to the one depicted in Figure 1

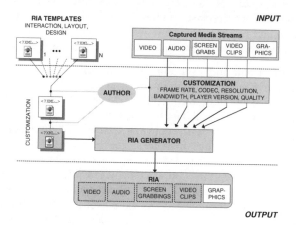

Fig. 8. Automation of the RIA generation process

4 Conclusions

While pure streaming solutions have advantages for both users and providers, they do not support certain navigational features required in the context of learning, especially with regard to efficient browsing within a document. We presented a distributed replay architecture which makes it possible to preload those media streams which are the most important ones for navigation, while streaming the other, more voluminous media. This allows learners to use features known from local applications, such as random visible scrolling, while avoiding the disadvantages of downloading large multimedia documents. The concept has been implemented as a Rich Internet Application using standard internet technologies.

The proposed replay model is not restricted to learning applications but can be transferred to other scenarios where Web-based delivery of multimedia contents consisting of more than one stream is required and certain navigational features are desired. The basic prerequisite is that the stream(s) directly involved in the navigation process are small enough (in terms of data volume) to be transferred as a whole at the initiation of a session. This requirement is usually met when the data consists of mostly symbolically represented information or drastically compressed binary data.

References

1. Abowd, G.D.: Classroom 2000: an experiment with the instrumentation of a living educational environment. IBM Systems Journal, Special issue on Pervasive Computing 38(4) (1999)
2. Brusilovsky, P.: Web lectures: electronic presentations in web-based instruction. Syllabus 13(5), 18–23
3. Macromedia (2006), http://www.macromedia.com/software/breeze
4. Brotherton, J., Abowd, G.D.: Lessons learned from eClass: assessing automated capture and access in the classroom. ACM Transactions on Computer-Human Interaction 11(2), 121–155 (2004)
5. Camtasia (2006), http://www.camtasia.com/
6. E-lectures, E-Lecture portal of the University of Freiburg (2006), http://electures.informatik.uni-freiburg.de
7. Gemmell, J., Bell, G.: Noncollaborative telepresentations come of age. In: Communications of the ACM, vol. 40(4), ACM Press, New York (1997)
8. Hürst, W., Müller, R.: A synchronization model for recorded presentations and its relevance for information retrieval. In: Proceedings of ACM Multimedia 1999, ACM Press, New York (1999)
9. Li, F., Gupta, A., Sanocki, E., He, L., Rui, Y.: Browsing digital video. In: Proceedings of the ACM conference on Computer Human Interaction (CHI), ACM Press, New York (2000)
10. Lauer, T., Müller, R., Trahasch, S.: Learning with lecture recordings: key issues for end-users. In: Proceedings of ICALT 2004, IEEE Press, Los Alamitos (2004)
11. RealNetworks (2006), http://www.realnetworks.com/
12. SCORM (2006), http://www.adlnet.org/
13. Zupancic, B., Horz, H.: Lecture recording and its use in a traditional university course. ACM SIGCSE Bulletin 34(3), 24–28 (2002)
14. Windows Media (2006), http://www.microsoft.com/windows/windowsmedia/

An E-Librarian Service That Yields Pertinent Resources from a Multimedia Knowledge Base

Serge Linckels and Christoph Meinel

Hasso-Plattner-Institut (HPI), University of Potsdam
Postfach 900460, D-14440 Potsdam, Germany
{linckels,meinel}@hpi.uni-potsdam.de

Abstract. In this paper we present an *e-librarian service* which is able to retrieve multimedia resources from a knowledge base in a more efficient way than by browsing through an index or by using a simple keyword search. We explored the approach to allow the user to formulate a complete question in natural language. Our background theory is composed of three steps. Firstly, there is the linguistic pre-processing of the user question. Secondly, there is the semantic interpretation of the user question into a logical and unambiguous form, i.e. $\mathcal{ALC}$ terminology. The *focus function* resolves ambiguities in the question; it returns the best interpretation for a given word in the context of the complete user question. Thirdly, there is the generation of a semantic query, and the retrieval of pertinent documents. We developed two prototypes: one about computer history (CHESt), and one about fractions in mathematics (MatES). We report on experiments with these prototypes that confirm the feasibility, the quality and the benefits of such an e-librarian service. From 229 different user questions, the system returned for 97% of the questions the right answer, and for nearly half of the questions only one answer, the best one.

Keywords: Multimedia, semantic search engine, natural language, information retrieval, performance, e-Learning.

1 Introduction

Our vision is to create an *e-librarian service* which is able to retrieve multimedia resources from a knowledge base in a more efficient way than by browsing through an index or by using a simple keyword search. Our premise is that more pertinent results would be retrieved if the e-librarian service had a *semantic search engine* which understood the sense of the user's query. This requires that the user must be given the means to enter semantics. We explored the approach to allow the user to formulate a complete question in natural langauge (NL). Linguistic relations within the user's NL question and a given context, i.e. an ontology, are used to extract precise semantics and to generate a semantic query. The e-librarian service does not return the answer to the user's question, but it retrieves the most pertinent document(s) in which the user finds the answer to her/his question.

The results of our research work are, firstly, a founded background theory that improves domain search engines so that they retrieve fewer but more pertinent documents.

J. Filipe and M.S. Obaidat (Eds.): ICETE 2006, CCIS 9, pp. 264–275, 2008.

It is based on the semantic interpretation of a complete question that is expressed in NL, which is to be translated into an unambiguous logical form, i.e. an $\mathcal{ALC}$ terminology. Then, a semantic query is generated and executed. Secondly, we provide empirical data that prove the feasibility, and the effectiveness of our underlying background theory. We developed two prototypes: CHESt (*Computer History Expert System*) with a knowledge base about computer history, and MatES (*Mathematics Expert System*) with a knowledge base about fractions in mathematics. We report on experiments with these prototypes that confirm the feasibility, the quality and the benefits of such an e-librarian service. From 229 different user questions, the system returned for 97% of the questions the right answer, and for nearly half of the questions only one answer, the best one.

In this paper we focus on the translation of a complete NL question into a semantic query. This process is done in three steps: the linguistic pre-processing (section 2), the mapping of the question to an ontology (section 3), and the generation of a semantic query (section 4). We present an algorithm (the focus function) that resolves ambiguities in the user question. The outcomes of the experiments are described in section 5. We present related projects in section 6, and conclude with some (dis)advantages in section 7.

2 Linguistic Pre-processing

The objective of the linguistic pre-processing step is to convert a stream of symbols into a structured stream of words, and to retrieve linguistic information about these words and the complete sentence. A search mechanism returns better results if the inference is done over a complete sentence by considering the relations between words — the syntax — than by only considering the isolated words. In fact, the syntactic structure of a sentence indicates the way words are related to each other, e.g. how the words are grouped together into phrases, which words modify which other words, and which words are of central importance in the sentence.

In our prototypes, the linguistic pre-processing is performed with a part-of-speech (POS) tagger; we use *TreeTagger* (IMS Stuttgart). The linguistic pre-processing step contributes in three points. Firstly, the word category of each word is made explicit, e.g. article, verb. Secondly, the tagger returns the canonical form (*lemma*) for each word (*token*). This considerably reduces the size of the ontology dictionary. Thirdly, the sentence is split into linguistic clauses. A linguistic clause is a triple of the form <subject;verb;object>. Each triple is then processed individually, e.g. the question $q =$ "Who invented the transistor and who founded IBM?" is split into the two clauses:

$$q_1' = [\text{Who invented the transistor?}]$$
$$conj = [\text{and}]$$
$$q_2' = [\text{Who founded IBM?}]$$

3 Ontology Mapping

In this section, we present the elaborated background theory for translating a linguistic pre-processed user question into a computer readable and unambiguous form w.r.t. a given ontology.

3.1 Ontology Preliminaries

The e-librarian service masters a domain language L_H over an alphabet Σ^*, which may or may not contain all the possible words L used by the user to formulate his question, so that $L_H \subseteq L \subseteq \Sigma^*$. The semantics are attached to each word by classification in the knowledge source, e.g. a dictionary, which is structured in a hierarchical way like *hyperonym*, *hyponym*, *synonym*, and *homonyms*. In most of the related projects (section 6), an existing knowledge source is used, normally *WordNet*. The major problem of such a knowledge source is that it is not dedicated to a domain. Like other large scale dictionaries, WordNet on the one hand lacks of specific domain expressions, but on the other hand contains too much knowledge about other domains. This increases the problem of ambiguous interpretations for a given word. We created our own dictionary, which is organized in a hierarchical way, similar to WordNet, and w.r.t. our ontology. Furthermore, the size of the dictionary is considerably reduced by the fact that it contains all words from the domain language L_H only in their canonical form. This reduces also the possibility of ambiguous interpretations.

Definition 1 (Concept Taxonomy). *A concept taxonomy $H = (V, E, v_0)$ is a directed acyclic graph where each node, except the root-node (v_0), has one or more parents. E is the set of all edges and V is the set of all nodes (vertices) with $V = \{(s, T) \mid s \in S\}$ where s is a unique label, S the set of all labels in the ontology, and T is a set of words from L_H that are associated to a node so that $T \subseteq L_H$.*

An example of a concept taxonomy about computer history is given in figure 1. Here, a document describing the transistor would be placed in the concept "EComponent" (electronic components), which is a hyponym of "Hardware".

A node v_i represents a concept. The words that refer to this concept are regrouped in T_i. We assume that each set of words T_i is semantically related to the concept that the node v_i represents. The example in figure 2 shows that words like "Transistor", "Diode" or "LED" semantically refer to the same concept, namely electronic components. Therefore, these three words are synonyms in the given ontology. Of course, a certain word can refer to different concepts, e.g. "Ada" is the name of a programming language but also the name of a person. Not all words in L_H must be associated with a concept. Only words that are semantically relevant are classified. In general, nouns and verbs are best indicators of the sense of a question. The difference between words that are semantically irrelevant and words that are not contained in L_H is that for the second ones, the system has absolutely no idea if they are relevant or not.

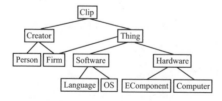

Fig. 1. Example of a concept taxonomy about computer history

Electronic components
$s = EComponent$
$T = \{\text{Transistor, Diode, LED}\}$

Fig. 2. Example of a node in the taxonomy about the concept EComponent (electronic components)

$$Clip \doteq \exists hasName.String \sqcap Creator \sqcup Thing$$
$$Creator \doteq Person \sqcup Firm$$
$$Person \doteq \exists wasBorn.Date \sqcap$$
$$\exists isDeceased.Date$$
$$Thing \doteq Firm \sqcup Software \sqcup Hardware \sqcup Net$$
$$\sqcap \exists wasInventedBy.Creator$$
$$Software \doteq Language \sqcup OS$$
$$Hardware \doteq EComponent \sqcup Computer$$

Fig. 3. Example of a concept taxonomy (TBox) about computer history as $\mathcal{ALC}$ terminology

3.2 Semantic Interpretation

The representation of context-independent meaning is called the *logical form*, and the process of mapping a sentence to its logical form is called *semantic interpretation* [1]. The logical form is expressed in a certain knowledge representation language; we use *Description Logics* (DL). Firstly, DL have the advantage that they come with well-defined semantics and correct algorithms. Furthermore, the link between DL and NL has already been established [13]. Finally, translating the user question into DL allows direct reasoning over the OWL-DL encoded knowledge base (section 4).

A DL terminology is composed, firstly, of *concepts* (unary predicates), which are generally nouns, question words (*w-words*) and proper names, and secondly, of *roles* (binary predicates), which are generally verbs, adjectives and adverbs. We use the language $\mathcal{ALC}$ [14], which is sufficiently expressive for our purposes. $\mathcal{ALC}$ concepts are built using a set of concept names (NC) and role names (NR). Valid concepts (C) are defined by the following syntax,

$$C ::= A \mid \top \mid \bot \mid \neg A \mid C_1 \sqcap C_2 \mid C_1 \sqcup C_2 \mid \forall R.C \mid \exists R.C$$

with $A \in$ NC is a concept name and $R \in$ NR is a role name (figure 3).

A core part of the semantic interpretation is a mapping algorithm. This step — commonly called *non-standard inference* [8] — maps each word from the user question to one or more ontology concepts, and resolves the arguments of each role by analyzing the syntactic structure of the sentence.

Definition 2 (Word Equivalence). *The function* $\pi : L, L \to \mathbb{R}$ *quantifies the similarity of two given words* $\pi(a, b)$ *so that* a *and* b *are said to be equivalent w.r.t. a given tolerance* ε, *written* $a \equiv b$, *iff* $\pi(a, b) \leq \varepsilon$.

Technically, for a given lemma from the user question, the equivalence function π uses the *Levenshtein function* to check if this word is contained in the ontology dictionary L_H given a certain allowed tolerance ε. That tolerance is calculated relative to the length of the lemma.

Definition 3 (Mapping). *The meaning of each word $w_k \in L$ is made explicit with the mapping function $\varphi : L \to V$ over an ontology dictionary $L_H \subseteq L \subseteq \Sigma^*$ and an $\mathcal{ALC}$ concept taxonomy $H = (V, E, v_0)$ so that $\varphi(w_k)$ returns a set of interpretations Φ defined as follows,*

$$\Phi = \varphi(w_k) = \{v_i \mid \exists x \in ft(v_i) : w_k \equiv x\}.$$

The function $ft(v_i)$ returns the set of words T_i associated to the node v_i (definition 1), and $w_k \equiv x$ are two equivalent words. This solution gives good results even if the user makes spelling errors. Furthermore, only the best matching is considered for the mapping, e.g. the word "comXmon" will be considered as "common", and not as "uncommon". Both words, "common" and "uncommon", will be considered for the mapping of "comXXmon". The ambiguity will be resolved in a further step (focus function).

Definition 4 (Semantic Relevance). *A word w_k is semantically relevant if there is at least one concept in the ontology H to which w_k can be mapped so that $\varphi(w_k) \neq \emptyset$.*

It is possible that a word can be mapped to different concepts at once, so that $|\Phi| > 1$. We introduce the notion of *focus* to resolve this ambiguity. The focus is a function (f), which returns the best interpretation for a given word in the context of the complete user question.

Definition 5 (Focus). *The focus of a set of interpretations Φ is made explicit by the function f which returns the best interpretation for a given word in the context of the complete question q. The focus, written $f_q(\varphi(w_k \in q)) = v'$, guarantees the following,*

1. *$v' \in \varphi(w_k)$; The focused word is a valid interpretation.*
2. *$|f_q(\varphi(w_k))| = [0, 1]$; The focus function returns 0 or 1 result.*
3. *$\top \leq v' \leq \bot$, if $f_q(\varphi(w_k)) \neq \emptyset$; If the focusing is successful, then the word is inside the context of the domain ontology.*
4. *$\pi(w_k, x \in ft(v')) \leq \pi(w_k, y \in ft(v_i \in \varphi(w_k)))$; The returned interpretation contains the best matching word of all possible interpretations.*

Let us consider as illustration the word "Ada", which is called a multiple-sense word. In fact, in the context of computer history, "Ada" can refer to the programming language named "Ada", but it can also be the name of the person "Augusta Ada Lovelace". The correct interpretation can only be retrieved accurately by putting the ambiguous word in the context of a complete question. For example, the context of the sentences "Who invented Ada?" and "Did the firms Bull and Honeywell create Ada?" reveals that here Ada is the programming language, and not the person Ada.

Technically, the focus function uses the role's signature. A role $r \in NR$ has the signature $r(s_1, s_2)$, where s_1 and s_2 are labels. The signature of each role defines the kind

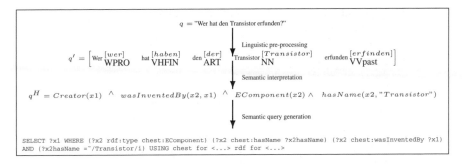

Fig. 4. Complete example for the generation of a semantic query from the user question "Who invented the transistor?"

of arguments that are possible. For example $wasInventedBy(Thing, Creator)$ is the role $r = wasInventedBy$ that has the arguments $s_1 = Thing$ and $s_2 = Creator$.

In the question $q =$ "Who invented Ada?" the following mappings are computed:

$$\varphi("Who") = \{Creator\}$$

$$\varphi("invented") = \{wasInventedBy(Thing, Creator)\}$$

$$\varphi("Ada") = \{Person, Language\}$$

The system detects an ambiguity for the word "Ada", which is mapped to an instance of the concept $Person$, but also to an instance of the concept $Language$. The focus function computes the following combinations to resolve the ambiguity:

1. Was Ada invented by who?*
2. Was Ada invented by Ada?
3. Was who invented by Ada?*
4. Was who invented by who?*

Cyclic combinations like (2) and (4) are not allowed. As for (3), it does not match the role's signature because $s_1 = Creator$ ("Who"), but $Thing$ is required. As for (1), s_1 can be $Person$ or $Language$ ("Ada"). The role's signature requires $Thing$, therefore $Person$ is excluded as valid interpretation because $Person \not\sqsubseteq Thing$. As $Language \sqsubseteq Thing$, a valid interpretation is found, and in the context of this question the word "Ada" refers to the programming language Ada. Finally, the result of the focus function is:

$$f_q(\varphi("Ada")) = Language.$$

In deed, (1) represents the question "Who invented Ada?".

It is still possible that the focus function cannot resolve an ambiguity, e.g. a given word has more interpretations but the focus function returns no result:

$$|\Phi| > 1 \text{ and } f(\varphi(w)) = \emptyset.$$

In a such case, the system will generate a semantic query for each possible interpretation. Based on our practical experience we know that users generally enter simple questions where the disambiguation is normally successful.

Definition 6 (Semantic Interpretation). *Let q be the user question, which is composed of linguistic clauses, written $q = \{q_1', ..., q_m'\}$, with $m \geq 1$. The sematic interpretation of a user question q is the translation of each linguistic clause into an $\mathcal{ALC}$ terminology w.r.t. a given ontology H written,*

$$q_i^H = \prod_{k=1}^{n} f_{q_i'} \left(\varphi(w_k \in q_i') \right)$$

with q_i' a linguistic clause $q_i' \in q$, and n the number of words in the linguistic clause q_i'.

If a user question is composed of several linguistic clauses, then each one is translated separately. The logical concatenation of the different interpreted clauses q_i^H depends on the conjunction word(s) used in the user question, e.g. "Who invented the transistor *and* who founded IBM?". If no such conjunction word is found, then the "or" operator is preferred over the "and" operator.

4 Query Generation

We will start with the assumptions that firstly, all documents in the knowledge base $\mathcal{K}$ are semantically described with OWL-DL metadata, w.r.t. an ontology H, and that secondly the user question q was translated into a DL terminology w.r.t. the same ontology H (section 3). Even if we currently do not profit from the full expressivity of OWL-DL, which is $\mathcal{SHOIN}(D+)$, it allows to have compatible semantics between the OWL-DL knowledge base, and the less expressive $\mathcal{ALC}$ user question. Logical inference over the non-empty ABox from $\mathcal{K}$ is possible by using a classical DL reasoner; we use *Pellet* [15]. The returned results are logical consequences of the inference rather than of keyword matchings.

An interpretation $\mathcal{I} = (\Delta^{\mathcal{I}}, \cdot^{\mathcal{I}})$ consists of a non-empty set $\Delta^{\mathcal{I}}$, the domain of the interpretation, and an interpretation function $\cdot^{\mathcal{I}}$ that maps each concept name to a subset of $\Delta^{\mathcal{I}}$ and each role name to a binary relation $r^{\mathcal{I}}$, subset of $\Delta^{\mathcal{I}} \times \Delta^{\mathcal{I}}$.

Definition 7 (Semantic Query). *A semantic query over a knowledge base $\mathcal{K}$ w.r.t. an ontology H, and an user question q is an ABox query, which means to search for models $\mathcal{I}$ of $\mathcal{K}$, written $\mathcal{K} \models q^H$.*

In other words, all documents from the knowledge base that satisfy the expression q^H are potential results. An individual α in $\mathcal{I}$ that is an element of $(q^H)^{\mathcal{I}}$ is a pertinent resource according to the user question.

Technically, an ABox query (in Pellet) is expressed in a query language; we use RDQL [10] via the Jena framework [3]. Firstly, for a complete question, each semantic interpretation, that is each translated linguistic clause, is transformed into a semantic query. Secondly, the nature of the question (*open* or *close*) reveals the missing part. An *open question* contains a question word, e.g. "Who invented the transistor?", whereas a *close question* (logical- or yes/no question) does not have a question word, e.g. "Did Shockley contribute to the invention of the transistor?". As for the first kind of questions, the missing part — normally not an individual but a concept — is the subject of the question and therefore the requested result. The result of the query is the set of all models $\mathcal{I}$ in the knowledge base $\mathcal{K}$. As for the second kind of questions, there is no missing part. Therefore, the answer will be "yes" if $\mathcal{K} \models q^H$, otherwise it is "no". A complete example is shown in figure 4.

5   Implementation and Experiments

Our background theory was implemented prototypically in two educational tools; one about computer history (CHESt), and one about fractions in mathematics (MatES). Both prototypes can be used at home or in a classroom either as Web application, or as stand-alone application (e.g. from a DVD/CD-ROM). The user can freely formulate a question in NL, and submit it to the e-librarian service. Then, the e-librarian service returns one (or more) document(s) which explain(s) the answer to the user's question (figure 5). The knowledge base is composed of short multimedia documents (*clips*), which were recorded with tele-TASK (http://www.tele-task.de) [12]. Each clip documents one subject or a part of a subject. The duration of each clip varies from several seconds to three or four minutes. This has two reasons, firstly, the younger the user, the shorter the time during which (s)he will concentrate on the information displayed on the screen [16]. Secondly, it is not easy to find the appropriate information inside a large piece of data, e.g. in an online lesson that lasts 90 minutes.

In a **first experiment** made in a secondary school with CHESt, we aimed to investigate, firstly, how useful our e-librarian service is as an e-learning tool, and secondly, in how far students accept to enter complete questions into a search engine instead of only keywords. Some 60 students took part in the assessment. In the first place, let us point out that nearly all students approved of the appealing multimedia presentations. They

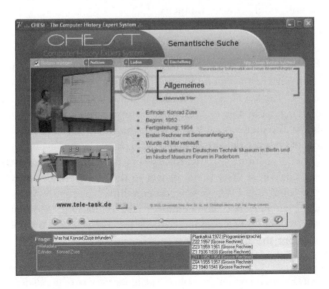

Fig. 5. CHESt with the question: 'What has Konrad Zuse invented?'

agreed that the explanations were sufficiently complete to understand the subject. Several appreciated the short length of the clips; a few stated that the clips were too long. Some added that they appreciated the short response time of the system. Finally, asked if they accepted to enter complete questions into a search engine, 22% of the students answered that they would accept, 69% accepted to enter complete questions instead of keywords only if this yielded better results, and 8% disliked this option.

In a **second experiment** we used MatES to measure the performance of our semantic search engine. A testing set of 229 different questions about this topic was created by a mathematic teacher, who was not involved in the development of the prototype. The teacher also indicated manually the best possible clip, as well as a list of further clips, that should be yielded as correct answer. The questions were linguistic correct, and short sentences like students in a secondary school would ask, e.g. "How can I simplify a fraction?", "What is the sum of $\frac{2}{3}$ and $\frac{7}{4}$?", "What are fractions good for?", "Who invented the fractions?", etc. This benchmark test was compared with the performance of a keyword search engine. The keyword search was slightly optimized to filter out stop words (words with no relevance, e.g. articles) from the textual content of the knowledge base and from the questions entered. The semantic search engine answered 97% of the questions (223 out of 229) correctly, whereas the keyword search engine yielded only a correct answer (i.e. a pertinent clip) in 70% of the questions (161 out of 229).

It is also interesting to notice that for 86 questions, the semantic search engine yielded just one – the semantically best matching – answer (figure 6). For 75% of the questions (170 out of 229) the semantic search engine yielded just a few results (one, two or three answers), whereas the keyword search yielded for only 14% of the questions less than 4 answers; mostly (138 questions out of 229) more than 10 answers. Our e-librarian service returned always at least one result. This is important because we learned from former experiments in school that students dislike getting no result at all.

For example, the semantic interpretation of the question "What is the sum of $\frac{2}{3}$ and $\frac{7}{4}$?" is the following valid $\mathcal{ALC}$ terminology:

$$Fraction(x1) \sqcap \exists hasOperation(x1, x2) \sqcap Operation(x2, sum).$$

Then the semantic query retrieves one clip, which explained how to add two fractions. This was the best clip that could be found in the knowledge base[1]. This means also that questions like "How can I add two fractions", "What is $\frac{11}{0.5}$ plus $\frac{5}{5}$, etc. would yield the same clip. The keyword search engine yields all clips, in which keywords like "sum" are found, e.g. a clip that explains how to represent a complex function in terms of additions, and a clip that explain how to describe situations with simple fractions.

The experiments revealed also two major weaknesses of our e-librarian service that should be improved in future. Firstly, the system is not able to make the difference between a question, where there is no answer in the knowledge base, and a question that is out of the topic, e.g. "Who invented penicillin?". Secondly, in its current state, the e-librarian service does not handle number restrictions, e.g. "How many machines did Konrad Zuse invent?". The response will be the list of Zuse's machines, but not a number. Furthermore, the question "What is the designation of the third model of Apple computers?" will yield a list of all models of Apple computers.

---

[1] Remember that the system returns clips that explain the answer to the student's question, but they do note give the precise answer, e.g. it does not compute the sum of the two fractions.

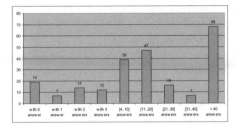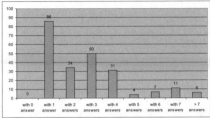

Fig. 6. Number of results yielded by a (1) keyword and by a (2) semantic search engine with a set of 229 questions

6 Related Work

START [5] is the first question-answering system available on the Web. Several improvements have been made since it came online in 1993 [7,6] which make of START a powerful search engine. However, the NLP is not always sound, e.g. the question "What did Jodie Foster before she became an actress?" returns "I don't know what Jodie fostered before the actress became an actress". Also, the question "Who invented the transistor?" yields two answers: the inventors of the transistor, but also a description about the transistor (the answer to the question: "What is a transistor").

AquaLog [9] is a portable question-answering system which takes queries expressed in NL and an ontology as input, and returns answers drawn from one or more knowledge bases. User questions are expressed as triples: <subject, predicate, object>. If the several translation mechanisms fail, then the user is asked for disambiguation. The system also uses an interesting learning component to adapt to the user's "jargon". AquaLog has currently a very limited knowledge space. In a benchmark test over 76 different questions, 37 (48.68%) where handled correctly.

The prototype PRECISE [11] uses ontology technologies to map semantically tractable NL questions to the corresponding SQL query. It was tested on several hundred questions drawn from user studies over three benchmark databases. Over 80% of the questions are semantically tractable questions, which PRECISE answered correctly, and recognized the 20% it could not handle, and requests a paraphrase. The problem of finding a mapping from the tokenization to the database requires that all tokens must be distinct; questions with unknown words are not semantically tractable and cannot be handled.

FALCON is an answer engine that handles questions in NL. When the question concept indicating the answer type is identified, it is mapped into an answer taxonomy. The top categories are connected to several word classes from WordNet. Also, FALCON gives a cached answer if the similar question has already been asked before; a similarity measure is calculated to see if the given question is a reformulation of a previous one. In TREC-9, FALCON generated a score of 58% for short answers and 76% for long answers, which was actually the best score.

LASSO relies on a combination of syntactic and semantic techniques, and lightweight abductive inference to find answers. The search for the answer is based on a form of indexing called paragraph indexing. The advantage of processing paragraphs instead of full documents determines a faster syntactic parsing. The extraction and evaluation of the answer correctness is based on empirical abduction. A score of 55.5% for short answers and 64.5% for long answers was achieved in TREC-8.

Medicine is one of the best examples of application domains where ontologies have already been deployed at large scale and demonstrated their utility. The generation, maintenance and evolution of a Semantic Web-based ontology in the context of an information system for pathology is described in [2]. The system combines Semantic Web and NLP techniques to support a content-based storage and retrieval of medical reports and digital images.

The MKBEEM [4] mediation system allows to fill the gap between customers queries (possibly expressed in NL) and diverse specific providers offers. They provide a consensual representation of the e-commerce field allowing the exchanges independently of the language of the end user, the service, or the content provider. The dynamic discovery mechanism converts the user query into an ontological formula, then into a concept description using DL. Finally, the relevant e-service is selected. The MKBEEM prototype has been validated with the languages Finnish, English, French, and Spanish, in two fields: business to consumer on-lines sales, and Web based travel/tourism services.

7   Conclusions

In this paper we presented an e-librarian service that allows the user to communicate by means of complete questions in NL, and that retrieves pertinent multimedia resources from a knowledge base. The background theory is composed of three steps: the linguistic pre-processing of the user's NL input, the semantic interpretation of the NL sentence into a logical form, and the generation of a semantic query. It uses Description Logics and Semantic Web technologies like OWL for the semantic interpretation of NL questions. We also presented an algorithm to resolve ambiguities in the user question. Experiments with two prototypes confirmed that this background theory is reliable and can be implemented, e.g. in an educational tool.

In our further work, we will try to improve the translation from the NL question into an $\mathcal{ALC}$ terminology, e.g. use number restrictions. We also want to investigate if a more precise grammatical analyze of the user question can help in the interpretation step, or if this would reduce the users liking of the interface (because of the smaller tolerance of the system). Another important topic is the maintenance facilities; how can unknown words from the user query (i.e. the user's "jargon") be included in the dictionary, and how can external "thrusted" knowledge sources been accessed by the e-librarian service?

References

1. Allen, J.: Natural Language Understanding. Addison-Wesley, Reading (1994)
2. Bontas, E.P., Tietz, S., Tolksdorf, R., Schrader, T.: Engineering a Semantic Web for Pathology. In: Koch, N., Fraternali, P., Wirsing, M. (eds.) ICWE 2004. LNCS, vol. 3140, pp. 585–586. Springer, Heidelberg (2004)

3. Carroll, J.J., Dickinson, I., Dollin, C., Reynolds, D., Seaborne, A., Wilkinson, K.: Jena: implementing the semantic web recommendations. In: 13th international conference on World Wide Web - Alternate Track Papers & Posters, New York, NY, USA, May 17-20, 2004, pp. 74–83 (2004)
4. Corcho, Ó., Gomez-Perez, A., Leger, A., Rey, C., Toumani, F.: An ontology-based mediation architecture for e-commerce applications. In: Intelligent Information Processing and Web Mining (IIS: IIPWM), Zakopane, Poland, pp. 477–486 (2003)
5. Katz, B.: Annotating the world wide web using natural language. In: 5th RIAO conference on computer assisted information searching on the internet, Montreal, Canada (1997)
6. Katz, B., Felshin, S., Yuret, D., Ibrahim, A., Lin, J.J., Marton, G., McFarland, A.J., Temelkuran, B.: Omnibase: Uniform access to heterogeneous data for question answering. In: 6th International Conference on Applications of Natural Language to Information Systems (NLDB), Stockholm, Sweden, June 27-28, 2002, pp. 230–234 (2002)
7. Katz, B., Lin, J.: Annotating the semantic web using natural language. In: 2nd Workshop on NLP and XML (NLPXML-2002) at COLING (2002)
8. Kusters, R.: Non-Standard Inferences in Description Logics. In: Küsters, R. (ed.) Non-Standard Inferences in Description Logics. LNCS (LNAI), vol. 2100. Springer, Heidelberg (2001)
9. Lopez, V., Pasin, M., Motta, E.: AquaLog: An Ontology-Portable Question Answering System for the Semantic Web. In: Gómez-Pérez, A., Euzenat, J. (eds.) ESWC 2005. LNCS, vol. 3532, pp. 546–562. Springer, Heidelberg (2005)
10. Miller, L., Seaborne, A., Reggiori, A.: Three implementations of SquishQL, a simple RDF query language. In: Horrocks, I., Hendler, J. (eds.) ISWC 2002. LNCS, vol. 2342, pp. 423–435. Springer, Heidelberg (2002)
11. Popescu, A.-M., Etzioni, O., Kautz, H.A.: Towards a theory of natural language interfaces to databases. In: 8th International Conference on Intelligent User Interfaces, Miami, FL, USA, January 12-15, 2003, pp. 149–157 (2003)
12. Schillings, V., Meinel, C.: tele-task: teleteaching anywhere solution kit. In: 30th annual ACM SIGUCCS conference on User services, Providence, Rhode Island, USA, November 20-23, 2002, pp. 130–133 (2002)
13. Schmidt, R.A.: Terminological representation, natural language & relation algebra. In: Ohlbach, H.J. (ed.) GWAI 1992. LNCS, vol. 671, pp. 357–371. Springer, Heidelberg (1993)
14. Schmidt-Schauβ, M., Smolka, G.: Attributive concept descriptions with complements. Artificial Intelligence 48(1), 1–26 (1991)
15. Sirin, E., Parsia, B.: Pellet: An owl dl reasoner. In: International Workshop on Description Logics (DL2004). CEUR Workshop Proceedings, Whistler, British Columbia, Canada, June 6-8, 2004, vol. 104 (2004), CEUR-WS.org
16. Williams, W.M., Markle, F., Sternberg, R.J., Brigockas, M.: Educational Psychology, Allyn & Bacon (2001)

PART IV
WINSYS

A Transceiver Concept Based on a Software Defined Radio Approach

Admir Burnic, Alex Vießmann, Tobias Scholand,
Arjang Hessamian-Alinejad, Guido H. Bruck, and Peter Jung

Lehrstuhl für KommunikationsTechnik, Universität Duisburg-Essen
47048 Duisburg, Germany
{Guido.Bruck,Peter.Jung}@KommunikationsTechnik.org

Abstract. In this communication, a software defined radio (SDR) transceiver design, termed FALCON, will be presented. The FALCON is entirely based on a modular signal processing concept; the FALCON receiver uses modules which process and generate log-likelihood ratio (LLR) signals, hence, providing the capability of a plug-and-play-type re-configurability. The authors' view on reconfigurability will be discussed in this communication. The FALCON currently deploys commercial radio frequency (RF) front-ends provided by Atmel, analogue and interface boards developed and implemented by the authors and DSP Starter Kits (DSK) based on TI TMS320C6416 DSPs (digital signal processors), which have been provided by Texas Instruments. The hardware/software integration has been done in the laboratory of the authors. Furthermore, the authors developed all signal processing modules in C language tailored for the TMS320C6416 DSPs. This paper will also illustrate measurement results obtained with the FALCON will be given. For an easy comparison of these results with widely published simulation results the authors will consider UMTS/W-CDMA. It will be shown that the FALCON provides a superb performance.

Keywords: Demonstrator, Digital Signal Processor (DSP), FALCON, Log-Likelihood Ratio (LLR), Reconfigurability, Software Defined Radio (SDR).

1 Introduction

Reconfigurability for transceivers for wireless access networks like Bluetooth, Wi-MAX (Worldwide Interoperability for Microwave Access) and W-LANs will become increasingly important in the forthcoming decade. Appropriately flexible and reliable hardware/software architectures, allowing the concurrent processing of different controlling tasks for wireless terminals will hence be important assets. The deployment of communication systems strongly depends on the availability of appropriate microelectronics. Therefore, the combined approach to communication and microelectronic system design is crucial [1]. The coming world of mobile communication will change dramatically in the future. Wireless networks will evolve their limited set of services to a great variety of applications, and the today's set of wireless terminal types will expand considerably [1], [2]. A single homogeneous network like UMTS (Universal Mobile Telecommunications System) will not provide such versatile services alone.

J. Filipe and M.S. Obaidat (Eds.): ICETE 2006, CCIS 9, pp. 279–289, 2008.

Only a heterogeneous network consisting of wired and wireless networks will form a catalyst for the evolution of such a diverse mobile world. Future mobile radio communication systems will hierarchically integrate a broad variety of wireless networks into a common structure encompassing e.g. WCDMA-based cellular mobile systems, OFDM-based radio LANs like IEEE 802.11a/b, and inexpensive personal-area networks like Bluetooth. It is recommendable to establish software defined radio (SDR) and cognitive radio (CR) concepts in wireless transceivers.

Reconfigurability in radio development is not a very new technique [2]. Already during the 1980s reconfigurable receivers were developed for radio intelligence in the short wave range. However, reconfigurability became familiar to many radio developers with the publication of the special issues on software radios of the IEEE Communication Magazine [3], [4].

In [2] the author refers to a transceiver as a software radio (SR), if its communication functions are realized as programs running on a suitable processor. An ideal SR directly samples the antenna output which does not seem feasible w.r.t. e.g power consumption and linearity as well as resolution requirements on analog-to-digital converters (ADCs). A software defined radio (SDR), however, is a practical and realizable version of an SR: The received signals are sampled after a suitable band selection filter, usually in the base band or a low intermediate frequency band [2].

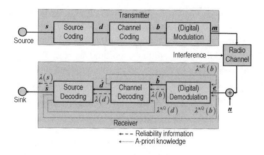

Fig. 1. Basic discrete-time structure of a digital radio communications system with a modular iterative receiver, cf. [16], Fig. 1.4, p. 11

In many available publications such as e.g. [5], [6], more or less inflexible implementation platforms or hardware oriented processing architectures for the control unit have been discussed rather than the software architecture and real-time operation of reliable reconfiguration. In [7], [8], the basic idea of reconfiguration in a wireless environment was addressed. However, the authors discussed procedures which are relevant to the network and the negotiation process for the updating. The hardware/software architecture and processing schemes inside terminals has not yet been considered in detail.

In order to obtain a flexible radio terminal, the modular receiver design is a viable asset. In particular, the physical layer (PHY) modules require inputs and outputs which facilitate a plug-and-play-type deployment. Devising PHY receiver modules which accept, process and generate log-likelihood ratios (LLRs) is a desirable approach because of the potential to implement optimum or near-optimum receiver strategies.

The concept of LLRs in receivers has been introduced in text-books already in the early 1970s, cf. e.g. Sect. 5.2, pp. 126ff. of [9]. It has been applied to e.g. demodulators, see e.g. [9], [10], channel decoders, cf. e.g. [11], and joint source-channel decoding (JSCD), see e.g. [12], [13]. However, the aforementioned publications do not consider implementation issues in an SDR context. Publications like [1], [2], [5], [6], [7], [8], focusing on SDRs, have not yet dealt with LLR based receiver realizations. Such receiver realizations are seldom and usually consider only parts of the receiver, often the channel decoder, cf. e.g. [14], [15].

The manuscript is organized as follows. The transmitter and receiver concepts deployed by the authors shall be briefly described in Sect. 0. The authors shall discuss their approach to the reconfiguarbility in Sect. 0. The FALCON setup implemented by the authors shall be discussed in Sect. 0. The measurement results obtained with the FALCON will be summarized in Sect. 0. Sect. 0 concludes the manuscript.

In what follows, the matrix-vector notation is used. Matrices are denoted as upper case characters in bold face italics, vectors are lower case characters in bold face italics. Furthermore, complex-valued variables are underlined.

2 LLR Based Receiver Concept

To the best knowledge of the authors, a complete view on LLR based receiver design and realization including iterative detection has first been given in [16], cf. e.g. Sect. 1.2, pp. 9ff. The basic discrete-time structure of a digital radio communications system with a modular iterative receiver is depicted in figure 1 in the case of a single transmitter and a single receiver and baseband modeling, cf. [15], Fig. 1.4, p. 11. Other signal sources are considered as interference. The source generates the information signal to be transmitted.

In figure 1, we assume a digital source signal, represented by the vector s. The transmitter consists of a source encoder, a channel encoder and a modulator. The source encoder encodes s and outputs the binary data vector d which is the basis for the channel coding, generating the binary channel encoded vector b. The channel encoder can e.g. be a turbo-code encoder as it is the case in many UMTS (universal mobile telecommunications system) services. The modulator puts out the complex modulated signal $\underline{m}$, the underline denoting a complex baseband signal which is then transmitted via the radio channel.

At the input of the receiver, the noise vector $\underline{n}$ is added, forming the received vector $\underline{e}$. The receiver inverts the transmitter operations and it therefore consists of a demodulator, a channel decoder and a source decoder. The receiver can be operated in a feed-forward manner as it was e.g. used in [14] in the case of a simple single-path AWGN (additive white Gaussian noise) channel without any fading. In this case, the demodulator generates the detected version $\hat{b}$ of b, together with corresponding exact or approximate LLR values contained in the reliability information vector $\lambda(b)$, both being processed by the channel decoder. The channel decoder puts out the detected data vector $\hat{d}$ and the reliability information vector $\lambda(d)$ which consists of the corresponding exact or approximate LLR values. Then, the source decoder delivers the detected source vector $\hat{s}$ to the sink. Also, the source decoder can put out the reliability information vector $\lambda(s)$ with the LLR values of s, which are not further needed in the further description.

The shown receiver can also be used in an iterative mode of operation when the channel decoder generates the a-priori knowledge estimate vector $\lambda^{a,K}(b)$ which can be used in the demodulation process. Also, the source decoder can be devised to produce a-priori knowledge estimate vectors $\lambda^{a,Q}(b)$ and $\lambda^{a,Q}(d)$ as further inputs of the demodulator and of the channel decoder, respectively.

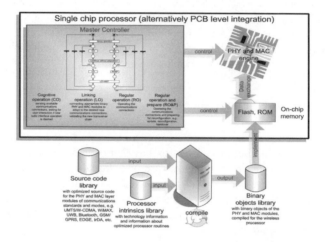

Fig. 2. Concept of the Master Controller for reliable reconfiguration of CRs

Fig. 3. FALCON transceiver

In what follows, we will illustrate which PHY modules of the UMTS terrestrial radio access (UTRA) FDD (frequency domain duplex) mode W-CDMA (wideband code division multiple access) correspond to the channel coding/decoding and the modulation/demodulation components of the structure shown in figure 1. The channel coding component shown in figure 1 consists of the CRC (cyclic redundancy check) generation, the Turbo Code encoding with the rate matching, the first interleaving, the radio frame and the physical channel segmentation and the second interleaving. The modulation component contains the pilot generation, the frame and the slot assembling, the serial-to-parallel conversion, the channelization code generation, the OVSF (orthogonal variable spreading factor) spreading, the scrambling code generation and allocation, the complex scrambling, the primary and secondary synchronization channel generation, the signal amplification and the signal summation, the root raised cosine (RRC) filtering, and the analog transmission section including the RF (radio frequency) transmit part.

The demodulation component of figure 1 contains the RF receive part, the RRC filtering, the adaptive RAKE receiver consisting of a searcher exploiting the synchronization channels for frame and slot synchronization as well as channel parameters identification and RAKE finger allocation, a variable number of adaptive RAKE fingers including the channel parameter tracking, the de-scrambling and the de-spreading, a maximal-ratio combining (MRC) unit including a signal-to-noise-and-interference ratio (SNIR) estimation unit, a parallel-to-serial conversion unit and an LLR computation unit, and, finally, the frame and the slot disassembling. The channel decoding component shown in figure 1 consists of the second de-interleaving, the radio frame and the physical channel de-segmentation, the first de-interleaving, the Turbo Code decoding with the rate de-matching, and the CRC (cyclic redundancy check) decoding. Similarly, the mapping of OFDM (orthogonal frequency division multiplexing) based concepts like WiMAX IEEE 802.16e can be done.

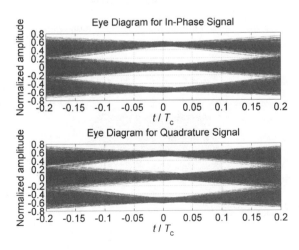

Fig. 4. Eye diagrams of the in-phase and quadrature signals at the input of the radio frequency (RF) board

3 Approach to the Reconfigurability

In order to achieve a best possible reconfigurability, the deployment of software definable hardware is beneficial. In particular, the deployment of digital signal processors (DSPs) in combination with dedicated mixed signal hardware which can be parameterized. In this case the reconfiguration of the transmitter can be easily accomplished by implementing e.g. the appropriate PHY signal processing algorithms mainly in software, allowing a highly flexible and reliable software architecture based strategy. This approach has been taken by the authors and shall be further described in the sequel of this communication.

The transmitter can be reconfigured by using known programming techniques, by using encoder and modulator software modules which can be parameterized in the anticipated ranges. This has been a standard strategy which will not be further considered here.

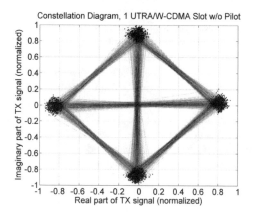

Fig. 5. Measured transmit constellation diagram

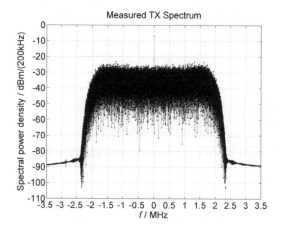

Fig. 6. Measured transmit spectrum

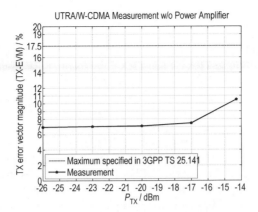

Fig. 7. Measured error vector magnitude values at the transmitter output

However, the use of LLR based reliability information in the receiver seems to be a novel idea; in particular in combination with iterative receiver strategies. LLR based reliability information makes a further re-scaling of soft values unnecessary. This fact facilitates a particularly simple reconfiguration of the receiver. When using this approach, single hardware/software modules can be replaced without affecting other modules, making the solution "plug-and-play".

In a future version of the FALCON, currently under development, the authors will further improve the reconfigurability by deploying an additional ARM controller which will run concurrent controlling tasks including the reconfiguration mode. The software architecture has been devised using Petri nets (PNs) [17], [18] and paves the way towards cognitive radio (CR) [2] concepts.

The way of reconfiguration of a terminal, in particular, the realization of a processor with master controller and a Petri net based approach, which allows concurrent mode of operation and high reliability and secure applications, has not yet been treated. The new approach proposed by the authors consists of a Master Controller, which is responsible for a reliable reconfiguration. In addition, there has to be a unit, which can communicate with the network, a PHY and MAC (medium access control layer) engine. This PHY and MAC engine needs software modules with signal processing algorithms for the data processing path. The third part is a memory, which contains these software modules. The Master Controller starts a cognitive operation in order to obtain the best reconfiguration and software modules needed for the SDR. The reconfiguration then consists in the linking of software modules, found in the memory, and installing them into the SDR to use the software modules in the regular signal processing chain.

Figure 2 shows the described concept of the Master Controller for reliable reconfiguration of CRs. The Master Controller works with the mentioned PN based software architecture. It needs a scalable control program which can e.g. be created by using e.g. Petri net compilers. As already mentioned, the implementation and validation of the Master Controller based concept on a PCB level integration will be done in the FALCON. In real terminals, an implementation in a single chip processor is conceivable.

4   The FALCON Setup

The FALCON currently consists of two identical transceivers (TRXs). Figure 3 shows a photograph of one of these TRXs. Each TRX consists of an RF front-end board with a single direct-downconversion RF chip, provided by Atmel, an analog TRX base-band board with filtering and signal conversion parts and a SPI (werial peripheral interconnection) interface for the DSP based programming of the RF chip, the mixed signal board carrying the ADC (analog-to-digital converter) and DAC (digital-to-analog converter) hardware, a USB (universal serial bus) interface board for the trans-fer of the information to the transmitter and of the detected information to the sink, and a TMS320C6416 DSP Starter Kit (DSK), provided by Texas Instruments, with a JTAG (joint test action group) interface for controlling and programming purposes. The RF front-end boards can provide transmit power values ranging from -26 dBm to -14 dBm without further power amplification and they have separate transmit and receive antenna connectors; in Figure 3, only the receive antenna is connected. The hardware/software integration has been done in the laboratory of the authors as well as the development of all the signal processing modules, which have been real-ized in C language tailored for the TMS320C6416 DSPs (digital signal processors).

The FALCON has been intended to address mid-range terminals and access points, in particular for cellular systems. Its functionality has bee validated for the UTRA/W-CDMA and OFDM based concepts like WiMAX IEEE 802.16e in indoor and laboratory environments with short delay spreads.

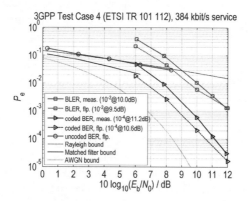

Fig. 8. Comparison of performance measurements and simulation results in the case of the 3GPP Test Case 4 channel model described in ETSI TR 101 112 in the case of the 384 kbit/s service

The FALCON e.g. provides programmable digital filtering, automatic frequency correction (AFC) and adaptive synchronization schemes which compensate impair-ments occurring in the analog domain. Measurements of the signal processing effort in MIPS (million instructions per second) have validated the real-time capability of the FALCON, both software and data fit into the DSP internal memories. In the case of indoor environments, a single RAKE finger is sufficient to provide the desired

UTRA FDD performance. In the case of the UTRA FDD 384 kbit/s service and a 720 MHz version of the TMS320C6416 DSP, the software implementation used by the authors consumes approx. 5.7 million processor cycles, the de-interleaving, rate de-matching and signal representation conversions require approx. 0.6 million processor cycles, totaling in a DSP load of about 96%. The remaining DSP capability is sufficient to accommodate the rest of the receive and the transmit signal processing.

5 Measurement Results

In this section, several measurement results obtained with the FALCON for the UTRA FDD 384 kbit/s service will be presented. First measurement results of transmit front-end characteristics will be considered. Figure 4 shows the eye diagrams of the in-phase and quadrature signals at the baseband input of the RF front-end chip and Figure 5 presents the corresponding constellation diagram. In both cases, now pilot transmission has been considered which is the reason for the occurrence of amplitude values around 0.

The measured transmit spectrum at the input of the transmit antenna is depicted in figure 6 in the case of -20 dBm transmit power and the measured values of the error vector magnitude (EVM) at the input of the transmit antenna versus the transmit power is shown in figure 7. The spectrum of figure 6 shows a nice agreement with the spectral mask required by the UMTS standard, the effect of the RRC filtering can be clearly observed. According to figure 7, the EVM is ranges between 7% and 8% for transmit power values between -26 dBm to -17 dBm. Only in the case of high transmit power values above -17 dBm, the EVM increases to approximately 10.5%. In all cases the EVM is well below the maximum allowed EVM of 17.5%, specified in the UMTS standard.

Figure 8 shows obtained simulation and measurement results in the case of the UTRA FDD 384 kbit/s service in the case of the transmission over the 3GPP Test Case 4 channel model which has been implemented in a channel simulator. The simulations were carried out with a floating point implementation of the signal processing algorithms done in C language. The measurements have been done with the digital implementation of the FALCON, the mixed signal and RF parts have not been considered.

The simulator determines the matched filter BER bound, which is the best possible performance in the case of the transmission of isolated bits over the channel and perfect knowledge of the channel at the receiver, together with the uncoded BER which can be obtained when considering the UTRA FDD 384 kbit/s service. The latter is of course worse than the matched filter bound. Furthermore, the simulator puts out the BER and the BLER (block error ratio) at the output of the Turbo-Code decoder. For reference purposes, we will consider the coded BER 10^{-4} and the coded BLER 10^{-2}, the latter meaning that 99% of all transmitted blocks have been received correctly, i.e. the throughput is equal to 99%. In the case of the 3GPP Test Case 4 channel, we require ≈ 10.6 dB to achieve the coded BER 10^{-4} and ≈ 9.5 dB to obtain the coded BLER 10^{-2}. The fixed point implementation in the FALCON leads to a small degradation of approximately 0.5 dB, and we yield ≈ 11.2 dB to achieve the coded BER 10^{-4} and ≈ 10.0 dB to obtain the coded BLER 10^{-2}.

In figure 8, the theoretical performance bounds of the BER (bit error ratio) are depicted as a function of the required signal-to-noise ratio $10\log_{10}\left(E_b/N_0\right)$ for the single path no fading ("AWGN bound") case,

$$P_e = Q\left(\sqrt{2\frac{E_b}{N_0}}\right),\tag{1}$$

$Q(\cdot)$ being the Q function, and the single path full fading ("Rayleigh bound") case,

$$P_e = \frac{1}{2}\left(1 - \sqrt{\frac{E_b}{E_b + N_0}}\right)\tag{2}$$

E_b being the average energy per bit, are depicted for reference purposes.

In general, we find that the simulated and the measures performance agree very well. Measurements of receive front-end characteristics, such as e.g. the intermodulation distortion (IMD) and, correspondingly, the effective number of bits (ENOB), are currently ongoing. Also, measurements of the BERs and BLERs in the case of the operation over the air, i.e. including the effects of the mixed signal and RF parts of the FALCON, are currently being done. The same accounts for the WiMAX transceiver operation.

6 Conclusions

In this communication, the authors presented the FALCON concept, entirely based on modular signal processing. The authors showed that the FALCON receiver deploys modules which process and generate LLR based reliability information which plays a key role when targeting reconfigurable hardware. Furthermore, the authors discussed a novel concept for the reconfigurability of transceivers which supports the way towards cognitive radios.

The FALCON currently deploys commercial radio frequency (RF) and DSP boards. Furthermore, it uses mixed signal and interface boards implemented by the authors. Also, the software development and the system integration, both hardware and software, has been done by the authors.

Finally, the authors presented selected measurement results obtained in the case of the UTRA FDD 384 kbit/s service. Further measurements are currently ongoing. It was shown that the FALCON provides a desirably performance and therefore proves that the concept of the FALCON is viable.

Acknowledgements

The authors wish to thank Atmel and Texas Instruments for their generous support. Furthermore, the authors are grateful to their colleagues for valuable support.

References

1. Grass, E., Tittelbach-Helmrich, K., Jagdhold, U., Troya, A., Lippert, G., Kruger, O., Leh-mann, J., Maharatna, K., Dombrowski, K.F., Fiebig, N., Kraemer, R., Mahonen, P.: On the single-chip implementation of a hiperlan/2 and IEEE 802.11a capable modem. IEEE Personal Communications 8(6), 48–57 (2001)
2. Jondral, F.K.: Software-defined radio – basics and evolution to cognitive radio. EURASIP Journal on Wireless Communications and Networking 3, 275–283 (2005)
3. Special Issue on software radio. IEEE Communications Magazine 33(5) (1995)
4. Special Issue on globalization of software radio. IEEE Communications Magazine 37(2) (1999)
5. Srikanteswara, S., Reed, J.H., Athanas, P., Boyle, R.: A soft radio architecture for recon-figurable platforms. IEEE Communications Magazine 38(2), 140–147 (2000)
6. Glossner, J., Iancu, D., Lu, J., Hokenek, E., Moudgill, M.: A software-defined communica-tions baseband design. IEEE Communications Magazine 41(1), 120–128 (2003)
7. Drew, N.J., Dillinger, M.M.: Evolution toward reconfigurable user equipment. IEEE Communications Magazine 39(2), 158–164 (2001)
8. Hoffmeyer, J., Park, I.-P., Majmundar, M., Blust, S.: Radio software download for com-mercial wireless reconfigurable devices. IEEE Radio Communications, S26–S32 (March 2004)
9. Whalen, A.D.: Detection of signals in noise. Academic Press, San Diego (1971)
10. Chiu, M.-C.: A low-complexity SISO multiuser detector for iterative decoding of asyn-chronous CDMA systems with convolutional codes. IEEE Transactions on Vehicular Technology 54, 516–524 (2005)
11. Hagenauer, J., Robertson, P., Papke, L.: Iterative ('Turbo') decoding of systematic convo-lutional codes with the MAP and SOVA algorithms. In: Proceedings of the ITG-Conference on Source and Channel Coding (SCC 1994), München, pp. 164–172 (1994)
12. Hagenauer, J.: Source-controlled channel decoding. IEEE Transactions on Communica-tions 43, 2449–2457 (1995)
13. Jung, P.: Analyse und Entwurf digitaler Mobilfunksysteme. B.G. Teubner, Stuttgart (1997)
14. Montorsi, G., Benedetto, S.: Design of fixed-point iterative decoders for concatenated codes with interleavers. IEEE Journal on Selected Areas in Communications 19, 871–882 (2001)
15. Faber, T., Jung, P.: Digital signal processing complexity of Turbo-Codes for UMTS on the TMS320C6416. In: Proceedings of the IEEE International Conference on Computers and Devices for Communication (CODEC 2004), Kalkota/India (January 2004)
16. Faber, T.: Turbo-Empfänger für digitale Mobilfunksysteme, gezeigt am Beispiel eines "Software Defined Radio"-Demonstrators. In: Jung, P. (ed.) Series: Selected Topics in Communications Technologies, Shaker, Aachen (2005)
17. Murata, T.: Petri nets: Properties, analysis and applications. Proceedings of the IEEE 77(4), 541–580 (1989)
18. Reisig, W.: Petri nets: An introduction. Springer, Berlin (1985)

Evaluation of an Orthogonal SFBC Channel Estimation Scheme for MIMO OFDM Wireless Systems

A.D. Marousis and P. Constantinou

Mobile Radio Communications Laboratory, School of Electrical and Computer Engineering
National Technical University of Athens, Greece
{amarous,fkonst}@mobile.ntua.gr

Abstract. This paper presents the design and evaluation of a channel estimation scheme that is efficient by means of both the mean square error (MSE) of channel estimation/tracking and its incorporation in a real MIMO system. The evaluation has been performed over the spatial channel model developed for MIMO simulations according to 802.16e case of 3GPP.25.996, taking also into account all IF and RF stages in the communication chain. Orthogonality has been applied in space-frequency dimension for both preamble and pilot symbols, as well as for the data symbols, with the application of Alamouti's scheme. In 4G multicarrier systems that use space-time-frequency coding, orthogonal design turns into a key factor for the performance of the system since the channel has to remain about constant during the transmission of one orthogonal block, something which becomes quite challenging in highly time-variant propagation channels. Furthermore, space-frequency block coding (SFBC) becomes more efficient as the number of subcarriers increases (802.16e, 802.20, etc). The modified channel estimation scheme applied to MIMO transceiver is also efficient in minimization of the processing requirements at the receiver side by estimating only those channel properties that have been changed assuming that the general channel conditions (low/high mobility) are known. The results presented refer to the normalized MSE of the channel estimator and the overall performance evaluation (BER) of the system in various propagations channels, data rates and forward error correction modes.

Keywords: MIMO transceivers, channel estimation and tracking, OFDM, space-frequency block coding, link level evaluation.

1 Introduction

Wireless broadband systems have to support services that demand information transmission with very high data rates over the wireless propagation medium. It has been proven [1] that the use of multiple antenna elements at both ends of a wireless link offers both capacity gain and improvement of robustness and reliability. Therefore, multiple input multiple output (MIMO) architecture has been incorporated in the development of various wireless systems operating in challenging propagation environments. In addition, the various sources of diversity should be properly exploited by means of coding and

J. Filipe and M.S. Obaidat (Eds.): ICETE 2006, CCIS 9, pp. 290–300, 2008.
© Springer-Verlag Berlin Heidelberg 2008

transmission scheme [2]. Temporal diversity is realized through FEC schemes (scrambling, Reed-Solomon, convolution, interleaving). Frequency diversity is exploited by orthogonal frequency division multiple (OFDM) access systems and spatial diversity is obtained by multiple antennas. Furthermore, the above diversity options are combined in space-time, space-frequency, or space-time-frequency codes where the orthogonal property and the ability to be preserved through the propagation channel is a key factor in the total system performance.

Optimum space-frequency coding schemes that maximize the diversity gain have been proposed in [3], but the processing requirements at the receiver are quite high. Space-time block codes proposed by Alamouti and extended in [4], provide a simple transmit diversity scheme with maximum diversity in flat fading MIMO channels, which are assumed about constant during the transmission of one orthogonal block. OFDM provides flat fading channel for each subcarrier, making space-time block codes well suited for OFDM systems assuming that the channel coefficients remain constant during two or more consecutive OFDM symbols.

In propagation environments with high Doppler shift loss of orthogonality, that is assembled in space-time domain, becomes possible, whilst in space-frequency structure the orthogonal design is not distorted. Furthermore, as the number of subcarriers increases, for a given total bandwidth of transmission, the probability of non constant affected neighbor subcarriers in severe frequency selective channels becomes quite small. Also, the greater number of subcarriers (WiMAX vs WiFi), the larger range is achieved, since larger delay spreads are tolerated (up to 10 times for WiMAX with respect to WiFi).

Channel estimation is a crucial design parameter in the performance of a real system since it has to estimate, track and compensate all channel distortions as well as the distortions caused in RF stages in transmitter and receiver units. Especially, in a MIMO-OFDM system the channel distortion is described by a complex factor per subcarrier requiring from the estimator $(N_{sym} \cdot N_c \cdot M_T \cdot M_R)$ estimations/compensations per frame (N_{sym}=number of OFDM symbols, N_c=number of subcarriers per OFDM symbol, M_T=number of transmit antennas, M_R=number of receive antennas). Such an operation can be particularly demanding in terms of computational effort [5]. Following the design of space-frequency orthogonality also for the preamble and pilot transmission the proposed approach causes a pilot overhead of 3.12% per OFDM symbol in which only phase estimation is used for the pilots that have been carefully placed in predefined positions.

In this paper, initially (section 2) the system model is depicted giving a detailed insight of transceiver architecture, as well as the channel models used for the evaluation. In section 3, the channel estimation is described giving rise to all advantages and trade offs caused by the low computational complexity at the receiver side. Finally (section 4), evaluation results of the channel estimation (MSE) and the overall system performance (BER) are given for 2x1 and 2x2 cases evaluated in various propagation models according to 802.16e (Mobile Broadband Wireless Access, MBWA) case of 3GPP.25.996 [6] using various FEC codes and mapping formats following the 802.16-2004 standard.

2   System Architecture

2.1   Transmission Scheme

The MIMO-OFDM transmitter with two branches employing space-frequency block coding (SFBC) is shown in fig.1. A binary data block $D[k]$ of k bits is scrambled, encoded by a concatenated Reed-Solomon and Convolutional encoder, followed by a puncturer and an interleaver. The resultant bit stream is mapped using a set of predefined constellation diagrams (BPSK-1/2, QPSK-1/2, QPSK-3/4, 16QAM-1/2, 16QAM-3/4, 64QAM-2/3, and 64QAM-3/4) giving a symbol stream $S[m]$ of m symbols. The same procedure is followed as well as for the frame control header (FCH) [7] with fixed QPSK mapping. These symbol streams are then frequency multiplexed with 8 pilot symbols and the output is SFB coded based on Alamouti's scheme. The output symbols are packetized in blocks of 200 symbols, zero padded and inserted in a 256-IFFT OFDM modulator. Subsequently, the outputs are time multiplexed with the OFDM output of the SFB coded preamble symbols P. The produced digital signals at the two chains are converted to analog ones and up-converted to the carrier frequency through RF stages with common oscillator. Hence, time synchronization and frequency offset compensation at the receiver are exactly the same as in the case of a SISO system.

2.2   Reception Scheme

At the receiver an equivalent procedure is followed. Alamouti's encoding scheme [8] (applied on a basis of 2 neighbor subcarriers) offers a simple combining scheme assuming that the channel estimates are available. Hence, extra attention has been paid in the channel estimation stage as shown in fig.2 (in which only one part of the 2×2 system has been depicted). The received signal at the frequency domain, either for data symbol stream, or for preamble symbol stream at the receiver chain is expressed as follows:

$$R_i^{(m_R)} = \sum_{j=1}^{M_T} H_i^{(m_R j)} \cdot S_i^{(j)} + N_i \tag{1}$$

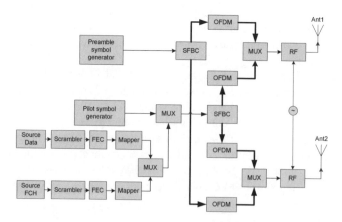

Fig. 1. Transmitter Block Diagram

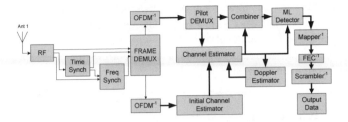

Fig. 2. Receiver Block Diagram

where i corresponds to the subcarrier index at the m_R-th receive antenna, j corresponds to the transmitter antenna index out of M_T transmit antennas ($M_T = 2$), N_i corresponds to additive complex Gaussian noise per subcarrier i with zero mean and variance σ_n^2. Also, $H_i^{(m_R j)}$ corresponds to the channel coefficient between the j-th transmit antenna and the m_R-th receive antenna for the i-th subcarrier [9].

The combiner outputs are fed to the maximum likelihood (ML) detector which estimates the most probable symbol stream according to the equation:

$$ J = \arg \min_{S_k \varepsilon C} = \sum_{k=1}^{N_c-1} \left\| R_k - \hat{H} \cdot S_k \right\|^2 \qquad (2) $$

where $C = [S_0, S_1, , S_{N-1}]$. Time and frequency synchronization are performed based on the time-correlation properties of the relative preamble (fig.3). The correction factor is fed back to the oscillator causing a delay. During this session, the analog automatic gain control (AGC) is adapted and remains constant during the subsequent frame period.

2.3   Channel Models

The evaluation of SFBC MIMO-OFDM scheme has been performed over realistic conditions taking into account not only the channel propagation characteristics, like time variability (Doppler shift) and multipath propagation (frequency selectivity), but also

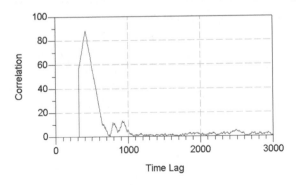

Fig. 3. Correlation of time synchronization preamble at the receiver

the correlations between the antennas at the transmitter and the receiver (described by Tx and Rx correlation matrices). The physical parameters used for link level modelling have been based on pedestrian level of mobility with line of sight (Rice factor K=6dB) according to the relative standard. Also, the proposed correlation values have been taken into account for an inter-element spacing of $\lambda/2$, where λ denotes the wavelength.

3   Channel Estimation

Channel state information (CSI) is acquired by the receiver on a two-step procedure (fig.2) whereas no CSI is fed back to the transmitter, establishing an open-loop system with equal transmission power on the antennas. The first step in the channel estimation procedure employs the OFDM preamble symbols which are orthogonal on a SFBC subcarrier basis. The estimation has been implemented using a MMSE approach. In the second step, the pilot symbols are used only for the phase estimation compensating the Doppler distortion. Then, using interpolation the correction factor for each subcarrier is taken into account in the preamble based estimation. The final channel estimates are used for both channel compensation and soft decision stages. Furthermore, Doppler estimation gives a figure of merit of the channel time variation which can be potentially used to increase the number of pilot symbols in time dimension or for adapting a higher order interpolation filter.

The MIMO channel estimation problem can be decomposed into several MISO channel estimations in parallel [9]. The initial channel estimation is based on the preamble OFDM symbols that have been transmitted from the 2 antennas in an orthogonal space-frequency format. Taking into account only the adjacent subcarriers i and $i + 1$ that convey pilot information in an orthogonal format it will be:

$$
\begin{aligned}
R_i^{(1)} &= H_i^{(11)} \cdot S_i^{(1)} + H_i^{(12)} \cdot S_i^{(2)} \\
R_{i+1}^{(1)} &= H_{i+1}^{(11)} \cdot S_{i+1}^{(1)} + H_{i+1}^{(12)} \cdot S_{i+1}^{(2)} \\
R_i^{(2)} &= H_i^{(21)} \cdot S_i^{(1)} + H_i^{(22)} \cdot S_i^{(2)} \\
R_{i+1}^{(2)} &= H_{i+1}^{(21)} \cdot S_{i+1}^{(1)} + H_{i+1}^{(22)} \cdot S_{i+1}^{(2)}
\end{aligned}
\tag{3}
$$

where $R_i^{(m_R)}$ is the received signal at m_R-th receive antenna in i-th subcarrier, $H_i^{(m_R m_T)}$ is the channel coefficient from the m_T-th transmit antenna to m_R-th receive antenna in i-th subcarrier, and $S_i^{(m_T)}$ is the transmitted symbol from m_T-th antenna in i-th subcarrier. Since, the Alamouti scheme has been adapted in space-frequency dimension the transmitted symbols in i-th and $(i + 1)$-th subcarriers will be: $P_a = S_i^{(1)}$, $P_a{}^* = S_{i+1}{}^{(2)}$, $P_b = S_i{}^{(2)}$, $-P_b{}^* = S_{i+1}{}^{(1)}$, where $(\cdot)^*$ denotes the complex conjugate operation. In addition, the channel is assumed constant for the subcarriers i and $i + 1$ giving:

$$
\begin{aligned}
H_i^{(11)} = H_{i+1}^{(11)} = H^{(11)}, \quad & H_i^{(21)} = H_{i+1}^{(21)} = H^{(21)} \\
H_i^{(12)} = H_{i+1}^{(12)} = H^{(12)}, \quad & H_i^{(22)} = H_{i+1}^{(22)} = H^{(2)}
\end{aligned}
\tag{4}
$$

Hence, eq.3 becomes:

$$\left.\begin{aligned}
R_i^{(1)} &= H^{(11)} \cdot P_a + H^{(12)} \cdot P_b \\
R_{i+1}^{(1)} &= -H^{(11)} \cdot P_b^* + H^{(12)} \cdot P_a^* \\
R_i^{(2)} &= H^{(21)} \cdot P_a + H^{(22)} \cdot P_b \\
R_{i+1}^{(2)} &= -H^{(21)} \cdot P_b^* + H^{(22)} \cdot P_a^*
\end{aligned}\right\} \Rightarrow$$

$$\begin{aligned}
R_i^{(1)} &= H^{(11)} \cdot P_a + H^{(12)} \cdot P_b \\
R_{i+1}^{(1)*} &= H^{(12)*} \cdot P_a - H^{(11)*} \cdot P_b \\
R_i^{(2)} &= H^{(21)} \cdot P_a + H^{(22)} \cdot P_b \\
R_{i+1}^{(2)*} &= H^{(22)*} \cdot P_a - H^{(21)*} \cdot P_b
\end{aligned}$$

(5)

Expressing the above formula in matrix notation, it will be:

$$\begin{bmatrix} R_i^{(1)} \\ R_{i+1}^{(1)*} \\ R_i^{(2)} \\ R_{i+1}^{(2)*} \end{bmatrix} = \begin{bmatrix} H^{(11)} & H^{(12)} \\ H^{(12)*} & -H^{(11)*} \\ H^{(21)} & H^{(22)} \\ H^{(22)*} & -H^{(21)*} \end{bmatrix} \cdot \begin{bmatrix} P_a \\ P_b \end{bmatrix}$$

(6)

$$\Leftrightarrow \mathbf{R}_p = \mathbf{H}_p \cdot \mathbf{S}$$

where the index p denotes the processed nature of the relative receive vector and the channel matrix. The matrix $\mathbf{H}_p$ has unitary properties, i.e.

$$\mathbf{H}_p^H \cdot \mathbf{H}_p =$$
$$\left(\left| H^{(11)} \right|^2 + \left| H^{(12)} \right|^2 + \left| H^{(21)} \right|^2 + \left| H^{(22)} \right|^2 \right) \cdot \mathbf{I}_2$$

(7)

$$= \mu \cdot \mathbf{I}_2$$

where $\mathbf{I}_2$ is the identity matrix of dimension 2, and $(\cdot)^H$ denotes the conjugate transpose matrix operation. For the case of perfect channel knowledge at the receiver, the output of the combiner representing the decision statistics (soft decisions) are given as follows:

$$\tilde{\mathbf{S}} = \frac{1}{\mu} \mathbf{H}_p^H \cdot \mathbf{R}_p = \frac{1}{\mu} \mathbf{H}_p^H \cdot (\mathbf{H}_P \cdot \mathbf{S} + \mathbf{N}) \Leftrightarrow$$
$$\tilde{\mathbf{S}} = \mathbf{S} + \mathbf{N}_m$$

(8)

which indicates that except the noise term the symbols have been recovered at the combiner's output. In a real system the MIMO channel has been estimated at the receiver non perfectly giving the following soft decision metric:

$$\tilde{\mathbf{S}} = \frac{1}{\mu} \hat{\mathbf{H}}_p^H \cdot \mathbf{R}_p = \frac{1}{\mu} \hat{\mathbf{H}}_p^H \cdot (\mathbf{H}_p \cdot \mathbf{S} + \mathbf{N}) \Leftrightarrow$$
$$\tilde{\mathbf{S}} = \mathbf{H}_{res} \cdot \mathbf{S} + \mathbf{N}_m$$

(9)

where the subscript res indicates the residual channel effect that have to be compensated by the ML decoder. In case of significant temporal channel variation during the transmission of an orthogonal scheme, the orthogonality is lost causing intersymbol interference. Hence, in order to preserve the orthogonality, the sampling theorem has to be applied determining the relative distances in time and frequency dimension that the pilots have to be placed. In space-time block codes the distance is proportional to the coherence time, while in space-frequency block coding is proportional to the coherence bandwidth. The channel tracking is performed through the phase estimation at the pilot positions based on the ML criterion according to the equation:

$$\hat{\theta}_c = \arg\min_{\angle \hat{H}} \sum_{i=1}^{8} \hat{H}_i \cdot \hat{H}_i^{(pre)*} \tag{10}$$

where $\hat{H}_i$ and $\hat{H}_i^{(pre)}$ are the current channel estimates at pilot positions and the estimates at the same subcarrier i during the preamble OFDM symbol respectively. The estimated phase difference updates the preamble based estimation. The final channel estimates at the pilot positions are interpolated (linearly in our case) in order to obtain the estimates in all subcarriers. A sample of the channel compensated symbols, just before the detector, is given in fig.4, where the blue dots are the transmitted ones before the SFBC encoder. The specific snapshot corresponds to a 2×2 MIMO-OFDM system with 16QAM and total coding (RS-CC) 3/4 in a channel type A (802.16e, 3GPP standard) operating in $E_b/N_o = 15$dB. In addition, QPSK modulation is observed due to the FCH symbols. Quantitatively, the maximum achievable diversity order is a product of the number of transmit antennas, the number of receive antennas, and the number of resolvable paths [3].

4   Evaluation Results

To study the impact of realistic channel estimation architecture on MIMO-OFDM performance, a 2×1 and 2×2 MIMO-OFDM system with orthogonal space frequency design has been designed, modelled and simulated, taking into account all stages in RF, IF and baseband level, as well as their relative requirements.

The simulated system achieves information data rates of 6.9Mbps at BPSK-1/2, of 13.8Mbps at QPSK-1/2, of 20.7Mbps at QPSK-3/4, of 27.7Mbps at 16QAM-1/2, of

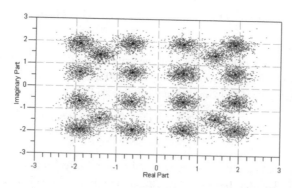

Fig. 4. Constellation map of the channel compensated symbols (red) with respect to the transmitted ones (blue)

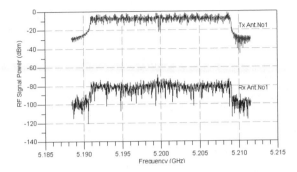

Fig. 5. Frequency spectrum at the Tx antenna (red) and the corresponding Rx one (blue) for 2×2 OFDM system

41.5Mbps at 16QAM-3/4, of 55.3Mbps at 64QAM-2/3, and of 62.2Mbps at 64QAM-3/4 in a frequency bandwidth of 20MHz at a center frequency of 5.2GHz. The relative frequency spectrum at a transmit antenna and a receive antenna is given in fig.5 for the 16QAM-3/4 case in a propagation channel of type A (802.16e) and for $E_b/N_o = 10$dB. The frequency selectivity is obvious, as well as the noise distortion is becoming quite severe.

The channel adaptation is based on 8 pilot symbols per OFDM symbol placed in blocks of 2 adjacent subcarriers. OFDM stages are based on a 256-point FFT/IFFT with cyclic prefix of 1/4. Each frame carries 2400 information bits and the evaluation is performed on the basis of achieving BER estimation relative variance of 0.0001 with an upper limit of 1000 frames.

The performance of the channel estimator with respect to the actual channel propagation conditions is based on normalized mean square error (NMSE), according to the formula (11) and the results are given in fig.6 for the 2×2 MIMO-OFDM case and for various propagation channels and data rates. Based on these results the channel estimator is characterized by an irreducible error floor at 3dB, achieving the limit at $E_b/N_o = 13$dB for all schemes and channel conditions tested.

$$NMSE = \frac{E\left[\left|H_i^{m_R m_T} - \hat{H}_i^{m_R m_T}\right|^2\right]}{E\left[\left|H_i^{m_R m_T}\right|^2\right]} \tag{11}$$

The total system performance of 2×1 and 2×2 MIMO-OFDM system has been evaluated based on the information bit error rate giving an insight at the sensitivity of the channel estimation errors in the efficiency of the system. For the probability of error P_e measurement to be statistically significant, the relative variance R_{var} of P_e is taken into account for N_t transmitted bits indicating the confidence interval of P_e. In fig.7 the probability of error has been produced for 2×1 case, in channel type A of 802.16e for all the modulation formats and coding modes. It is worth noticing that for the information data rate of 6.9Mbps a value of $E_b/N_o = 4.5$dB is enough to achieve $Pe = 10^{-4}$, while the same value for 62.2Mbps requires almost 10dB increase in E_b/N_o.

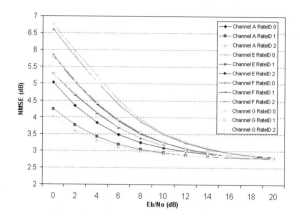

Fig. 6. Normalized MSE of the overall channel estimation in various propagation channels and data rates for 2×2 MIMO-OFDM case

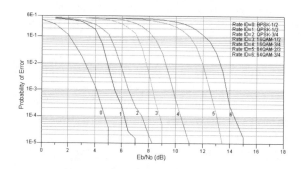

Fig. 7. Probability of error for a 2×1 OFDM system in propagation channel type A

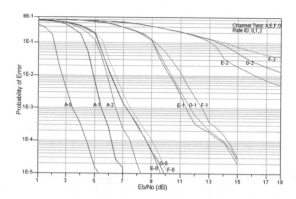

Fig. 8. Performance of a 2×1 OFDM system in various propagation channels and data rates

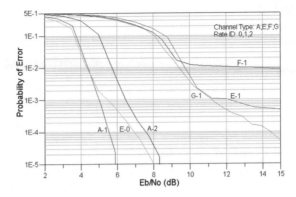

Fig. 9. Performance evaluation of a 2×2 OFDM system

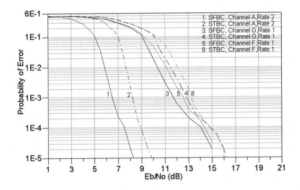

Fig. 10. Comparison between SFBC (solid) and STBC (dash) schemes for 2×1 case

In fig.8 the performance of a 2×1 OFDM system has been evaluated for various channel types of 802.16e standards. The system performs better for channel type A, but for more demanding channels (E,F,G), with higher mobility or frequency selectivity, the system fails to support increased data rates in relatively small values E_b/N_o.

In fig.9 the performance of 2×2 MIMO OFDM system has been depicted for various propagation channels and data rates indicating that the proposed scheme is quite efficient in propagation channels that follow the channel models of type A, E, or G. Furthermore, the proposed scheme is characterized by bit error rate achievable floors as E_b/N_o increases in channel models with increased frequency selectivity.

Finally, for comparison reasons, the system has been also implemented with space-time block coding (STBC) and for the 2×1 OFDM case the results are given in fig.10. The performance gain for the SFBC scheme at a probability of error $P_e = 10^{-3}$ is about 2dB for a data rate of 20.7Mbps in a channel of type A, whilst for 13.8Mbps the gain is about 1.5dB in channels of types G and F.

5 Conclusions

In this paper a MIMO multicarrier system has been designed and evaluated giving rise to space-frequency orthogonality. In addition, all the RF stages at the transmitter and the receiver were taken into account approaching a real architecture as close as possible. An efficient channel estimation scheme was incorporated in the system achieving not only a good efficiency, but also low computational requirements since the processing is performed in one OFDM symbol and the channel estimation during the frame is limited only in the varying propagation characteristics. The overall system performance of SFBC MISO/MIMO OFDM was evaluated for various propagation channels resulting in very good performances for propagation conditions that are characterized by low frequency selectivity, since the pilot overhead is only 3.12%.

References

1. Adjoudani, A., et al.: Prototype Experience for MIMO BLAST Over Third-Generation Wireless System. IEEE Journal on Selected Areas in Communications 21(3), 440–451 (2003)
2. Tarokh, V., Seshadri, N., Calderbank, A.: Space-Time Codes for High Data Rate Wireless Communication: Performance Criterion and Code Construction. IEEE Trans of Information Theory 44, 744–765 (1998)
3. Bolcskei, H., Paulraj, A.: Space-Frequency Codes for Broadband Fading Channels. In: IEEE International Symposium on Information Theory, June 2001, p. 219 (2001)
4. Tarokh, V., Jafarkhani, H., Calderbank, A.: Space-Time Block Codes for orthogonal designs. IEEE Trans of Information Theory 45, 1456–1467 (1999)
5. Li, Y., Seshadri, N., Ariyavisitakul, S.: Channel Estimation for OFDM Systems with Transmitter Diversity in Mobile Wireless Channels. IEEE Journal of Selected Areas in Communications 17(3), 461–471 (1999)
6. 3GPP TR 25.996 v6.1.0, Spatial Channel Model for Multiple-Input Multiple Output Simulations (2003-2009)
7. IEEE Std 802.16.2-2004, Recommended Practice for Local and metropolitan area networks (March 17, 2004)
8. Alamouti, S.: A Simple Transmit Diversity Technique for Wireless Communications. Journal of Selected Areas in Communications 16(8) (October 1998)
9. Stuber, G., Barry, J., Mclaughlin, S., Li, Y., Ingram, M., Pratt, T.: Broadband MIMO-OFDM Wireless Communications. Proceedings of the IEEE 92(2) (February 2004)
10. Agilent, MIMO Wireless LAN PHY Layer [RF] Operation & Measurement, Application Note 1509 (September 16, 2005)

A New Signal Detection Method for TR-UWB: By Time Delayed Sampling and Correlation (TDSC)

Muriel Muller, Yang Ni, Roger Lamberti, and Charbel Saber

GET-Institut National des Télécommunications 9,
rue Charles Fourier 91011 Evry France
{muriel.muller,yang.ni}@int-evry.fr

Abstract. This paper introduces a new signal detection method for Low cost, Low power and Low complexity (L3) TR-UWB systems for medium to low data rate applications such as sensors networks. This new detection method is based on a time_to_space conversion realizable by an analog waveform sampler. This method overcomes the major difficulties in a traditional TR-UWB detection methods based on wide band delay lines. Finally the relaxed timing precision needed in symbol synchronization contributes further to lower the system power consumption. This concept has been validated by simulation with real data from experimental setup. The results will be presented and compared also with other solutions.

Keywords: Ultra-Wideband (UWB) communications, Transmitted Reference (TR) UWB, non-coherent detection.

1 Introduction

Many applications [8], [11], [16] require low cost, low power and low complexity (L3) short range wireless communications means. Most of the current wireless communications systems are designed for the data transmission in a computer related context and do not satisfy completely these criteria. Our motivation in this research activity is to design wireless communications devices with L3 characteristics based on Impulse Radio (IR) UWB concept. The apparent hardware simplicity of an UWB system hides a lot of design challenges [1]. The high switching speed for the short duration UWB signal generation and the high timing resolution for UWB signal detection and synchronization between transmission and reception generate a considerable extra hardware complexity associated with very important power consumption overhead.

In an impulse radio based UWB system, the pulse generation can be implemented by using fast switching devices such step recovery diode (SRD) with a reasonable power consumption and complexity. This is not the case for UWB pulse detection.

Two main UWB detection methods can be distinguished.

The coherent detection method, based on a signal correlation between the incoming UWB signal and a local generated template [15], [9], is requiring channel estimation.

The other one is based on non-coherent energy detection method [2], [14]

J. Filipe and M.S. Obaidat (Eds.): ICETE 2006, CCIS 9, pp. 301–311, 2008.

Theoretically speaking the coherent method gives better detection result than that of the non-coherent one.

But in reality, the high precision synchronization and local template generation in a multi-path environment are extremely difficult to be implemented with simple hardware.

Many UWB receivers use some number of analog correlators to collect the signal energy in front-end rake receiver architecture. The need to capture a large amount of the transmitted energy involves to use a great number of paths, besides the propagation which deforms the pulses shape, path to path, leads to a very high complexity both on hardware and software (estimation channel) [3].

Some non-coherent detection based simple systems use signal energy detection which consists of measuring the energy in the incoming signal. The detection efficiency of this method is conditioned by the degree of the temporal energy concentration of an UWB signal. This detection method is usually implemented by using fast switching devices such as Schottky diodes or tunnel-effect diodes.

In spite of obvious hardware simplicity, this type of methods presents several limitations. The necessary low-pass post-filtering decreases considerably the amplitude of the signal at the output of the detector, spreads out this same signal over the axis of time. This leads to a much lower temporal discrimination power than that of initial UWB impulses and results in an unacceptably low sensitivity. Fig. 1 gives the comparison between the instant signal power and the low pass filtered signal. We can observe an important loss of signal amplitude due to the energy dilution in time.

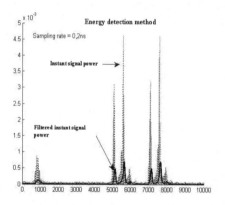

Fig. 1. Energy detection systems

From these observations, we think that the Transmitted-Reference (TR) UWB architecture [13], [6] could be a solution to our L3 UWB systems for several reasons. Firstly in TR-UWB system, each transmitted signal pulse is preceded or followed by a reference pulse. Due to the short time duration between these pulses, the propagation channel can be considered as constant and the two pulses will keep a strong correlation at the reception point even in a strong multi-path environment. So the TR-UWB signal can be detected by using a pseudo coherent scheme where the TR-UWB signal is correlated with a time delayed copy of this signal as shown in Fig. 2. Secondly the time delay between the signal pulse and the reference pulse can be seen as a parameter of signal diversification for channel coding and multiplexing. Besides TR-UWB can be as efficient as Rake-receiver for energy collection [17], but with a much simpler hardware.

Despite the advantages of TR-UWB, the major difficulty in the realization is the broadband delay line with wide bandwidth, highly linear phase, perfect impedance adaptation and highly stable delay [5]. An implementation using transmission line presents several problems, especially the delay precision and stability. The lack of real-time programmability is another limitation in a real exploitation of TR-UWB. Moreover, a real transmission line presenting an exploitable delay value remains impossible to integrate in a miniature circuit simply because of its physical dimension.

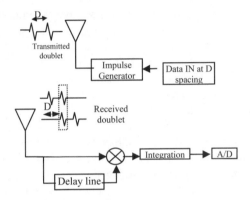

Fig. 2. Simplified TR-UWB communication system

In this article we proposed a very different approach based on a time-space conversion using an analog sampler. The TR-UWB signal is sampled by two analog waveform samplers with pre-defined delay which matches the time delay between the pulses in a TR-UWB frame. The signal detection will be done by applying a waveform correlation between the two TR-UWB signal samples. We called this new concept for UWB data transmission, the Time Delayed Sampling and Correlation (TDSC) which will be detailed in section II. In section III, we will report the first experimental validation results made in different propagation conditions. These results demonstrate the potential advantages of this TDSC concept in L3 UWB communications systems. Finally in section IV, we will give some conclusions and perspectives in this research works.

2   TDSC - A New Approach for TR-UWB Signal Detection

Recently, other fields such as the physics of high energy particles use high speed waveform samplers in order to capture and record highly impulsive signals from different detectors. These signals have the similar temporal and electrical properties as those of UWB. The most significant work is done by [7] in CMOS technology. The realized circuit can capture several hundred points of a signal at 10 GHz sampling rate.

Our proposed TDSC detection scheme is highly inspired from this work. The analog waveform sampler as shown in Fig. 4 uses an asynchronous delay line composed of simple inverters to generate the sampling commands at the different moments. This asynchronous implementation permits a sampling rate much higher with much lower power consumption than that of a synchronous design by using a global and explicit clock.

By using two waveform samplers as shown in Fig. 3, one is activated at the instant T and the other at T+D, two time delayed and sampled waveforms of a TR-UWB signal can be obtained. If a TR-UWB signal pulses fall in these sampling windows, we will have two similar waveforms because the double pulses in a TR-UWB frame have the same waveform distortion after the propagation in a time invariant channel as explained in section I. The absence of TR-UWB signal will result in two totally independent waveforms from the samplers. By consequent, the TR-UWB signal detection here can be easily done by using a simple correlation operation between the time delayed sampled waveforms. This principle is called Time Delayed Sampling and Correlation. Fig. 5 gives a graphical representation of this detection concept.

By using this method, we can see that the TR-UWB will be sampled twice with a constant time delay. The role of the broadband delay line is replaced by a time delayed double sampling which removes completely the need of an explicit analog signal delay line and all the design difficulties associated with. In this case, the delay is only applied to the sampler's command digital signals, which can be generated easily and programmably in real-time from the system clock with an extremely high precision and high stability. So the parameter D in TR-UWB can be used for channel coding and multiplexing. Fig. 3 gives the overall structure of TDSC [12].

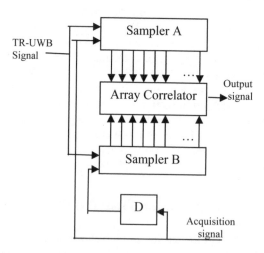

Fig. 3. General scheme of Time Delayed Sample & Correlation system, based on two samplers temporally delayed

Acquisition signal

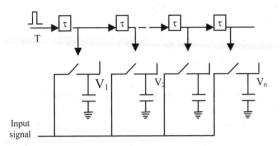

Fig. 4. The principle of an asynchronous delay line based analog waveform sampler

The TDSC detection cannot be done continuously in time. So a synchronisation be-tween the TDSC operation and the incoming TR-UWB signal is needed. But in con-trast to other detection methods [15] TDSC method imposes much lower constraint on the precision of this synchronisation. As shown in Fig. 5, when the UWB pulses fall inside the sampling windows, it can be detected reliably.

This means that the timing precision for this synchronisation is indexed at the TR-UWB frame duration which is much larger than that for pulse detection.

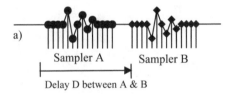

Waveforms of the Time Delayed Sampled TR-UWB signal

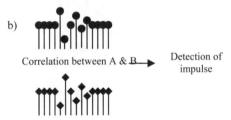

Signal detection by the Correlation between the Time Delayed
Samples

Fig. 5. Principle of TDSC method. a) Waveforms of the time delayed sampled TR-UWB sig-nals captured by the samplers A and B. b) The detection of impulse doublet is obtained with a simple correlation operation of the two delayed sampled waveforms.

This low timing precision necessary in detection synchronisation reduces not only considerably the signal acquisition time but also the complexity of synchronisation track-ing. This characteristic is particularly interesting for sensor networks like applications where the data transmission is sporadic with very low duty cycle. The fast acquisition and tracking can reduce significantly the system power consumption by reducing the activation time which is often conditioned by acquisition time for small data packages.

3 Experimental Validation

TDSC detection method has been validated by using simulation on the data captured from an experimental setup. This experimental setup gives realistic input signals for the TDSC simulation program in order to be as close as possible to the real TR-UWB working conditions. The results of the validation give some design guide to further VLSI implementation.

3.1 Experimentation Setup

The experimentation setup is shown in Fig. 6. We used a off the shelf pulse generator in order to generate a rectangular pulses train as shown in Fig. 7. The symmetric rising and falling edge transition time is less than 5ns (Pulse Generator E-H research laboratories model 137A), and we set the rectangular pulse width to 100 ns.

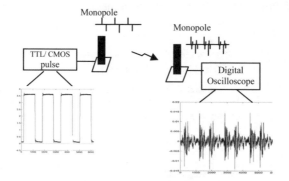

Fig. 6. Experimentation setup: A off the shelf pulse generator, two monopole antennas and a digital oscilloscope as sampler, were used

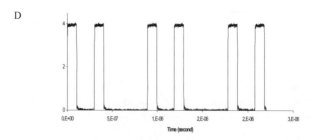

Fig. 7. Rectangular input signal. The temporal delay D between the two pulses of the doublet is around 100ns. Two doublets will be separated by 300ns. A silence space between two couple of doublets is equal to 500ns.

A simple thick monopole antenna has been used for this experimentation. The inevitable ringing in this kind of antenna permits to test the tolerance of TDSC detection method vis-à-vis to the impedance adaptation problems in real implementation. Monopole antennas will reshape the digital pulses into wide band limited pulses. So the rising and falling edges of each digital pulse will generate an impulse doublet with opposite polarities and a temporal delay D corresponding to the digital pulse width. Then, the impulse doublets are sent, propagated in an indoor environment and received by a digital oscilloscope with memory of 300MHz bandwidth. An example of the captured TR-UWB signal is shown in Fig. 8. Finally, we use the Matlab software to simulate the TDSC detection method on these sampled TR-UWB signals.

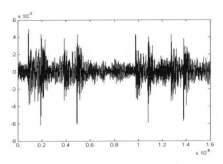

Fig. 8. Real output doublets sampled and recorded thanks to a digital oscilloscope. The reference pulse and the data pulse are separated by a temporal delay D.

3.2 Experimentation Results

In the TDSC principle, the TR-UWB signal detection is done by correlating two temporally delayed sampled TR-UWB signal. This is simulated by applying cross-correlation function to two temporal windows on the recorded TR-UWB signal. These temporal windows correspond to the double time delayed waveform samplers.

In order to skip at first the problem of synchronisation, these windows will slide on the recorded TR-UWB signal in a contiguous way, as shown in Fig. 9-a. In the same figure (Fig. 9-b), the result of the simulated TDSC detection method with a TR-UWB signal sampled at 5 GHz rate (200ps), is represented. It is demonstrated that the basic cross correlation function gives a satisfied results and the virtually null output during TR-UWB signal absence makes the decision threshold setting very easy.

In order to evaluate the performance of TDSC method, different configurations and parameters have been tested.

In the above example, the receiving antenna was placed 250 cm away from the transmitting antenna with the same height.

Many others measurements were carried out where the distance varied from 80 cm to 5 meters, with constant emission power. The sampling rate also varied from 200ps to 2ns. For all these cases, the TDSC method gave very good detection performance. Note that above a 2ns sampling rate, the TDSC detection failed. This is consistent with Shannon theorem.

These results are very promising for the TDSC concept and the future realization circuits. Based on these promising results we decided to investigate others properties of TDSC method.

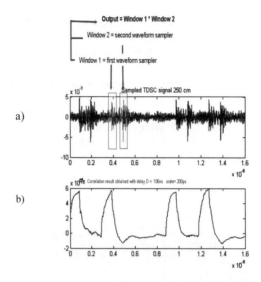

Fig. 9. a) Principle of the algorithm used to validate the TDSC concept. One sampling window is sliding on another window about a fixed temporal delay equal to D. b) Correlation result between the two sampled signals. Here the sampling rate was equal to 0,2ns.

3.2.1 Synchronisation Tolerance and Temporal Discrimination

The high speed impulses used in IR-UWB need a high precision temporal synchronisation between the transmitter and the receiver. In a classic IR-UWB system, this temporal synchronisation precision should be higher than the minimum pulse width. This requirement represents one of the major challenges in a real hardware implementation.

In the TDSC method, the detection can be effective when the impulse doublet falls inside the temporal sampling windows. This means that the temporal synchronisation precision is indexed to the symbol rate but not that of individual impulses. The maximum width of the sampling window is to the delay D and this gives a large synchronisation facility and tolerance.

But another interesting point here is that this large synchronisation tolerance has no impact on the temporal discrimination power of the TDSC detection because the temporal discrimination power of the TDSC method is conditioned by the cross-correlation function applied onto the sampled signals. This high temporal discrimination capability is illustrated by the following aspect: - the separation between two pulses inside a TR-UWB doublet.

In order to code one data bit, two pulses are transmitted, separated by a known delay D. This delay can be seen as selectivity parameter (similar to frequency in a frequency division system) at the reception. A high selectivity based on this parameter can not only reduce noise but also give higher channel capacity for coding and multiaccess.

In order to validate this selectivity, we carried out simulations by varying the delay D at TDSC detection stage for a recorded TR-UWB signal with D=127ns at transmission here. We varied the value of D +/-10 sampling points around its nominal value.

The simulation result is shown in Fig. 10. Here the sampling period is 200ps, the temporal discrimination can be evaluated at +/-2ns.

This characteristic can not be found in other detection methods. For example, an energy detector integrates all incoming energies and results in a low temporal discrimination. Besides, some information on the incoming signal can be lost, such as pulse polarity. The coherent detection method gives a theoretically better performance but the difficulties in the local template generation and ultra-high precision synchronisation make it impractical in simple low cost and low power systems.

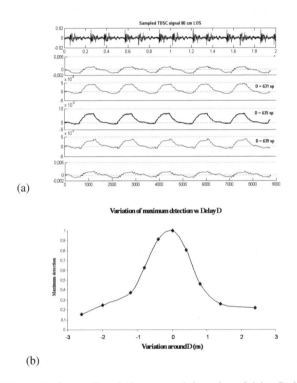

(a)

(b)

Fig. 10. a) TDSC results for small variations around the value of delay D. b) The variation of the maximum detection versus D.

3.2.2 Detection and MP Energy Collection under LOS and NLOS Contexts

We conducted experiments with and without a line of sight propagation path in order to evaluate the performance of TDSC detection in the two cases. For the first case (Fig. 11), the two monopole antennas are in line-of-sight, at a distance of about 2,50 meters. The second case (Fig. 12), is performed with a metallic obstacle between the two monopole antennas, in order to obtain a non line-of-sight scheme.

In a multi-path (NLOS) context, the received TR-UWB impulse doublets can be strongly confused together as shown by the upper waveform in Fig. 12. When the

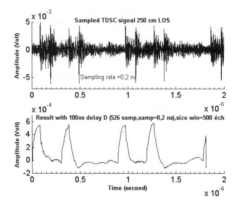

Fig. 11. Simulation result for LOS experiment

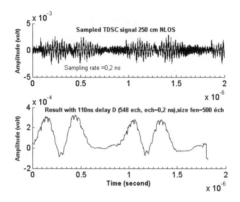

Fig. 12. Simulation result for NLOS experiment

TDSC method is applied to this signal, the successive TR-UWB doublet can be clearly separated and detected, despite the energy spreading as shown in the lower waveform in Fig. 12.

4   Conclusion and Perspectives

In this paper, we have introduced a new TR-UWB signal detection concept -The Time Delayed Sampled and Correlation (TDSC). This method has been presented in details and validated experimentally. This detection method gives numerous advantages such as large synchronisation tolerance, high multipath signal energy collection efficiency in strong multi-path environment, high signal selectivity and modular CMOS friendly design with low power consumption, etc. Actually this validation has been done in 300MHz band, a CMOS waveform sampler circuit capable to operate at 10GHz is on the way and this circuit will permit a full validation at the lower end of FCC UWB band. In parallel, the theoretical investigations on this method by using different channel models proposed by IEEE P802.15-WPANs [4], [10] are on the way.

References

1. Bettayeb, M., Shah, S.F.A.: State of the art ultra-wideband technology for communication systems: a review. In: Proceedings of the 2003 10th IEEE International Conference on Electronics, Circuits and Systems, vol. 3, pp. 1276–1279 (2003)
2. Doré, J.B., Uguen, B., Paquelet, S., Mallégol, S.: UWB Non-Coherent High Data Rates Transceiver Architecture and Implementation. In: International workshop on convergent technologies (IWCT) (2005)
3. Durisi, G., Benedetto, S.: Comparison between coherent and noncoherent receivers for UWB communications. EURASIP journal on applied signal processing UWB state of the art 3, 1–9 (2005)
4. Foerster, J.: Channel Modeling Sub-committee Report Final, IEEE P802.15-02/490r2-SG3a, 2003 IEEE P802.15 Working Group for Wireless Personal Area Networks (WPANs) (2003)
5. Goeckel Dennis, L., Zhang, Q.: Slightly Frequency-Shifted Transmitted-Reference Ultrawideband Radio: TR-UWB without the Delay Element. In the 2005 IEEE Military Communications Conference (MILCOM 2005) (2005)
6. Hoctor, R., Tomlinson, H.: Delayed-hopped transmitted-reference RF communications. IEEE Conference on UWB systems and technologies, 265–270 (2002)
7. Kleinfelder, S.: GHz Waveform Sampling and Digitization Circuit Design and implementation. IEEE Transactions on Nuclear Science 50(4) (2003)
8. Metha, V., Zarki, M.E.: An Ultra Wide Band (UWB) based Sensor Network for Civil Infrastructure Health Monitoring. EWSN (2004)
9. Mielczarek, B., Wessman, M.O., Svensson, A.: Performance of coherent UWB Rake receivers with channel estimators. In Vehicular Technology Conference. In: IEEE 58th, vol. 3, pp. 1880–1884 (2003)
10. Molisch, A., Foerster, J.R.F., Pendergrass, M.: Channel models for ultrawideband personal area networks. Wireless Communications 10(6), 14–21 (2003)
11. Oppermann, I., Stoica, L., et al.: UWB Wireless Sensor Networks: UWEN — A Practical Example. Communications Magazine, IEEE 42(12), S27 - S32 (2004)
12. NI, Y.: Récepteur UWB et procédé et système de transmission de données. Brevet Français déposé par GET/INT 0500886 (2005)
13. Rushforth, C.K.: Transmitted-reference techniques for random or unknown channels. IEEE Trans. Inf. Theory 10(1), 39–42 (1964)
14. Stoica, L., Tiuraniemi, S., Oppermann, I.: An ultra-wideband low complexity circuit transceiver architecture for sensor networks. In: Circuits and Systems, ISCAS. IEEE International Symposium on, pp. 364–367 (2005)
15. Time Domain, PulsON Technology Overview, Time Domain (2001), http://www.timedomain.com
16. Duo, X., Torikka, T., Zheng, L.-R., Ismail, M., Tenhunen, H., Tjukanoff, E.: A DC-13 GHz LNA for UWB RFID applications. In: Norchip Conference, 2004. Proceedings, 8-9, pp. 241–244 (2004)
17. Zasowski, T., Althaus, F., Wittneben, A.: An Energy Efficient Transmitted-Reference Scheme for Ultra Wideband Communications. In: International Workshop on Ultra Wideband Systems (IWUWBS) Joint with Conference on Ultra Wideband Systems and Technologies (UWBST), Kyoto, Japan (2004)

Image Transmission with Adaptive Power and Rate Allocation over Flat Fading Channels Using Joint Source Channel Coding

Greg H. Håkonsen, Tor A. Ramstad, and Anders Gjendemsjø

Department of Electronics and Telecommunications
Norwegian University of Science and Technology
O.S. Bragstads plass 2B, 7491 Trondheim, Norway
{hakonsen,ramstad,gjendems}@iet.ntnu.no

Abstract. A joint source channel coder (JSCC) for image transmission over flat fading channels is presented. By letting the transmitter have information about the channel, and by letting the code-rate vary slightly around a target code-rate, it is shown how a robust image coder is obtained by using time discrete amplitude continuous symbols generated through the use of nonlinear dimension changing mappings. Due to their robustness these mappings are well suited for the changing conditions on a fading channel.

Keywords: Joint source channel coding, nonlinear mappings, fading channel, image coder.

1 Introduction

For transmission over wireless channels it is important to have a robust system as the channel conditions vary as a function of time. Traditional *tandem systems* use a channel code that is designed for a worst case *channel signal-to-noise ratio* (CSNR) where it can guarantee a *bit error rate* (BER) below a certain level. A source coder is then matched to the bit rate for which the channel code is designed. There are two main problems with this system. One is that this system breaks down very fast if the true CSNR falls below the design level. On the other hand, if the true CSNR is much higher than the design level, this system suffers from what is called the *leveling-off effect*. As the CSNR rises, the BER decreases, but the performance of the system remains constant after a certain threshold. This is due to the lossy part of the source coder: the design of the quantizer sets a certain distortion level which yields the target rate of the channel code.

To increase the average bit rate over a channel, one strategy is to divide the CSNR range into a set of regions and use different constellations for the different regions, see e.g. [1]. This does not, however, combat the problem that most channel codes need to group very long bit sequences into blocks to perform well. So switching fast between these constellations becomes a problem.

Shannon's *separation theorem* [2], says that a source coder and channel coder can be separately designed and still obtain an optimal communication system. To achieve this, the two coders have to have infinite complexity and infinite delay. When taking

J. Filipe and M.S. Obaidat (Eds.): ICETE 2006, CCIS 9, pp. 312–321, 2008.

complexity and delay into account, *joint source channel coding* (JSCC) is a promising solution. The idea in JSCC is to optimize the source and channel codes together, and in that manner make the source information better adapted to the channel. Work on JSCC can be split into three main categories, one is fully digital systems, where the different parts of the source is given unequal error protection (UEP) on the channel, see e.g. [3]. A second is hybrid digital-analog (HDA) systems, where some digital information is sent, but an analog component is sent as refinement, see e.g. [4]. In this paper the focus is on continuous amplitude systems, where the main information is sent without any kind of channel code. We use nonlinear Shannon mappings to adapt the transmission of an image over a flat fading channel without the use of any quantization or channel codes. This image communication system is partly based on the system presented for an *additive white Gaussian noise* (AWGN) channel in [5].

2   System Overview

The system considered in this paper is a joint source channel coder for image transmission over flat fading channels. The structure of the system is as seen in Figure 1.

We assume that the return channel from the receiver to the transmitter has no delay, so that the transmitter has the same information as the receiver about the channel. To be able to decode the main information, the receiver needs some side information. The side information sent from the transmitter is assumed to be error free. At least at high rates, the size of the side information will have little impact on the total bandwidth. Any further investigation of the size of the side information is outside the scope of this paper. Transmission and coding are based on the use of nonlinear dimension changing mappings. The properties for these mappings will not be analyzed here, but can be found in e.g., [5,6]. The channel samples are transmitted as amplitude continuous, time discrete PAM symbols. The mappings work by taking g *source samples* and represent these samples by b *channel samples*, where g and b are integers such that $\hat{r} = b/g$. The resulting ratio $\hat{r}$, will from now on be denoted as the rate of the mapping. A mapping of $\hat{r} = 2$ represents each source sample as 2 channel samples, thus adding redundancy to protect that sample.

A mapping of $\hat{r} = 1/2$ is shown in Figure 2. Compression is achieved by representing two source samples by one channel sample. A $2D$ vector composed of two source samples is represented by (*). This point is then mapped to the closest point on the

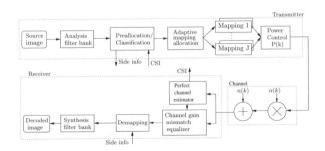

Fig. 1. Proposed image transmission system

spiral, represented by (o). This point will then be transmitted as a continuous amplitude PAM symbol. Points on the dotted line can be represented by negative channel
symbols, while points on the solid line can be represented by positive channel symbols.
Channel noise will move this point so that the received point will have a different value,
represented by ($\Diamond$). The total distortion in the reconstructed sample will be due to the
approximation and channel noise.

Figure 2 can also be used to explain a mapping of $\hat{r} = 2$. Letting the spiral represent
the source space, a source sample, represented by ($\Diamond$), can take any value along the
spiral. By representing this sample as a $2D$ vector, the value of each coordinate can be
transmitted as a continuous amplitude PAM symbol. After noise is added, the resulting
$2D$ vector has been moved in the noise-space, represented by (*). The receiver knows
that the original point has to be on the spiral, and maps it into the closest point along
the spiral, represented by (o).

Designing good mappings for large dimension changes is increasingly more difficult
as the dimensionality goes up, due to the high number of parameters that need to be
optimized, similar to vector quantization [7]. Due to this, the mappings we use in this
paper have rates

$$\hat{r}_j \in \{0, \frac{1}{4}, \frac{1}{2}, \frac{2}{3}, 1, 2\}, j = 0, \ldots, 5. \qquad (1)$$

Each mapping can be optimally designed for a set of given CSNRs, $\{\gamma_m\}_{m=1}^M$. The
obtained signal representations are robust, so the system improves and degrades the
performance gracefully around the design CSNR.

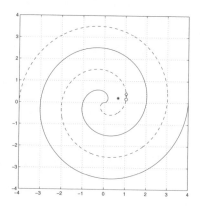

Fig. 2. Example of mapping with $r_j = \frac{1}{2}$. $2D$ input vector marked by (*) is mapped to the
closest point (o) in the channel space (the spiral). The channel noise will move the point along
the spiral ($\Diamond$).

2.1 Source Description

The source in this paper is an image which is decorrelated by using a *filter bank* designed by Balasingham in [8]. This filter bank consists of an 8×8 band uniform filter
bank, and three different 2×2 band filter banks, used in a tree structure so each filter

is applied to the low-low band of the previous stage. The filter bank is *maximally dec-imated* which keeps the number of pixels equal before and after filtering. Images have non-zero means, which implies a non-zero mean in the resulting low-low band, so to reduce the power of the image, the mean is subtracted from this band and sent as side information.

To cope with the local statistical differences within each band, the subband filtered image is split into N blocks. By using small blocks, the local statistics are captured better, but then the number of blocks will be larger, resulting in larger side informa-tion. To be able to decode the transmitted signal the receiver needs knowledge about the variances of all the source blocks. This information is sent as side information. Tak-ing practical considerations into account, we have found 8×8 subband pixels to be a suitable block size. The variance $\sigma^2_{X_n}$ of each block is estimated using the RMS value.

We assume that the transform coefficients within a block can be modeled by a Gaus-sian pdf [9]. For a given distortion μ, the block variance can then be used to find the rate (bits/source sample), for each sub-source(block) from the following expression [10],

$$R_n = \frac{1}{2} \log_2 \left(\frac{\sigma^2_{X_n}}{\sigma^2_{D_n}} \right) \text{ bits/source sample,} \tag{2}$$

where $\sigma^2_{D_n} = \min(\mu, \sigma^2_{X_n})$.

Assuming that all the N blocks are independent, the total average rate is given by

$$R = \frac{1}{2N} \sum_{n=0}^{N-1} \log_2 \left(\frac{\sigma^2_{X_n}}{\sigma^2_{D_n}} \right) \text{ bits/source sample.} \tag{3}$$

The overall *signal-to-noise ratio* (SNR) is given by

$$\text{SNR} = \frac{\sum_{n=0}^{N-1} \sigma^2_{X_n}}{\sum_{n=0}^{N-1} \sigma^2_{D_n}}. \tag{4}$$

By using (4), it is possible to find the value of μ that yields a wanted SNR. This can be the scenario if the receiver needs a certain quality in the received image. Another scenario is when there is a time requirement, i.e. the transmission has be be finished within a certain time. This will put a rate constraint on (3), and the corresponding μ for this rate needs to be found. Large values of μ imply that some of the source blocks are discarded according to rate distortion theory [10].

2.2 Channel Adaptation

We consider a frequency-flat fading channel where it is assumed that the received signal $y(k)$ can be written as

$$y(k) = \alpha(k)v(k) + n(k), \tag{5}$$

where $\alpha(k)$ is a stationary channel gain, $v(k)$ is the sent signal and $n(k)$ is AWGN.

Let $\bar{P}$ denote the average transmit power and $N_0/2$ be the noise density on the chan-nel of bandwidth B. The instantaneous CSNR, $\gamma(k)$, is defined as

$$\gamma(k) = \frac{\bar{P}|\alpha(k)|^2}{N_0 B}, \tag{6}$$

and let the expected value of the CSNR, $\bar{\gamma}$, be

$$\bar{\gamma} = \frac{\bar{P}}{N_0 B}. \tag{7}$$

To avoid an infinite amount of *channel state information* (CSI), the CSNR range is divided into $M + 1$ regions, similar to e.g. [1]. In this paper we choose to let a set of parameters $\{\gamma_m\}_{m=1}^M$ represent the different CSNR regions where we transmit, and let the region with worst CSNR represent outage. These regions will be denoted as channel states. The representation points γ_m, are placed inside each channel region similar to representation points in scalar quantization. The reason why this system is optimized for a representation point within a region instead of the edges which is common in *adaptive coded modulation* (ACM), is that the mappings used in this system degrades and improves gracefully in an area around the design CSNR instead of breaking down as is the case of conventional digital codes. So a mismatch between the CSNR for which a mapping is coded, and the actual CSNR, does not have so big impact as it would in traditional systems.

For a channel state γ_m, the instantaneous channel capacity is then given by, for $m = 1, \ldots, M$,

$$C_m = \frac{1}{2} \log_2 (1 + \gamma_m) \text{ bits/channel sample}. \tag{8}$$

2.3   Matching Source to Channel

Since the source is represented by source blocks, and the channel is divided into discrete channel states, it is interesting to look at the instantaneous rate, given by

$$r_{n,m} = \frac{\log_2 \left(\frac{\sigma_{X_n}^2}{\sigma_{D_n}^2} \right)}{\log_2 (1 + \gamma_m)} \text{channel/source samples}. \tag{9}$$

For a given channel state γ_m, (9) gives the rate-change needed to be able to transmit a source block with variance $\sigma_{X_n}^2$ and distortion μ. Using a continuous set of dimensional changing mappings is, however, highly impractical, so in practice $r_{n,m}$ has to be approximated to the closest match in (1). And since the mappings are not ideal, the actual performance of each mapping has to be considered.

To set up a reasonable strategy for source-channel adaptation, the different source blocks are *preallocated* to the different channel states so that the block with largest variance is matched with the best channel state. The preallocation is done using the long term statistics of the channel. For a single transmission the channel does not behave exactly according to the statistics. So if, during transmission, there are no more blocks preallocated to a given state, blocks from a better channel state are transmitted, but then a new mapping has to be used calculated from (9). In this way the system can adapt to the varying conditions of the channel.

2.4   Finding the Representation Points

Since the source blocks are preallocated to different channel states, it is natural to include them in the calculation of channel representation points γ_m. Finding the best representation points γ_m will also include finding the best thresholds $\hat{\gamma}_m$ that defines the different channel regions $R_m = \{\gamma : \hat{\gamma}_m < \gamma \leq \hat{\gamma}_{m+1}\}$.

Since the rate-change needed is given by the ratio between the source rate and instantaneous channel capacity, (9), it is natural to include this into the optimization problem. By looking at the total average rate-change needed in a given channel state m

$$r_{\mathrm{avg}_m}(\gamma_m) = \frac{\frac{1}{|I_m|} \sum_{n \in I_m} \log_2\left(\frac{\sigma_{X_n}^2}{\sigma_{D_n}^2}\right)}{\log_2(1 + \gamma_m)}, \tag{10}$$

where I_m is the set of source blocks allocated to the m'th channel state, we can find the mean squared error (MSE) denoted, ϵ, for all the M transmission channel states and all source blocks by

$$\epsilon = \sum_{m=1}^{M} \int_{R_m} \left(r_{\mathrm{avg}_m}(\gamma) - r_{\mathrm{avg}_m}(\gamma_m)\right)^2 p_\gamma(\gamma) d\gamma. \tag{11}$$

Minimization of ϵ with respect to R_m and γ_m has to be done through an iteration process, since the number of blocks in each channel state varies.

2.5 Optimization of Power Distribution

The mapping rate, $\hat{r}_n$, for each block, does not match the needed rate $r_{n,m}$ exactly. This leads to a variation in the resulting distortion that is not necessarily optimal. It is possible to minimize the distortion after the source blocks have been preallocated to a channel state and mapping rate by adjusting the power allocation. With a power constraint, and when taking the real distortions of each mapping into account, a Lagrangian can be set up

$$\mathcal{L} = \sum_{n=0}^{N-1} \sigma_{X_n}^2 D_n(P_n) + \lambda \frac{\sum_{n=0}^{N-1} P_n \hat{r}_n}{\Psi}, \tag{12}$$

where, for practical mappings, $D_n(P_n)$ is the tabulated distortion of the mapping the n'th block is given, with power P_n, and Ψ is the total rate given by

$$\Psi = \sum_{n=0}^{N-1} \hat{r}_n \left(1 + \frac{p_o}{p_t}\right), \tag{13}$$

where p_o and p_t are the probabilities of being in outage or transmit mode respectively.

To find the optimal P_n, (12) is differentiated and set to zero.

$$\frac{d\mathcal{L}}{dP_n} = \sigma_{X_n}^2 D_n'(P_n) + \frac{\lambda \hat{r}_n}{\Psi} = 0 \tag{14}$$

$$\Updownarrow$$

$$-D_n'(P_n) = \frac{\lambda \hat{r}_n}{\sigma_{X_n}^2 \Psi}. \tag{15}$$

The optimal λ, has to be found by checking the total power used by inserting the P_n^* from the optimal $D_n'(P_n)$ into

$$\bar{P} = \frac{\sum_{n=0}^{N-1} P_n^* \hat{r}_n}{\Psi}. \tag{16}$$

3   Reference System

To check the performance of the system we have chosen to compare with a traditional tandem source and channel coding system. As a source coder we have chosen to use JPEG2000 [11][1]. For transmission, the reference system employs an ACM scheme consisting of M transmission rates (bit/channel symbol), each assumed to achieve AWGN capacity for a given CSNR. To further maximize the *average spectral efficiency* (ASE) continuous power adaptation to is used within each CSNR region [12].

The examples of the proposed coder are given for a certain CSNR, $(\bar{\gamma})$, and an overall target compression-rate, r_{avg} (channel samples/pixel). To be able to compare with the reference system, a bitrate in bits/channel sample, R_c, is found for a given $\bar{\gamma}$ for the channel code, and the resulting source bitrate, R_s, in bits/pixel is found and given as a parameter to the reference image coder through

$$R_s = r_{avg} R_c. \tag{17}$$

4   Results

The following results are for images transmitted over a Rayleigh fading channel. The Doppler frequency is set to $f_d = 100$ Hz, and the carrier frequency, f_c, is set to 2 GHz, resulting in a mobile velocity of 15 m/s. The channel is simulated according to the Jakes' correlation model [13]. The number of channel states with transmission, M, is set to four for the proposed system and the reference system, thus allowing one outage state for both cases.

The quality of the received image is measured by *peak signal-to-noise ratio* (PSNR), defined as the ratio between the squared maximum pixel value, and the mean squared error (MSE) on a pixel basis for the whole image.

From Figure 3 and Figure 4 we see that the proposed system performs slightly poorer compared to the reference system. When comparing the two systems, it is however important to remember that the reference system uses near capacity achieving channel transmission. In practice the reference system would require infinite complexity and infinite delay.

Looking at robustness we can see from Figure 5, that even without any error protecting or correcting code, the robustness in the proposed system is quite high. Where as the reference channel transmission system will break down without perfect channel knowledge, the proposed system degrades gradually. In Figure 4, we have included the case where the transmitter does not have perfect channel knowledge. Two cases

---

[1] Version 5 of executables is downloaded from www.kakadusoftware.com

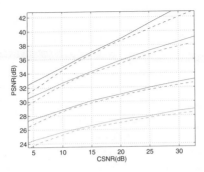

Fig. 3. Performance of proposed system (dashed) compared to reference system (solid). "Gold-hill" image. r_{avg} in channel samples/pixel, from below: $0.03, 0.1, 0.3, 0.5$.

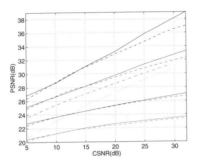

Fig. 4. Performance of proposed system (dashed) compared to reference system (solid). "Bridge" image. r_{avg} in channel sample/pixel, from below: $0.03, 0.1, 0.3, 0.5$. Proposed system for $r_{avg} = 0.3$ with channel information every 1000'th (dash-dotted), and 20000'th channel symbol (dotted).

are included, one where the transmitter only knows the channel state for every 1000'th channel symbol, and one for every 20000'th symbol. For $r_{avg} = 0.3$ the total number of channel symbols is about 78300 for a 512×512 image. We will however not analyze this any further in this paper. It should noted that the reference system uses an optimal threshold for outage, while the proposed system uses a fixed outage threshold of $\hat{\gamma}_1 = 2$ for simplicity.

It should be emphasized that the performance for the proposed system is an average. Due to the limited number of symbols needed to transmit an image, the channel will not be fully ergodic. The result of this can be seen in the distribution of the average rate r_{avg} in Figure 6. The assumed rate is based on the preallocation of the blocks, but since the probabilities of each channel state will vary, the number of channel symbols will also vary. Since r_{avg} varies, the actual CSNR will vary slightly as well. So when reading the results in Figure 3 and Figure 4, one should keep in mind that the CSNR and PSNR is plotted as an average. An estimated distributions of the PSNR for different r_{avg} is given in Figure 5.

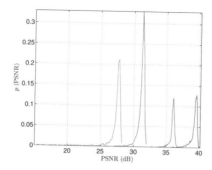

Fig. 5. Estimated distributions of PSNR for target average rate r_{avg}, from left: $0.03, 0.1, 0.3, 0.5$. For $\bar{\gamma} = 22$ dB. "Goldhill" image.

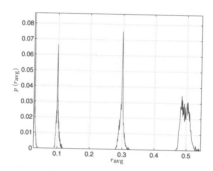

Fig. 6. Estimated distributions of average transmission rates r_{avg} for target average rate from left: $0.03, 0.1, 0.3, 0.5$. For $\bar{\gamma} = 22$ dB. "Goldhill" image.

In Figure 3 and Figure 4, it can be seen that the performance of the proposed coder is not parallel with the performance of the reference coder. For high CSNR values this is due to the number of mapping rates available is to low in the rate-range of 0 to 2. For low CSNR values, there is a need for mappings with rates higher than 2.

5   Conclusions

We have shown how a joint source channel image coder system can achieve robust performance for transmission over a Rayleigh fading channel, when allowing the average rate to vary slightly around a target rate. This is done by choosing nonlinear mappings best suited for the current channel condition, the importance of the transmitted image block, and by allocating the power to minimize the distortion. The proposed system has been shown to be comparable to a reference tandem system using capacity-approaching codes.

References

1. Holm, H., Øien, G.E., Alouini, M.-S., Gesbert, D., Hole, K.J.: Optimal design of adaptive coded modulation schemes for maximum spectral efficiency. In: Proc. Signal Processing Advances in Wireless Communications (SPAWC), pp. 403–407 (2003)
2. Shannon, C.E.: A mathematical theory of communication. Bell Syst. Tech. J. 27, 379–423 (1948)
3. Tanabe, N., Farvardin, N.: Subband image coding using entropy-coded quantization over noisy channels. IEEE J. Select. Areas Commun. 10, 926–943 (1992)
4. Mittal, U., Phamdo, N.: Hybrid digital-analog(hda) joint source-channel codes for broadcasting and robust communication. IEEE Trans. Inform. Theory 48, 1082–1102 (2002)
5. Coward, H., Ramstad, T.: Robust image communication using bandwidth reducing and expanding mappings. In: Conf. Record 34th Asilomar Conf. Signals, Syst., Comput., Pacific Grove, CA, USA, vol. 2, pp. 1384–1388 (2000)
6. Fuldseth, A., Ramstad, T.A.: Bandwidth compression for continuous amplitude channels based on vector approximation to a continuous subset of the source signal space. In: Proc. IEEE Int. Conf. on Acoustics, Speech, and Signal Proc (ICASSP), vol. 4, pp. 3093–3096 (1997)
7. Gersho, A., Gray, R.M.: Vector Quantization and Signal Compression. Kluwer Academic Publishers, Boston (1992)
8. Balasingham, I.: On Optimal Perfect Reconstruction Filter Banks for Image Compression. PhD thesis, Norwegian University of Science and Technology, Norway (1998)
9. Lervik, J.M., Ramstad, T.A.: Optimality of multiple entropy coder systems for nonstationary sources modeled by a mixture distribution. In: Proc. IEEE Int. Conf. on Acoustics, Speech, and Signal Proc (ICASSP), Atlanta, GA, USA, vol. 4, pp. 875–878. IEEE, Los Alamitos (1996)
10. Berger, T.: Rate Distortion Theory: A Mathematical Basis for Data Compression. Prentice Hall, Englewood Cliffs (1971)
11. Taubman, D., Marcellin, M.: JPEG 2000 Image compression fundamentals, standards and practice. Kluwer Academic Publishers, Dordrecht (2001)
12. Gjendemsjø, A., Øien, G.E., Holm, H.: Optimal power control for discrete-rate link adaptation schemes with capacity-approaching coding. In: Proc. IEEE Global Telecommunications Conference, St. Louis, MO, pp. 3498–3502 (2005)
13. Jakes, W.C.: Microwave Mobile Communication. Wiley, New York (1974)

Directional Spectrum Modelling in Inhomogeneous Forests at 20 and 62.4 GHz

Telmo R. Fernandes[1], Rafael F. S. Caldeirinha[1],
Miqdad O. Al-Nuaimi[2], and Jürgen Richter[2]

[1] ESTG-Leiria/Institute of Telecommunications-DL
Alto do Vieiro - Morro do Lena, 2411-911 Leiria, Portugal
telmo@estg.ipleiria.pt, rfcaldei@estg.ipleiria.pt
[2] Radiowave Propagation and System Design Research Unit, School of Electronics
University of Glamorgan, Treforest, CF37 1DL, United Kingdom
malnuaim@glam.ac.uk, jrichter@glam.ac.uk

Abstract. This paper presents a radiowave propagation model for inhomogeneous forests based on the Radiative Energy Transfer theory (RET) model. This model, which is a discretised version of the RET, is able to simulate the behaviour of radiowaves inside a forest which contains various types of vegetation and free space gaps. The forest is divided into non-overlapping square cells, each one with different propagation characteristics. The propagation properties of each cell rely on specific propagation parameters, which are extracted from vegetation using an appropriate measurement method which is also described. The model performance is assessed through comparison between predicted values and directional spectrum measurements carried out in an isolated inhomogeneous forest at 20 and 62.4 GHz. This forest, located in South Wales, is formed by 6 different species of trees of various sizes and leaf types. The measurements were performed with the trees in-leaf.

Keywords: Radiative Energy Transfer, Micro and Millimetre Wave Propagation, Vegetation, Foliage Attenuation.

1 Introduction

The growth of fixed and mobile radio networks experienced in the last decades, has led to an increased need for cost effective, and enhanced utilisation of the available bandwidth and system coverage. This enhancement can be accomplished through a more efficient use of the available radio spectrum. A more efficient use of the radio spectrum relies on accurate radio planning tools which allow system planners to effectively predict the behaviour of their radio communication systems in terms of coverage and interference on existing systems.

The radiowaves interact with the obstacles and surrounding environment present in the radio path creating undesirable effects which need to be accurately modelled. From these obstacles, vegetation is very likely to be present in sub-urban and rural environments, causing degradation in the performance of the radio systems. To this extent, the understanding of the interaction between radiowaves and vegetation media is very important.

J. Filipe and M.S. Obaidat (Eds.): ICETE 2006, CCIS 9, pp. 322–333, 2008.

Various propagation models have been applied to vegetation with different degrees of success [9]. From these, the *Radiative Energy Transfer* theory (RET) has yielded good results for micro- and millimeter wave frequencies [9,6]. In [9], results from an extensive measurement campaign are used to compare the predictions of the RET with actual measurement data in the 1 to 60 GHz frequency band. This work has established a generic model for radiowave propagation in vegetated areas which was recently appended to the ITU-R recommendation in force [6]. Although this model is based on three different propagation mechanisms, it is reported that the scattered component, which is modelled with the RET, is dominant in terms of the received signal level.

The first known application of the RET theory to model the radiowave propagation in vegetation media was reported in [7] which is based on the RET modelling presented in [5]. Both of these RET formulations present some approximations which limit the applicability of the model, *e.g.* the model considers a homogeneous medium; the medium is not physically limited and special geometry conditions must be met. The vegetation media is normally inhomogeneous in nature as leafs tend to grow more in the periphery of the forest due to the increased sunlight exposure. Another limitation is that vegetation normally appears in limited or isolated groups, and forest volumes are normally limited by the ground and the top of the vegetation.

To overcome the issues presented above, a discretised version of the RET (dRET) was presented in [2]. A development of this model as well as a complete assessment was performed in [3] using an idealised scaled-down version of a forest formed by 16 *Ficus Benjamina* plants inside an anechoic chamber at 20 and 62.4 GHz.

In order to apply the dRET, the vegetation volume is divided into non overlapping square cells each one presenting distinct propagation characteristics. The signal flow in each of the cells is subsequently calculated using an iterative algorithm which evaluates the interactions between the different cells.

In this paper, the dRET formulation is used to simulated the behaviour of a full scale outdoor forest formed by 6 different species of trees. The assessment of the model is performed by comparing the predicted values with the actual measurement data obtained from outdoor measurements at 10 locations inside the test forest.

In section 2, the RET based scattering propagation models which are used during this paper as well as the differences between the original RET and its discretised version are presented. The model input propagation parameters are also described. The site specifics, including both the geometry and the tree characteristics, used to validate the proposed model is also presented. The experimental procedures used to extract the vegetation parameters as well as the overall model validity in terms of excess attenuation caused by tree is also outlined. Section 4 presents and discusses the measurement results. Finally in section 5 the conclusions of the paper are presented.

2   The Scattering Propagation Models

2.1   The Radiative Energy Transfer (RET)

The RET models vegetation as a homogeneous medium randomly filled with similar scatterers, which are characterised by the following set of parameters:

- The **Extinction Coefficient** or k_e. This parameter specifies the amount of energy which is lost due to absorption and scattering;
- The **Scattering Coefficient**, k_s, which specifies the scattered energy;
- The scatter directional profile $p(\hat{s}, \hat{s}')$, known as **Phase Function** [5], with $\hat{s}'$ and $\hat{s}$ representing the directions of the energy entering and emanating from each scatterer, respectively.

The phase function is normally modelled according to Eq. 1 [7,5] which represents a Gaussian function superimposed to an isotropic background level:

$$p(\gamma) = \alpha \left(\frac{2}{\beta}\right)^2 e^{-\left(\frac{\gamma}{\beta}\right)^2} + (1 - \alpha),\tag{1}$$

where α is the ratio between the forward lobe power and the total power of the phase function, β represents the half power beamwidth of the forward lobe and γ is the angle subtended by $\hat{s}$ and $\hat{s}'$.

The RET equation is normally expressed in its differential form, presented in Eq. 2.

$$\frac{dI}{ds} = -k_e I + k_s \int_{4\pi} p(\hat{s}, \hat{s}')I dw,\tag{2}$$

where the left hand side (LHS) describes the spatial variability (*i.e.* derivative) of intensity over one scatterer, while the first term on the right hand side (RHS) accounts for the reduction in intensity due to the absorption and scattering. The second term on the RHS represents the increase of intensity resulting from the scattering contributions of surrounding scatterers [7]. In [7], the overall intensity I is divided into two different intensities: the reduced intensity, I_{ri} and the diffuse intensity I_d. I_{ri} is the attenuated incident intensity whereas I_d accounts for the contributions from incoherent scattered components inside the vegetation medium.

2.2 The dRET Formulation

The discrete RET (dRET) was originally proposed by [2], as a method to overcome the RET limitations in terms of applicability to isolated vegetation volumes. In the dRET modelling, the vegetation volume is divided in non-overlapping square cells and an iterative algorithm is used to gather all the interactions between these primary cells, allowing for the computation of the intensity across the entire tree formation. This approach of splitting the vegetation in discrete elementary volumes, allows one to assign different scattering parameters to every cell, consequently enabling an inhomogeneous vegetation volume to be more accurately represented. This is depicted in Fig. 1.

The dRET approach presented in [3] and used here, comprises 4 major improvements compared to the algorithm given in [2]. These are summarised as follows: (i) the improved dRET version yields results for angles other than those which are integer multiples of $45°$; (ii) it accounts for the effect of the receiving antenna radiation pattern; (iii) the dRET differential equation is more readily solved, which means that piecewise linear approximation is no longer needed, so that the algorithm can cover larger cell sizes; and (iv) the cell parameters can be defined individually, thus allowing one to define inhomogeneous scenarios.

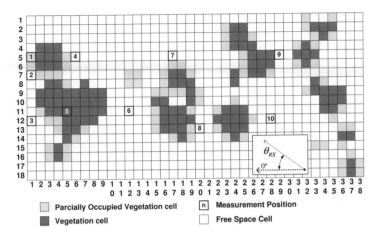

Parcially Occupied Vegetation cell   [n] Measurement Position

Vegetation cell   Free Space Cell

Fig. 1. 2D cell structure

3 Experimental Procedure

An experimental program was designed to evaluate the performance of the dRET model in a real outdoor environment. This program involved two main tasks: the dRET parameter extraction and the evaluation of the excess attenuation caused by trees at several locations inside the test forest.

3.1 Description of the Measurement Site

The measurement site is located in the North-East of Cardiff in South Wales. The test forest is an isolated group of trees formed by 6 different species. To completely characterise the test forest, precise locations of each tree and the mean canopy diameters were measured using a theodolite. Using this data, a 2D representation of the forest is

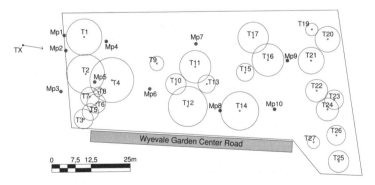

Fig. 2. Scaled drawing of the Wyevale Garden Center test site

presented in Fig. 2. The transmitter location (TX) and the direction where it was pointed in the measurements are also presented.

The red dots which are labeled *Mpx*, represent the received signal measurement locations. The tree species present in the test forest as well as the dimensions of the trees are presented in Table 1.

Table 1. Tree species of Wyevale Garden Center site

Tree Label	Common Name	Canopy Diameter (m)	Tree Height (m)
T1	Oak	11.4	10.9
T2	Oleaster	12.1	16.5
T3	Ornamental Cherry	6.1	3.5
T4	Oleaster	14.0	17.7
T5	Ornamental Cherry	5.2	3.5
T6	Ornamental Cherry	6.0	3.5
T7	Ornamental Cherry	6.0	3.5
T8	Ornamental Cherry	3.0	3.0
T9	Silver Birch	4.5	8.4
T10	Silver Birch	6.5	6.4
T11	Silver Birch	10.0	10.0
T12	Oleaster	12.5	15.6
T13	Silver Birch	5.6	5.5
T14	Oleaster	12.0	15.0
T15	Oak	5.6	2.5
T16	Oak	10.1	7.2
T17	Gean	9.6	7.3
T19	Pecan	3.9	8.9
T20	Oak	8.0	9.6
T21	Pecan	8.3	5.2
T22	Pecan	7.0	7.0
T23	Oak	6.1	7.8
T24	Oak	7.2	6.8
T25	Pecan	6.8	13.0
T26	Pecan	6.2	14.3
T27	Pecan	3.9	4.3

For each of the species, the leaf size parameters were measured. These mean sizes are presented in Table 2.

Table 2. Tree leaf sizes of Wyevale Garden Center site

Common Name	Leaf Size Length (cm)	Width (cm)
Oak	13	8
Oleaster	9	0.8
Ornamental Cherry	10	6
Silver Birch	4	2.5
Gean	15	6
Pecan	9	3

3.2 Directional Spectrum Measurements

To evaluate the excess attenuation caused by the vegetation, the RX antenna was placed at each of the locations shown in Fig. 2 and the directional profile of the received signal was evaluated. This evaluation was performed positioning the receiver antenna at 5.5 m high, which represent approximately one half of the mean canopy height of the trees which form the test forest. At each location, the RX antenna was rotated clockwise 360° around its vertical axes (θ_{RX}) in $1°$ incremental steps.

The TX antenna was placed outside the forest in the position shown in Fig. 2 at 13 m distance from the air to vegetation interface. To achieve an almost uniform illumination of the interface, very broad 50° (10 dBi) half power beamwidth antennas were used at both test frequencies. At the receiver side, high gain directional antennas were used. At 20 GHz the RX antenna was of the lens horn type with 33 dBi and $4°$ of HPBW, while at 62.4 GHz a lens horn antenna with 36 dBi and $2.8°$ of HPBW was used.

3.3 Parameter Extraction and Scaling

The dRET input parameters must be extracted from specific measurement data. This data is obtained from received signal measurements in specific locations around the tree as explained in Fig. 3. The distances $d_{1,2,3}$ were chosen so that 100% of the canopy width could be illuminated within the HPBW of the TX antenna, and at the same time, the RX antenna was placed as close as possible to the tree canopy.

At each of the 3 measurement locations presented in Fig. 3 (labeled M_n) the receiver antenna was rotated around the vertical axes in a $\pm45°$ range in $1°$ steps.

The extraction of k_e was based on the measurement of the insertion loss caused by the tree, and consequently relied on measurements M_1 and M_3. The ratio between the maximum received powers at these locations was used to calculate k_e using Eq. 3.

$$\frac{P_{3\,\max}}{P_{1\,\max}} = e^{-k_e(d_3-d_1)} \left(\frac{d_3}{d_1}\right)^2, \tag{3}$$

where $P_{1\,\max}$ and $P_{3\,\max}$ are the maximum receiver powers at positions M_1 and M_3, respectively, and d_n is the distance between the TX and the nth measurement location in meters.

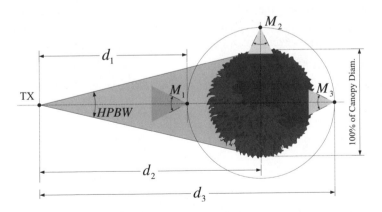

Fig. 3. Parameter extraction measurement setup

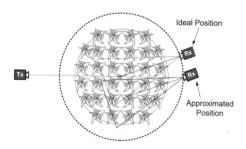

Fig. 4. Approximated method to measure parameter β

To extract the phase function parameters α and β, a modified version of the re-radiation indoor measurement procedure [3] was used. This modified version overcomes some of the inaccuracies reported in [8] and is simpler to carry out. The β optimisation is based in measurement M_3, where the ideal measurement position is replaced by a more convenient approximated position, as explained in Fig. 4.

The optimisation of α uses the side scatter level of the tree obtained from measurement M_2, which is subsequently used to optimise α in Eq. 1. Finally, k_s is extracted by modelling the tree as a single dRET cell. As there are no interactions involved between cells a simple version of the dRET diffuse intensity equation [3] is used to optimise k_s, providing the measured side scatter level.

The parameter extraction was performed for 5 of the 6 species present in the test forest. The trees chosen to carry out the parameter extraction were: T_1, T_3, T_{11}, T_{12} and T_{17}. These were chosen due to their location at the border of the forest, thus avoiding the possible contamination of measured results caused by interference from the other species. The extracted parameters are presented in Tables 3 and 4 for 20 and 62.4 GHz respectively. Some parameters were impossible to calculate, specially for the larger trees, due to the high attenuation of the coherent signal component. In these cases average parameter values were assigned to the corresponding trees.

To limit the *stair case* error due to the discretisation of the forest, while maintaining a reasonable computational time, a 2.5 m vegetation cells division was used, as depicted in Fig. 1. In order for the phase function parameters to remain valid, these have to be adapted to the new vegetation volumes by performing an appropriate scaling. The

Table 3. Input parameter values extracted from selected vegetation blocks at 20 GHz

Tree Label	20 GHz			
	k_e	k_s	α	β
T_1	0.38	0.28	0.36	10.7°
T_3	0.99	0.25	0.13	7.0°
T_{11}	0.75	NA	0.05	13.7°
T_{12}	0.68	NA	NA	15.9°
T_{17}	0.45	NA	0.13	19.5°
Mean	**0.65**	**0.26**	**0.17**	**13.4°**

Table 4. Input parameter values extracted from selected vegetation blocks at 62.4 GHz

Tree	62.4 GHz			
Label	k_e	k_s	α	β
T_1	0.31	0.13	0.08	4.7°
T_3	1.26	1.02	0.07	15.5°
T_{11}	0.81	NA	NA	12.1°
T_{12}	0.51	0.10	0.15	14.9°
T_{17}	0.50	0.38	0.04	11.1°
Mean	**0.68**	**0.41**	**0.09**	**11.7°**

scaling method used here is explained in [4], which suggests a linear behaviour of α and β with the variation of the vegetation volume.

4   Measurement Results

The assessment of the dRET propagation model results was performed comparing the predicted results with directional spectrum measurements were carried out at 10 locations inside the forest according to the procedure explained before. The measured excess attenuation can subsequently be compared with the predictions calculated by the dRET algorithm for the test forest depicted in Fig. 2 when modelled with the cell structure presented in Fig. 1.

A comparison between the measured received signal and the predicted signal values obtained at MP_2 is presented in Figs. 5 and 6, at 20 and 62.4 GHz, respectively. In these measurements, which were performed at the air to vegetation interface, the RX signal level is strongly influenced by the direct path between the TX and the RX antennas. Hence, the plots present a signal shape which is very close to the radiation pattern of the receiver antennas, particularly in the angular region around 0° where the RX antenna is pointing to the TX. Although a good overall agreement between predicted and measured

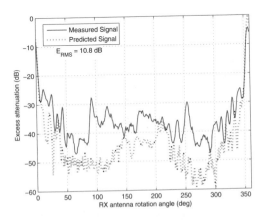

Fig. 5. Measured and predicted signals in MP_2 at 20 GHz

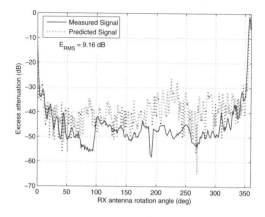

Fig. 6. Measured and predicted signals in MP_2 at 62.4 GHz

curves can be observed, specially when the RX and TX antennas are aligned, a slightly increased error is present in the prediction of the signal which is scattered from the forest. This may be explained due to some inaccuracy in the estimation of k_s parameter corresponding to the surrounding trees during the parameters extraction phase.

Figs. 7 and 8, present the results for MP_4, which is located behind tree number 1. The results for 20 GHz (Fig. 7) also present a good agreement between the measured and the predicted received signal values. Nevertheless, there is a tendency to underestimate the scattered signal from tree number 1. This effect is present in the 220 to 330° angular range and might be due to the incorrect estimation of the beamwidth of the scattering profile of tree number 1. The underestimation of this parameter will concentrate the scattered radiation in the forward scattering region ($\theta_{RX} = 340°$) leading to the mentioned inaccuracy. Around $\theta_{RX} = 200°$ the dRET model predicts a peak in the received signal which corresponds to the signal scattered from tree number 9. The misalignment between this peak

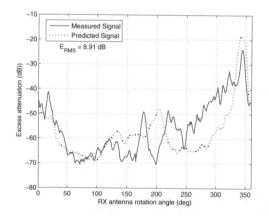

Fig. 7. Measured and predicted signals in MP_4 at 20 GHz

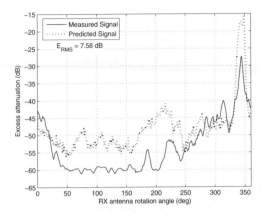

Fig. 8. Measured and predicted signals in MP_4 at 62.4 GHz

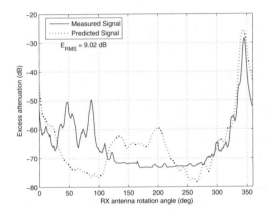

Fig. 9. Measured and predicted signals in MP_9 at 20 GHz

and the correspondent peak in the measured signal is likely to be due to the approximation in discretisation of the tree position inherent to the cell division process.

The 62.4 GHz plot (Fig. 8) presents an absolute error of 10 to 13 dB in the forward scattering region (around $340°$). This can be due to some blockage which was taken into account in the k_e extraction. In fact, k_e is extracted by measuring the excess attenuation caused by the tree, using a radial path which is different from the line used to measure the attenuation. Attenuation differences between different radial paths of 20 dB have been published in literature [1]. This may help to explain this discrepancy.

Figure 9 presents the measured and predicted received signal values in position MP_9 at 20 GHz. A good correspondence between the two values is present in the forward scattering region around $\theta_{RX} = 330°\pm70°$. In the angular region where the RX antenna is pointing away from the test forest, i.e. $30° \leq \theta_{RX} \leq 110°$ the measured signal shows an increased received signal level which appears to be due to scattering in the vegetation structures surrounding the test forest. These structures, lying outside the test forest were

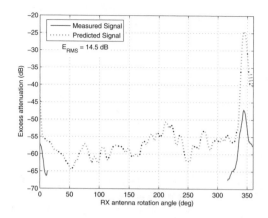

Fig. 10. Measured and predicted signals in MP_9 at 62.4 GHz

not modeled and consequently are not taken into account by the dRET modelling thus explaining why the model seems to be unable to predict accurately the signal level within this angular region.

At 62.4 GHz the signal level in position MP_9 was relatively low and could only be measured for a narrow angular region. Outside this region the received signal was too close to the receiver noise level, which is around -70 dBm, to be measured. The measured and predicted values seem to exhibit a level offset which seems to be due to a vertical misalignment of the RX antenna. This offset generates a larger RMS error when compered with the remaining measurement positions.

The overall RMS error for the complete set of measurement performed at 20 and 62.4 GHz is shown in Table 5. The RMS error is consistently below 15 dB except at a few locations in the forest. The mean overall RMS error is 12.2 and 10.7 dB at 20 and 62.4 GHz, respectively. Although the RMS error values are slightly above figures found in

Table 5. Model performance assessment using the RMS error criterion

Measurement Position	RMS error (dB) 20 GHz	62.4 GHz
MP_1	11.8	9.0
MP_2	10.8	9.2
MP_3	13.9	7.8
MP_4	8.9	7.6
MP_5	12.5	16.5
MP_6	13.5	13.5
MP_7	9.6	6.7
MP_8	18.7	11.8
MP_9	9.0	14.5
MP_{10}	13.2	NA
Mean	**12.2**	**10.7**

other published results, these can be considered reasonably low. They also demonstrate the benefits of dRET modelling, particularly when considering inhomogeneous media.

5 Conclusions

This paper presents a model for radiowave propagation in inhomogeneous vegetation media for micro and millimeter waves, which is based on the RET. The model relies on 4 vegetation dependent propagation parameters and a method to extract and scale these parameters is also presented. The input parameters are extracted from the different vegetation volumes forming the test forest using the proposed method at 20 and 62.4 GHz. Subsequently these parameters are used in the model to generate excess attenuation predictions at several locations inside the test forest. Finally, the predicted and measured results are compared using the RMS error criterion. This is shown to be consistently below 15 dB. Although this RMS error value is within the range of other published results, in some measurement locations the error was found to be as high as 18.7 dB. This is thought to be due to localised blockages, inaccuracies in the parameter extraction method and also misalignment of the RX antenna during the attenuation measurement phase. An improved parameter extraction method is thus being investigated to eliminate higher error discrepancies.

References

1. Caldeirinha, R.F.S.: Radio characterisation of single trees at micro- and millimetre wave frequencies. PhD thesis, University of Glamorgan (2001)
2. Didascalou, D., Younis, M., Wiesbeck, W.: Millimeter-wave scattering and penetration in isolated vegetation structures. IEEE Transasctions on Geoscience and Remote Sensing 38, 2106–2113 (2000)
3. Fernandes, T., Caldeirinha, R., Al-Nuaimi, M., Richter, J.: A discrete RET model for millimeter-wave propagation in isolated tree formations. IEICE Transactions on Communications E88-B(6), 2411–2418 (2005)
4. Fernandes, T., Caldeirinha, R., Al-Nuaimi, M., Richter, J.: A practical method for vegetation scattering function parameter extraction and scaling. In: Loughborough Antennas and Propagation Conference - LAPC, UK, vol. 1, pp. 105–109 (2006)
5. Ishimaru, A.: Wave propagation and scattering in random media. IEEE Press, Los Alamitos (1997)
6. ITU-R: Recommendation ITU-R P.833-5, Attenuation in vegetation. ITU-R (2005)
7. Johnson, R.A., Schwering, F.: A transport theory of millimeter wave propagation in woods and forest. Technical Report CECOM-TR-85-1, Forth Monmouth (1985)
8. Richter, J., Caldeirinha, R., Al-Nuaimi, M.: Phase function measurement for modelling radiowave attenuation and scatter in vegetation based on the theory of radiative energy transfer. In: Proceeding of PIMRC 2002, pp. 146–150 (2002)
9. Rogers, N.C., Seville, A., Richter, J., Ndzi, D., Caldeirinha, R., Shukla, A., Al-Nuaimi, M., Craig, K., Austin, J.: A generic model of 1-60GHz radio propagation trough vegetation - Final report. Technical report, Radiocommunications Agency (2002)

Use of AGPS Call Data Records for Non-GPS Terminal Positioning in Cellular Networks

Semun Lee[1], Jeongkeun Lee[1], Taekyoung Kwon[1], Yanghee Choi[1],
Tae Joon Ha[2], and Tae-il Kim[2]

[1] School of Computer Science & Engineering, Seoul National University
San 56-1 Shilim-dong, Kwanak-gu, Seoul, South Korea
{smlee,jklee,tk,yhchoi}@mmlab.snu.ac.kr
[2] Radiant Technologies, Inc.
Il-yang Bldg 206, Nonhyeon 1-dong. Gangnam-gu, Seoul, South Korea
{tjha,happyti}@radiantech.net

Abstract. This paper presents a novel method of user terminal positioning in cellular networks. A pattern matching technology based on received-signal-strength (RSS) from the pilot channels of cell towers has been the most popular network-based positioning method. In response to a position request, a terminal measures RSSs of pilot channels from surrounding cell towers and then the terminal's RSS pattern is compared with a pattern database to find the most correlated one which indicates the position of the terminal. Although the pattern matching method can provide accurate positioning, its database construction and maintenance require a high overhead of periodic labor-intensive pattern collection. In this paper, we propose to exploit the call data records (CDRs) that are uploaded by Assisted Global Positioning System (AGPS) terminals as inputs to the pattern database, which removes or reduces the pattern collection overhead. In AGPS systems, terminals measure satellite signals and cellular network parameters (such as RSS) and relay them to the cellular infrastructure, which in turn calculates the terminal position using both that satellite and cellular network data. The proposed AGPS CDR based pattern matching method takes advantage of the increasing number of AGPS terminals in service: non-AGPS terminals can obtain more precise positioning results in areas where more AGPS calls are generated (e.g. hotspots). To do so, we analyze the characteristics of RSS patterns and AGPS CDRs. Based on the analysis, a pattern-distance metric and an AGPS CDR based pattern matching system are proposed and their performances are evaluated by examining field data of several urban downtown areas of Seoul, Korea. We obtain promising results: the position of the user terminal can be estimated with the accuracy (or, positioning error) at the level of 96.5m and 149.8m for the 67% and the 95% confidence interval, respectively.

Keywords: Positioning, Pattern Matching, AGPS CDRs, cellular network.

1 Introduction

[1]The geographic position of a user terminal is valuable and critical information to provide ubiquitous/intelligent services such as location-based emergency terminal service.

---

[1] Korea patent pending.

J. Filipe and M.S. Obaidat (Eds.): ICETE 2006, CCIS 9, pp. 334–346, 2008.

Many researchers and engineers have made great efforts to obtain accurate user terminal position information with or without Global Positioning System (GPS).

Although GPS is able to provide excellent position accuracy, position fixes require lines of sight (LOS) to multiple satellites, long first fix time (at least 30s), and high processing power. Assisted GPS, or AGPS [1], is a technology that uses an assistance server in a cellular infrastructure to cut down the time needed to fix the position. In AGPS systems, the terminal, being limited in processing power, communicates with the assistance server that has high processing power. In response to position queries, AGPS terminals measure satellite signals and cellular network parameters (such as RSS) and relay them to the assistance server. The server uses those data to calculate the position of the terminal and send the calculated position back to the terminal. In urban areas, however, AGPS does not work (like GPS) under heavy tree cover or indoors where the terminal cannot receive a sufficient number of satellite signals. Moreover, equipping a terminal with AGPS module raises terminal production cost. That's why some proposed positioning technologies exploit the inherent radio parameters of the cellular network rather than relying on GPS technologies.

The network parameters open up several possibilities for positioning methodology. Simply, every cellular system provides some information identifying the serving cell (Cell-ID) enabling a coarse-grained position estimate. For more accurate positioning, a number of proposed solutions have utilized the propagation delay, time-difference-of-arrival (TDOA), antenna orientation or received-signal-strength (RSS). The propagation time (or time-of-arrival) to the cell tower is only available in TDMA systems and UMTS. And in cases without LOS view between the transmitter and the receiver, the distance from the propagation time is overestimated. TDOA among several cell towers could be measured and the terminal position can be obtained by solving the hyperbolic system. Hyperbolic systems require time synchronization among cell towers, which is feasible not in GSM and UMTS but in only CDMA networks. Additional hardware can compensate for the time asynchronity but raises costs. The hyperbolic systems also suffer from the inaccurate TDOA measurements mainly caused by the near-far problem: Idle Periods in Downlink (IPDL) is proposed to mitigate the problem while it costs downlink capacity and additional complexity [12]. The information of sector antenna orientation and angle opening can be used to increase the positioning accuracy. Many service providers, however, do not maintain the information of each sector antenna. And radio waves may arrive from outside the opening angle due to antenna side lobes, reflections, and diffractions especially in dense urban areas.

Compared to the above-mentioned parameters, RSS is the commonly available basic parameter for all types of wireless cellular systems. Shadowing and multipath fading, however, make RSS an unreliable metric to estimate the exact transmitter-receiver distance. Moreover, the RSS-to-distance function (propagation model) is highly affected by environment/system specific factors such as height of surrounding buildings, walls and operation RF frequency. Thus, rather than RSS-based triangulation, RSS database pattern matching algorithm is in use. It overcomes the above-mentioned problems by using a database built from measurements or predictions. The position of the terminal is then determined by comparing the terminal's RSS measurements to the database entries and finding the best-matching position. Making appropriate measurements over wide cellular network areas is very expensive and therefore not considered applicable. Moreover, the change of cell towers' locations, antenna angles, and surrounding buildings mandates frequent update of the database. Thus, the pattern matching approach is more practical by wireless LAN based small-area/indoor positioning services. Prediction data, on the other hand, can be obtained from wave propagation simulation tools and remove the database maintenance overhead. Accurate prediction, however, requires precise 3-D maps over large areas and accurate/detailed network parameters including antenna loss, height, tilt, transmission power, etc., which are not commonly and easily obtained. And the maps and parameters also require frequent update.

In this paper, we propose to exploit the call data records (CDRs) uploaded by Assisted Global Positioning System (AGPS) terminals as inputs to the pattern database, which removes or reduces the pattern collection overhead. The characteristics of RSS patterns and AGPS CDRs are analyzed and reflected in designing a pattern-distance metric and pattern matching system, respectively. The main contributions of this paper are:

- Database cost reduction: we show that the AGPS CDRs can be utilized to build and maintain a pattern database for positioning of non-AGPS terminals.
- Pros and cons of the use of the AGPS CDRs
  - As the number of AGPS users increase, non-AGPS terminals obtain more accurate position results. It means that non-AGPS terminals can obtain more accurate positioning results in the area where more AGPS calls are generated (position information of non-AGPS terminals will be requested much more frequently).
  - Absence of AGPS CDRs in indoor areas may reduce the coverage of pattern matching positioning area. However, we show that indoor positioning by the proposed method is possible even with outdoor AGPS CDRs.
- The analysis of RSS pattern characteristics: we design a pattern-distance metric based on the analysis.

The performance of the pattern-distance metric and the AGPS CDRs based pattern matching system are evaluated by examining the field data of urban downtown area of Seoul, Korea. Field trials provide promising results: the position of a user can be estimated with the accuracy at the level of 96.5m and 149.8m for the 67% and the 95% confidence interval, respectively.

The remainder of this paper is organized as follows. In the next section, we present related work. Section 3 introduces the proposed pattern matching localization, and Section 4 details the proposed pattern distance metric. In Sections 5 and 6, experimental results and concluding remarks are given.

2   Related Work

Cell-ID, time-difference-of-arrival (TDOA), GPS are the traditional localization methods in cellular networks [12], [1], [2]. In Cell-ID systems, the position of user terminal is determined as the position of serving cell tower. This method is simple and applicable to every cellular network, but it offers only coarse-grained position information because the cell area is typically wide. TDOA uses the time difference of the radio signal propagation to estimate the distance between the user terminal and the adjacent cell towers. By using these distance data, TDOA triangulates the position of the user terminal. This method can provide a more accurate position than the Cell-ID method, but its application is limited to synchronized networks or it introduces an additional hardware cost to measure the asynchrony. GPS provides specially coded satellite signals that can be processed in a GPS receiver, enabling the receiver to calculate the position, the velocity and the time; accuracy of GPS is fairly high. By attaching a GPS receiver on a user terminal, GPS can be employed in cellular networks. However, GPS is not available in indoors or deep urban canyons, because it requires LOS to satellites. In cellular networks, on the other hand, AGPS is used to reduce the time required to find the position of the user terminal.

Pattern matching localization method is proposed to overcome the limitations of traditional methods [9], [3], [4], [5]. Under the pattern matching method, a user terminal measures the radio signal pattern, and then, seeks for the most similar pattern in the pattern database, which consists of the radio signal patterns gathered at the specified positions a priori. In this way, the position of the user terminal is estimated. [9] proposes a pattern matching method for wireless local area networks, while [3], [4], [5] employ the pattern matching in cellular networks.

Under the pattern matching method, because the signal pattern database should be updated periodically in order to adapt to the ever-changing radio environment, the maintenance cost is significant. Accordingly, a number of research efforts have been made to reduce the maintenance cost. [6], [8] employ the radio signal propagation model to predict the radio signal patterns at the specific positions. Measured field data can complement the radio signal propagation model: it therefore reserves accuracy of the signal pattern database with a low pattern database maintenance cost. This prediction method is orthogonal to our proposed AGPS CDR base method, thus, they can be used together with our method. Accurate propagation modeling, however, requires precise 3-D maps over large areas and detailed network parameters including antenna loss, height, tilt, transmission power, etc. [10], [11] propose special algorithms exploiting spatial correlation of patterns in wireless LAN environments. Although they are proved to work well in indoor wireless LAN systems, we observed that it is inappropriate to apply them to cellular network systems because of cellular systems' larger cell coverage and more dynamic radio environment than those of small-area wireless LAN systems.

3   Pattern Matching Localization

3.1   Basic Pattern Matching System

Figure 1 depicts the basic pattern matching system architecture. In basic pattern matching systems, operators use dedicated measurement terminals and collect signal patterns at positions (whose positions are already known) in advance. And the patterns are stored in the signal pattern database. Signal patterns at a position may vary with the change of radio propagation environment or cell planning. Therefore, operators are required to periodically measure signal patterns to maintain the signal pattern database up-to-date. We call a collected signal pattern stored in signal pattern database as a *seed*. That is,

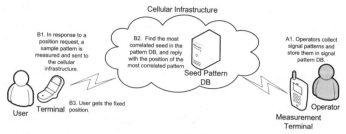

Fig. 1. Basic pattern matching architecture. Process A is the pattern database construction process, and process B is the user terminal positioning process.

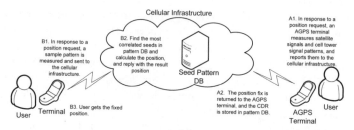

Fig. 2. AGPS CDR based pattern matching architecture. Process A is the pattern database construction process using AGPS user terminals, and process B is the user terminal positioning process.

the seed is the entry in the signal pattern database. On the other hand, we call a signal pattern in a position request from a terminal as a *sample*.

In order to determine the position of a user terminal, the user terminal first measures the signals from surrounding cell towers, and sends the sample pattern to the infrastructure to find the most correlated pattern which is used to estimate the position where the terminal's pattern is measured.

Collecting seed patterns over the wide area of the cellular network is labor-intensive work. Suppose we collect seeds at every 50 m grid point in $1km^2$ range, 400 times of measurement are needed, and in case of $5km^2$ urban area range, 10,000 times. Furthermore, operators should measure seed patterns periodically to maintain the database up-to-date. Moreover, in order to obtain the more accurate position fix, the more and the denser seed patterns are needed. Therefore, we propose a novel pattern matching system to automate the construction of the signal pattern database.

3.2 Proposed Pattern Matching System

The proposed AGPS CDR based pattern matching architecture is illustrated in Figure 2. In the proposed system, we make use of the CDRs uploaded by AGPS terminals as seed patterns for positioning non-AGPS terminals. In general, AGPS is accurate within 50 meters when users are indoors if GPS signals are received and 15 meters when they are outdoors [1], so that we can leverage the AGPS result as the actual position of a

Table 1. The result error distances (m) on the time variation. This table shows the mean positioning accuracy and the accuracies (in meters) for the 67% (1 sigma) and 95% (2 sigma) confidence interval, respectively.

Measurement date of sample	Mean	1 Sigma	2 Sigma
12/15/2005	87.7	110	169
2/8/2006	93.2	121	196

terminal. An AGPS CDR includes the call time as well as the signal pattern and an AGPS positioning result [13]. From the CDMA (IS-95) system of the company A in Korea, we have obtained this log data without any modification on the system. In this way, we are able to construct and maintain a pattern database at low cost.

In some cases, the size of the seed pattern database may be too large to manage, since the number of AGPS terminals is increasing and many users exploit AGPS for the location based service. Then, the database lookup time and, eventually, position fix time will increase. In this case, we can reduce the time by doing spatial and temporal filtering for the incoming CDRs. For example, we can designate regional databases for each area unit, and each database maintains CDRs generated from its assigned area. When we choose candidate seed patterns from the database to compare with the sample pattern, we can filter out old seeds. We can also consider the specific time interval (a day of the week, a time in a day) at which the sample and seed patterns are measured in choosing most appropriate seed patterns in a manageable size.

On the other hand, in a particular area, or a particular cellular network where AGPS terminals are generating calls not so frequently, there may not be sufficient number of seeds in the pattern database. In this case, the seeds should be accumulated in the pattern database for a long time to offer required accuracy in that area. This incurs a question on the seed valid time. We investigate this question: how long the seed is valid, by using two sample sets of 55-day difference, which is somewhat long time if we consider the rapid change of outdoor radio environment especially in urban area. We collected the seed set on Dec. 15, 2005, and used two sample set: one was measured on Dec. 15, 2005, and the other on Feb. 8, 2006. The seeds and samples were collected from about 100 spots of downtown area of Seoul (near the *Gangnam station*, one of the most crowded areas in Korea, with many high buildings) and the area size is approximately $1km \times 1km$. The result error distance of our proposed method is shown in Table 1. The mean error of former sample set (with 'fresh' seeds) is 87.7 m, while that of the latter sample set (with '55-day-old' seeds) is 93.2 m. Despite of the 55 day gap between the two sets, the positioning accuracy results do not make a considerable difference. This demonstrates that the duration of the seed validity could be very long than our presumption. Therefore, when AGPS terminals are generating calls not so frequently, we can store seeds in the pattern database for a long time to maintain the density of seeds in the pattern database.

The basic pattern matching picks up only one seed (and its measurement position) in determining the position of a sample pattern. Consequently, the result of the basic pattern matching will become unstable as the variations of the radio signals increase (due to slow fading and fast fading). In order to mitigate the effect of the variations, we select

Table 2. An example of RSS pattern (unit: dBm)

Location	RSS from cell 1	RSS from cell 2	RSS from cell 3	RSS from cell 4
(37.5085, 127,0335)	-4.43	-7.23	-10.22	-20.46

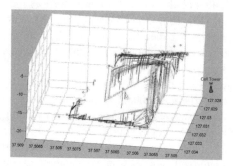

Fig. 3. Signal strength at various positions received from a cell sector antenna. Cell tower is at (37.50504, 127.02527).

multiple seeds and use them together in determining the position of user terminals. We introduce a metric of the pattern distance, which will be detailed in Section 4, and select multiple seed patterns in terms of the pattern distance. We then estimate the centroid of the selected seeds as the position of a user terminal. The field trial test in Section 5 shows that this centroid method exhibits with less deviating positioning results.

4 Pattern Distance Metric

We define a radio signal pattern as a set of the received-signal-strengths (RSSs) of adjacent cell towers (Table 2). User terminals commonly measure the RSS of the pilot channel to determine when to handoff to other cells, or to control transmit power in any cellular network, i.e., GSM, CDMA, WCDMA networks.

Before designing a pattern distance metric, we analyze the characteristics of RSS patterns. First we look at the distribution of RSS values measured from one cell tower as illustrated in Figure 3. X, Y, and Z axes represent latitude, longitude, and RSS value in dBm, respectively. Circular points indicate measurement locations. In Figure 3, as the user terminal goes far from the cell tower, the measured RSS value decreases while the RSS values measured near the cell tower are not decreasing fast. Although there are some fluctuation of RSS values due to slow and fast fading, in general, the difference between two RSS values measured at two positions increases in proportion to the distance between the positions. With these characteristics of the RSS, we reach the following observation.

– **Observation 1.** In general, as the distance between two measurement positions increases, the difference between the two measured RSS values increases. The pattern distance metric should reflect the difference between RSSs of two patterns (i.e., a seed and a sample), then eventually indicate the distance between the two measurement positions.

Therefore, in order to take RSS difference into an account to pattern distance metric, we use the Euclidean distance as follows.

$$\sqrt{\sum_{k=1}^{n} (RSS_{A_k} - RSS_{B_k})^2}.$$

where n is the number of RSSs in two patterns and RSS_{A_k} is the kth RSS value of the pattern A and RSS_{B_k} is the kth RSS value of the pattern B.

Because RSSs of the points at the same distance from a cell tower are similar (as shown in Figure 3), if a pattern (sample or seed or both of them) contains only one RSS measurement value from one cell, the pattern with a single RSS may appear at a number of positions. In that case, the picked-up position of the most correlated seed based on the above metric may be far from the position of the sample pattern. However, as the number of RSS values from different cells increases, an RSS pattern will have a fewer number of candidate positions. In addition to Observation 1, we come to another observation.

– **Observation 2.** Let S_A and S_B denote the set of cells whose pilot signals are received by user A and user B, respectively. As the number of cells in their intersection increases, we can say that the similarity (the distance between A and B) between two patterns becomes more substantial. Therefore, comparing two patterns, we need to consider the number of cells common in the two patterns.

Patterns may have RSSs from a different set of cells. Let us take an example of Table 3, in which pattern A has RSSs from cell 1, cell 2, and cell 4, and pattern B has RSSs from cell 1, cell 2, and cell 3. In this example, we cannot calculate Euclidean distance between patterns A and B. We call the RSS from the cell whose RSS is measured by only one pattern (not in the other pattern) as *hole*. In the example of Table 3, the pattern A contains a RSS from cell 4 but the pattern B does not: the RSS entry of cell 4 is a hole in pattern B. Likewise, the RSS entry of cell 3 is a hole in pattern A. As

Table 3. An example of hole RSS. (unit : dBm)

	RSS from cell 1	RSS from cell 2	RSS from cell 3	RSS from cell 4
Pattern A	-3.42	-5.23	*hole*	-16.78
Pattern B	-6.23	-13.25	-8.43	*hole*

we have observed, if the number of holes of a pattern pair is large, the two patterns' measurement positions are far apart.

In order to calculate the Euclidean distance between them, we assign a certain constant value to holes: *hole RSS*. Through an experiment given in Section 5, we find that a constant somewhat lower than the smallest RSS in the pattern database (also in the sample patterns) is appropriate for the hole RSS. According to Observation 2, we should give some penalty to holes, and the proposed hole RSS method gives penalty by assigning a small value to the hole: as the hole RSS becomes smaller, a distance metric value becomes larger.

We have tested our proposed metric by observing the correlation coefficient between the pattern distance metric and the actual geographic distance. High coefficient value (close to one) indicates the proposed pattern distance metric reflects the actual geographic distance well. From the data set (both seed and sample) of section 5, all possible pattern pairs are examined: we calculate the correlation coefficient between the vector of pattern distance metric and the vector of geographic distance (between measurement positions). The results show that a promising value of a coefficient of 0.7.

The another application of the proposed distance metric is to infer confidence level of a position fix. If the sample and the picked-up most correlated seed has a small pattern distance metric, the measurement position of the seed patten is close to the sample measurement position, i.e., the position fix is accurate with a high probability.

5   Experimental Results

We have performed extensive experiments with data gathered from the commercial CDMA network of the company A in the urban area of Seoul, Korea. The gathered data sets are as follows.[1]

- **Seed Pattern Database:** The pairs of the position and the signal pattern were gathered by the CDRs uploaded by AGPS terminals in the urban area (near the *Gangnam station*) of Seoul. The area size is $1km \times 1.8km$, and we obtained seed patterns of 283 positions in that area.
- **Sample Data Set:** We measured signal patterns at 30 points in the area covered by the signal pattern database. We measured 5 samples at one point, indoors/outdoors separately at the same point [2]; 300 samples in total were measured. We retrieved the real latitude and longitude of each point using the digital map, which enabled us to calculate the error distances of localization results.

Choice of Hole RSS. First, we have performed an experiment to determine the appropriate value of the hole RSS. We figured out under which value it shows the best accuracy, varying the hole RSS from -50 dB to -25 dB. Figure 4 shows that, with -45 dB of the hole RSS, we can achieve the best accuracy; in this case, the mean error distance is 87.4 m and 2 sigma (the accuracy for the 95% confidence interval) is 175.2m.

---

[1] In our experiments, the CDRs contain the SINR values (Ec/Io) from the adjacent cell towers, and we have used the SINR values as signal pattern instead of the RSS.

[2] For example, samples were measured inside and outside of a building entrance with a distance of several meters, or measured under the roof and on the roof of a building.

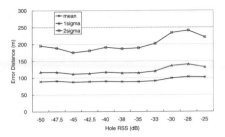

Fig. 4. Experiment result with various hole RSS. 1 sigma means the accuracy for the 67% confidence interval and 2 sigma means the accuracy for the 95% confidence interval.

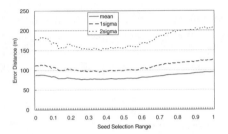

Fig. 5. Experiment result with various seed selection range

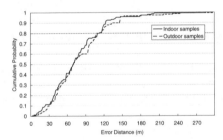

Fig. 6. Cumulative distribution function (CDF) accuracy of proposed pattern matching that used with indoor and outdoor samples separately. Hole RSS is -45 dB and seed selection range is 0.37.

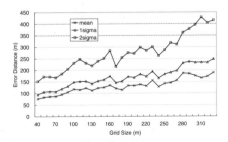

Fig. 7. Experiment result with various grid size (seed density). Hole RSS is -45 dB and seed selection range is 0.37.

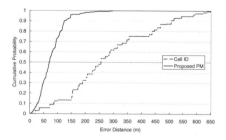

Fig. 8. Cumulative distribution function (CDF) accuracy of proposed pattern matching and Cell ID method. Hole RSS is -45 dB, and seed selection range is 0.37, and all seeds are used.

In our experiment environment, the minimum RSS that a user terminal can detect is around -32 dB: -45 dB is somewhat lower value than the minimum RSS. From this result, we can infer that the somewhat lower value than the minimum RSS which a user terminal can detect is eligible when applying our proposed method to other wireless networks.

Effect of Multiple Top Seeds. Next, we have figured out the effect of seed selection when determining the position of a user terminal. The basic pattern matching uses only the most similar seed (top seed), and determines the position of that seed as the user terminal's position. However, because of the momentary fluctuation of the radio signal caused by shadowing, the result of the basic pattern matching is not stable. This is the reason why we propose to exploit several similar seeds when estimating the position of a user terminal in the previous section. We perform an experiment, varying the seed selection range based on the top seed metric. The seed selection range will be denoted by S. Let m be the top seed metric, then we will consider the positions of the seeds whose metric is less than $m \times (1 + S)$. Then we determine the position of a user terminal as the centroid of those seeds. We use -45 dB as the hole RSS in all following experiments.

Figure 5 shows the error distances with varying the value of the seed selection range. When the seeds are selected within the appropriate seed selection range, the accuracy of the result is better than that of the case that only top seed is selected, i.e., when the seed selection range is zero. From the graph, we find that the accuracy of the result is the best when the seed selection range is 0.37, in which case, the mean error distance is 76.8 m and the 2 sigma result was 149.8m. In particular, the 2 sigma result shows more improvement (180m to 150m) while the mean value exhibits relatively small improvement (90m to 77m): this centroid method decreases the deviation, and thus, has a stabilization effect.

Indoor vs. Outdoor. Throughout the previous experiments, we have used the mixture of both the indoor and the outdoor samples. Now, we test whether our proposed pattern matching is suitable for the indoor samples. Figure 6 shows the cumulative distribution function (CDF) accuracy of our proposed pattern matching with indoor and outdoor samples separately. Although the indoor samples are usually collected from several meters inside from building entrances and do not include deep basement samples, it shows almost the same accuracy values in both indoor and outdoor samples, from which we could conclude our proposed pattern matching is suitable for both the indoor and the outdoor samples.

Effect of Seed Density. The accuracy of our proposed pattern matching shows some dependency on the density of the seeds (the number of seeds in the seed database per unit area). Through experiments, we examine the relation between the density of seeds and the accuracy of our method. In the experiment, we divide a range into grids, and leave only one seed in a grid. Figure 7 shows the experiment result. As the grid size increases, the accuracy of the proposed pattern matching method becomes lower. Particularly, above 70 m of the grid size, the accuracy of our proposed pattern matching decreases rapidly. Hence, in our proposed pattern matching, the appropriate density of seeds has to be maintained to achieve the high accuracy.

Comparison with Cell-ID. Finally, we have compared the accuracy of our proposed method with the Cell-ID method. Figure 8 shows the cumulative distribution function (CDF) accuracy of our proposed pattern matching and Cell-ID method. As Figure 8 shows, the accuracy of our proposed pattern matching is much higher than Cell-ID method.

6 Conclusions

In this paper, we have proposed a novel pattern matching localization method for the cellular network, by exploiting the CDRs uploaded by AGPS terminals as inputs to the pattern database. We have analyzed the characteristics of RSS patterns from AGPS CDRs, and designed the pattern-distance metric and the new pattern matching method using that metric. The proposed positioning method reduces the pattern collection overhead by automating the construction of the RSS pattern database. The experiment results demonstrate that 1) the accuracy of the proposed positioning method is much higher than that of the Cell-ID method 2) the proposed AGPS CDR based method works well for indoor users as well as for outdoor users 3) the density of seed patterns is closely related to the positioning accuracy. For the future work, we will investigate how to leverage other GPS-free positioning methods together with the proposed AGPS CDR based pattern matching method.

References

1. Djuknic, G., Richton, R.: Geolocation and Assisted GPS. In: IEEE Computer Magazine, February 2001, IEEE press, Los Alamitos (2001)
2. Zhao, Y.: Standardization of Mobile Phone Positioning for 3G Systems. In: IEEE Communications Magazine, July 2002, IEEE press, Los Alamitos (2002)
3. Laitinen, H., Lähttenmäki, J., Nordström, T.: Database Correlation Method for GSM Location. In: VTC, IEEE press, Los Alamitos (2001)
4. Ahonen, S., Laitinen, H.: Database Correlation Method for UMTS Location. In: VTC, IEEE press, Los Alamitos (2003)
5. Borkowski, J., Lempiäinen, J.: Pilot correlation positioning method for urban UMTS networks. In: European Wireless Conference (2005)

6. Zhu, J., Durgin, G.D.: Indoor/outdoor location of cellular handsets based on received signal strength. In: Electronics Letters, vol. 41(1), IEEE press, Los Alamitos (January 2005)
7. Daniel Wong, K.: Get-Location in Urban Areas Using Signal Strength Repeatability. In: IEEE Communications Letters, October 2001, vol. 5(10), IEEE press, Los Alamitos (2001)
8. Roos, T., Myllymäki, P., Tirri, H.: A Statistical Modeling Approach to Location Estimation. In: IEEE Transactions on Mobile Computing, January–March 2002, vol. 1(1), IEEE press, Los Alamitos (2002)
9. Bahl, P., Padmanabhan, V.N.: RADAR: An In-Building RF-based User Location and Tracking System. In: INFOCOM 2000, IEEE press, Los Alamitos (2000)
10. Smailagic, A., Kogan, D.: Location Sensing and Privacy in a Context-Aware Computing Environment. In: IEEE Wireless Communications, October 2002, IEEE press, Los Alamitos (2002)
11. Lim, H., Kung, L., Hou, J.C., Luo, H.: Zero-Configuration, Robust Indoor Localization: Theory and Experimentation. In: INFOCOM 2006, IEEE press, Los Alamitos (2006)
12. 3GPP, Stage 2 functional specification of User Equipment (UE) positioning in UTRAN (Release 4). 3GPP (2002)
13. 3GPP2, Position Determination Service Standard for Dual Mode Spread Spectrum Systems. 3GPP2 (2001)

A Telephony Application for Manets: Voice over a MANET-Extended JXTA Virtual Overlay Network

Luis Bernardo, Rodolfo Oliveira, Sérgio Gaspar, David Paulino, and Paulo Pinto

Faculdade de Ciências e Tecnologia, Universidade Nova de Lisboa
P-2829-516 Caparica, Portugal
lflb@fct.unl.pt, rado@fct.unl.pt, sergiomgaspar@gmail.com,
david.paulino@gmail.com, pfp@fct.unl.pt

Abstract. This paper presents MANET-VoVON, a new Internet application for mobile ad-hoc networks (MANETs) providing voice over virtual overlay networks. A MANET-enabled version of JXTA peer-to-peer modular open platform (MANET-JXTA) is used to support user location and optionally, audio streaming over the JXTA virtual overlay network. Using MANET-JXTA, a client can search asynchronously for a user, and delay the call setup until a path is available to reach the user. The application uses a private signalling protocol based on the exchange of XML messages over MANET-JXTA communication channels. Nevertheless, it is fully interoperable with normal SIP clients through an embedded gateway function. This paper describes a prototype implementation of the proposed application and of the MANET-JXTA, and presents some performance measurements.

Keywords: Internet Telephony service, Mobile Ad-hoc Networks, Peer-to-Peer computing.

1 Introduction

Internet telephony services based on SIP (*Session Initiation Protocol*) [12] were designed for stable networks. The original IETF's approach relied on a registration service to handle client's mobility and availability. The call setup is forwarded by a proxy server, which queries the registration service for the current user location. Peer-to-peer (p2p) services were proposed for replacing the centralized registration service: Skype [16], [2] uses Kazaa's p2p infrastructure for storing the user's location, and P2P-SIP [14] uses a Chord p2p infrastructure for the same purpose. However, both p2p approaches were designed for the Internet and assume complete and stable connectivity.

Unstable mobile ad-hoc networks (MANETs) present a challenge for the existing applications because they are composed by scattered islands of nodes, with limited connectivity. Under these conditions it is costly to create and maintain a Chord distributed hash table (DHT) with a ring topology that does not match the MANET topology. A Chord link may connect two nodes that geographically are several hops distant. It is also costly to create and maintain a virtual overlay network (VON) connecting Kazaa supernodes. [8] shows that for these conditions the p2p infrastructures above collapse for high node's speeds. For a MANET it is also not acceptable to base

J. Filipe and M.S. Obaidat (Eds.): ICETE 2006, CCIS 9, pp. 347–358, 2008.
© Springer-Verlag Berlin Heidelberg 2008

the telephony call's success upon the connectivity to a centralized node. Instead, a new asynchronous tolerant approach is needed. The "location service" must be capable of storing the user's "call desires", and opportunistically establish the call when the network topology allows it. Therefore, the call establishment is not immediate but can take some time after the user gives the command.

We have implemented MANET-VoVON (MANET Voice over VON), a partition tolerant telephony service. The prototype is based on a new p2p architecture [9] that was implemented as an extension of the JXTA platform version 2.3.2 [7] optimized for unstable MANETs (we call it MANET-JXTA in this paper). This service interoperates with external SIP clients through a gateway, and within the MANET using MANET-JXTA services. It can stream audio directly end-to-end, or through the p2p VON. An evaluation of the MANET-JXTA overhead is presented in this paper.

The remainder of this paper is organized as follows: Section two introduces MANET-JXTA main characteristics. Section three presents the proposed internet telephony architecture, and its interoperation with SIP based services. Section four gives an overview of the prototype software implemented, and some performance measurements. Finally, some conclusions are drawn in section five.

2 MANET-JXTA

MANET-JXTA defines an extended set of the JXTA core p2p protocols and services [6], on top of which applications can be implemented. These protocols provide the basic functionality for peer and resource discovery, communication and organization.

2.1 JXTA

Applications run on a JXTA VON, which is a set of peers grouped on peer groups created by exchanging advertisements. All entities and resources (peers, groups, pipes, endpoints, queries, services, etc.) in JXTA are represented by advertisements. Advertisements are XML documents having unique IDs. JXTA core p2p services manipulate advertisements caching them and using searching procedures when caching fails.

JXTA defines a set of protocols adapted for searching advertisements on the Internet [6]. Basic query–reply message exchanges are supported by the Resolver Service (RS), which implements the Peer Resolver Protocol (PRP). RS is then used to implement other application specific resolution services. When no cache information is available, PRP uses a search service to look for advertisements. The most basic search service is the Rendezvous service and besides PRP other higher level search services also use it (e.g. Peer Discovery service, Pipe Binding Protocol). Additionally, JXTA supports a loosely-consistent DHT of advertisements (Rendezvous peer view service) implemented by a subset of Rendezvous peers. A Rendezvous (RV) peer is the equivalent to the Kazza's supernode: it acts as an advertisement concentrator supporting searches for a subset of non-RV peers.

Inter-peer communication in JXTA is usually implemented by exchanging XML messages over a communication channel created by the pipe service. The pipe service defines a one-to-one or one-to-many non-reliable peer-to-peer channel that transport messages through the VON connecting the peer-nodes, crossing NAT routers and firewalls. JXTA 2.0 defines two additional communication layers that are not adapted to telephony applications: endpoint service implements static connections; JXTA sockets implement reliable communication.

Pipes use logical identifiers at system level that are associated and resolved to physical addresses by the Endpoint Routing Protocol (ERP) at run-time, and when the connection is lost. Therefore, they identify univocally an application and a peer, independently of how many network interfaces the peer's machine has, or if their IP addresses change. However, pipes introduce an important message overhead that results from all the JXTA headers included by the JXTA core protocols and the application protocols. The minimum set includes the Endpoint Router header, which has the source and destination endpoint addresses, and a tentative route to the destination. [1] evaluates the JXTA's communication performance on a Fast Ethernet, and shows that JXTA overhead can be very high for small packet sizes. On the other side, a minimum of five percent throughput degradation is achievable on a Fast Ethernet for large packet sizes.

2.2 MANET-JXTA

MANET-JXTA handles queries preferentially using searching, because cached information tends to be outdated too fast on MANETs. It is also capable of using the original JXTA mechanism to interoperate with pure, non MANET-JXTA peers. MANET-JXTA adds the MANET rendezvous protocol (MANET-RVP) [9], a p2p protocol that uses a cross-layering flooding approach for propagating query messages through rendezvous peers in real-time. Query messages are flooded directly into the wireless LAN (WLAN) using IP multicast. It does rely on any existing VON topology. That might not be adapted to the physical topology. Due to peer movement, several RV peers may be located on the same network region. A clustering protocol is used to reduce the flooding overhead on these conditions. Each RV peer sends beacons periodically. Using the beacon information, RV peers are capable of selecting a subset of the RV peers as broadcast group leaders, responsible for broadcasting the query messages through all RV peers. Beacons are also used to detect the appearance of new neighbours. Notice that for a MANET almost all the peers must be RV peers because the topology may change continuously.

MANET-JXTA also modifies the Resolver Service (RS), responsible for answering advertisement queries. A TTL (*Time-To-Live*) parameter was added to the query message, allowing applications to specify time limited asynchronous queries.

After the query message reaches a RV peer, it is successively flooded using MANET-RVP protocol until it reaches all connected RV peers, within the specified maximum number of network hops. The response message is sent back to the query originator reversing the query message path. If the path is broken (a peer in the path is out of range), the route resolver protocol uses RS to search for another path using the destination endpoint addresses. Besides answering to the query with local information, RV peers add the query message to a finite length active query table. When a RV peer previously out of range (peer 3 in figure 1) is detected, the queries in the table are repropagated to it, and to the RV peers in the island it belongs to, eventually being stored by all RV peers that ever get in touch with a covered peer island.

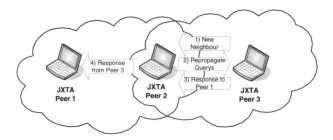

Fig. 1. Query resolution after user 3 discovery

For MANET-JXTA, the VON connecting the peers is created on-demand after MANET-RVP is used to answer a query. VON links are defined by the path elements contained in the answer message headers. Therefore, after a query resolution it matches the physical MANET topology, with minimum communication overhead. All neighbour peers in the VON are within radio coverage. If peers move from their original position, MANET routing protocols can be used to maintain the VON links as long as the application pipes are alive.

JXTA reference implementation [7] only supported TCP and HTTP transport protocols. MANET-JXTA added an UDP transport protocol module. The use of UDP links eventually reduces the end-to-end jitter on the application pipe's communications over 802.11 error prone WLANs [18]. However, no quality of service guarantees are provided by the existing 802.11 MAC protocols on ad-hoc mode, and the implemented UDP module does not support any traffic differentiation mechanisms either.

3 MANET-VoVON Application

The MANET-Voice over VON (VoVON) application implements a telephony application on a MANET enabled version of JXTA service. Figure 2 shows the overall VoVON architecture.

Within MANET-JXTA enabled peers, VoVON supports asynchronous telephony call setup to a remote peer. VoVON application publishes a VoVON ModuleSpecificAdvertisement, which specifies the control receiving pipe advertisement. Therefore, using MANET-JXTA resolver service, other VoVON peers can search for VoVON advertisements, and can establish a call using the pipe advertisement.

If a MANET-JXTA RV peer exists interconnecting the MANET to the Internet (forming a meshed wireless network), the application supports synchronous call setup using standard JXTA protocols and services.

The model also includes a JXTA-SIP gateway (figure 2), which allows standard SIP clients to make calls to JXTA peers and to receive calls from JXTA peers, without modifying the user agent. The gateway associates a DNS domain name to the VoVON's JXTA name space, and encapsulates the RTP audio stream into XML messages, when needed. It supports direct interaction with SIP users, or indirect interaction, through SIP proxies.

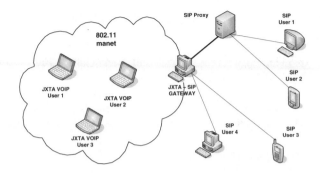

Fig. 2. MANET-VoVON architecture

3.1 Signalling

The VoVON's signalling messages were defined as a XML mapping of the SIP messages. In order to handle JXTA pipe unreliability, all VoVON messages are confirmed. A timer is used to retransmit them if no acknowledge is received and up to nine attempts are made. Table 1 presents a subset of the messages supported by Vo-VON.

Call setup original three-way hand-shake was mapped into a four-way VoVON message hand-shake over a pipe channel. *Call_Req* message includes the classical INVITE fields (e.g. Session Description Protocol (SDP) field), but adds a TTL field that defines for how long the call request is valid. *Call_Reply* message acknowledges the reception of *Call_Req*, and is equivalent to SIP's "100 trying" message. *Call_OK* message implements the "200 OK" SIP's message, with the corresponding fields (including the SDP field), and the SIP codec negotiation rules are followed. VoVON adds two *Call_Connect* messages to initialize audio streaming on each way, containing private pipe advertisements (see figure 3).

The SDP field was modified, to allow the definition of either a RTP endpoint (RTP protocol, IP address and the port number); or a JXTA pipe (receptor pipe advertisement string). Through pipes audio is transmitted over the VON links crossing firewalls and NAT routers, reaching any peer within JXTA VON. Pipes usage also minimizes the network setup time on a MANET – no MANET routing overhead exists. On the other hand, RTP streams introduce an initial routing overhead – it is necessary to discover the IP route between both peers before sending the audio samples. Depending on the MANET routing algorithm [10] discovering an IP route for a remote peer several hops away may mean: flooding the entire MANET with a "route request" packet for on-demand protocols (e.g. AODV, DSR, etc.); or continuously updating a routing table for proactive protocols (e.g. DSDV, OLSR). However, pipes may introduce a huge bandwidth overhead [1].

VoVON call termination is implemented by a two way message hand-shake. No REGISTER message is included in VoVON signalling. Instead, all peer associations are made using MANET-JXTA RS (resolver service), more adapted to the unstable nature of the MANETs.

Table 1. MANET-VoVON signalling messages and their mapping to SIP messages

SIP	MANET-VoVON
INVITE	Call_Req / Call_Reply
200 OK (for INVITE)	Call_OK
	Call_Connect
ACK (for INVITE)	Call_Status_Reply_OK
BYE / 200 OK	Call_End / Call_End_ACK

3.2 SIP Interoperation

SIP interoperation with VoVON is supported by JXTA-SIP gateways. A JXTA-SIP gateway publishes a JXTA-SIP gateway advertisement instead of a VoVON advertisement, which includes additional gateway specific information. Therefore, using the MANET-JXTA RS, other VoVON peers can search for JXTA-SIP advertisements, and can use them to establish a call to a SIP client.

A JXTA-SIP gateway is associated with a DNS domain name and implements the SIP protocol stack to communicate with SIP users and SIP proxies. Each JXTA user is associated with a VOVON uniform resource identifier (URI) within the JXTA network. Thus URI can be associated with a SIP URI identifying the domain when seen through a JXTA-SIP gateway:

vovon:(name JXTA)
sip:(name JXTA) @ domain DNS

When a VoVON client requests a call setup to a SIP URI, the VoVON application uses MANET-JXTA RS to search for VoVON advertisements with the URI's name component. If the search fails, MANET-JXTA RS is then used to find JXTA-SIP gateway advertisements. A bidirectional connection is established to one of the JXTA-SIP gateways.

Figure 3 shows the messages exchanged through the control pipes during a call setup from a MANET-JXTA client to a SIP user agent connected to a SIP proxy. JXTA-SIP gateway runs the VoVON setup message hand-shake at the JXTA interface with the VoVON user, and perform the translations described above.

JXTA-SIP gateway maintains all audio encoding specifications in the SDP audio fields it sends to the SIP proxy or to the SIP user. Although, it swaps all domain names with references to its domain name (IP address) and to a dynamic UDP port, which is allocated in response to a new VoVON client request. Therefore, the JXTA-SIP gateway always intermediates the audio streams from VoVON users and SIP users, converting the encapsulation formats and the addresses between the VoVON user (XML message or RTP packets) and the SIP user (RTP packets). In case of JXTA-SIP gateway failure, all active connections are torn down, and VoVON clients have to select a new MANET-JXTA gateway and create new connections (possibly associated with a different DNS domain).

Calls can be disconnected by any of the call participants. When SIP's "BYE" or VoVON's *Call_End* messages are received, JXTA-SIP end the audio streaming, and completes the disconnection signalling exchanges for each connection.

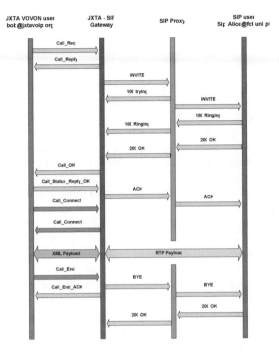

Fig. 3. Call setup from JXTA to SIP using a SIP proxy

3.3 Interaction with SIP Proxy

JXTA-SIP gateway can be configured to register itself on a SIP Proxy. However, the usual SIP procedure of sending a REGISTER message for each VoVON user cannot be used since the SIP-Proxy does not know who is available in the MANET.

Instead, JXTA-SIP gateway sends the SIP Proxy a domain REGISTER message associating itself with all names within a DNS domain name. A SIP proxy handles an INVITE request by trying to match a registered full URI. If none exists, it tries to match a registered domain. In this case, it forwards the call to the gateway and decrements the "Max-header" field in the SIP header.

When a JXTA-SIP gateway receives a call to the JXTA-SIP's DNS domain, it answers back with a "100 trying" message and starts a MANET-JXTA RS query looking for a VoVON user with the URI name. This query carries a zero TTL value, meaning that it only accepts calls when the VoVON user is reachable at that instant. If the user is located, the messages exchange follow a pattern similar to the one presented in figure 3. Otherwise the call is rejected.

4 Application

A VoVON prototype application is currently being implemented over a prototype implementation of MANET-JXTA. MANET-JXTA current prototype extended a previous prototype presented in (Oliveira, 05b) with the RS and the MANET-RVP presented above.

4.1 VoVON Prototype

We implemented a MANET-JXTA application which combines the VoVON user application and the JXTA-SIP gateway application.

VoVON signalling is exchanged using two control unidirectional pipes: one receiver pipe to receive connection requests from remote client pipes and other signalling messages; one client pipe for connecting to remote control VoVON receiver pipes. Audio can be transmitted using two JXTA pipes (one for each direction), or using two RTP streams over UDP.

Audio is handled using Java Media Framework (JMF) version 2.1.1e [5]. The application captures and formats audio into RTP format using two JMF modules. VoVON application always tries to select the GSM codec, due to its compression rate (13 Kbit/s), but it is compatible with any format supported by JMF.

Audio is transmitted over a JXTA pipe with the RTP header, encapsulated in a XML message. Therefore the JXTA pipe acts as a tunnel that transparently sends audio samples through the JXTA VON. JMF objects are connected to JXTA pipes using a local UDP socket. JMF objects stream audio to a local UDP socket, where the RTP packets are received and sent through an audio JXTA pipe. RTP packets are extracted from JXTA messages and sent to the JMF objects using the same UDP socket. Therefore, the architecture is not optimised for sending audio over JXTA pipes because it introduces additional jitter due to local socket transmissions at the sender and at the receiver side.

The audio player is capable of compensating some jitter, by storing the received audio samples on a circular buffer and delaying their presentation. However, if an audio sample is received after its presentation time, it is discarded. By default, JMF uses an audio buffer length of 250 ms, but it can be configured to a maximum value of 1000 ms.

The graphical interface, presented in figure 4, supports the application configuration and the call initiation and termination. The user is allowed to define its JXTA name (*My Name*), the JXTA group it joins (*Name*), if it is a rendezvous peer (in *RendeVouz* menu), and the gateway configuration (RTP port and IP address, and the DNS domain name, in the *Gateway* menu). The application presents a list of known VoVON peers in a table, but also allows the introduction of a SIP or VOVON URI (by default is a SIP URI) to start a new call.

The Current MANET-JXTA implementation can only use one of the transport protocols for all JXTA: TCP or UDP. It cannot use both in parallel. When the application is run for the first time, it opens a MANET-JXTA configuration menu where the transport module and the transport parameters are chosen. The application stores the configuration in a ".jxta" directory for the next run.

4.2 Performance Measurements

VoVON application initial performance tests focused on its overhead, compared to other Voice over IP applications, and on its SIP interoperability.

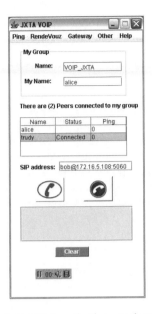

Fig. 4. VoVON application user interface

Audio can be sent using RTP packets over UDP transport protocol, or using JXTA pipes over UDP or TCP protocols. For GSM audio encoding, 50/3 messages with audio samples per second are sent. Using the Ethereal protocol analyser [3], we measured the total number of bytes sent, represented in table 2. JXTA pipes send two IP packet fragments per sample, and TCP sends an acknowledge packet. As expected, JXTA pipes introduce a huge overhead that results from the presence of an Endpoint Router and a VoVON headers, and from the XML encoding overhead. This conclusion is consistent with [1], confirming that pipe encapsulation is only valuable when bandwidth is not a problem, the connection requires NAT or firewall crossing, or the connection has a short life, dissuading any extra MANET-route discovery delay.

Table 2. JXTA Pipes communication overhead for GSM audio encoding

Audio Encoding	Message size [Bytes]
RTP	153 Bytes/message
JXTA Pipes over UDP	1799 Bytes/message
JXTA Pipes over TCP	1818 Bytes/message

Even with this large bandwidth overhead, it is only possible to send audio over a JXTA pipe if the end-to-end jitter introduced by the encoding and decoding process is not significant, compared with using RTP channels. Jitter is usually defined by equation 1 [13]. Jitter is the mean deviation (smoothed absolute value) of the difference D between the arrival time and the sender time tag. The smoothing factor of 1/16 is used to reduce the effect of huge isolated deviation peaks, common on 802.11b WLANs.

$$J(i) = J(i-1) + (|D(i-1,i)| - J(i-1))/16 \tag{1}$$

Table 3 presents the average jitter value measured at the receiver side for two SIP Communicator user agents [15] using RTP streams over UDP, and for two VoVON applications communicating on a network with only two peers, using a TCP JXTA pipe. Jitter was measured using Ethereal protocol analyser (which uses equation 1), capturing the packets just before they are received by the JMF object. The results show that the use of JXTA TCP pipes introduces an average jitter overhead of about 10 msec (52.8 %) for one JXTA hop. This value can be compensated using JMF buffering, and is clearly below the maximum end-to-end delay defined by ITU-T for telephony applications (150 msec).

Table 3. Average jitter for an unloaded Ethernet, measured using Ethereal

Audio encapsulation and network	Jitter [ms]
RTP	19,23
RTP over JXTA TCP pipes	29,39

Table 4 presents the average jitter value measured for an extensive set of experiments, with two VoVON applications communicating on a network with only two peers, for four different setups. The jitter on the JXTA pipe was measured when the XML audio messages are received from the pipe (excluding the jitter introduced at the last local socket retransmission), using a measuring function included in the VoVON application. The pipes' jitter measurements show that 802.11b network is responsible for a 28% increase on the average jitter for UDP pipes, and a 1% increase for TCP pipes, comparing them to the Fast Ethernet measurements. This behaviour difference is probably due to a high overhead handling fragmented 802.11b UDP packets on MS Windows XP. Unfortunately, it was not possible to test MANET-VoVON on Linux because the kernel does not handle fragmented multicast UDP packets, required for MANET-RVP. It also shows that TCP congestion control effects are not noticeable possibly because traffic bandwidth is very low.

VoVON JXTA-SIP gateway interoperability was tested by connecting a VoVON client to a VoVON JXTA-SIP gateway and to a SIP Communicator [15] user agent, using 802.11b WLANs and Fast Ethernet. The system was also tested with JAIN-SIP Proxy [4]. In all cases, it was possible to start calls from the VoVON clients and the SIP Communicator clients.

Table 4. Jitter measurements for unloaded networks using VoVON and JXTA pipes

Audio encapsulation and network	Jitter [ms]
Pipes over UDP on Fast Ethernet	16,18
Pipes over TCP on Fast Ethernet	16,45
Pipes over UDP on 802.11b	20,75
Pipes over TCP on 802.11b	16,68

5 Conclusions and Further Work

This paper shows that MANET-JXTA peer-to-peer open platform can be used to implement real-time applications on a MANET or on meshed networks. It shows that using MANET-RVP deferred search, it is simple to have call setup triggered by connection availability in a simple way. Other alternative approaches, like using SIP events [11], would be complex. A centralized approach would require a connection to a third party: the location server. A decentralized approach would require periodic flooding of searches or replies, controlled by the application.

Internet Telephony based on p2p architectures (i.e. Skype and P2P-SIP) has focused primarily on the user's location tracking. This paper proposed and analysed the possibility of also using the p2p network for streaming audio, concluding that due to the huge bandwidth overhead, its use should be restricted to extreme situations: NAT and firewall crossing, or short-lived connections. Results show that the end-to-end jitter is acceptable when audio is sent through a p2p VON.

Future work includes the continuation of the design and implementation of MANET-JXTA and MANET-VoVON. Quality of service can be improved by introducing message differentiation mechanisms in JXTA pipes, and by introducing advanced flow control mechanisms based on network state measurements. Further prototype tuning is also necessary on the JXTA UDP transport module and on the audio pipe communication. The audio pipe's communication jitter can be reduced by connecting the JMF classes directly to the JXTA pipes using the JMF RTP socket interface. Finally, comprehensive MANET multi-hop tests will be done and reported on a future paper.

References

1. Antoniu, G., Hatcher, P., Jan, M., Noblet, D.: Performance Evaluation of JXTA Communication Layers. In: GP2PC 2005. International Workshop on Global and Peer-to-Peer Computing (May 2005)
2. Baset, S., Schulzrinne, H.: 2004. An Analysis of the Skype Peer-to-Peer Internet Telephony Protocol. Technical Report CUCS-039-04, Computer Science Department, Columbia University, New York, USA (September 2004)
3. Ethereal: A Network Protocol Analyser (2006), Retrieved from
   http://www.ethereal.com/
4. NIST-SIP. A JAIN-SIP Proxy for the People (2003), retrieved from
   http://snad.ncsl.nist.gov/proj/iptel/
5. JMF. Java Media Framework API (JMF) (2006), retrieved from
   http://java.sun.com/products/java-media/jmf/
6. JXTA. Project JXTA: JXTA v2.0 Protocols Specification (2004), retrieved from
   http://spec.jxta.org/nonav/v1.0/docbook/JXTAProtocols.html
7. JXTA. JXTA: Get Connected (2006), retrieved from http://www.jxta.org
8. Oliveira, R., Bernardo, L., Pinto, P.: Flooding Techniques for Resource Discovery on High Mobility MANETs. In: IWWAN 2005. International Workshop on Wireless Ad-Hoc Networks (May 2005)

9. Oliveira, R., Bernardo, L., Ruivo, N., Pinto, P.: Searching for PI resources on MANETs using JXTA. In: AICT-SAPIR-ELETE 2005, Advanced Industrial Conference on Telecommunications/Service Assurance with Partial and Intermittent Resources Conference/E-Learning on Telecommunications Workshop, pp. 371–376. IEEE Press, Los Alamitos (2005b)
10. Perkins, C.: Ad Hoc Networking. Addison Wesley, Reading (2001)
11. Roach, A.: Session Initiation Protocol (SIP)-Specific Event Notification. IETF RFC 3265 (June 2002)
12. Rosenberg, J., Schulzrinne, H., Camarillo, G., Johnston, A., Peterson, J., Sparks, R., Handley, M., Schooler, E.: SIP: Session Initiation Protocol. IETF RFC 3261 (June 2002)
13. Schulzrinne, H., Casner, S., Frederick, R., Jacobson, V.: RTP: A Transport Protocol for Real-Time Applications. IETF RFC 3550 (July 2003)
14. Singh, K., Schulzrinne, H.: Peer-to-Peer Internet Telephony using SIP. In: NOSSDAV 2005, International Workshop on Network and Operating Systems Support for Digital Audio and Video, pp. 63–68. ACM Press, New York (2005)
15. SipCommunicator. SIP Communicator - the Java VoIP and Instant Messaging client (2006), retrieved from https://sip-communicator.dev.java.net/
16. Skype. Skype Explained (2006), retrieved from http://www.skype.com/products/explained.html
17. Smith, J.: The book, The publishing company, 2nd edn., London (1998)
18. Zhang, X., Schulzrinne, H.: 2004. Voice over TCP and UDP. Technical Report CUCS-033-04, Computer Science Department, Columbia University, New York, USA (September 2004)

A Context-Aware Architecture for Mobile Knowledge Management

Olaf Thiele[1], Hartwig Knapp[1], Martin Schader[1], and Nicolas Prat[2]

[1] University of Mannheim - Department of Information Systems,
68131 Mannheim, Germany
{thiele,knapp,martin.schader}@uni-mannheim.de
[2] Essec Business School - Information and Decision Systems Department
Avenue Bernard Hirsch, B.P.50105 - 95021 Cergy cedex, France
prat@essec.fr

Abstract. In many professional activities (e.g., medical diagnosis, construction, or sales), the ability to retrieve and store knowledge in a mobile situation is crucial. This need, together with the progress of mobile devices, has led to the emergence of mobile knowledge management. The mobile situation imposes specific constraints on traditional knowledge management activities (e.g., knowledge retrieval or presentation). Therefore, a key research question for mobile knowledge management is how context should be taken into account.

In this paper, we propose a context-aware knowledge management architecture for mobile environments. The key aspect is the "Contextualizer" middleware that takes care of knowledge storage and retrieval as well as contextually adapted knowledge presentation on mobile devices. In contrast to existing concepts, we suggest a broader approach, where the middleware serves as the mediator to different mobile devices. We implemented the architecture in a fitted use case. Our roadside assistance use case demonstrates the architecture's strength for presenting both text and graphics stemming from several knowledge sources.

Keywords: Mobility, knowledge management and context-aware computing.

1 Introduction

The issues of knowledge management and mobility have often been explored separately. In this paper, we combine the increased importance of intellectual capital in today's business life with the rapidly changing properties and requirements of mobile devices. The world of mobile consumer electronics has changed enormously over the last years. While cell phones, for example, display high-resolution video streams and location-based services offer numerous interesting opportunities, business life, on the other hand, evolves in an analogous way but much slower. Business applications are usually more specialized and therefore more complex and more costly than standardized consumer software. Some applications like e-mail messaging or word processors can be used for both private and business tasks. Still, this kind of application is mostly implemented in a proprietary way (e.g. Blackberry). Research in this area mainly addresses just one kind of mobile device or application. Most user interfaces are constructed especially for the

J. Filipe and M.S. Obaidat (Eds.): ICETE 2006, CCIS 9, pp. 359–370, 2008.

targeted device (e.g. special PalmOS devices; also see [2]) or functionality is limited (e.g. WML; also see [17]).

Our generalized approach towards mobile knowledge management aims at both, contextually adapted queries to knowledge sources as well as contextually adapted presentation of knowledge on mobile devices. This includes modified communication with the mobile client according to network variables. While most research focuses on certain aspects of the problem, we present a complete architecture, which builds upon previous work in the fields of knowledge management and mobility. A middleware component called the Contextualizer serves as the main building block of the architecture. The Contextualizer is complemented by components that reside on the mobile device and in the back-end. This reduces the resources needed to include a new mobile device or knowledge source into the system. The main advantage is that modifications to the knowledge source (databases, unstructured knowledge sources, etc.) or to the mobile devices need only be applied to the Contextualizer instead of modifying all knowledge sources and devices.

In the next section, we present the mobile knowledge management environment and point out the technical prerequisites. In Section 3, we highlight our proposed architecture and explain its main components. Section 4 shows parts of our prototypical implementation while we draw the outline of other works in Section 5. Finally, we conclude with a resume and an outlook.

2   Mobile Knowledge Management Environment and Properties

In this section, we highlight the main aspects of knowledge management and mobility relevant to our work.

2.1   Knowledge Management

Knowledge management is often described as a system of activities to permit the utilization of organizational knowledge by the members of that organization [11]. Possible knowledge management techniques and approaches usually fall into one of the five categories: expert finder, virtual teamwork, lessons learned databases, case-based reasoning, or virtual/augmented reality [6]. The first approach is often used to identify and contact a relevant expert for a specific problem. The second one refers to work that is conducted by geographically distributed coworkers. The next approach refers to the concept of maintaining positive and negative experiences in a problem-solving process (see also [18]). The fourth looks for similar issues in the past and retrieves these solutions. The last approach assists the user by means of virtual reality. Due to the fact that knowledge management is a vast field of research, further definitions can be found in the referred work or in the books by Davenport and Prusak [5] or Nonaka and Takeuchi [16].

In this paper, we focus on four general knowledge management processes that are relevant to our more technical view. On the one hand, these are knowledge presentation and acquisition, which evolve around human interaction with the system. Knowledge presentation comprises both displaying data on the device as well as interacting with it. If this interaction leads to some sort of knowledge storage or if the user deliberately enters information through a form or just as plain text, we categorize these activities as belonging to knowledge acquisition. On the other hand, knowledge retrieval and storage are relevant to our work. We use these terms analogous to their technical counterparts.

2.2   Mobility Aspects

Classical knowledge management applications were programmed for desktop use. With the introduction of mobility, sophisticated adaptation to the mobile context becomes more important. In general, the unique properties of mobile devices are a major influencing factor in the proposed system. With a growing number of different device types, the heterogeneity grows enormously as most devices differ in their capabilities from PCs (e.g. screen size) and from other mobile device types (e.g. cell phones and PDAs). Critical factors include the display size and resolution, the memory size and accessibility, the processing power, connection protocols like GPRS, UMTS, or EDGE, interaction techniques like the stylus and supported standardized programming interfaces like Java or C (see [15] and more recently [1]). Key properties are the ubiquity and the ability to adapt to the user's context, given the current position and other preferences (e.g. user profiles).

To sum up, benefits of joining the fields of knowledge management and mobility are "anytime, anywhere information access" [10], mobile-added values like ubiquity or context-sensitivity [6], and automatic context incorporation (e.g., knowledge is accessed in an adapted way and context variables such as location are stored automatically).

2.3   Requirements

While the limitations of technology supporting knowledge management activities have already been discussed elsewhere (see for example [6]), the requirements for mobile devices and their communication partners are a field, which deserves further description. As mentioned above, mobile devices are limited in several key features that are normally fulfilled by common PCs or workstations (e.g. screen size). Other mobile restrictions include network issues like bandwidth or communication protocols. Because of this fact, we introduced an intelligent middleware - the Contextualizer -, which serves the function to convert a data stream from the server side into a client-readable format and back. Therefore, the Contextualizer has a rough understanding of device types with their properties and clients transfer their specific needs (e.g., exact device identification, resolution, display size, colors, free memory, number of presentable letters in a row, etc.) during the communication's initialization phase. The middleware, which will be presented in more detailed in Section 3 receives a response from one or more of the databases and converts it into the client's contextually adapted format. In the other direction, the middleware has to translate a client's request for knowledge into a database-understandable format. This is also described in Section 3.

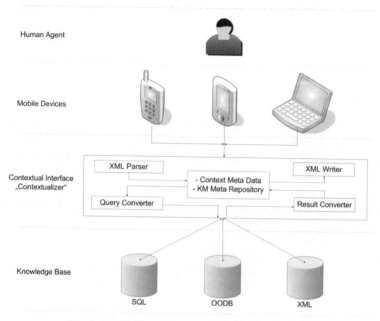

Fig. 1. Mobile Knowledge Management Architecture

3   Mobile Knowledge Management Architecture

In this section, we introduce our mobile knowledge management architecture and its underlying components. Subsequently, we explain how the context mapping works and afterwards, we present the Contextualizer middleware in more detail in Section 4.

3.1   Introduction

Our proposed architecture for mobile knowledge management, shown in figure 1 on the next page, is divided into four layers. The first layer contains the mobile users or mobile agents. This human agent interacts with the system to access knowledge. The human agent then utilizes this knowledge, transfers it to others or enters some new knowledge back into the system. The knowledge management activities, knowledge presentation and acquisition are the interface between layers one and two. The second layer consists of Java-enabled mobile devices like mobile phones, PDAs, or laptop computers. These three device types are the most common today and usually all devices of a certain type share similar properties (e.g., reduced set of keys on cell phones compared to a complete keyboard on notebook computers). We programmed client-side pieces of software for each device type. They serve as small agents on the device, which automatically determine device properties such as screen resolution, color table, or bandwidth. If the device supports determination of the location (by GPS), this data is collected as well and sent to the Contextualizer, which resides on the third layer. The implemented middleware serves as the connecting link between the adjoining layers - it is the main focus of our work. It translates the data flow coming from the mobile devices to a database query and the response is then adapted according to the mobile context and sent back to the device. The interfacing activities between the third and fourth layer are knowledge storage and retrieval. The fourth layer contains the knowledge source which is built up of different database types. We chose the three most popular types: relational (SQL), object-oriented (OODB), and XML databases. Due to the fact that most of the intelligence and complexity of our application reside on the third layer, we explain this component more detailed in the next subsection.

3.2 Outline of the Contextualizer

The Contextualizer is a middleware component, which serves as a mediator between the human agent and existing knowledge bases. It takes care of communication with the knowledge base (knowledge storage and retrieval) as well as linking the server and client side according to the context (knowledge presentation and acquisition). In general terms, if the Contextualizer receives an XML query from a mobile device, it parses the request and analyzes the context according to the following four context elements: user dependency, technological environment, situation, and task. Subsequently, all relevant databases are queried, the results are transformed according to the four context elements, and, finally, the result is sent back to the client application. All four context elements are described thoroughly in the following subsections. Table 1 gives on overview of typical context elements.

Not all context elements need to be considered for all knowledge management activities. The role of a user within the organization, for example, has significant impact on what type of knowledge can be accessed (retrieval of knowledge) but is independent of the knowledge presentation. Furthermore, context elements may change during the

Table 1. Overview of Context Elements by Category

Context Elements	Subelements
User Dependency	Role in the Organization (function, hierarchical position), User Preferences (technical, application specific)
Technological Environment	Handheld Device (screen size, processing power, available memory), Network (bandwidth, current network load)
Situational Elements	Time (time and time zone), Location (automatically via GPS or manually by zip code)
Task-Specific Elements	Heavily dependent on the task and therefore hard to predetermine

execution of a task and therefore need special attention. Again, the role of the user will usually remain stable but the location or network load may well change. Thus, the distinction between static and dynamic context elements is important to our architecture. Finally, some context elements need to be determined either on the client or the server side. While the user's role has to be retrieved on the server side to prevent misuse, the location (e.g. by GPS use) is usually retrieved on the mobile device. Some elements require server and client side effort (e.g. measuring network load).

We carefully designed this integrated architecture to meet all our needs. Lei and Georganas distinguish three different areas (client, proxy, or server), where an adaptation could be placed in a context-aware architecture [13]. Several arguments support our approach to include some logic on the client and the back-end with a sophisticated mediator like the Contextualizer in between. Thus, we combine all three approaches with an emphasis on the proxy. For one, we need to collect as much context parameters as possible. These are only available on the client. Therefore, we need a minimum application on the client if not a more complex agent software. Furthermore, a unified language for accessing knowledge sources allows for selecting chunks of knowledge as they are needed for the actual context. Driving instructions could be textual, verbal, sketch-based, or full-size maps. Performing all transformations on the client, for example, would exceed the processing power of most cell phones, whereas an implementation centered around only one knowledge source would hinder spreading the architecture to different tasks.

3.3   User Dependency

User dependent elements form the first type of context elements. They include technical preferences as well as the agent's role within the organization. Most technical preferences are represented through the user's profile. A typical user profile includes data on preferred color themes as well as favored font sizes. Profile information is stored on the client and is transferred to the Contextualizer in the initialization phase. In addition to the profile, the role of the user within the organization needs to be taken into account. On the one hand, not all members of an organization work with all available knowledge. The users' role determines what knowledge they are allowed to and need to access. Authentication and authorization is incorporated within the startup phase. For example, all available data would lead to an information overflow for executive members of the organization. They need an abstract overview of the accessible knowledge.

3.4   Technological Environment

The technical environment comprises elements of the device and the network. The device plays a major role for the Contextualizer. Variables like the screen size, processing power, available colors, or programming interfaces are key determinants for putting the knowledge into context. Two major types of applications need to be considered: text and graphical knowledge representations. Text can be displayed in many ways. Font size, text formatting and navigational elements within texts (e.g. hyperlinks) as well as ways for changing screens (e.g. scrolling) can be varied between mobile devices depending on their capabilities. As for graphical knowledge representation, display facilities vary a lot between devices. While some devices like laptops or PDAs offer powerful standardized programming interfaces, smaller devices like cell phones or smartphones usually have limited custom interfaces.

The network connection is another important influencing factor. The available bandwidth determines the transferable data size. Pictures, for example, need to be compressed or simplified before transfer. Furthermore, interaction techniques usually rely on broadband connections. But the available bandwidth may differ due to increased network traffic. In this case, the bandwidth parameters need to be dynamically adjusted. Finally, the costs for network traffic might be a limiting factor. Some users might prefer a low-end knowledge representation over a more expensive one.

3.5 Situational Elements

Situational elements are those connected with time and location. The time variable includes the actual time as well as the corresponding time zone. Depending on the time of day, knowledge queries might return different results. Moreover, the time zone is important when retrieving time-critical information from databases in far away countries.

The other important situational element is the location. The position of the user on the globe is one of the most prominent contextual elements and is used in many mobile applications. The location can be determined automatically (via GPS) or manually. The position of the user is especially interesting for graphical knowledge representation in maps or sketches. The dynamic nature of this element is also important in navigational tasks. Both the Contextualizer and client need to keep up with a driving vehicle to deliver timely knowledge.

3.6 Task-Specific Elements

All other context element implementations, as described above, are universal and can be used for most task types, but elements specific to the task need to be adjusted for each task type. To ease the programming effort needed for implementing new tasks, we developed a semantic XML description format (similar to Topic Maps), which can be used to semantically express what knowledge should be retrieved from which database. The semantic description is situated in the part named KM meta repository and further includes information on interrelated topics. Basically, the client sends a request to the server, which determines the resources to access by using these descriptions. Within the Contextualizer, all data is represented in a uniform XML format, regardless of the data source (relational, object-oriented, or native XML).

4 Prototype Implementation

We implemented a sample use case prototype to validate our mobile knowledge management architecture and to illustrate its features. First, a technical overview of the implementation is given. Subsequently, we then present the basic idea of our use case and we introduce the implemented clients as well as the corresponding server side.

4.1   Overall Implementation

Generally, all applications (client and server side) are programmed in Java. The many advantages of Java include the wide variety of available client programming interfaces as well as a free choice of the server side operating system. The often mentioned performance drawback is not as significant for our applications but might play a role when using more or larger images. The client-side application has been programmed using the J2ME programming interfaces. The widely available components include APIs for handling images as well as storing information on the device for caching purposes. The server side and especially the Contextualizer were programmed using J2EE. The Java 2 Enterprise Edition APIs offer the capabilities for handling multiple connections with clients as well as databases. The Contextualizer is therefore scalable and performant.

4.2   Roadside Assistance Use Case

The main idea behind the use case is helping both professionals and car drivers in assessing problems related to a car that broke down. The look and feel of the application is depicted in figure 2.

The welcome screen is shown in the left half and a typical GUI element in the right half of the screenshot. Due to the high screen resolution and processing power of modern cell phones (here the Nokia6230i) we present these screenshots. The adaptations for PDAs and laptop computers look similar to those known from analogous applications (e.g. [22]). The main idea of the use case led to two basic scenarios: In the first one, a professional mechanic drives to a remote location to solve a car breakdown. In order to find the location, he uses a map given by our application. Our implementation is shown in figure 3.

Both, the actual position and the location of the accident or breakdown are shown on the map. The cursor keys may be used to navigate on the map. Once the mechanic arrives at the destination, the application helps him to spot the failure by querying several databases (e.g. the manufacturer's one and reports by colleagues). The mechanic as well as the car driver might use either a cell phone, a PDA, or a laptop to access the knowledge management system. The second scenario includes the driver of the car, who wants to find a nearby garage while the car is still on the road or he intends to mark his

Fig. 2. Screenshots from the application GUI

Fig. 3. Illustrations from Scenario 1

Fig. 4. Screenshots of Scenario 2

position on a map. Furthermore, the driver might describe his situation using the client, which sends the request to the Contextualizer. There, the request is parsed and sent to the databases according to the predefined semantic map. The results are then transferred back to the mobile client. A possible request to the system is shown in figure 4.

First, the user describes the problem in short keywords. Afterwards, several databases are questioned and the results are then transferred back to the device. In both scenarios, some knowledge on possible solutions is transferred back into the system. The outside temperature, for was helpful in solving the problem might ease future use of the system.

4.3   Contextual Adaptation

The implemented use case adapts knowledge according to all four context elements. User dependent elements include a user profile and organizational role. The user is able to choose a certain skin and save favored top menu items. The organizational role determines, which parts of the system may be accessed by the user. The mechanic has more access to different knowledge sources than a regular driver (e.g., excerpts from a professional database are not easily understandable). Technical context elements in the use case include the color, interaction style, screen size, and bandwidth. The images sent to the device are adapted according to the given color table. Certain keywords in responses are highlighted if colors are supported. The graphics are sent in total if the device supports interaction types like the stylus or mouse movements. Only parts of a picture are sent to a cell phone due to the limited interaction capabilities and the smaller screen. The screen size and bandwidth determine how much of the map is sent at a time. Devices with a slow network connection receive smaller pieces of the map. The bandwidth of a regular cell phone posed a problematic situation when moving fast while viewing high resolution images. Situational elements include the time and place. Problems differ at night, especially in winter time. Furthermore, a much smaller set of garages is open after hours. The location plays a major role in this scenario and is monitored constantly. The task specific elements were mainly described above and included map navigation and problem solving.

5 Related Work

While knowledge management and mobility are well-established research fields, the combination of both raises questions and uncertainties. On the more technical side, for example, we face the problem that connections between mobile devices and databases are not dependable; a connection and session management has to be introduced to guarantee a complete and timely data exchange. Some [12] attend to the question how a database query might be answered completely and discuss several disconnection modes while others (see for example [3]) dwell on weak or partial connection modes. Further work revolves around the question how the amounts of data sent back and forth can be minimized in order to avoid large data transfers in non-broadband networks (see [4] or [14]).

Work similar to our approach was carried out by Fagrell et al. as early as 2000 [8]. As mobile devices had much less processing power back then, context elements such as user dependency or automatic location detection were not considered. The work of Wei and Prehofer focuses more on distributed context repositories, which are queried for decision making [21]. Derballa and Pousttchi present the idea of mobile-added values [6]. Their approach is rather abstract and they do not offer a technical implementation roadmap. Focusing on similar issues are Grimm et al., who are working on the MUMMY project (see [10] or [9]). They developed applications for several tasks (e.g. mobile facility management, trade fair information). Finally, Adipat and Zhang develop an adaptable framework for mobile knowledge management [1]. Their main focus lies on web content adaptation according to user preferences.

Further research on contextual awareness is carried out in the field of human computer interaction. Dourish [7] gives a comprehensive overview of the field's history and current research. An approach towards mobile knowledge management from that research field is presented by Shen [20] or Bardram and Hansen [2]. Finally, work on mobile knowledge management exists that centers around peer to peer exchange of knowledge. Schwotzer and Geihs present an architecture for topic map exchange [19].

6   Conclusions

Mobile knowledge management is a key application area for mobile computing in general and context-aware computing in particular. In this paper, we have presented a context-aware mobile knowledge management architecture. The key component of the architecture is the Contextualizer. This middleware implements the knowledge management activities (e.g., knowledge storage, retrieval, presentation, and acquisition) by taking into account the context elements, namely the user, the technical environment, the situation (i.e. time and place) and the specific task at hand. Moreover, in contrast to existing approaches, the Contextualizer comprises a meta-repository, which decides dynamically where the requested knowledge resides. We have implemented a prototype of our mobile knowledge management architecture and applied it to a scenario.

Our prototype architecture needs to be extended in order to take into account all mobile knowledge management activities (e.g. better knowledge acquisition techniques like forms and recording audio). The scalability of the architecture requires further testing (a wider range of devices and media types) and applications to real-life situations (e.g. handheld audits). We are currently working on these issues.

References

1. Adipat, B., Zhang, D.: Developing adaptive and personalized mobile applications: A framework and design issues. In: Proceedings of the Eleventh Americas Conference on Information Systems (AMCIS 2005), August 11–14, 2005, Omaha, Nebraska (2005)
2. Bardram, J.E., Hansen, T.R.: The aware architecture: supporting context-mediated social awareness in mobile cooperation. In: CSCW 2004: Proceedings of the 2004 ACM conference on Computer supported cooperative work, pp. 192–201. ACM Press, New York (2004)
3. Chan, D., Roddick, J.: Context-sensitive mobile database summarisation. In: ACSC 2003. Twenty-Sixth Australasian Computer Science Conference (2003)
4. Chang, T.-Y., Velayutham, A., Sivakumar, R.: Mimic: raw activity shipping for file synchronization in mobile file systems. In: MobiSys 2004: Proceedings of the 2nd international conference on Mobile systems, applications, and services, pp. 165–176. ACM Press, New York (2004)
5. Davenport, T.H., Prusak, L., Prusak, L.: Working Knowledge: How Organizations Manage What They Know. Harvard Business School Press, Boston (1997)
6. Derballa, V., Pousttchi, K.: Extending knowledge management to mobile workplaces. In: ICEC 2004. Sixth International Conference on Electronic Commerce, pp. 583–590 (2004)
7. Dourish, P.: What we talk about when we talk about context. Personal Ubiquitous Comput. 8(1), 19–30 (2004)
8. Fagrell, H., Forsberg, K., Sanneblad, J.: Fieldwise: A mobile knowledge management architecture. In: CSCW 2000, pp. 211–220 (2000)
9. Grimm, M., Tazari, M.-R., Balfanz, D.: Towards a Framework for Mobile Knowledge Management. In: Karagiannis, D., Reimer, U. (eds.) PAKM 2002. LNCS (LNAI), vol. 2569, pp. 326–338. Springer, Heidelberg (2002)
10. Grimm, M., Tazari, M.-R., Balfanz, D.: A reference model for mobile knowledge management. In: Proceedings of I-KNOW 2005, Graz, Austria (2005)
11. Hannig, U.: Zwei Welten wachsen zusammen. In: Knowledge Management and Business Intelligence, Springer, Berlin (2002)

12. Holliday, J., Agrawal, D., El Abbadi, A.: Disconnection modes for mobile devices. Wireless Networks 8, 391–402 (2002)
13. Lei, Z., Georganas, N.: Context-based media adaptation in pervasive computing. In: Canadian Conference on Electrical and Computer Engineering, 2001, vol. 2, pp. 913–918. IEEE Press, Los Alamitos (2001)
14. Lindemann, C., Waldhorst, O.P.: Exploiting epidemic data dissemination for consistent lookup operations in mobile applications. SIGMOBILE Mob. Comput. Commun. Rev. 8(3), 44–56 (2004)
15. Lum, W.Y., Lau, F.C.M.: A context-aware decision engine for content adaptation. IEEE Pervasive Computing 1(3), 41–49 (2002)
16. Nonaka, I., Takeuchi, H.: The Knowledge-Creating Company: How Japanese Companies Create the Dynamics of Innovation. Oxford University Press, Oxford (1995)
17. Picco, G.P., Murphy, A.L., Roman, G.-C.: Developing mobile computing applications with lime. In: ICSE 2000: Proceedings of the 22nd international conference on Software engineering, pp. 766–769. ACM Press, New York (2000)
18. Probst, G., Raub, S., Romhardt, K.: Wie Unternehmen ihre wertvollste Ressource optimal nutzen, Wissen managen, Gabler, Wiesbaden (1997)
19. Schwotzer, T., Geihs, K.: Shark - a system for management, synchronization and exchange of knowledge in mobile user groups. In: 2nd International Conference on Knowledge Management (I-KNOW 2002), Graz, Austria, pp. 149–155 (2002)
20. Shen, J.: Utilizing mobile devices to capture case stories for knowledge management. In: CHI 2003: CHI '03 extended abstracts on Human factors in computing systems, pp. 688–689. ACM Press, New York (2003)
21. Wei, Q., Prehofer, C.: Context management in mobile environments. In: Proceedings of ANwire Workshop, Paris (2003)
22. Yue, W., Mu, S., Wang, H., Wang, G.: Tgh: a case study of designing natural interaction for mobile guide systems. In: MobileHCI 2005: Proceedings of the 7th international conference on Human computer interaction with mobile devices & services, pp. 199–206. ACM Press, New York (2005)

Author Index